O-Parts HUNTER

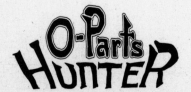

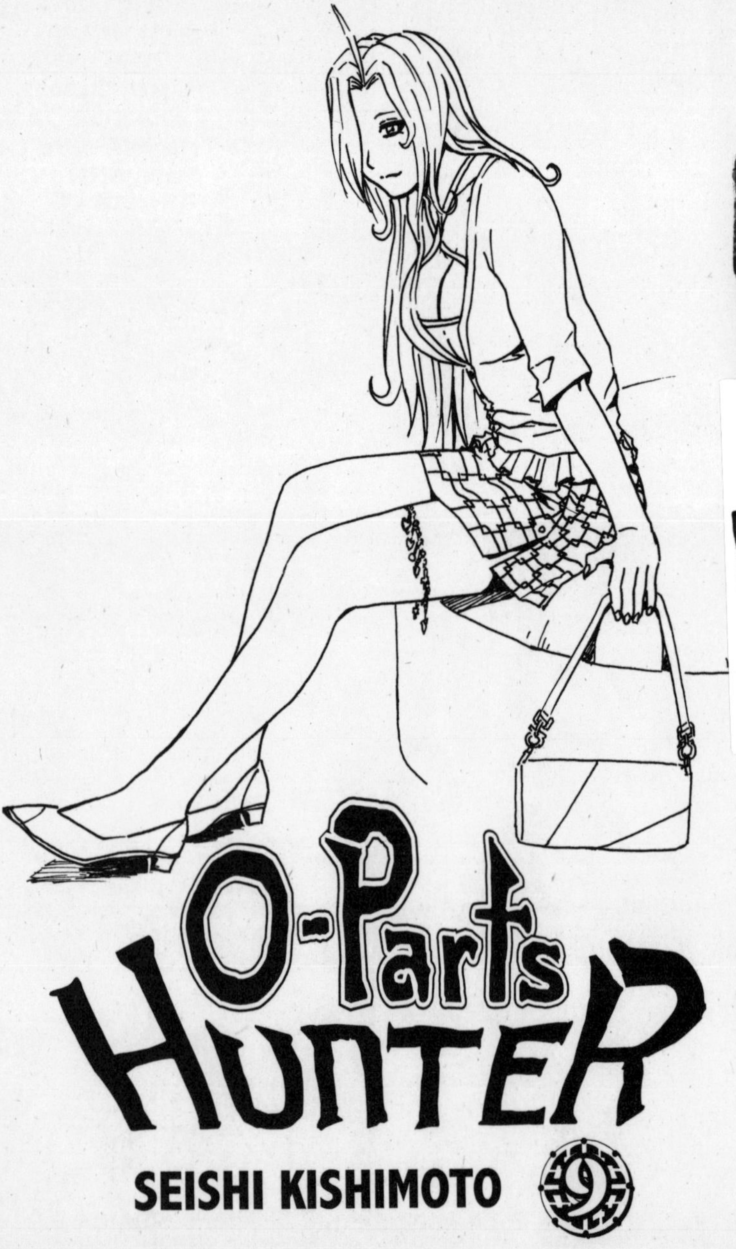

O-Parts HUNTER

SEISHI KISHIMOTO

9

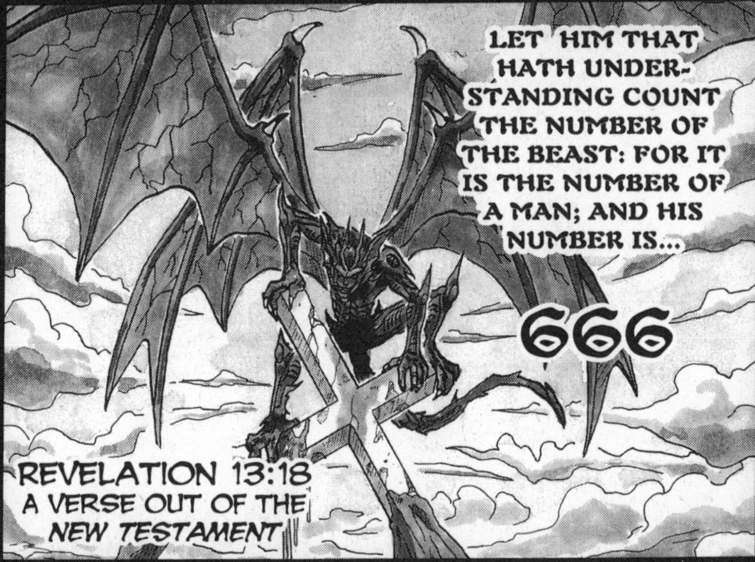
LET HIM THAT HATH UNDER-STANDING COUNT THE NUMBER OF THE BEAST: FOR IT IS THE NUMBER OF A MAN; AND HIS NUMBER IS...
666
REVELATION 13:18 A VERSE OUT OF THE *NEW TESTAMENT*

O-Parts Hunter

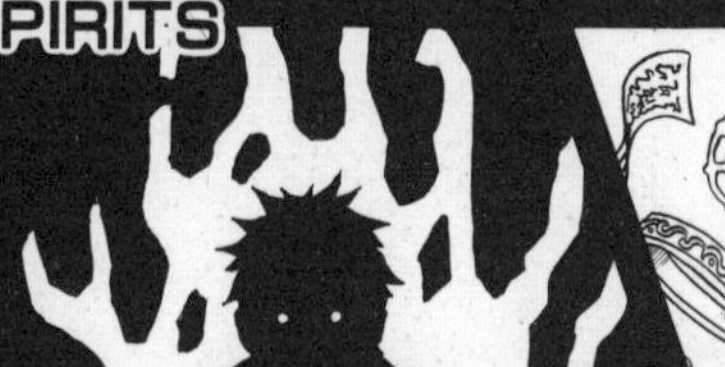
SPIRITS

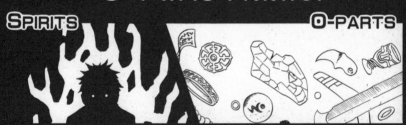

Spirit: A special energy force which only the O.P.T.s have. The amount of Spirit they have within them determines how strong of an O.P.T. they are.

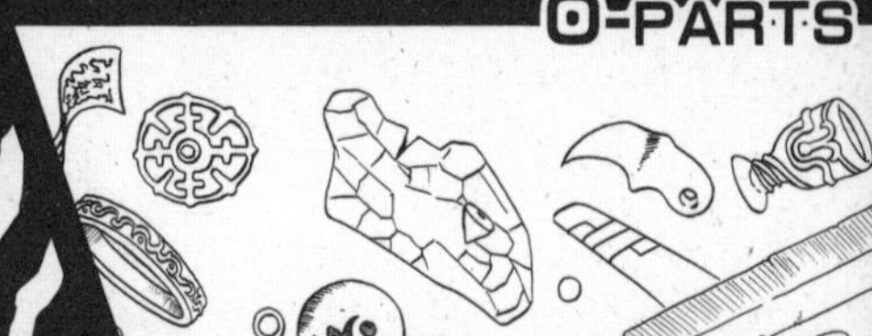
O-PARTS

O-Parts: Amazing artifacts with mystical powers left from an ancient civilization. They have been excavated from various ruins around the world. Depending on their Effects, O-Parts are given a rank from E to SS within a seven-tiered system.

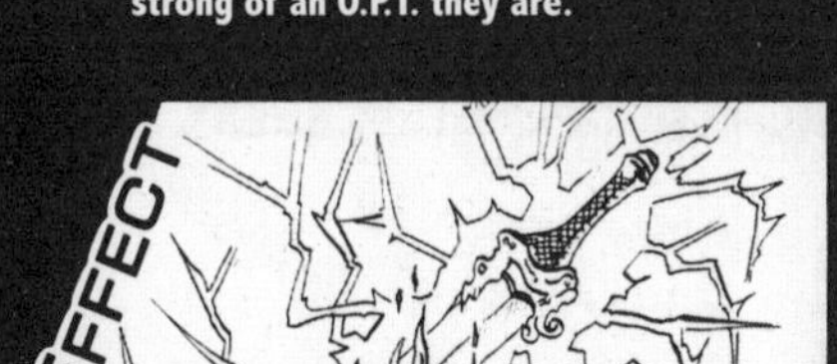
EFFECT

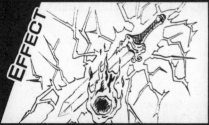

Effect: The special energy (power) the O-Parts possess. It can only be used when an O.P.T. sends his Spirit into an O-Part.

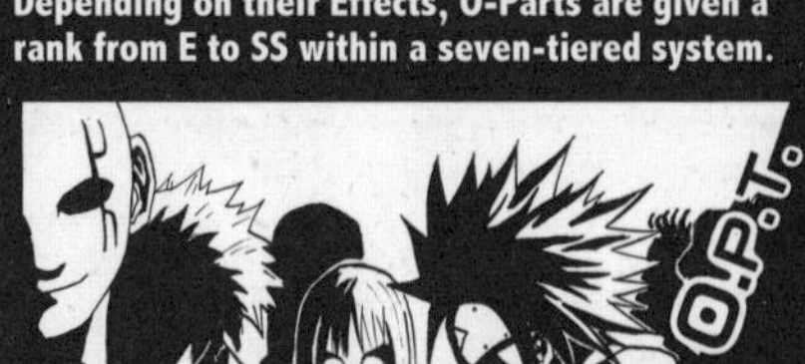
O.P.T.

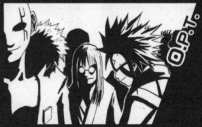

O.P.T.: One who has the ability to release and use the powers of the O-Parts. The name O.P.T. is an abbreviated form of O-Part Tactician.

CHARACTERS

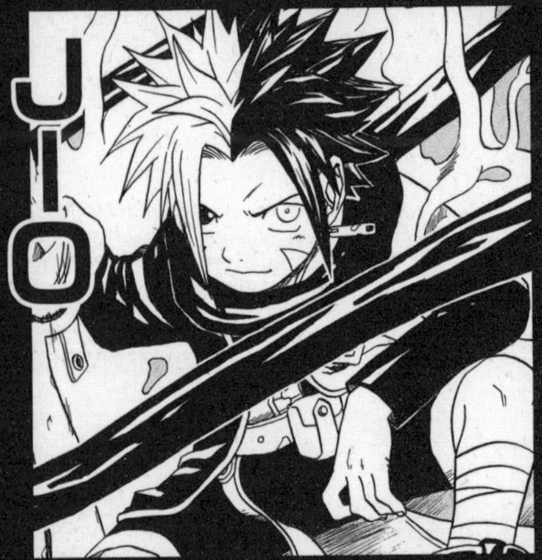
JIO

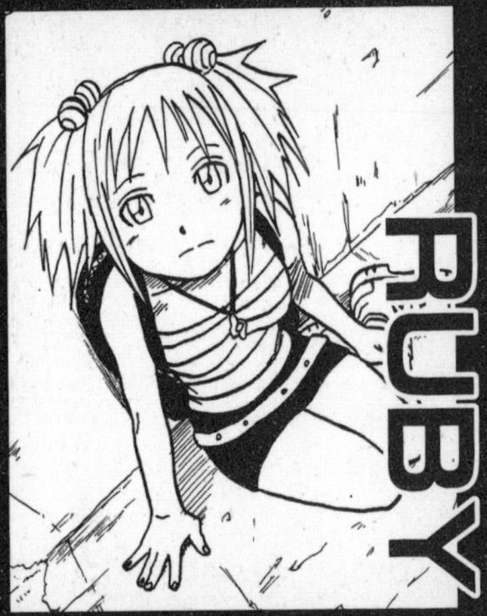
RUBY

Jio Freed
A wild O.P.T. boy whose dream is world domination! He has been emotionally damaged by his experiences in the past, but is still gung-ho about his new adventures! O-Part: New Zero-shiki (Rank B)
Effect: Triple (Increasing power by a factor of three)

Ruby
A treasure hunter who can decipher ancient texts. She meets Jio during her search for a legendary O-Part.

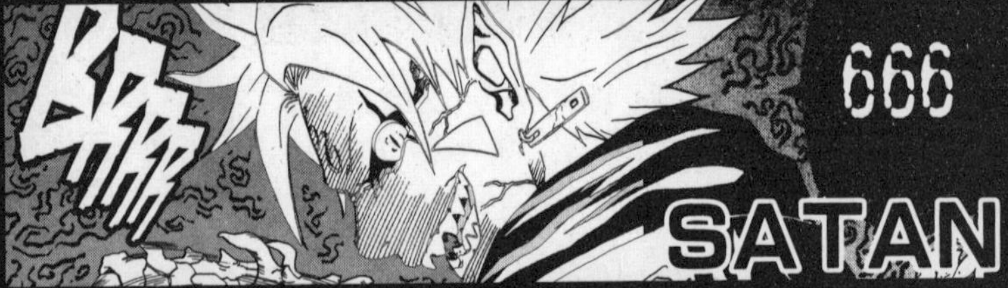
666
SATAN

Satan
This demon is thought to be a mutated form of Jio. It is a creature shrouded in mystery with earth-shattering powers.

STORY

Ascald: a world where people fight amongst themselves in order to get their hands on mystical objects left behind by an ancient civilization...the O-Parts.

In that world, a monster that strikes fear into the hearts of the strongest of men is rumored to exist. Those who have seen the monster all tell of the same thing–that the number of the beast, 666, is engraved on its forehead.

***

Jio, an O.P.T. boy who wants to rule the world, travels the globe with Ball, a novice O.P.T., Kirin, a mentor figure with a penchant for pickles, and Ruby, a girl searching for a legendary O-Part and her missing father. On a quest to find the Kabbalah before the Stea Goverment can use it for world domination, our heroes meet Cross, a young but formidable O.P.T. who has hunted Satan all his life. Cross doesn't recognize Satan in Jio, and the two part ways... but then Jio's team stumbles onto the city of Rock Bird where Olympia, a deadly world tournament for O.P.T.s, is being held. Jio and Ball enter, but will they leave alive? Meanwhile, Cross meets with a strange hacker known as "Invisible" to gather information for his personal quest to eradicate Satan...

O-Parts HUNTER

Table of Contents

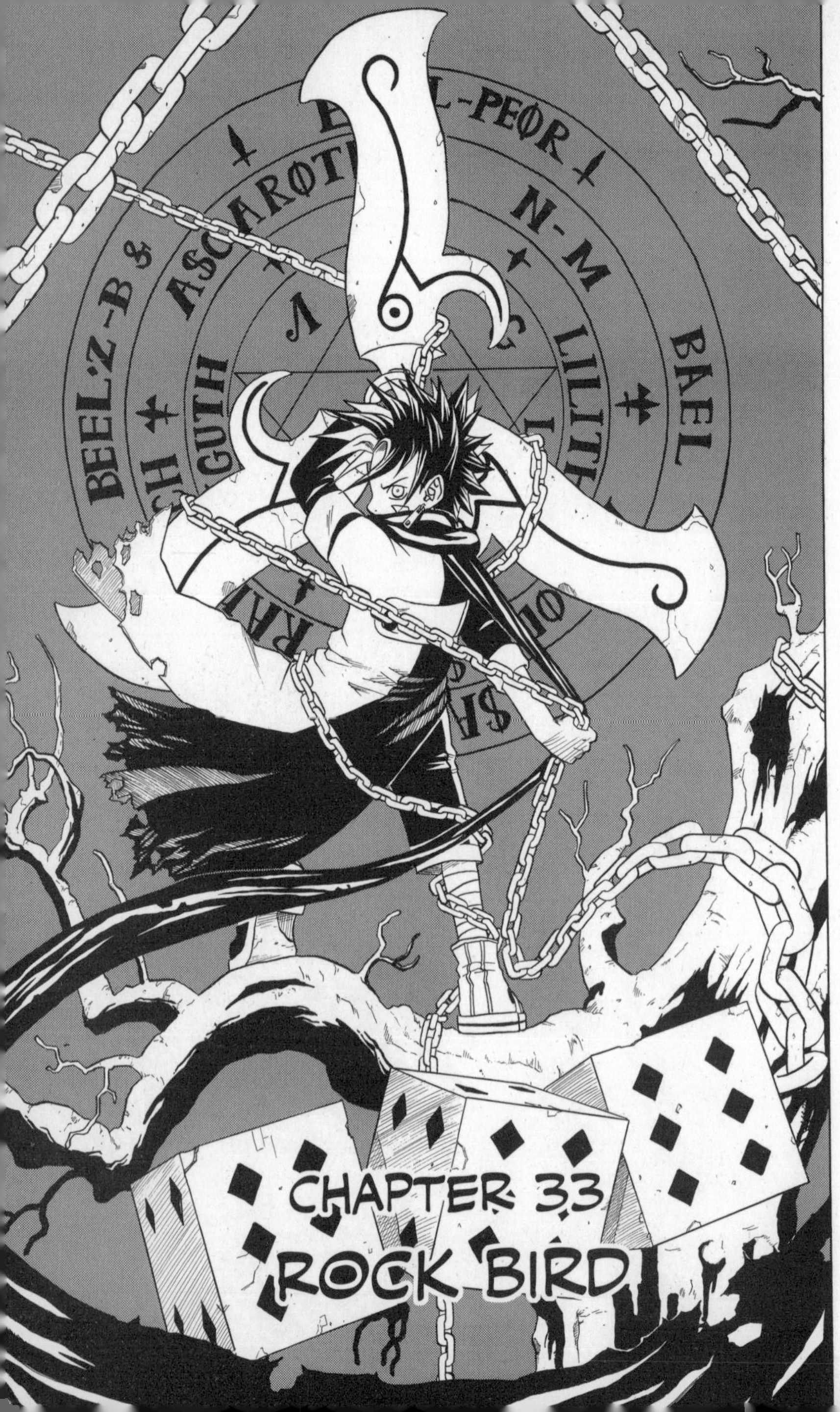
CHAPTER 33
ROCK BIRD

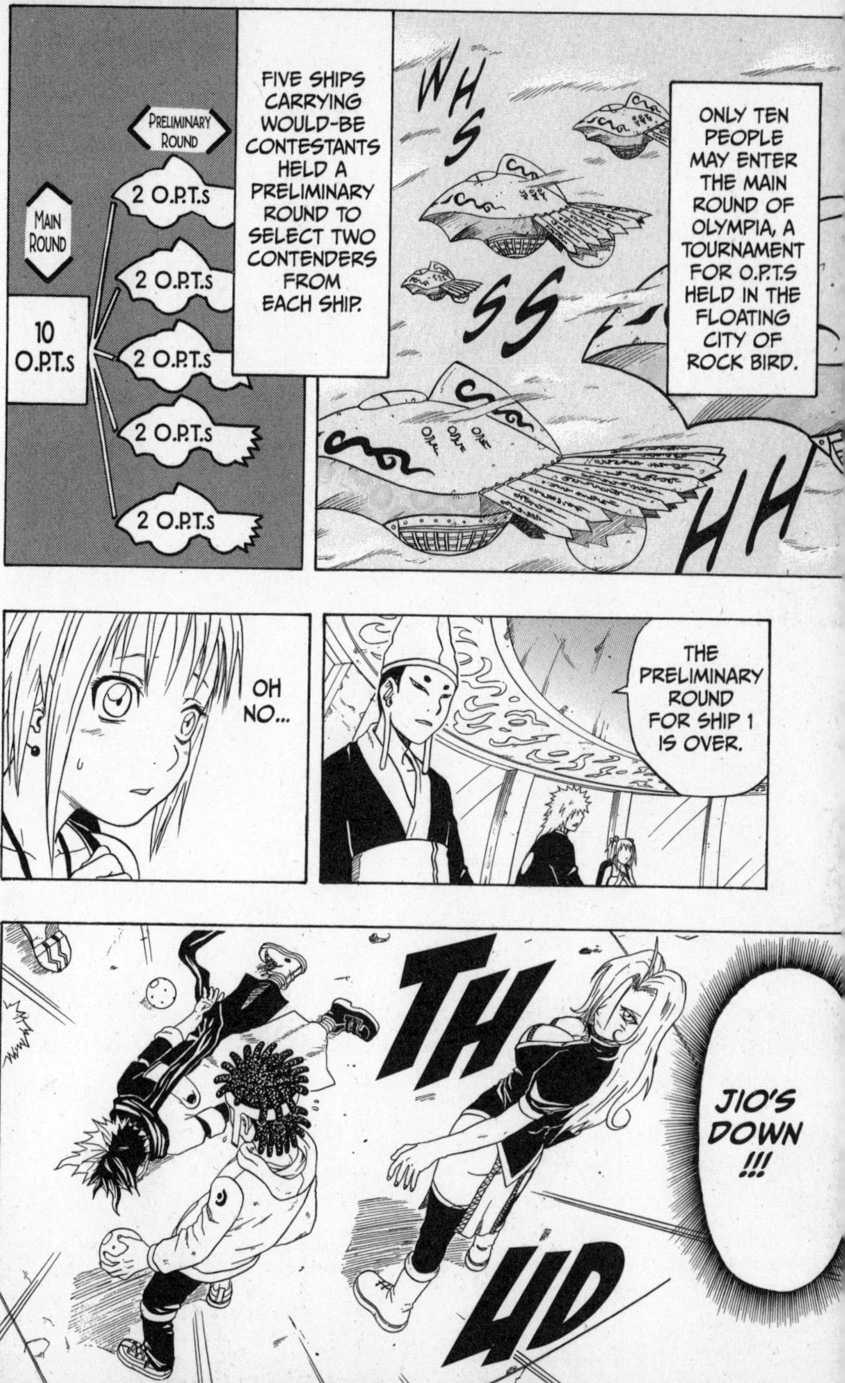
ONLY TEN PEOPLE MAY ENTER THE MAIN ROUND OF OLYMPIA, A TOURNAMENT FOR O.P.T.S HELD IN THE FLOATING CITY OF ROCK BIRD.
WHSSSHH
FIVE SHIPS CARRYING WOULD-BE CONTESTANTS HELD A PRELIMINARY ROUND TO SELECT TWO CONTENDERS FROM EACH SHIP.
PRELIMINARY ROUND
MAIN ROUND
2 O.P.T.s
2 O.P.T.s
2 O.P.T.s
2 O.P.T.s
2 O.P.T.s
10 O.P.T.s
THE PRELIMINARY ROUND FOR SHIP 1 IS OVER.
OH NO...
JIO'S DOWN !!!
THUD

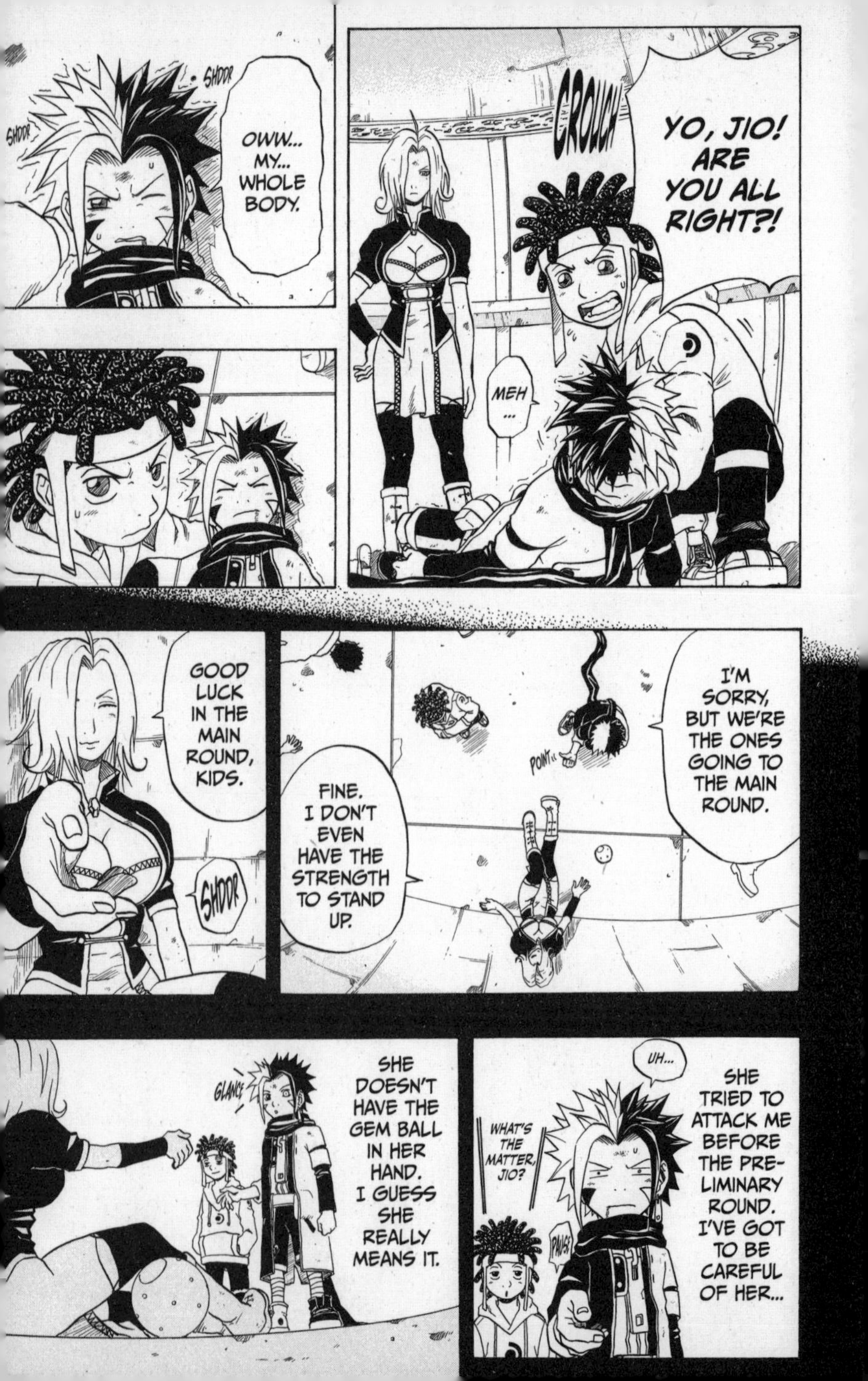
CRUNCH
YO, JIO! ARE YOU ALL RIGHT?!
MEH...
SHDDR
SHDDR
OWW... MY... WHOLE BODY.
I'M SORRY, BUT WE'RE THE ONES GOING TO THE MAIN ROUND.
POINT
FINE. I DON'T EVEN HAVE THE STRENGTH TO STAND UP.
GOOD LUCK IN THE MAIN ROUND, KIDS.
SHDDR
UH...
SHE TRIED TO ATTACK ME BEFORE THE PRE-LIMINARY ROUND. I'VE GOT TO BE CAREFUL OF HER...
WHAT'S THE MATTER, JIO?
PAUSE
GLANCE
SHE DOESN'T HAVE THE GEM BALL IN HER HAND. I GUESS SHE REALLY MEANS IT.

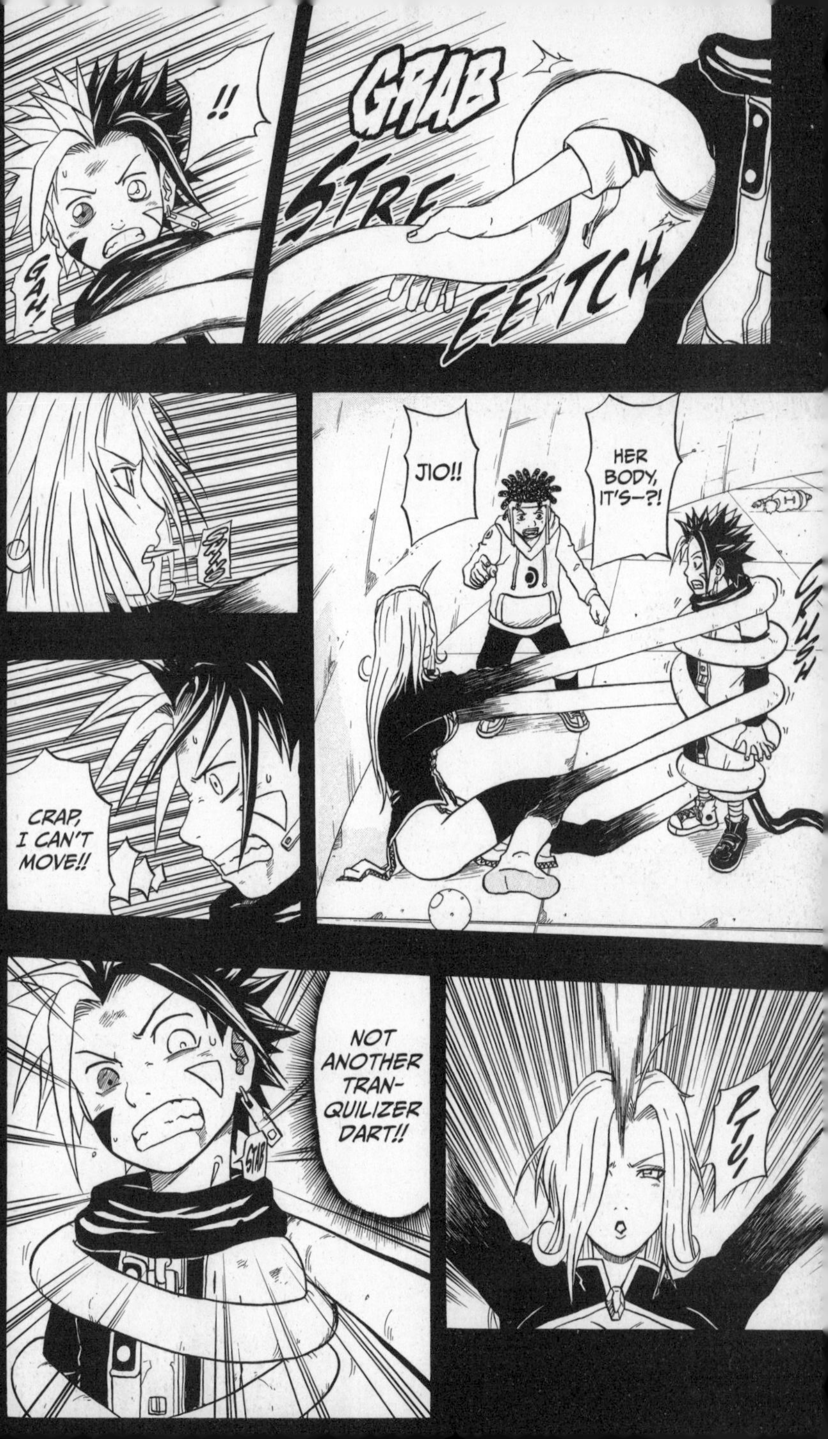
GRAB
STRE EETCH
!!
GAH!
HER BODY, IT'S—?!
JIO!!
CRUSH
CRAP, I CAN'T MOVE!!
PTUI
NOT ANOTHER TRAN-QUILIZER DART!!
STAB

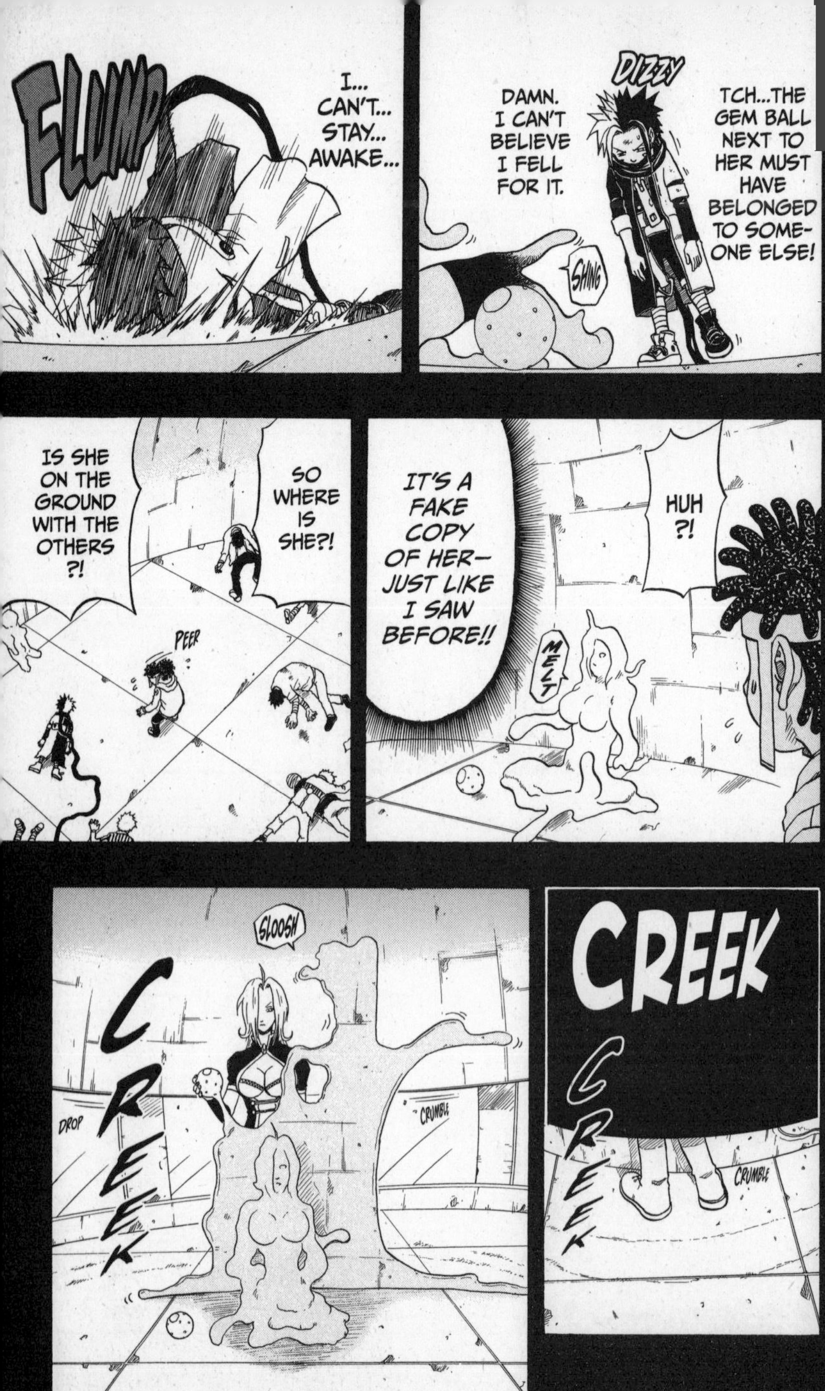
DIZZY
TCH...THE GEM BALL NEXT TO HER MUST HAVE BELONGED TO SOME-ONE ELSE!
DAMN. I CAN'T BELIEVE I FELL FOR IT.
SHING
I... CAN'T... STAY... AWAKE...
FLUMP
HUH?!
IT'S A FAKE COPY OF HER— JUST LIKE I SAW BEFORE!!
MELT
SO WHERE IS SHE?!
IS SHE ON THE GROUND WITH THE OTHERS?!
PEER
CREEK
CREEEK
CRUMBLE
SLOOSH
CRUMBLE
CREEEK
DROP

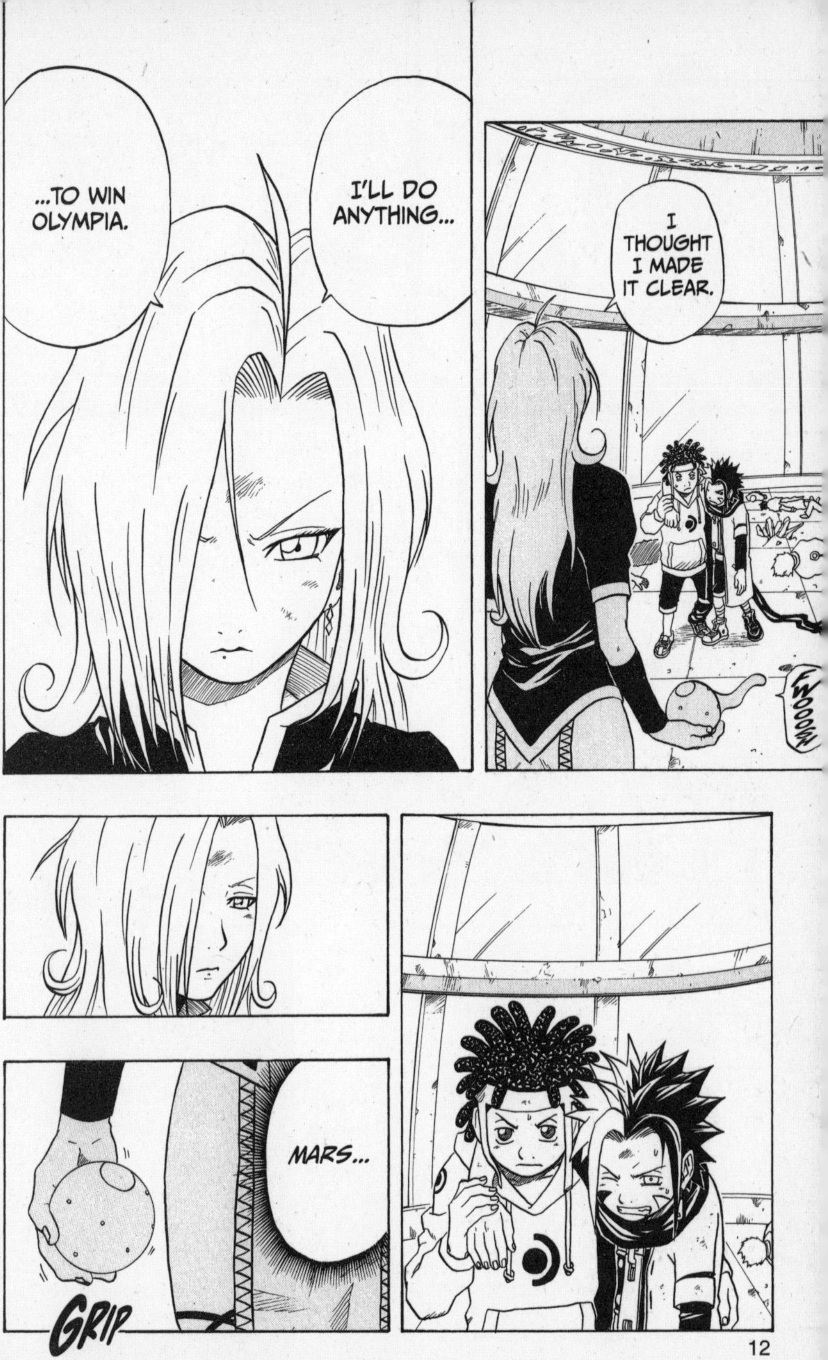
I THOUGHT I MADE IT CLEAR.
FWOOOSH
I'LL DO ANYTHING...
...TO WIN OLYMPIA.
MARS...
GRIP

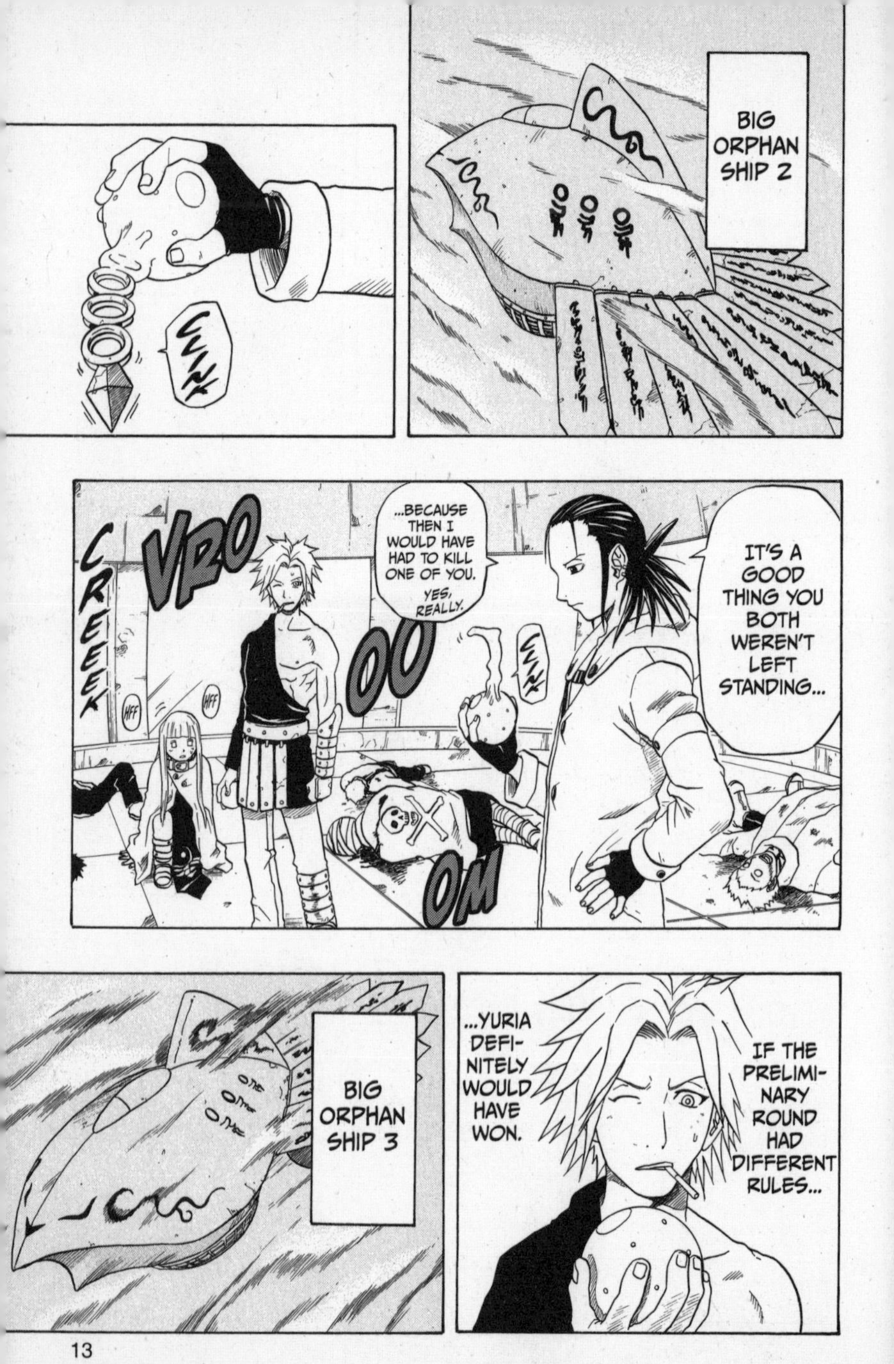
BIG ORPHAN SHIP 2
CLINK
IT'S A GOOD THING YOU BOTH WEREN'T LEFT STANDING...
...BECAUSE THEN I WOULD HAVE HAD TO KILL ONE OF YOU.
YES, REALLY.
CLINK
VROOOOM
CREEEK
HFF
HFF
IF THE PRELIMINARY ROUND HAD DIFFERENT RULES...
...YURIA DEFINITELY WOULD HAVE WON.
BIG ORPHAN SHIP 3

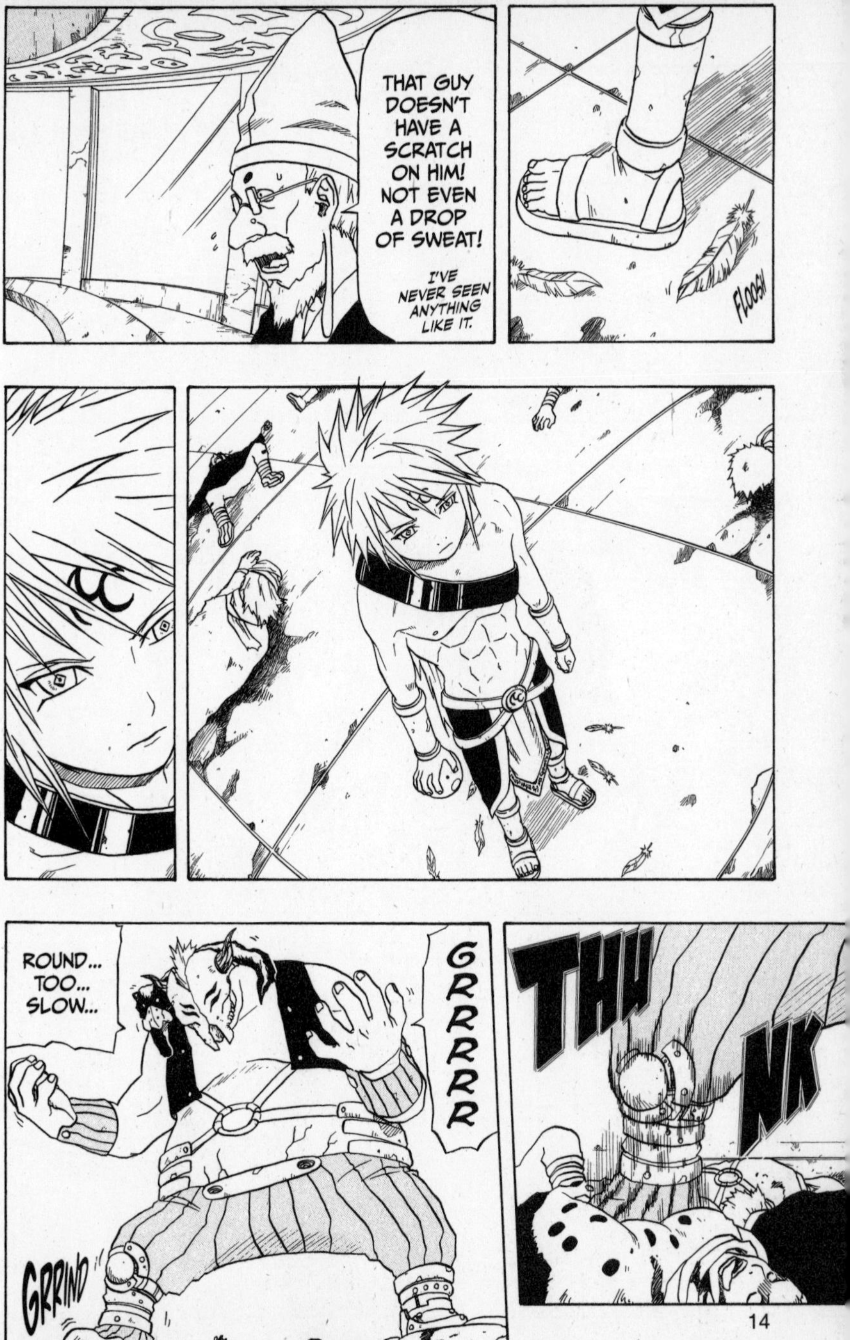
FLOOSH
THAT GUY DOESN'T HAVE A SCRATCH ON HIM! NOT EVEN A DROP OF SWEAT!
I'VE NEVER SEEN ANYTHING LIKE IT.
THUNK
GRRRRR
ROUND... TOO... SLOW...
GRRIND

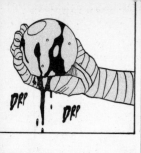

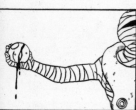

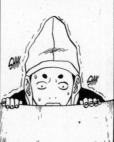

BIG ORPHAN SHIP 4
WH-WHO IS THAT GUY? HE'S GOING TO KILL ME NEXT. I KNOW IT!
SHHK
SHAK
DRP
DRP
OOPS. I GOT TOO EXCITED...
...AND KILLED THEM ALL.
GRAAAAAAH
DRP
DRP

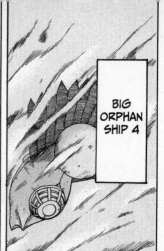

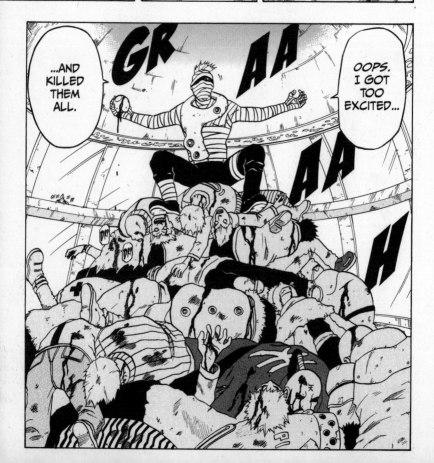

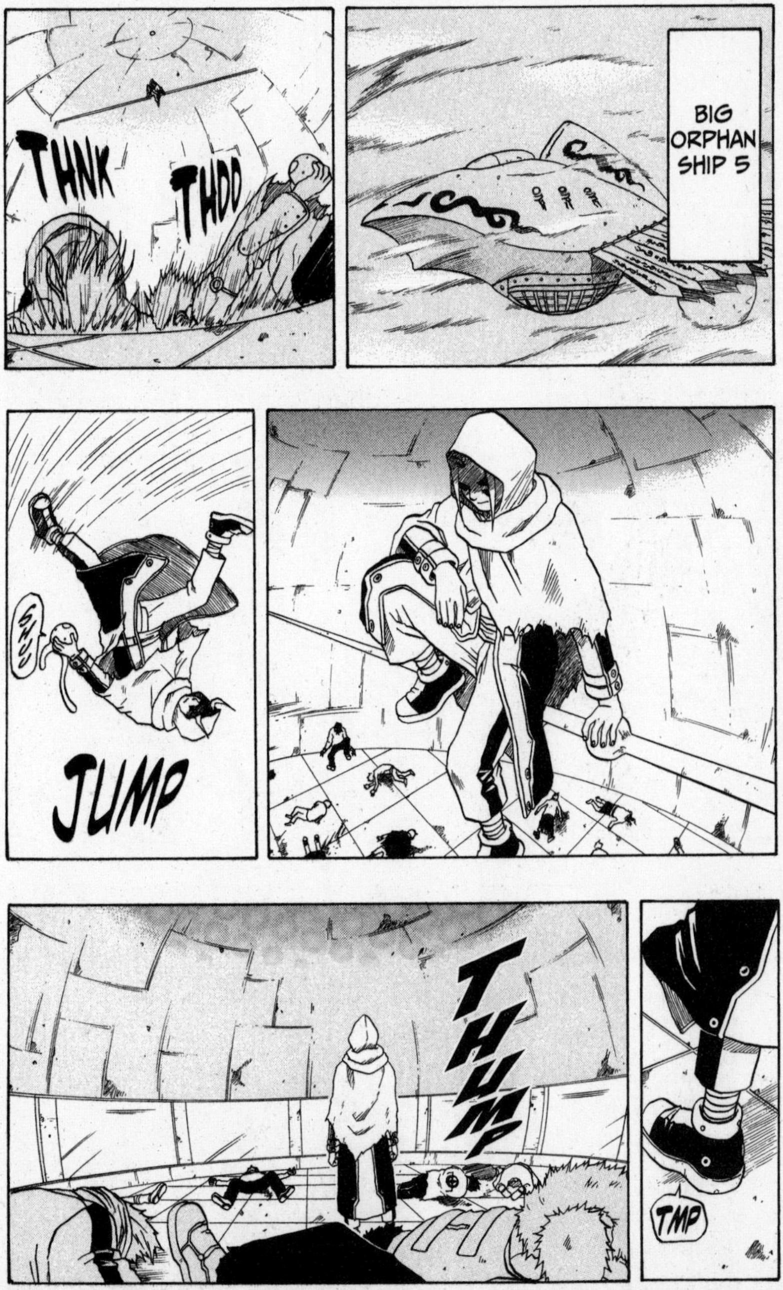
BIG ORPHAN SHIP 5
THNK
THDD
SHUU
JUMP
TMP
THUMP

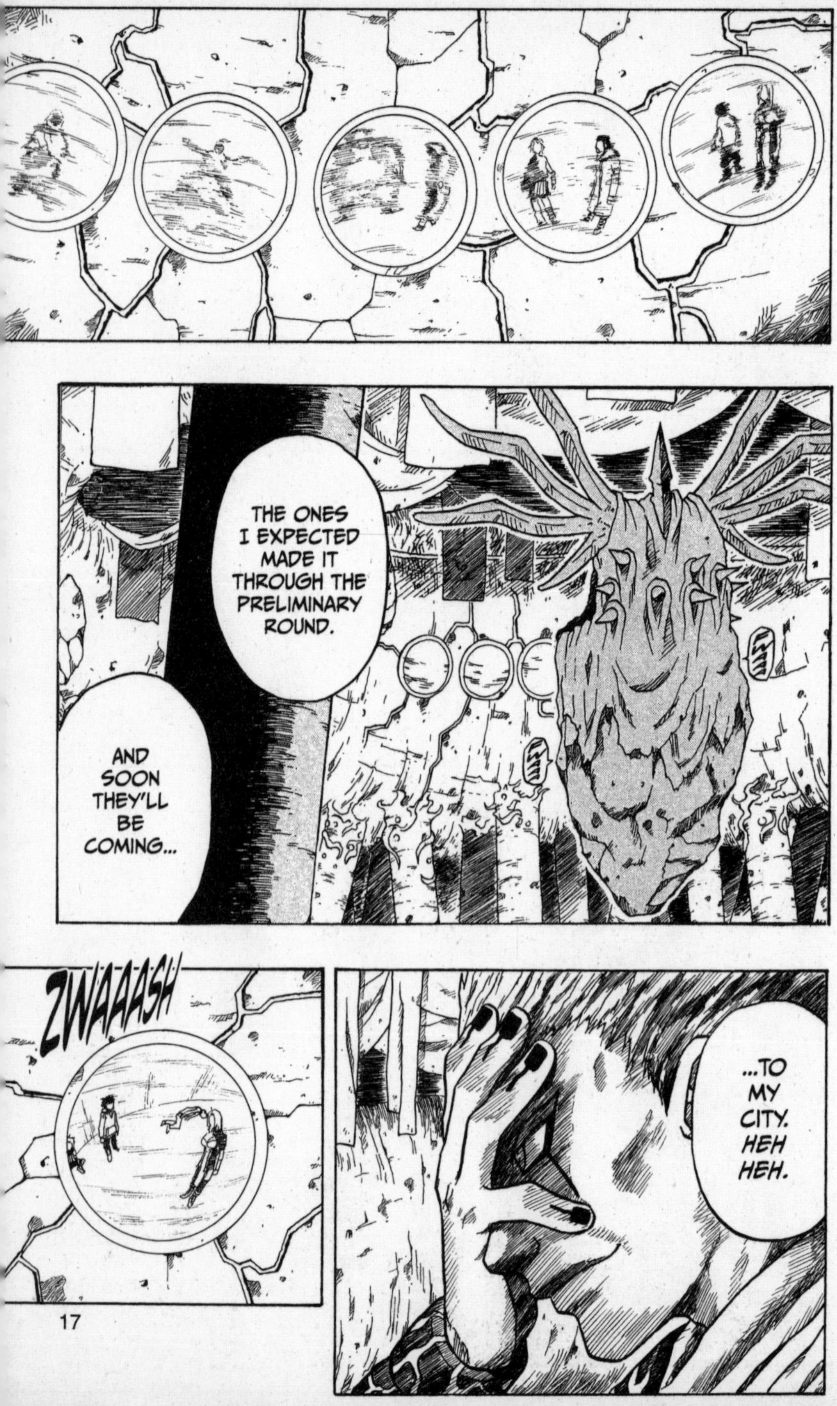
THE ONES I EXPECTED MADE IT THROUGH THE PRELIMINARY ROUND.
AND SOON THEY'LL BE COMING...
...TO MY CITY. HEH HEH.
ZWAAASH

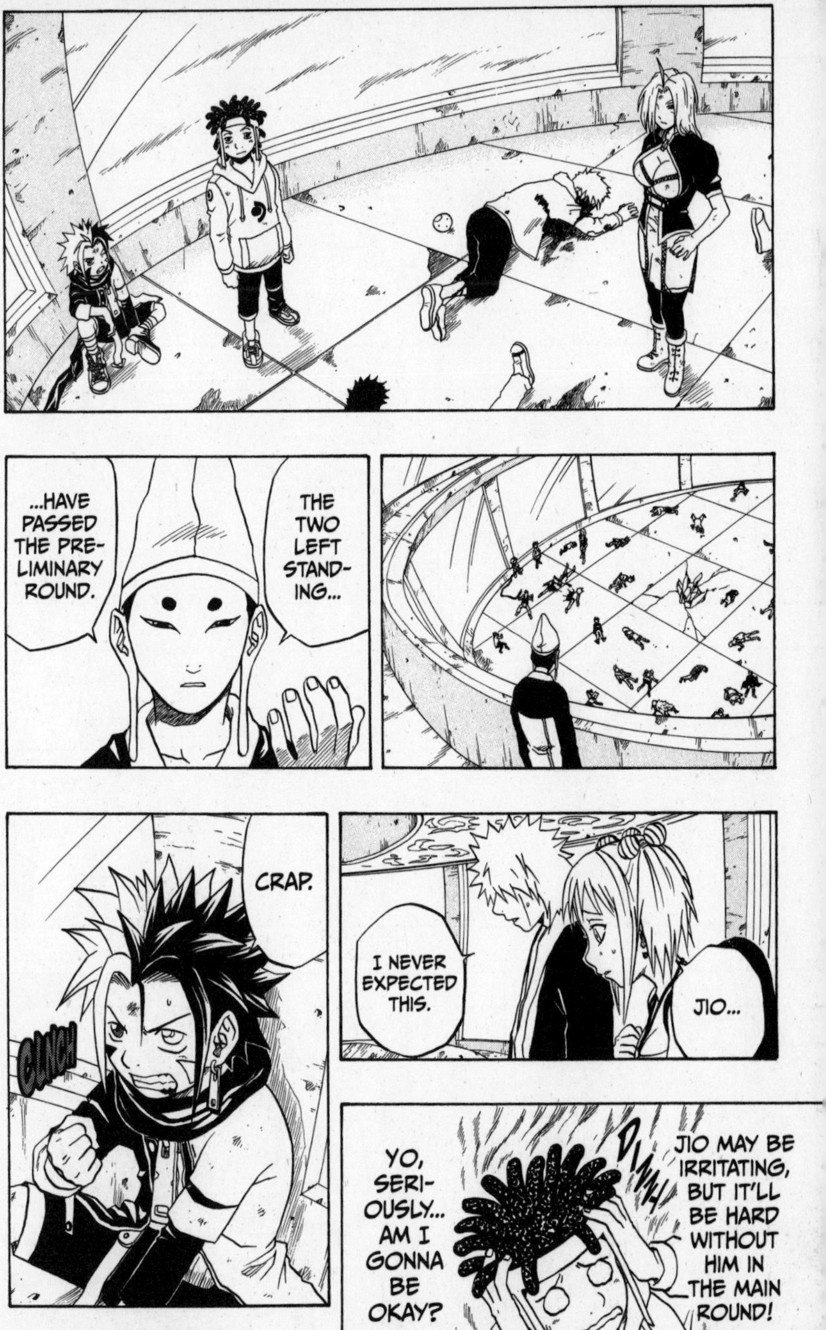
THE TWO LEFT STANDING...
...HAVE PASSED THE PRELIMINARY ROUND.
JIO...
I NEVER EXPECTED THIS.
JIO MAY BE IRRITATING, BUT IT'LL BE HARD WITHOUT HIM IN THE MAIN ROUND!
YO, SERIOUSLY... AM I GONNA BE OKAY?
CRAP.
CLINCH

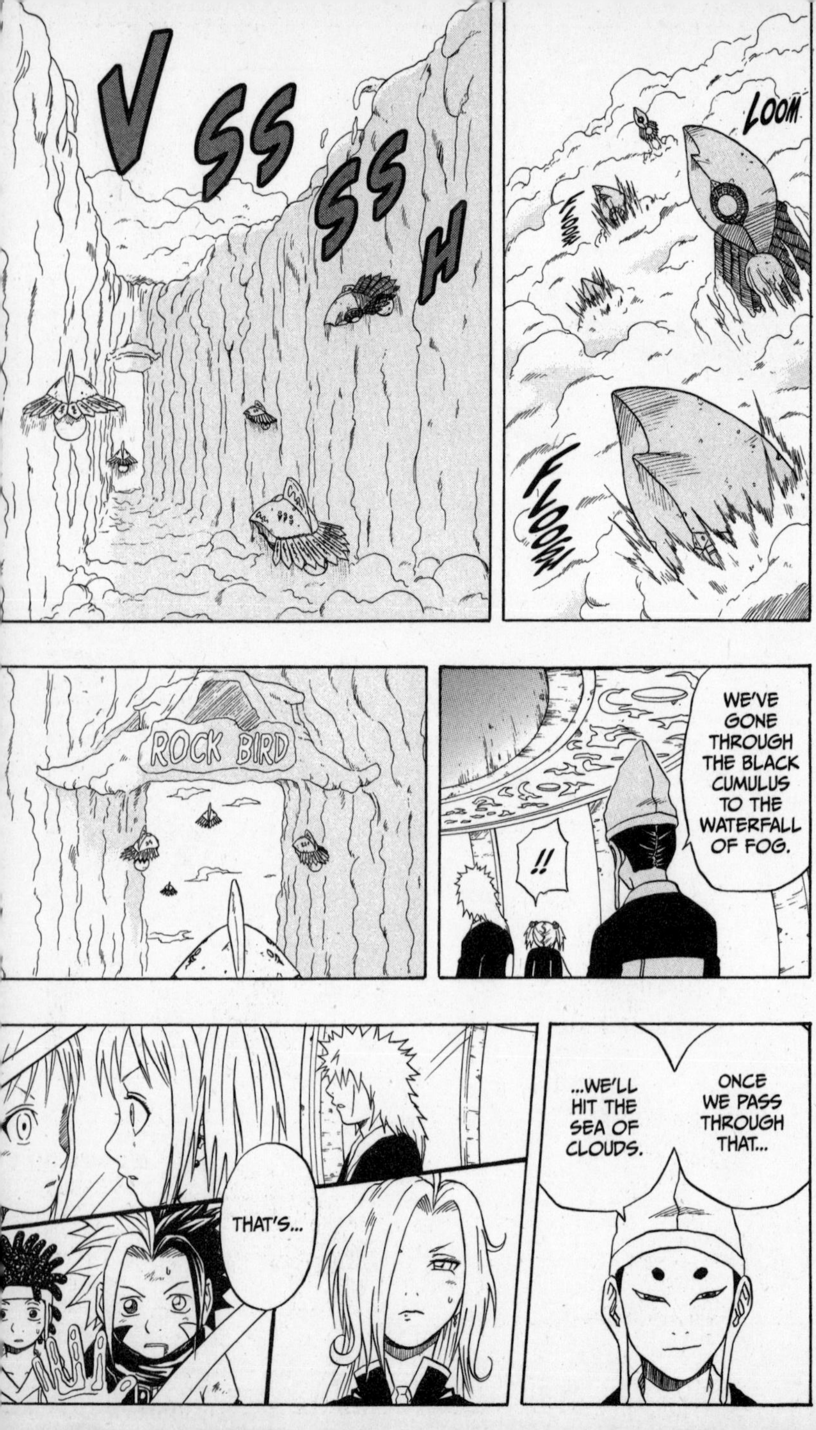
LOOM
VWOOM
VSSSSH
WE'VE GONE THROUGH THE BLACK CUMULUS TO THE WATERFALL OF FOG.
!!
ROCK BIRD
ONCE WE PASS THROUGH THAT...
...WE'LL HIT THE SEA OF CLOUDS.
THAT'S...

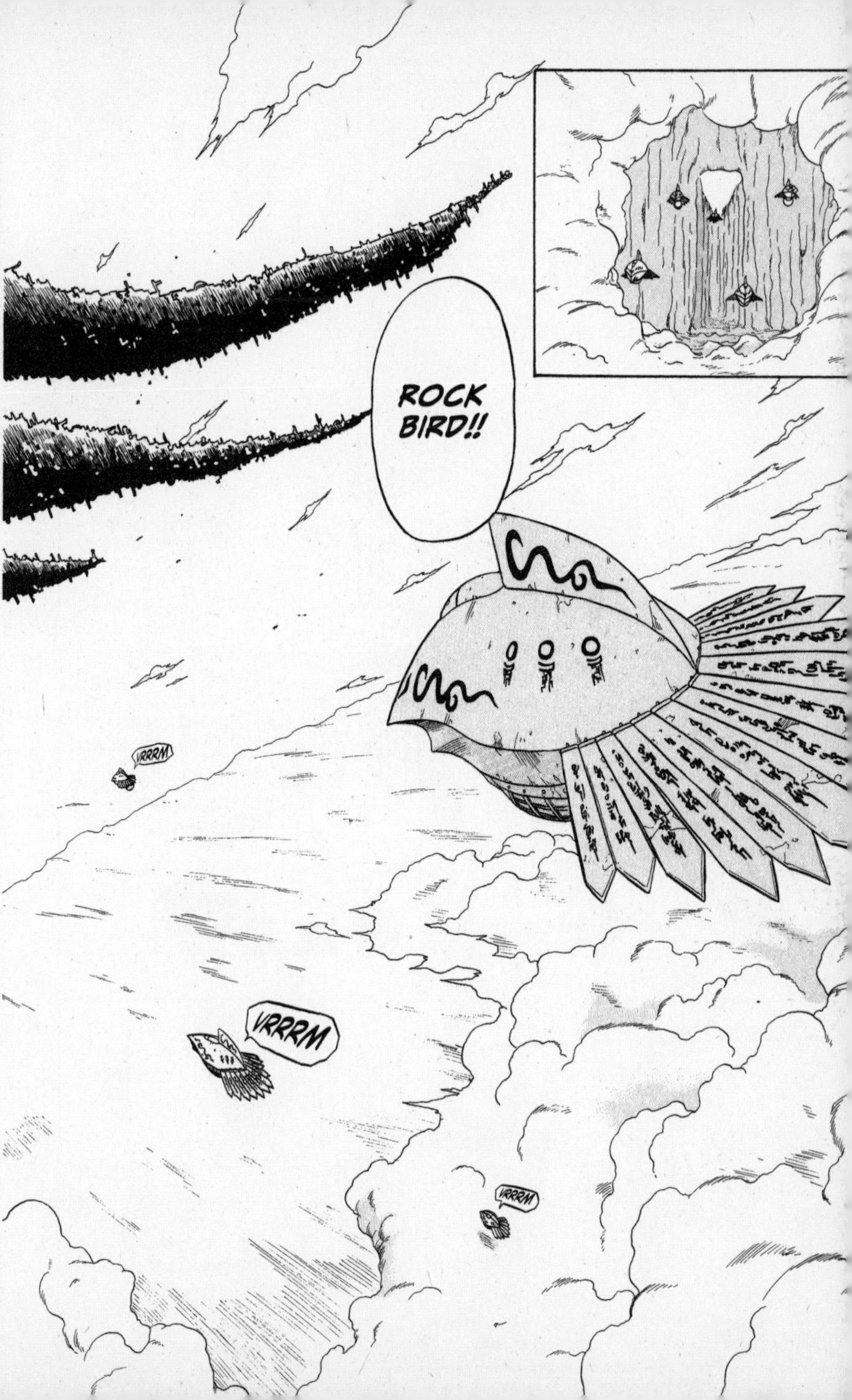
ROCK BIRD!!
VRRRM
VRRRM
VRRRM

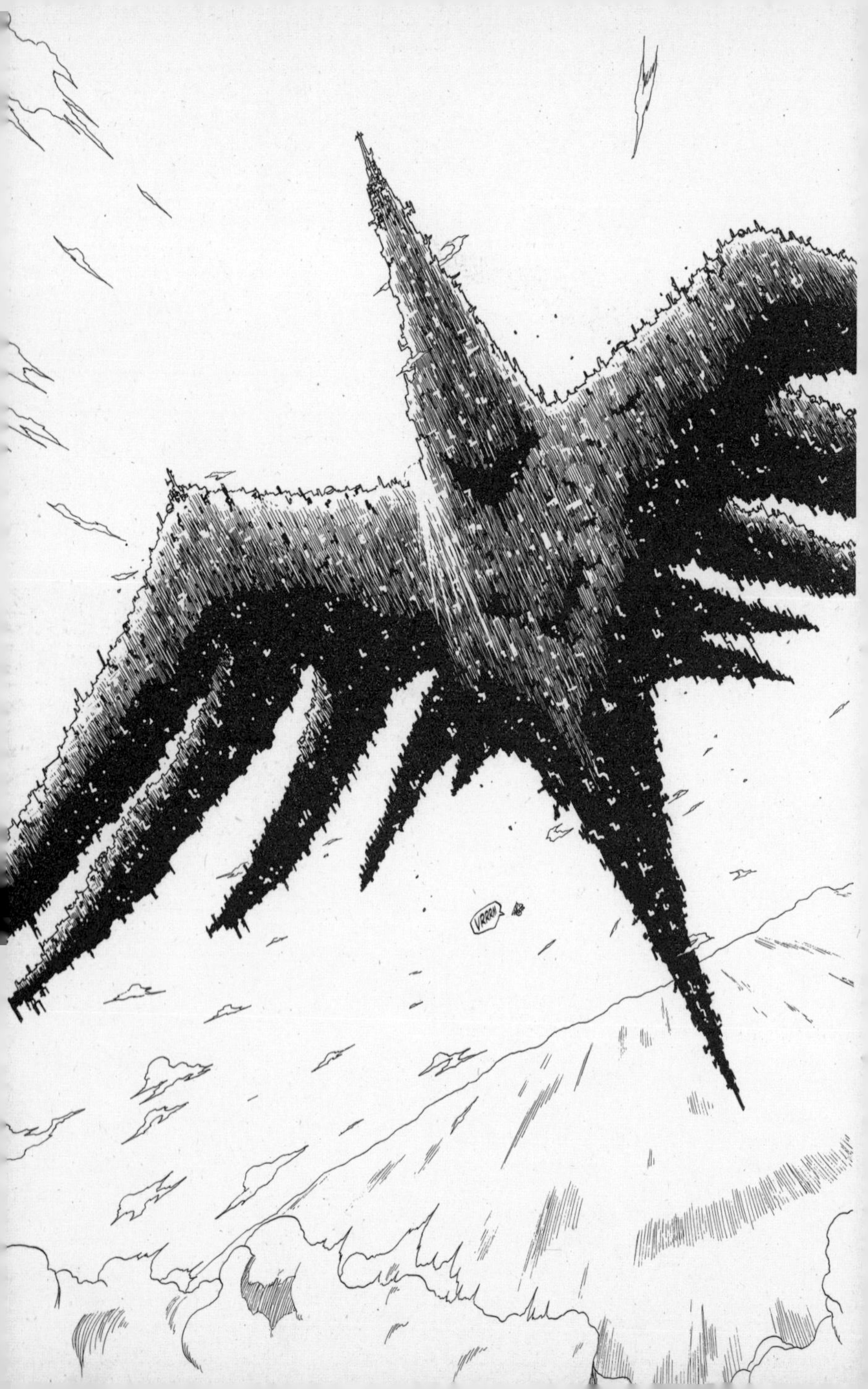
VRRRM

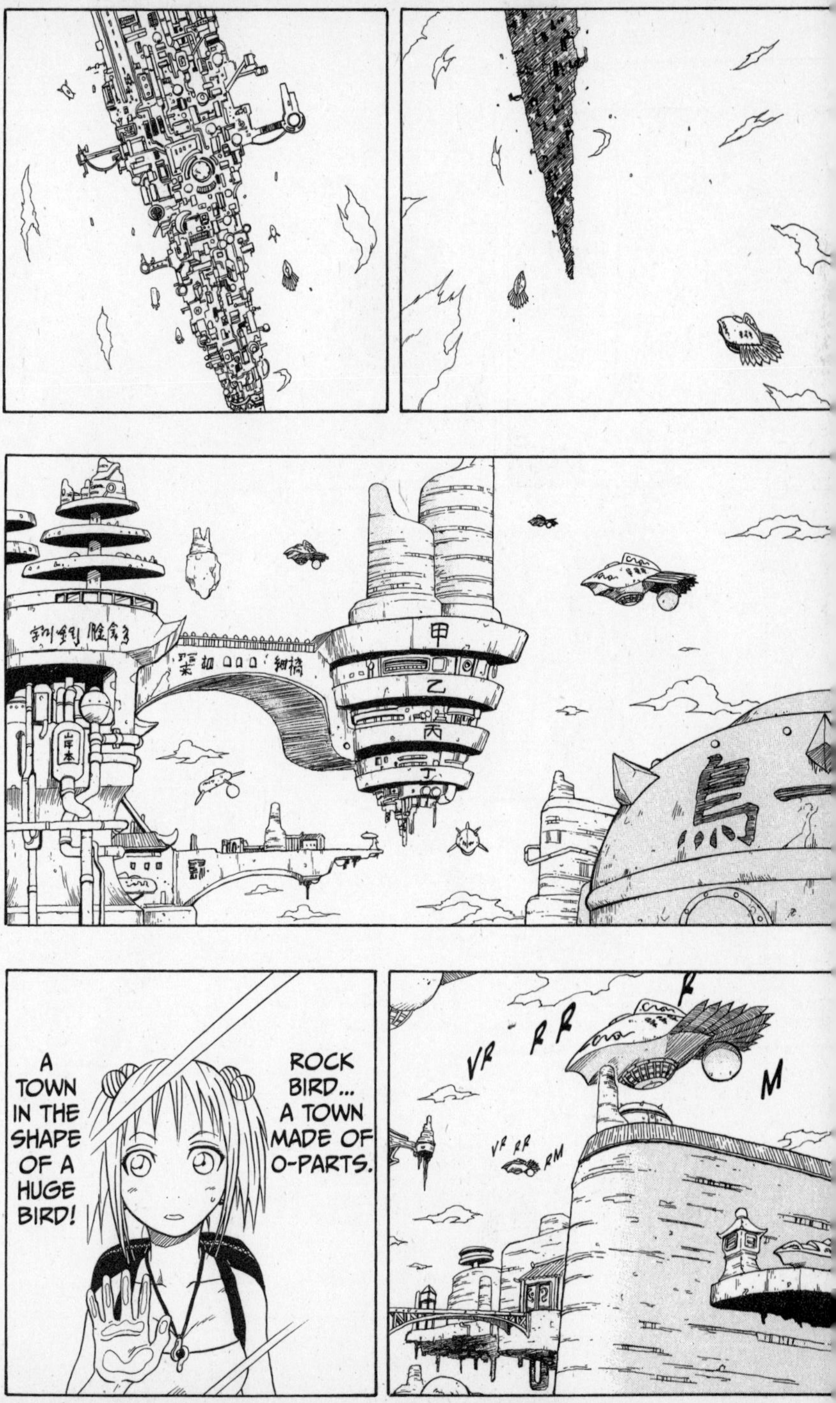

甲
乙
丙
丁
鳥
VR RR R M
VR RR RM
ROCK BIRD... A TOWN MADE OF O-PARTS.
A TOWN IN THE SHAPE OF A HUGE BIRD!

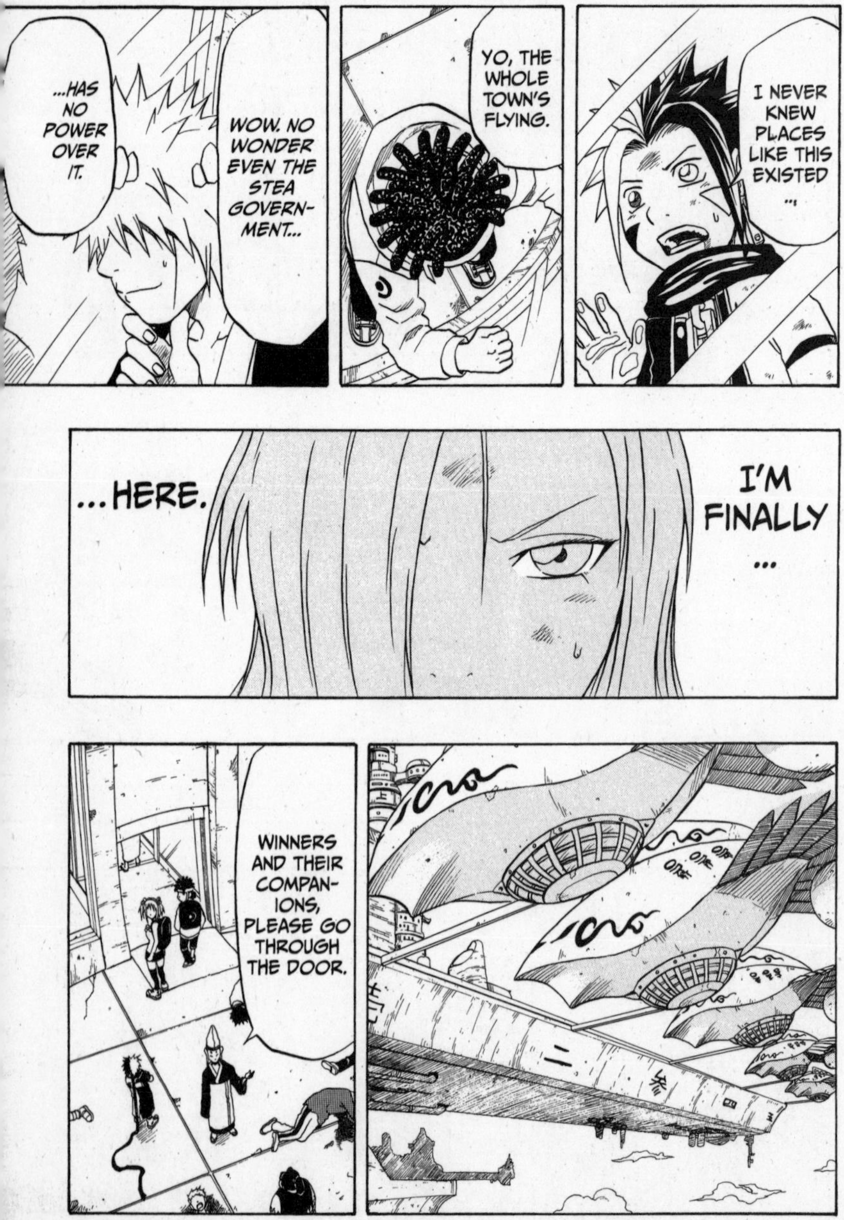
I NEVER KNEW PLACES LIKE THIS EXISTED ...
YO, THE WHOLE TOWN'S FLYING.
WOW. NO WONDER EVEN THE STEA GOVERNMENT...
...HAS NO POWER OVER IT.
I'M FINALLY ...
...HERE.
WINNERS AND THEIR COMPANIONS, PLEASE GO THROUGH THE DOOR.

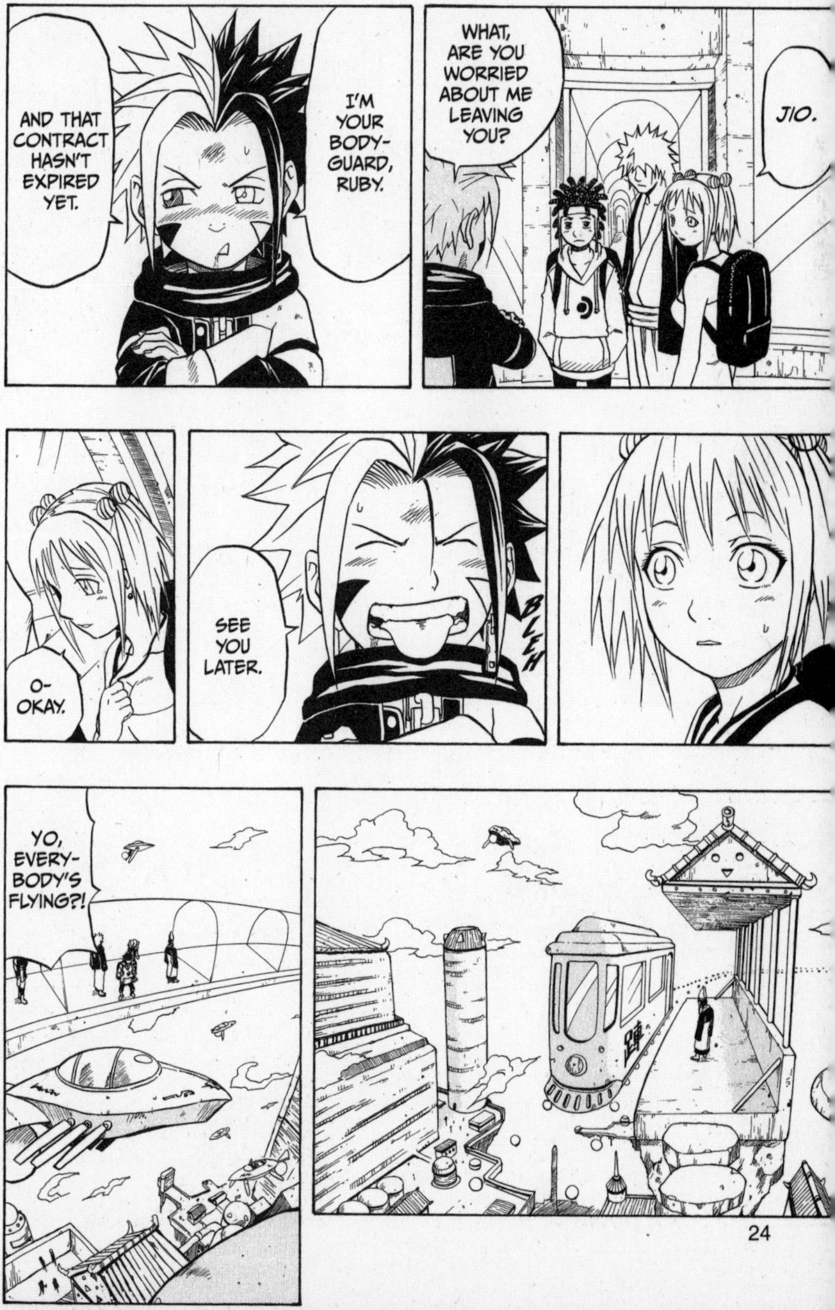
JIO.
WHAT, ARE YOU WORRIED ABOUT ME LEAVING YOU?
I'M YOUR BODY-GUARD, RUBY.
AND THAT CONTRACT HASN'T EXPIRED YET.
SEE YOU LATER.
BLEH
O-OKAY.
YO, EVERY-BODY'S FLYING?!

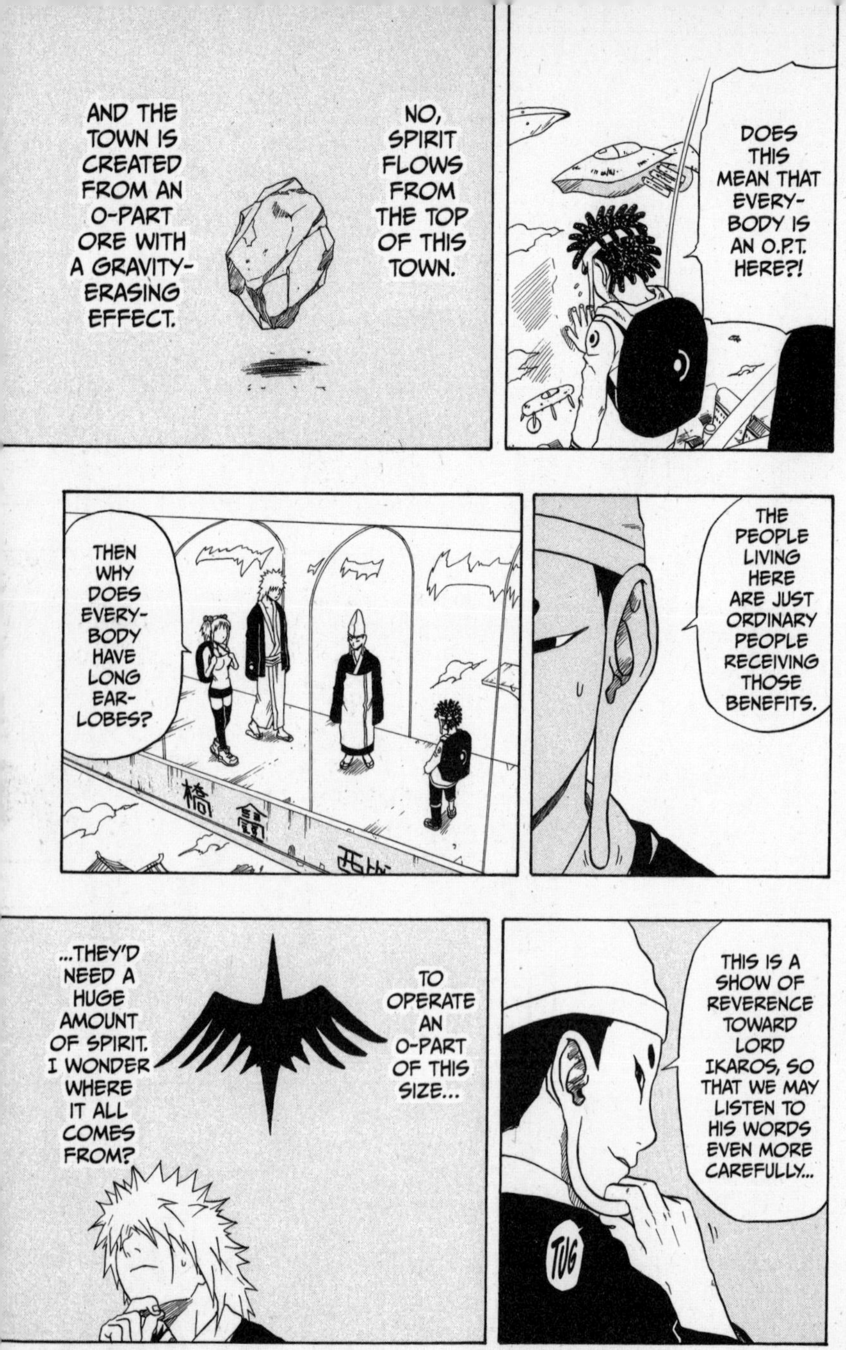
DOES THIS MEAN THAT EVERYBODY IS AN O.P.T. HERE?!
NO, SPIRIT FLOWS FROM THE TOP OF THIS TOWN.
AND THE TOWN IS CREATED FROM AN O-PART ORE WITH A GRAVITY-ERASING EFFECT.
THE PEOPLE LIVING HERE ARE JUST ORDINARY PEOPLE RECEIVING THOSE BENEFITS.
THEN WHY DOES EVERYBODY HAVE LONG EARLOBES?
THIS IS A SHOW OF REVERENCE TOWARD LORD IKAROS, SO THAT WE MAY LISTEN TO HIS WORDS EVEN MORE CAREFULLY...
TUG
TO OPERATE AN O-PART OF THIS SIZE...
...THEY'D NEED A HUGE AMOUNT OF SPIRIT. I WONDER WHERE IT ALL COMES FROM?

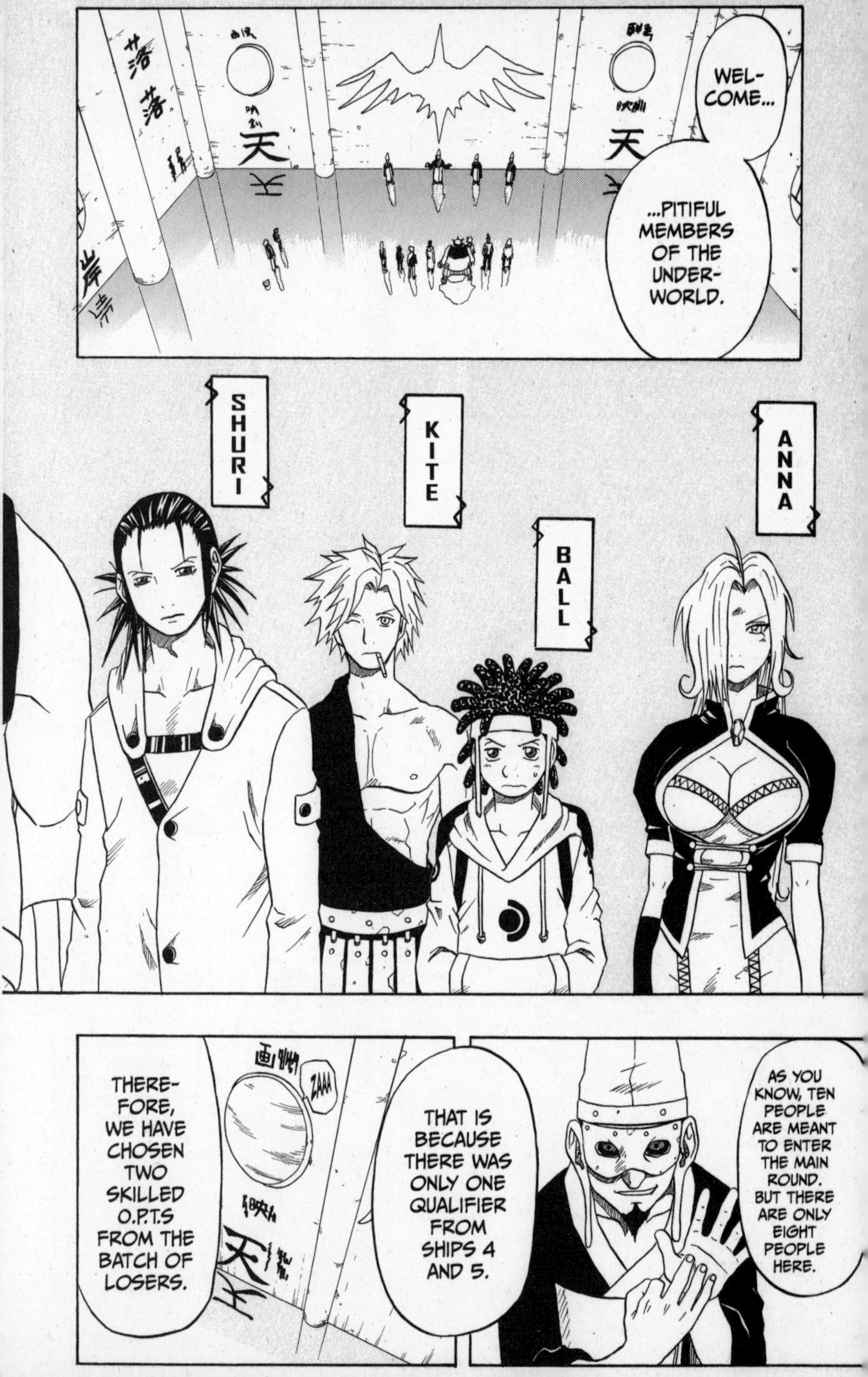
WEL-COME...
...PITIFUL MEMBERS OF THE UNDER-WORLD.
ANNA
BALL
KITE
SHURI
AS YOU KNOW, TEN PEOPLE ARE MEANT TO ENTER THE MAIN ROUND. BUT THERE ARE ONLY EIGHT PEOPLE HERE.
THAT IS BECAUSE THERE WAS ONLY ONE QUALIFIER FROM SHIPS 4 AND 5.
ZAAA
THERE-FORE, WE HAVE CHOSEN TWO SKILLED O.P.T.S FROM THE BATCH OF LOSERS.

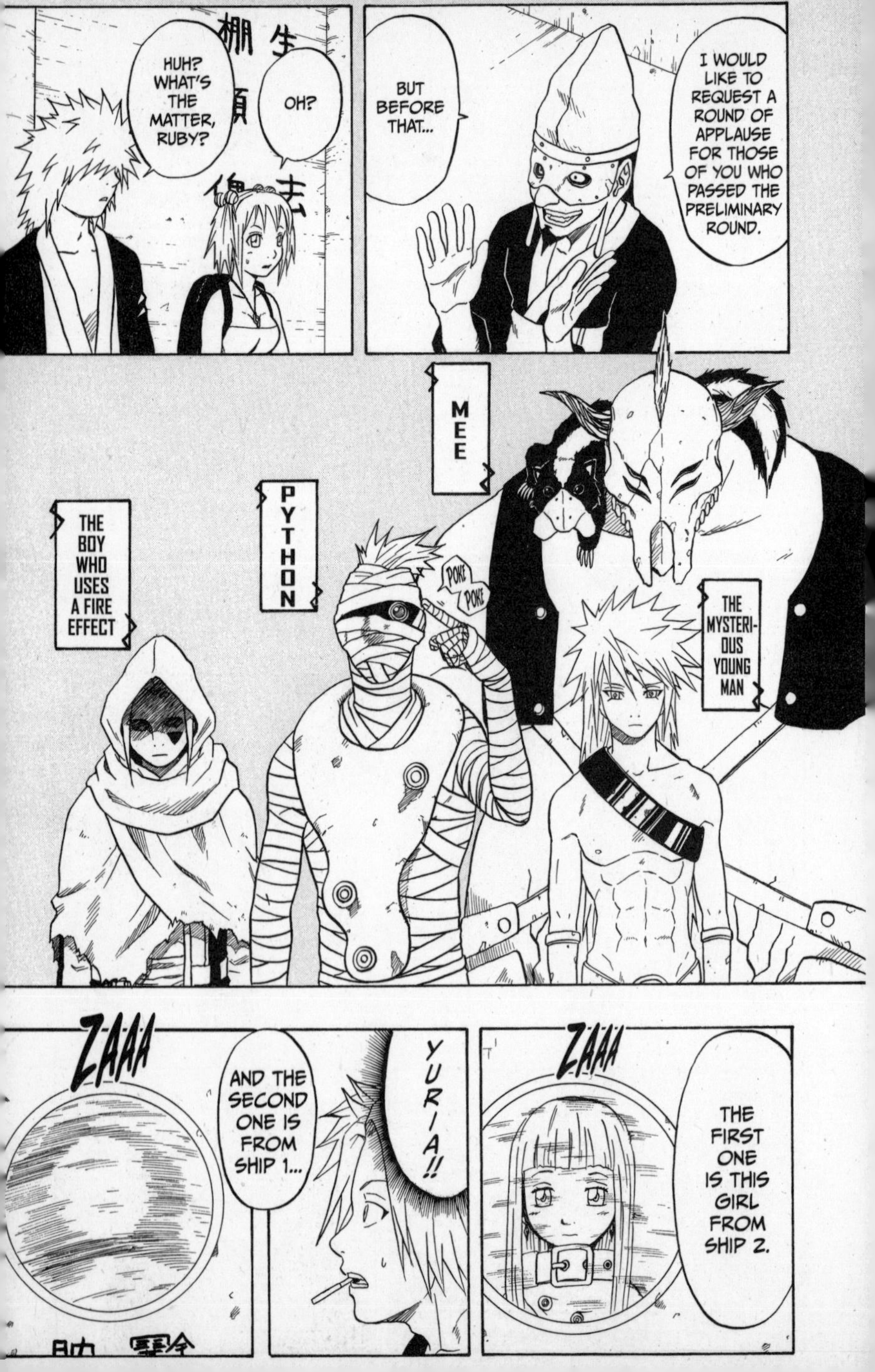
I WOULD LIKE TO REQUEST A ROUND OF APPLAUSE FOR THOSE OF YOU WHO PASSED THE PRELIMINARY ROUND.
BUT BEFORE THAT...
OH?
HUH? WHAT'S THE MATTER, RUBY?
MEE
THE MYSTERIOUS YOUNG MAN
PYTHON
POKE
POKE
THE BOY WHO USES A FIRE EFFECT
ZAAA
THE FIRST ONE IS THIS GIRL FROM SHIP 2.
YURIA!!
AND THE SECOND ONE IS FROM SHIP 1...
ZAAA

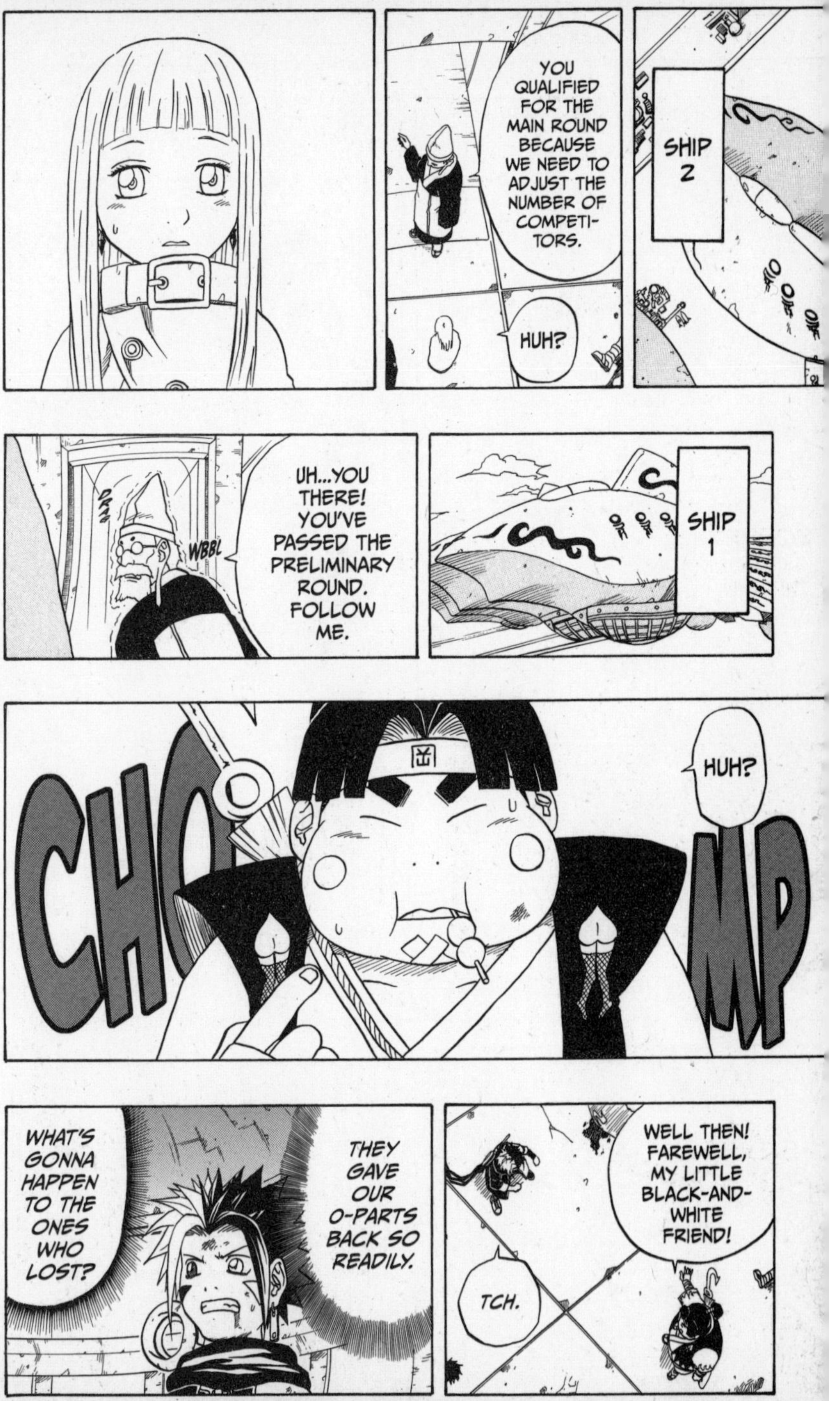
SHIP 2
YOU QUALIFIED FOR THE MAIN ROUND BECAUSE WE NEED TO ADJUST THE NUMBER OF COMPETI-TORS.
HUH?
SHIP 1
UH...YOU THERE! YOU'VE PASSED THE PRELIMINARY ROUND. FOLLOW ME.
WBBL
CHOMP
HUH?
WELL THEN! FAREWELL, MY LITTLE BLACK-AND-WHITE FRIEND!
TCH.
THEY GAVE OUR O-PARTS BACK SO READILY.
WHAT'S GONNA HAPPEN TO THE ONES WHO LOST?

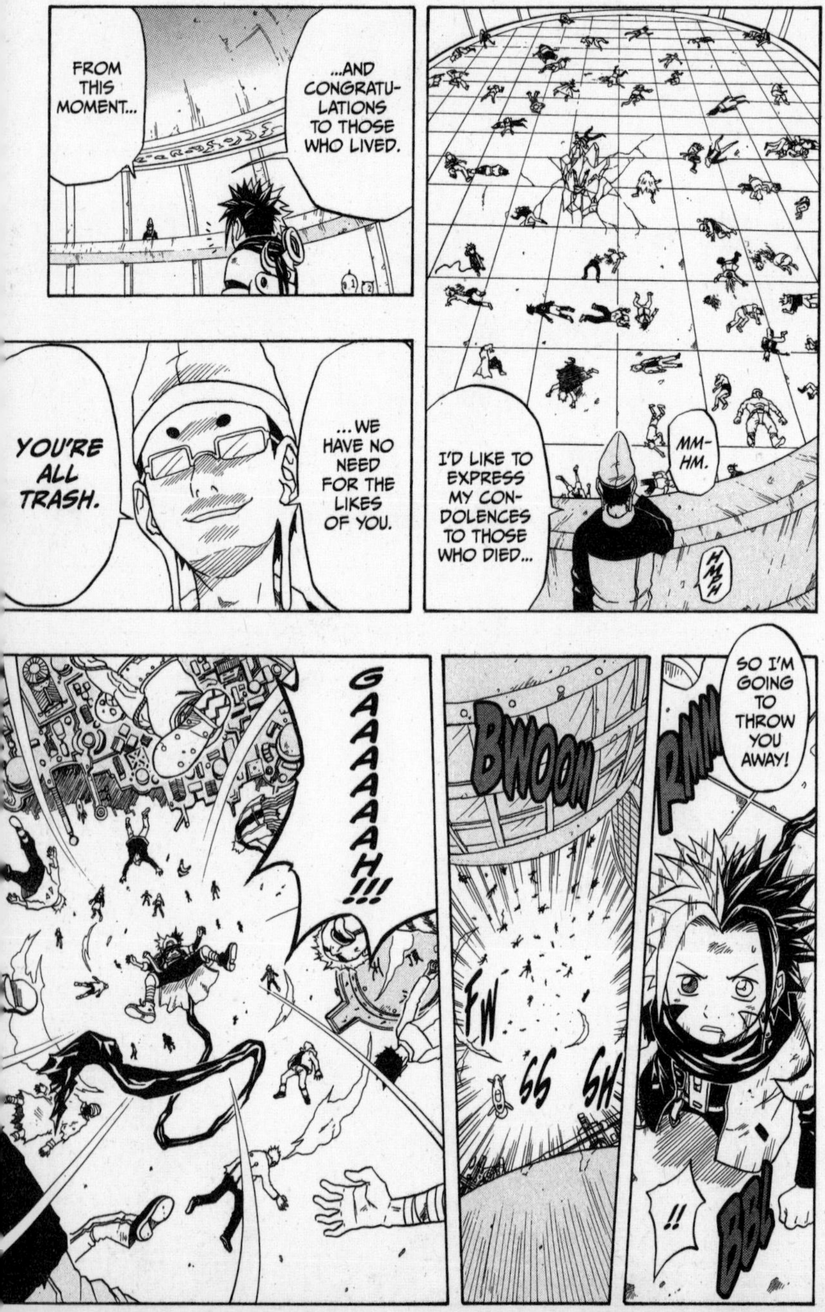
MM-HM.
I'D LIKE TO EXPRESS MY CONDOLENCES TO THOSE WHO DIED...
HMMH
...AND CONGRATULATIONS TO THOSE WHO LIVED.
FROM THIS MOMENT...
...WE HAVE NO NEED FOR THE LIKES OF YOU.
YOU'RE ALL TRASH.
SO I'M GOING TO THROW YOU AWAY!
RMM
!!
BBL
BWOOM
FW
SS
SH
GAAAAAAAH!!!

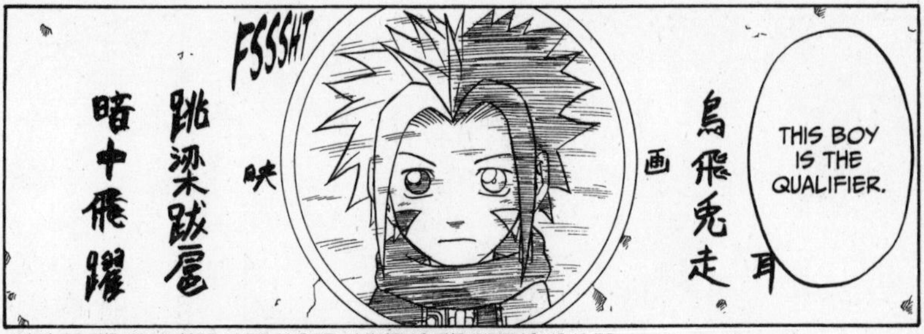
THIS BOY IS THE QUALIFIER.
鳥飛兎走
耳
画
映
跳梁跋扈
暗中飛躍
FSSSHT

MUCH OF THE KANJI USED IN ROCK BIRD, INCLUDING THE WRITING NEXT TO JIO'S PICTURE ABOVE, IS PURELY STYLISTIC WITH NO REAL MEANING. –ED

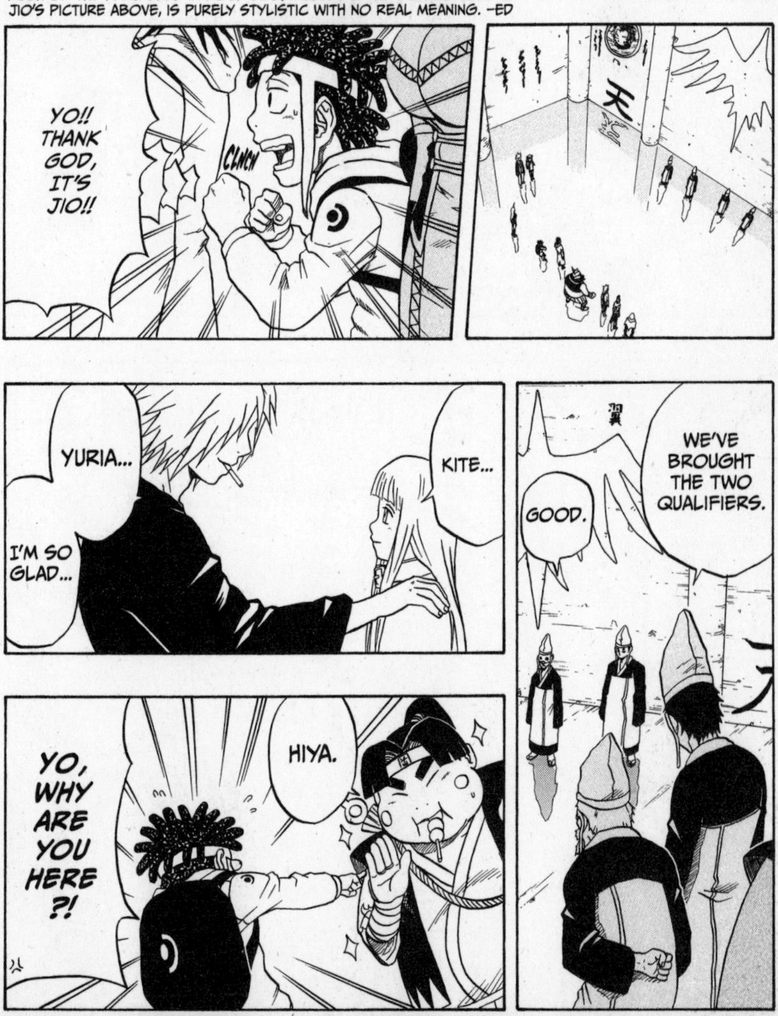
天
YO!! THANK GOD, IT'S JIO!!
CLNCH
WE'VE BROUGHT THE TWO QUALIFIERS.
GOOD.
KITE...
YURIA...
I'M SO GLAD...
HIYA.
YO, WHY ARE YOU HERE?!

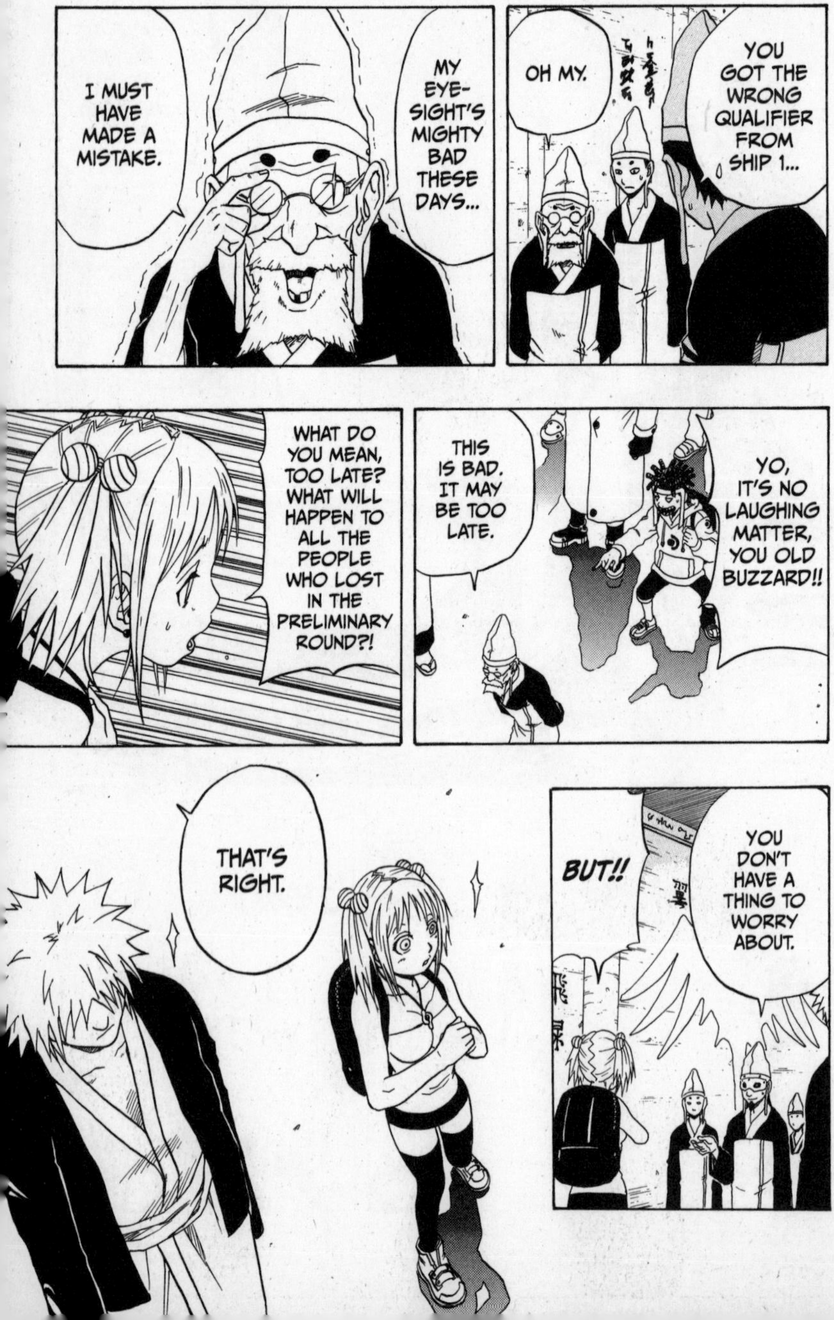
YOU GOT THE WRONG QUALIFIER FROM SHIP 1...
OH MY.
MY EYE-SIGHT'S MIGHTY BAD THESE DAYS...
I MUST HAVE MADE A MISTAKE.
YO, IT'S NO LAUGHING MATTER, YOU OLD BUZZARD!!
THIS IS BAD. IT MAY BE TOO LATE.
WHAT DO YOU MEAN, TOO LATE? WHAT WILL HAPPEN TO ALL THE PEOPLE WHO LOST IN THE PRELIMINARY ROUND?!
YOU DON'T HAVE A THING TO WORRY ABOUT.
BUT!!
THAT'S RIGHT.

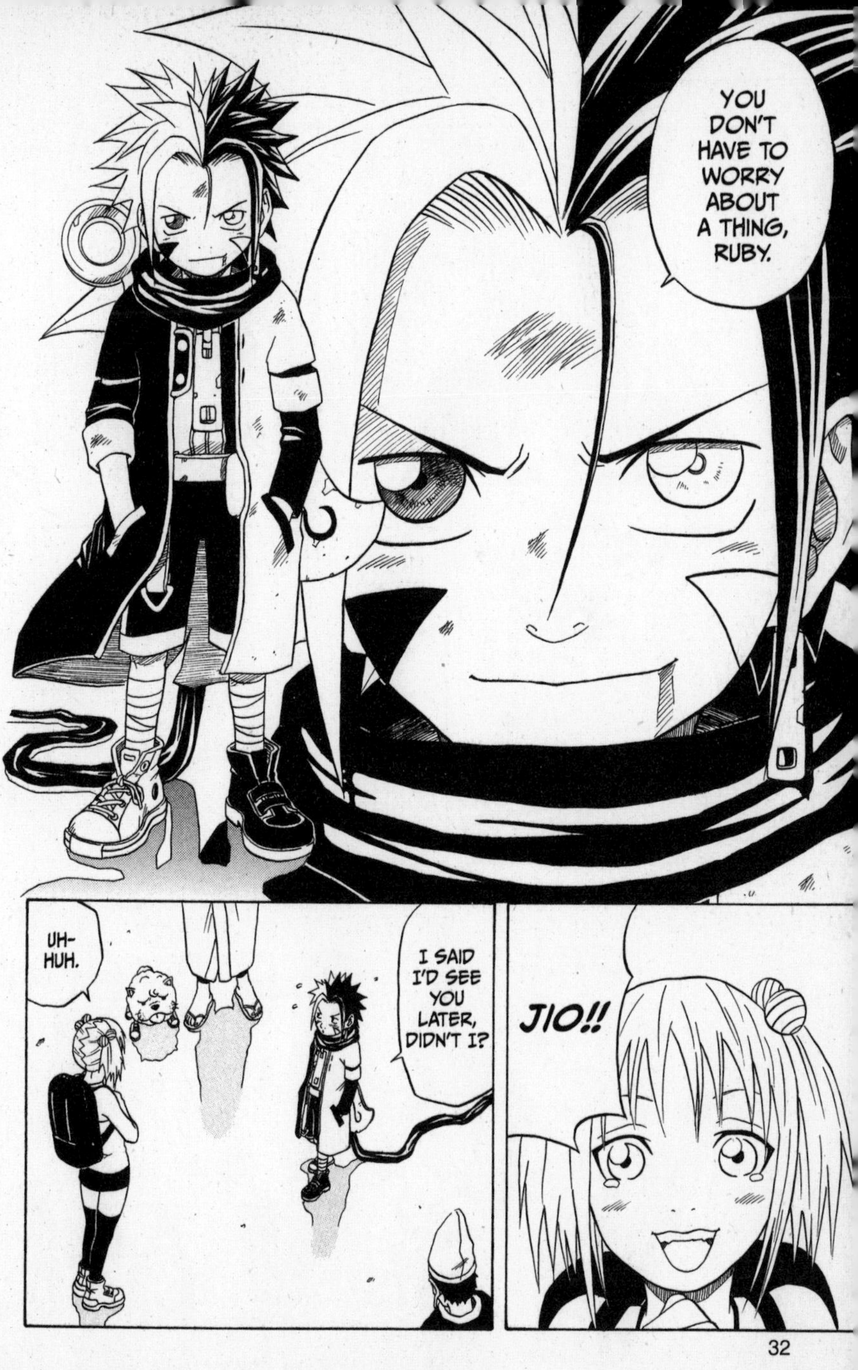
YOU DON'T HAVE TO WORRY ABOUT A THING, RUBY.
JIO!!
I SAID I'D SEE YOU LATER, DIDN'T I?
UH-HUH.

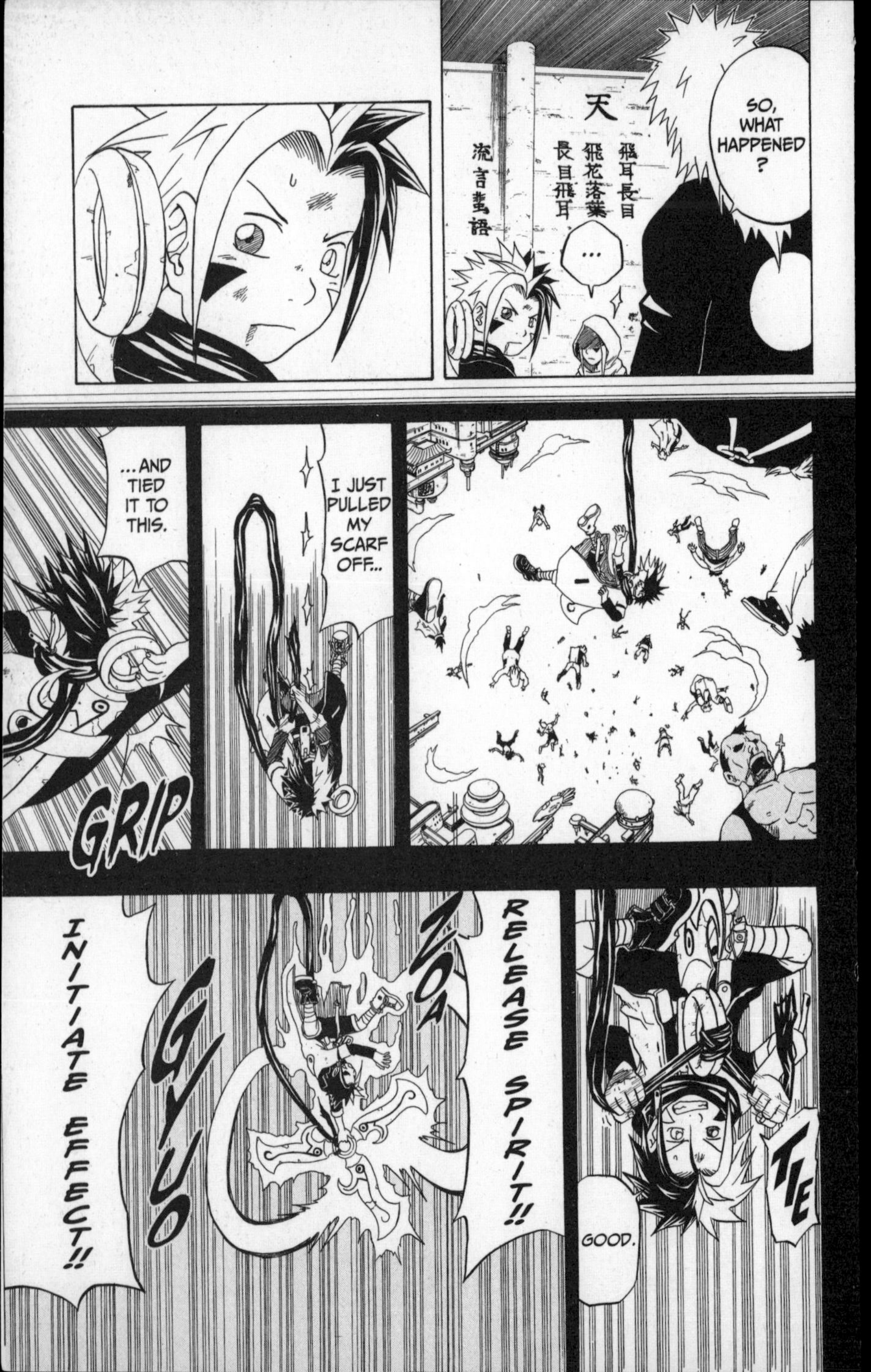
SO, WHAT HAPPENED?
天
飛耳長目
飛花落葉
長目飛耳
流言蜚語
...
I JUST PULLED MY SCARF OFF...
...AND TIED IT TO THIS.
GRIP
TIE
GOOD.
RELEASE SPIRIT!!
ZOA
GYUO
INITIATE EFFECT!!

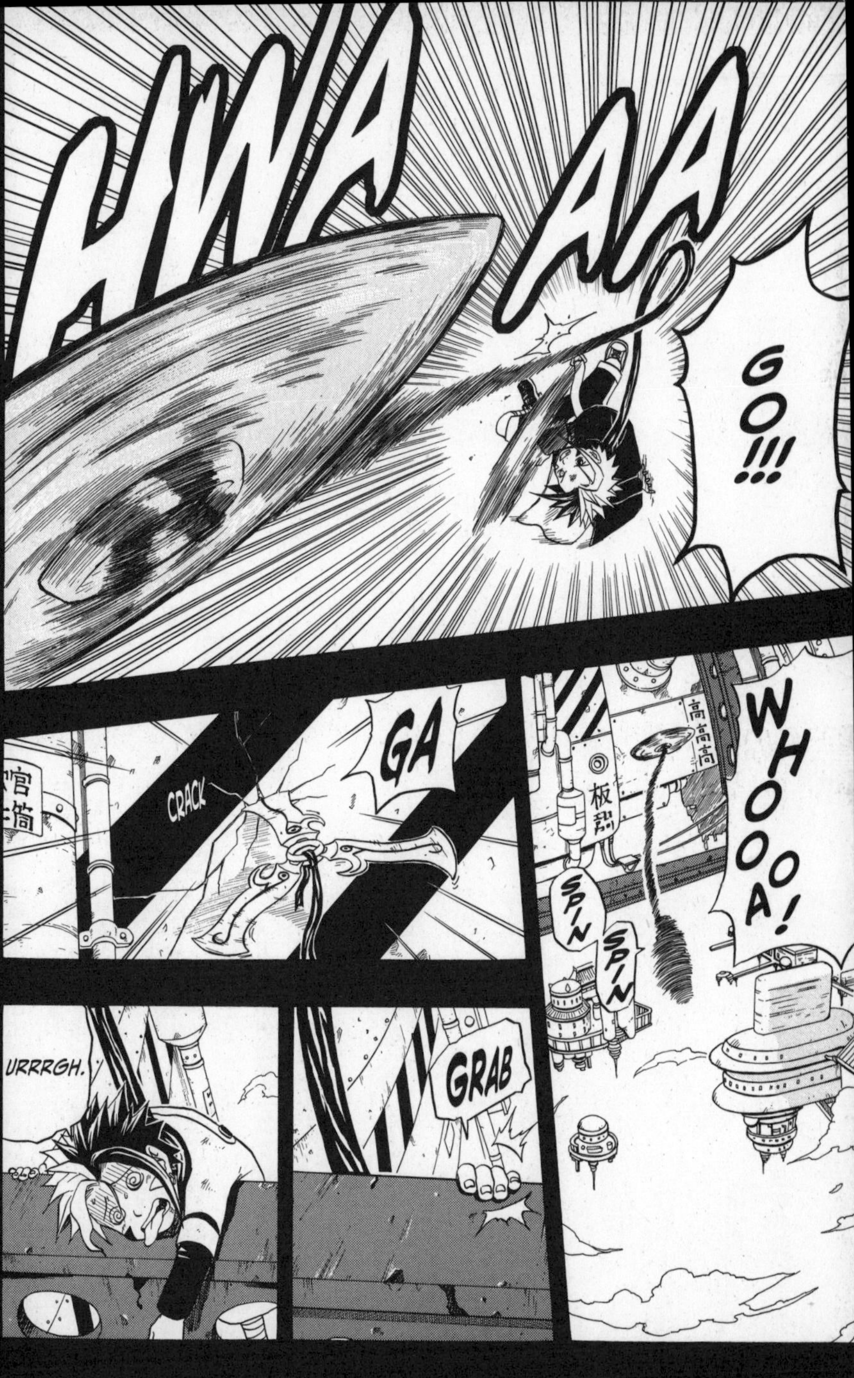

HWAAA
GO!!!
WHOOOA!
高高高
SPIN
SPIN
GA
CRACK
GRAB
URRRGH.

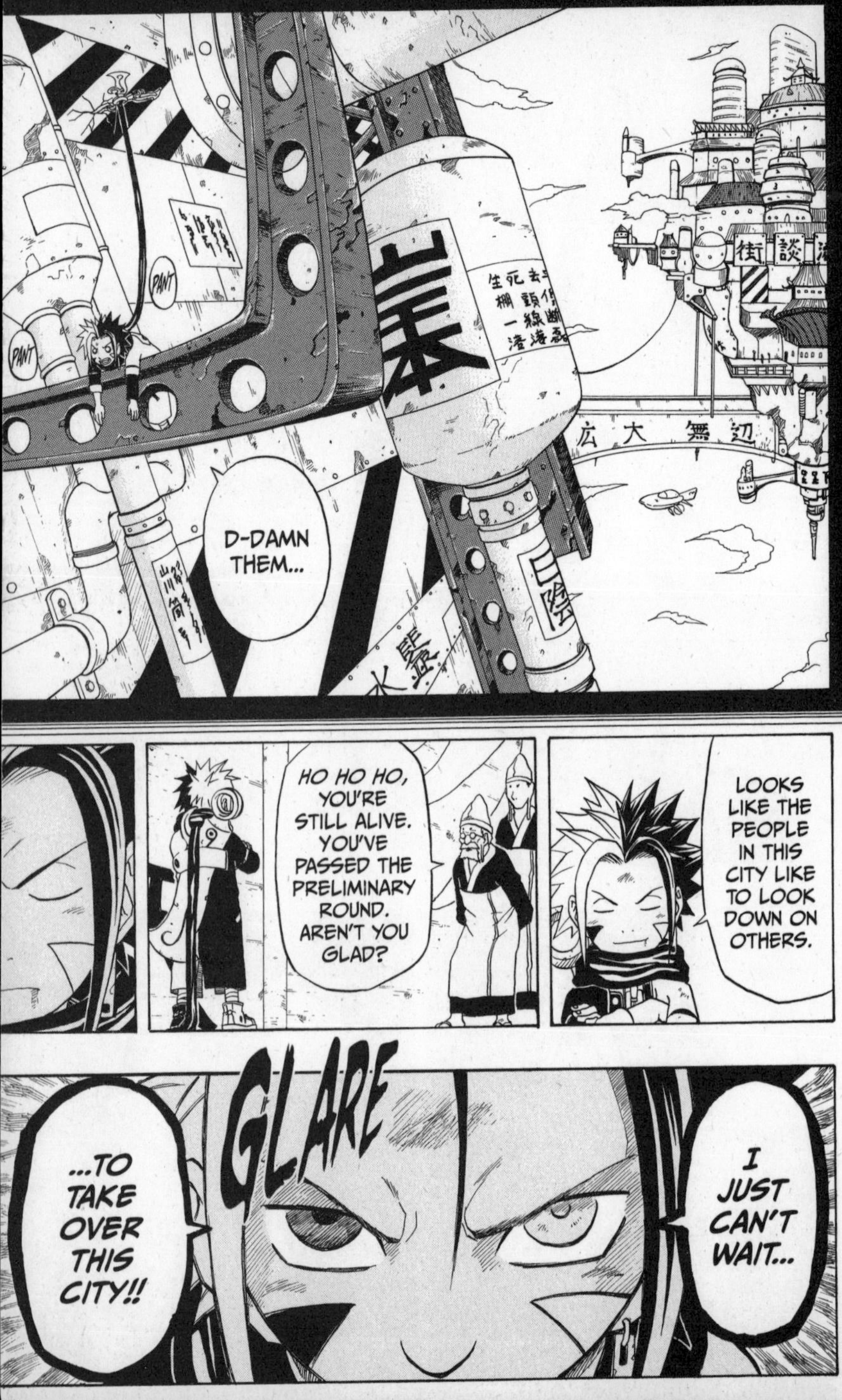

広大無辺
PANT
PANT
D-DAMN THEM...
LOOKS LIKE THE PEOPLE IN THIS CITY LIKE TO LOOK DOWN ON OTHERS.
HO HO HO, YOU'RE STILL ALIVE. YOU'VE PASSED THE PRELIMINARY ROUND. AREN'T YOU GLAD?
I JUST CAN'T WAIT...
GLARE
...TO TAKE OVER THIS CITY!!

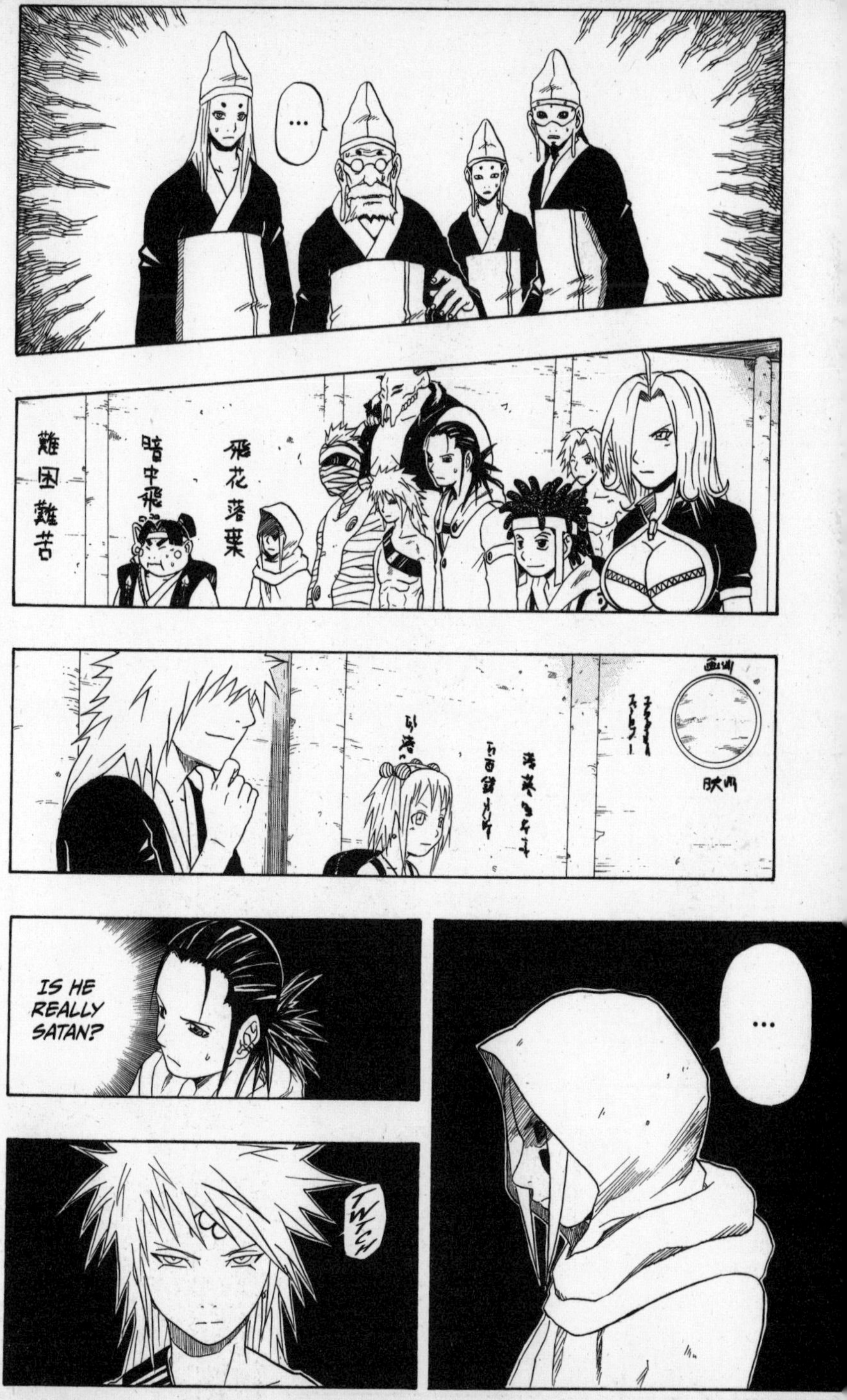
...
飛花落葉
暗中飛躍
...
IS HE REALLY SATAN?
TWITCH

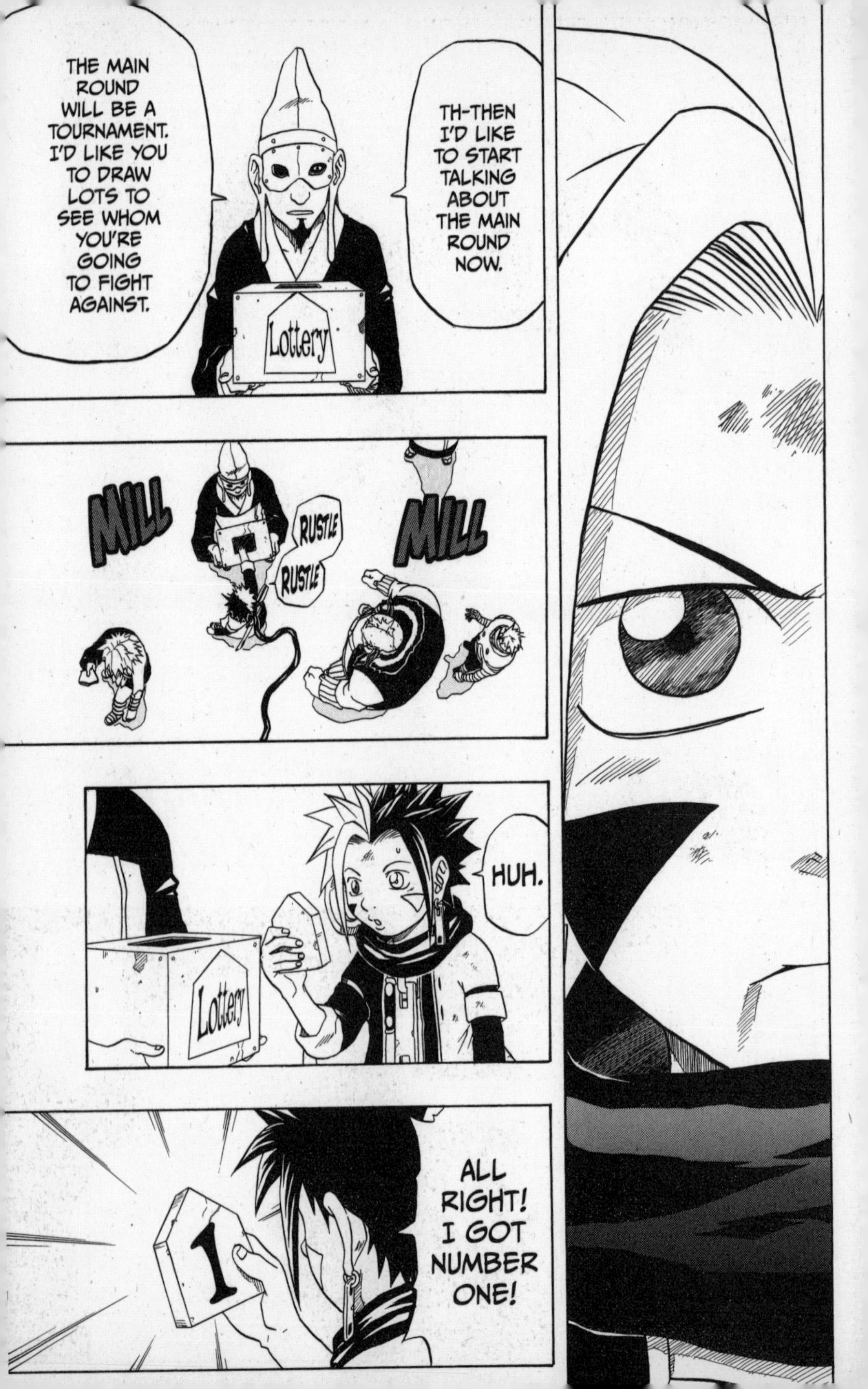
TH-THEN I'D LIKE TO START TALKING ABOUT THE MAIN ROUND NOW.
THE MAIN ROUND WILL BE A TOURNAMENT. I'D LIKE YOU TO DRAW LOTS TO SEE WHOM YOU'RE GOING TO FIGHT AGAINST.
Lottery
MILL
RUSTLE
RUSTLE
MILL
HUH.
Lottery
ALL RIGHT! I GOT NUMBER ONE!
1

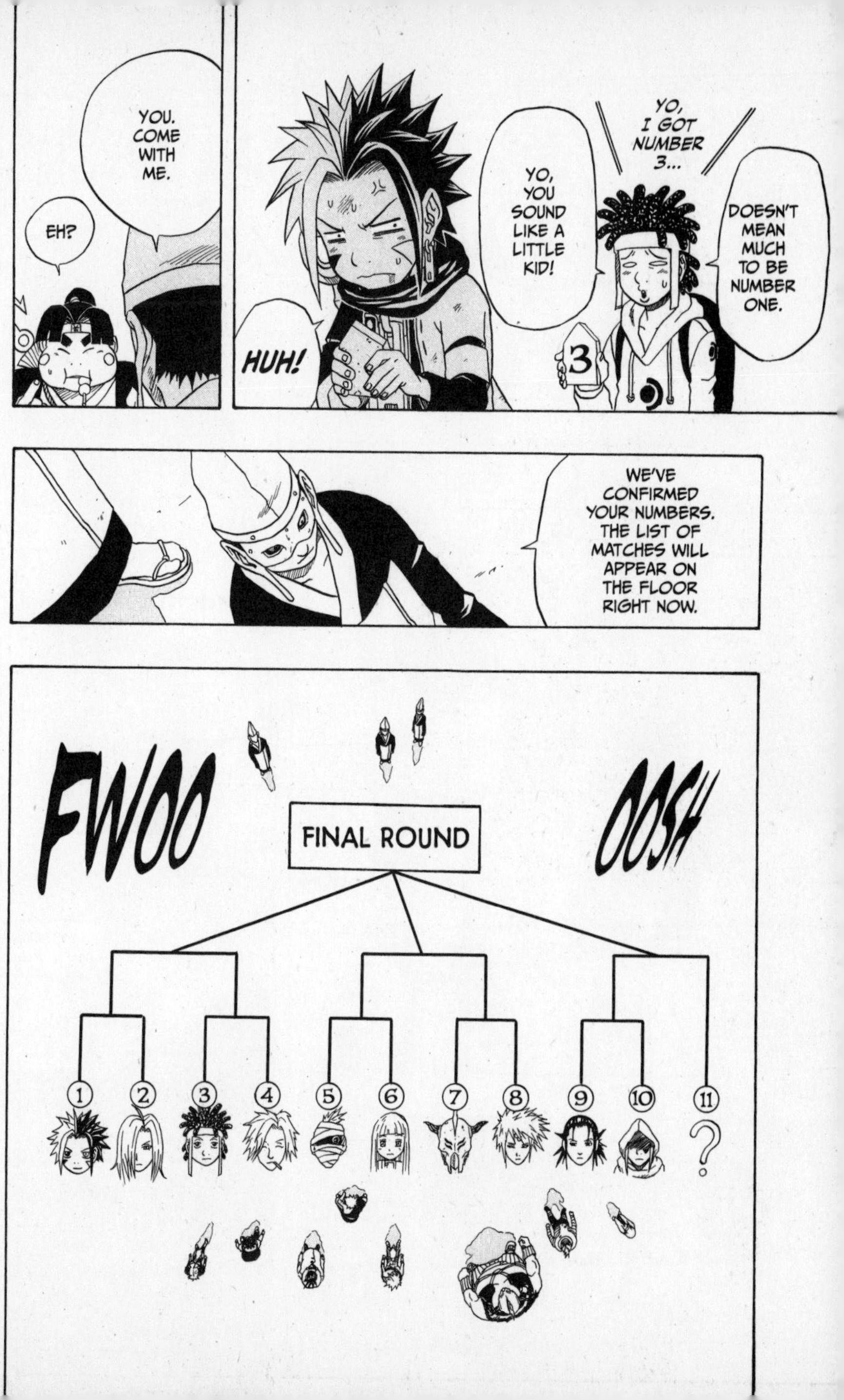
YO, I GOT NUMBER 3...
DOESN'T MEAN MUCH TO BE NUMBER ONE.
3
YO, YOU SOUND LIKE A LITTLE KID!
HUH!
YOU. COME WITH ME.
EH?
WE'VE CONFIRMED YOUR NUMBERS. THE LIST OF MATCHES WILL APPEAR ON THE FLOOR RIGHT NOW.
OOSH
FWOO
FINAL ROUND
1
2
3
4
5
6
7
8
9
10
11
?

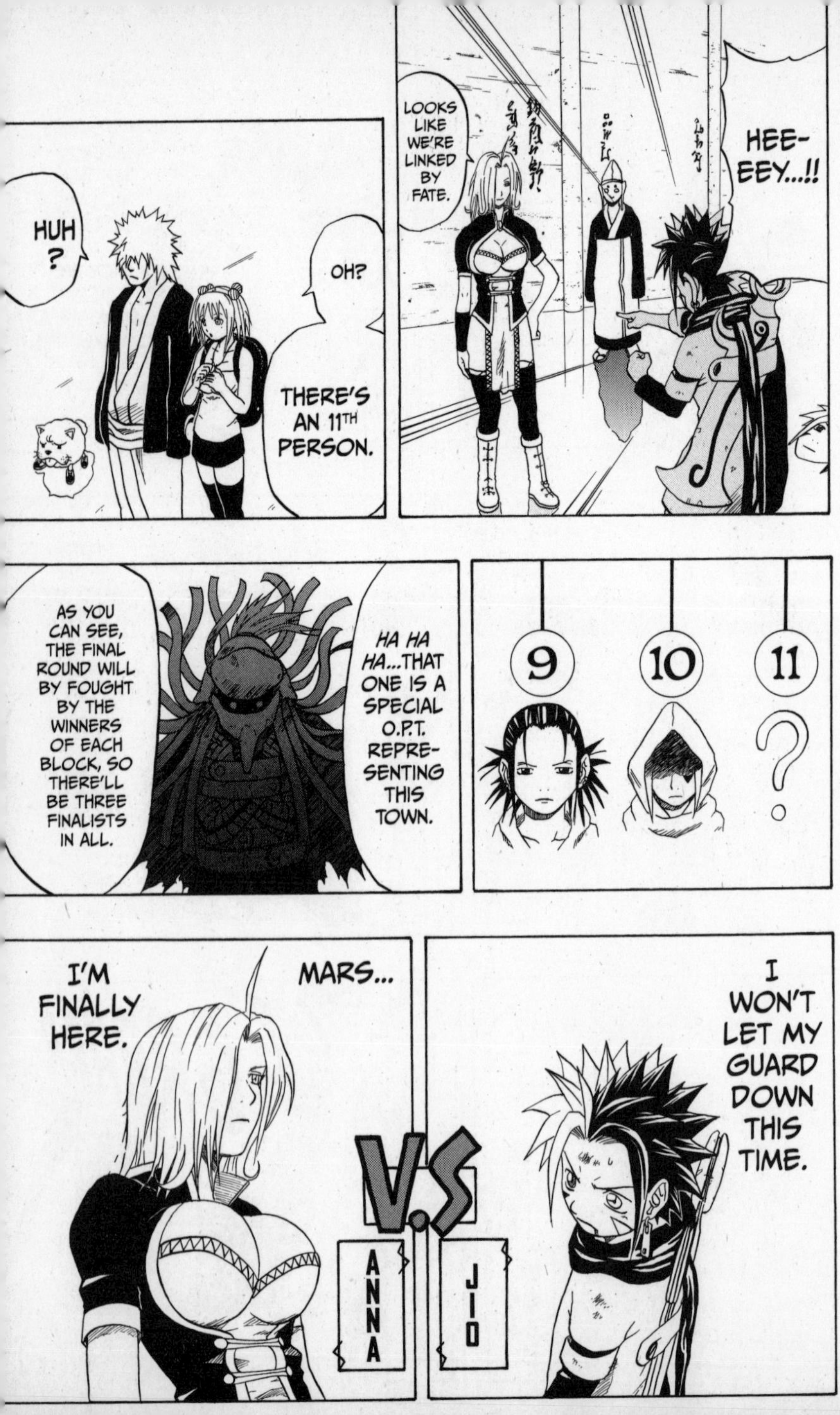
HEE-EEY...!!
LOOKS LIKE WE'RE LINKED BY FATE.
OH?
THERE'S AN 11TH PERSON.
HUH?
9
10
11
?
HA HA HA...THAT ONE IS A SPECIAL O.P.T. REPRESENTING THIS TOWN.
AS YOU CAN SEE, THE FINAL ROUND WILL BY FOUGHT BY THE WINNERS OF EACH BLOCK, SO THERE'LL BE THREE FINALISTS IN ALL.
I WON'T LET MY GUARD DOWN THIS TIME.
JIO
V.S
MARS...
I'M FINALLY HERE.
ANNA

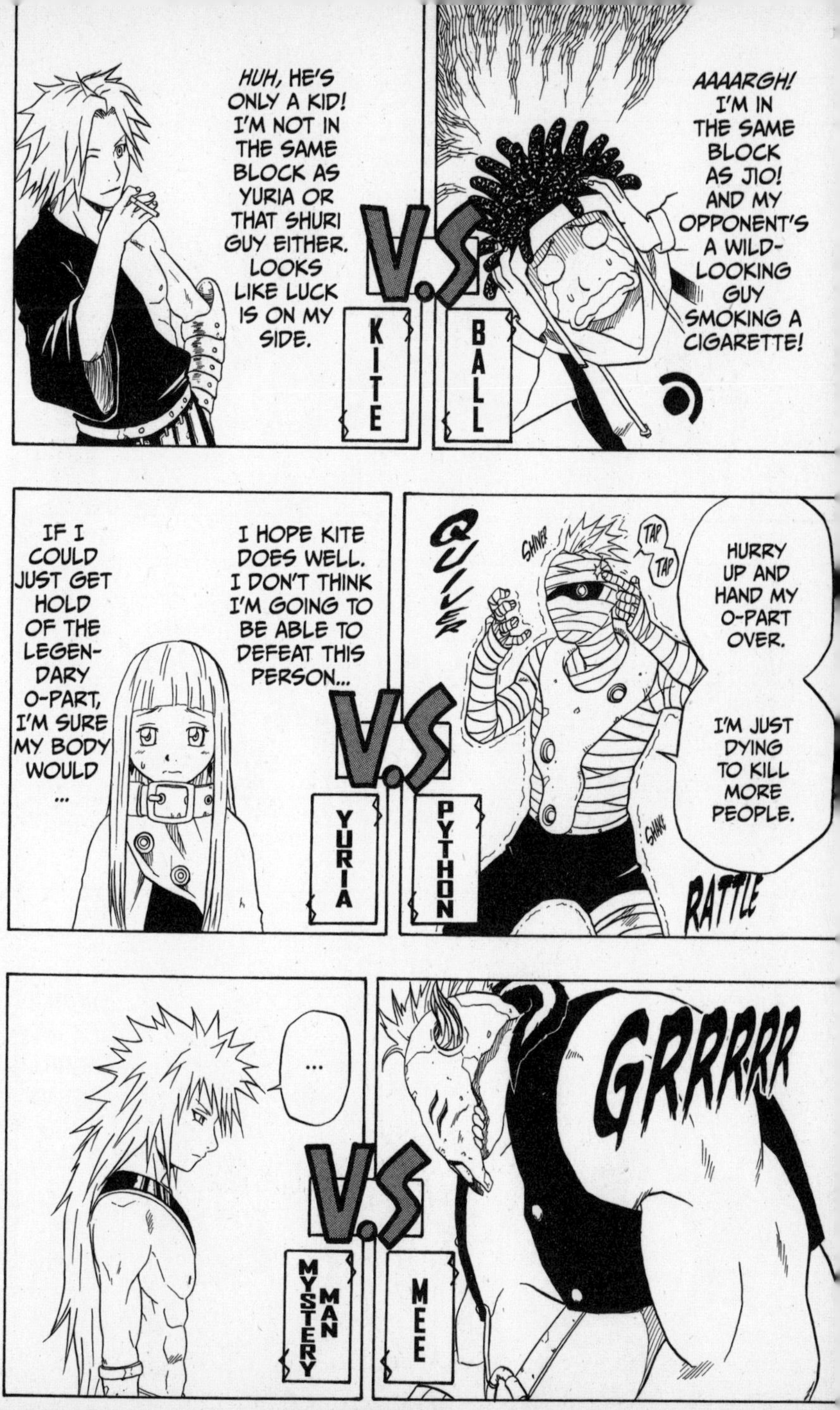
AAAARGH! I'M IN THE SAME BLOCK AS JIO! AND MY OPPONENT'S A WILD-LOOKING GUY SMOKING A CIGARETTE!
BALL
V.S
KITE
HUH, HE'S ONLY A KID! I'M NOT IN THE SAME BLOCK AS YURIA OR THAT SHURI GUY EITHER. LOOKS LIKE LUCK IS ON MY SIDE.
HURRY UP AND HAND MY O-PART OVER.
I'M JUST DYING TO KILL MORE PEOPLE.
TAP
TAP
SHIVER
QUIVER
SHAKE
RATTLE
PYTHON
V.S
YURIA
I HOPE KITE DOES WELL. I DON'T THINK I'M GOING TO BE ABLE TO DEFEAT THIS PERSON...
IF I COULD JUST GET HOLD OF THE LEGEN-DARY O-PART, I'M SURE MY BODY WOULD ...
GRRRRR
MEE
V.S
MYSTERY MAN
...

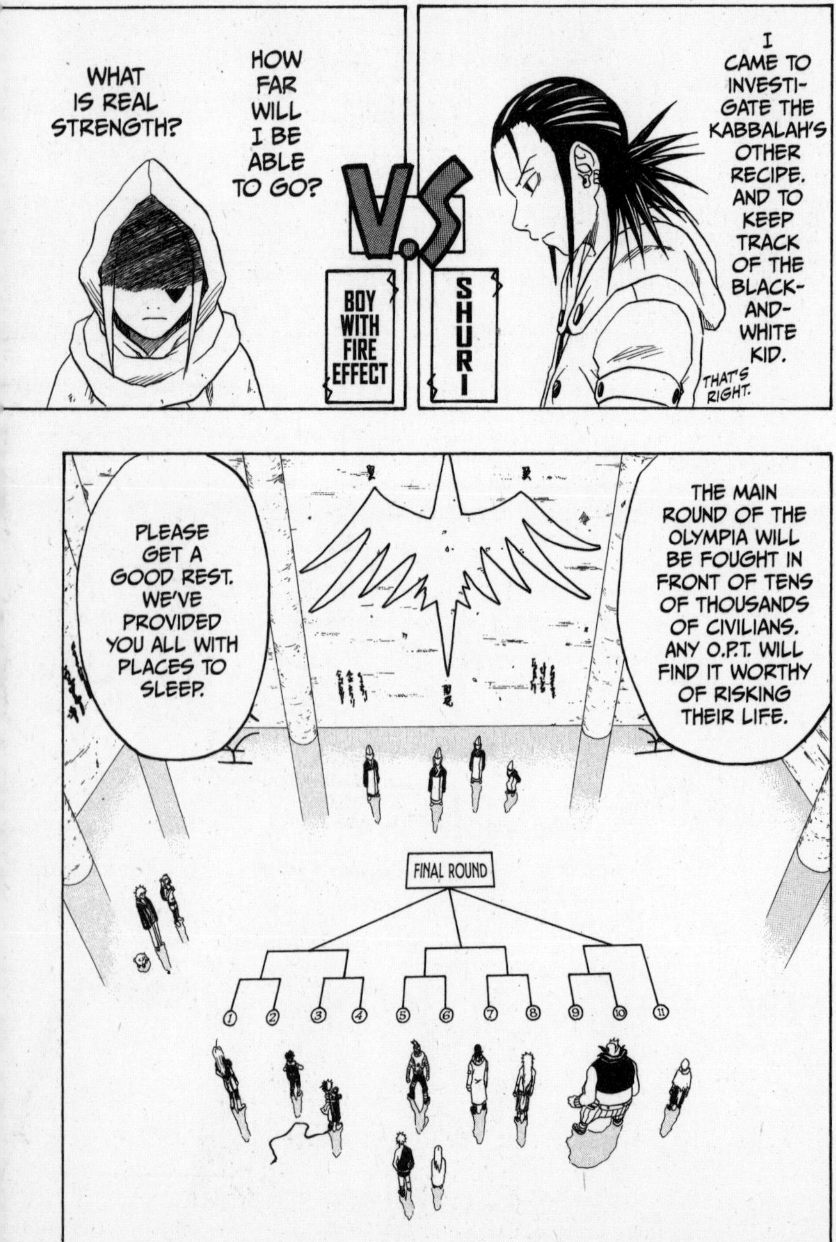
I CAME TO INVESTIGATE THE KABBALAH'S OTHER RECIPE. AND TO KEEP TRACK OF THE BLACK-AND-WHITE KID.
THAT'S RIGHT.
SHURI
V.S
BOY WITH FIRE EFFECT
HOW FAR WILL I BE ABLE TO GO?
WHAT IS REAL STRENGTH?
THE MAIN ROUND OF THE OLYMPIA WILL BE FOUGHT IN FRONT OF TENS OF THOUSANDS OF CIVILIANS. ANY O.P.T. WILL FIND IT WORTHY OF RISKING THEIR LIFE.
PLEASE GET A GOOD REST. WE'VE PROVIDED YOU ALL WITH PLACES TO SLEEP.
FINAL ROUND
1 2 3 4 5 6 7 8 9 10 11

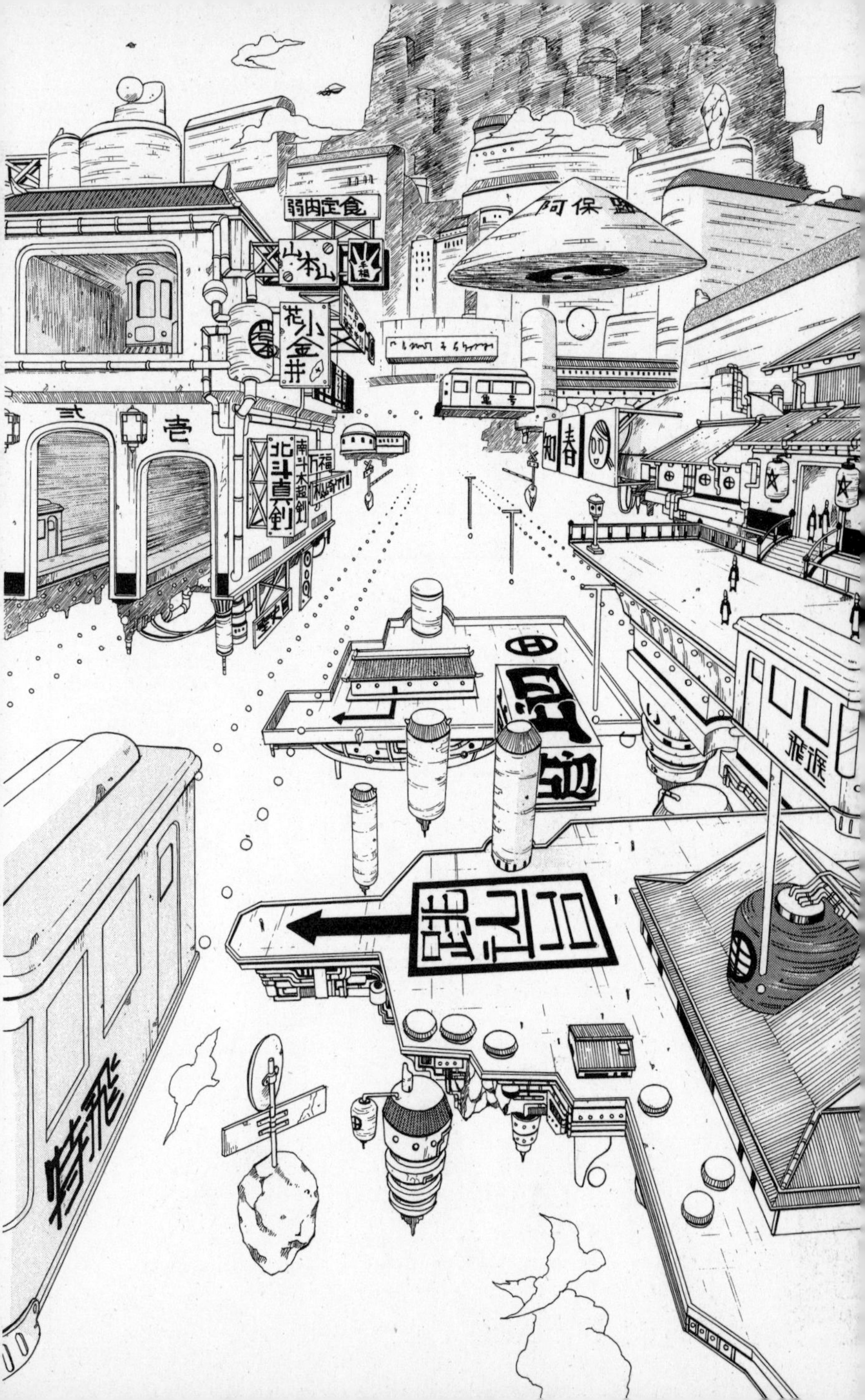
弱肉定食
山本山
花
小金井
北斗真剣
壱
知春
阿保

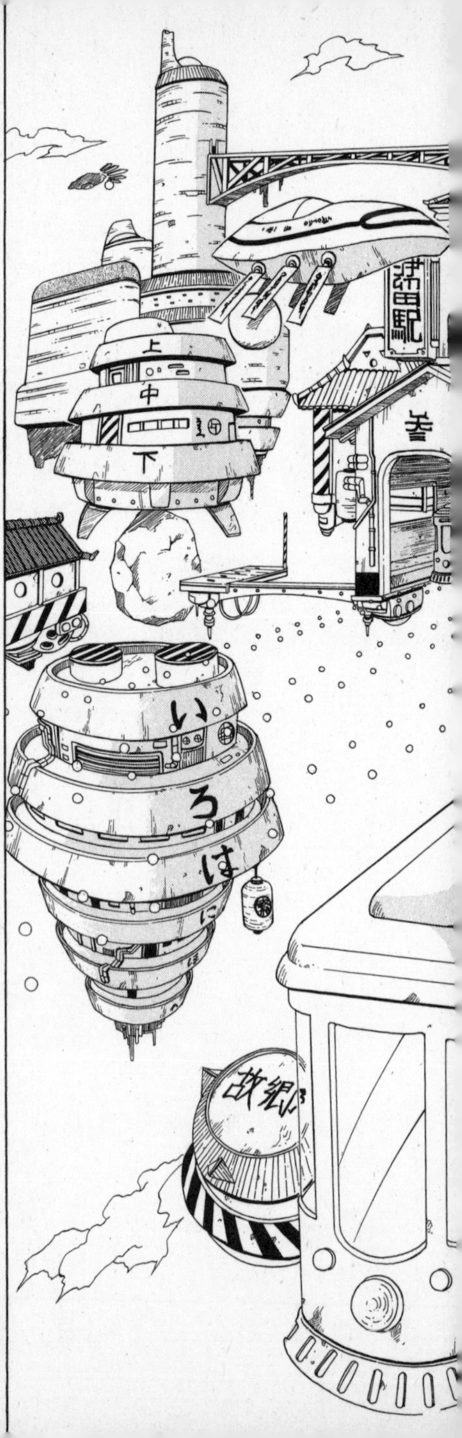
上
中
下
いろは
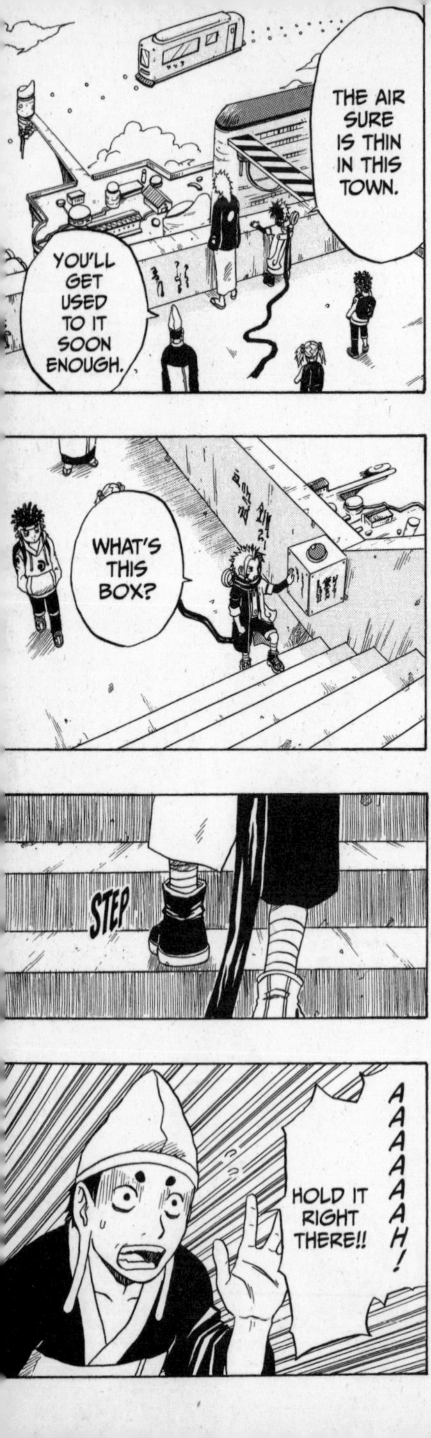
THE AIR SURE IS THIN IN THIS TOWN.
YOU'LL GET USED TO IT SOON ENOUGH.
WHAT'S THIS BOX?
STEP
AAAAAAAH!
HOLD IT RIGHT THERE!!

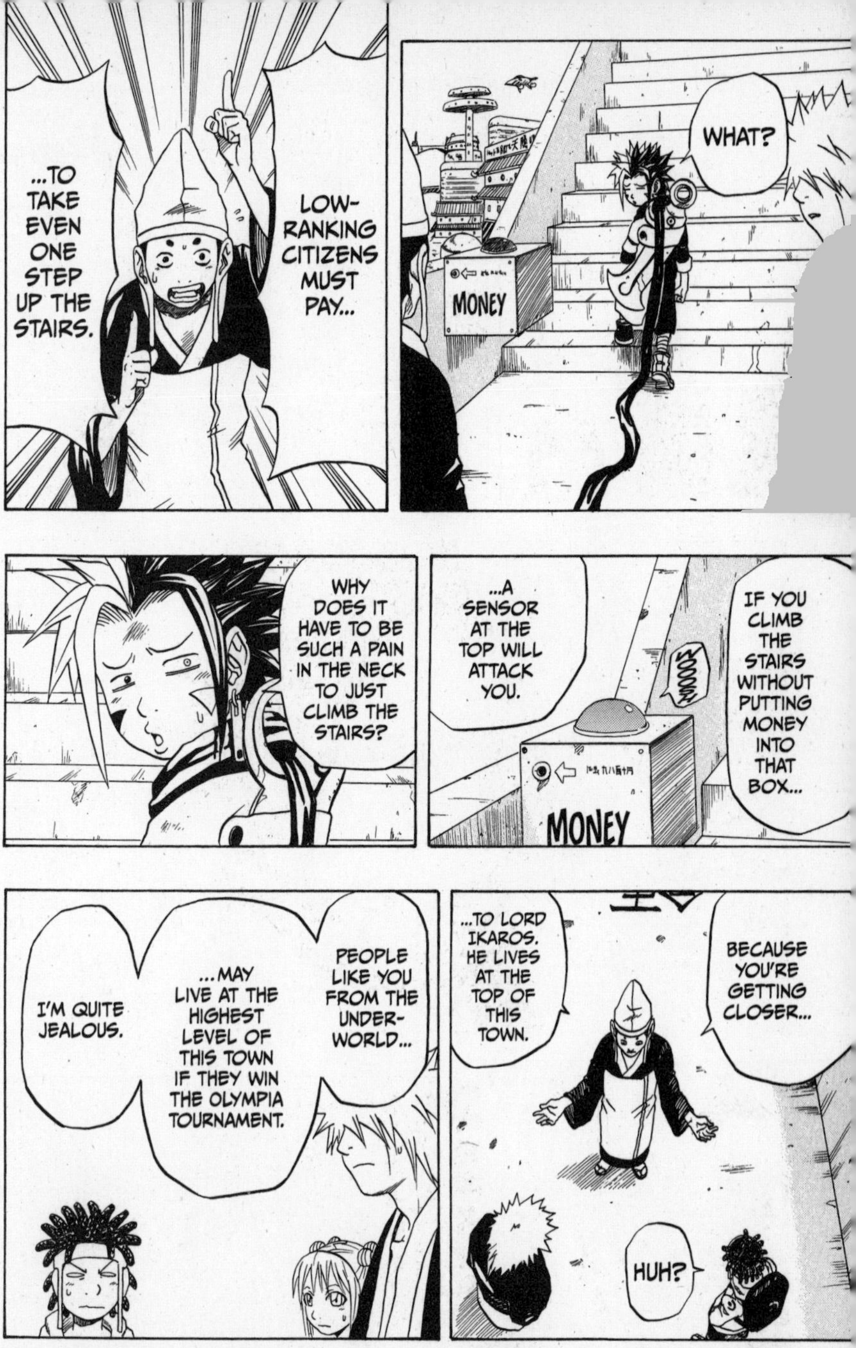
WHAT?
MONEY
LOW-RANKING CITIZENS MUST PAY...
...TO TAKE EVEN ONE STEP UP THE STAIRS.
IF YOU CLIMB THE STAIRS WITHOUT PUTTING MONEY INTO THAT BOX...
...A SENSOR AT THE TOP WILL ATTACK YOU.
MONEY
WHY DOES IT HAVE TO BE SUCH A PAIN IN THE NECK TO JUST CLIMB THE STAIRS?
BECAUSE YOU'RE GETTING CLOSER...
...TO LORD IKAROS. HE LIVES AT THE TOP OF THIS TOWN.
HUH?
PEOPLE LIKE YOU FROM THE UNDER-WORLD...
...MAY LIVE AT THE HIGHEST LEVEL OF THIS TOWN IF THEY WIN THE OLYMPIA TOURNAMENT.
I'M QUITE JEALOUS.

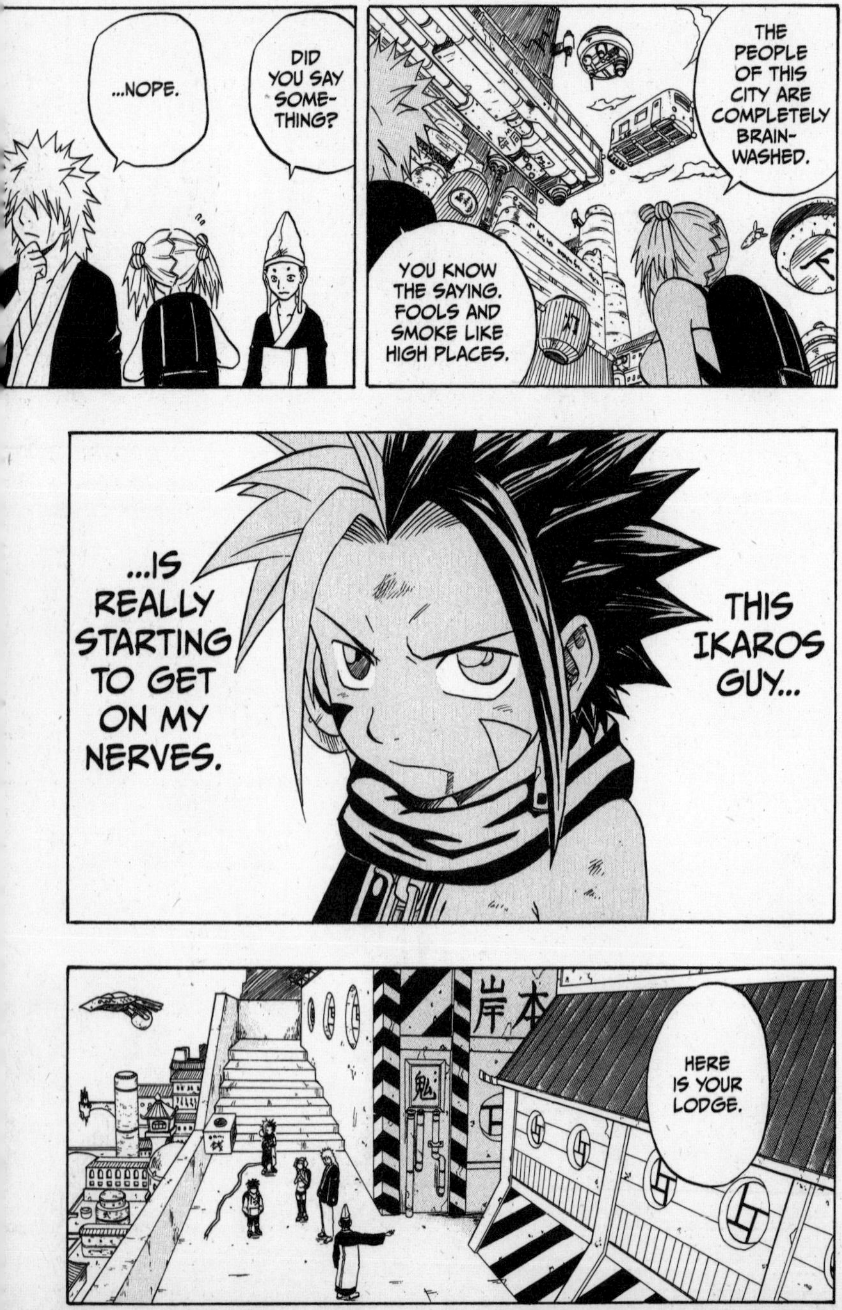
THE PEOPLE OF THIS CITY ARE COMPLETELY BRAIN-WASHED.
YOU KNOW THE SAYING. FOOLS AND SMOKE LIKE HIGH PLACES.
DID YOU SAY SOME-THING?
...NOPE.
THIS IKAROS GUY...
...IS REALLY STARTING TO GET ON MY NERVES.
HERE IS YOUR LODGE.

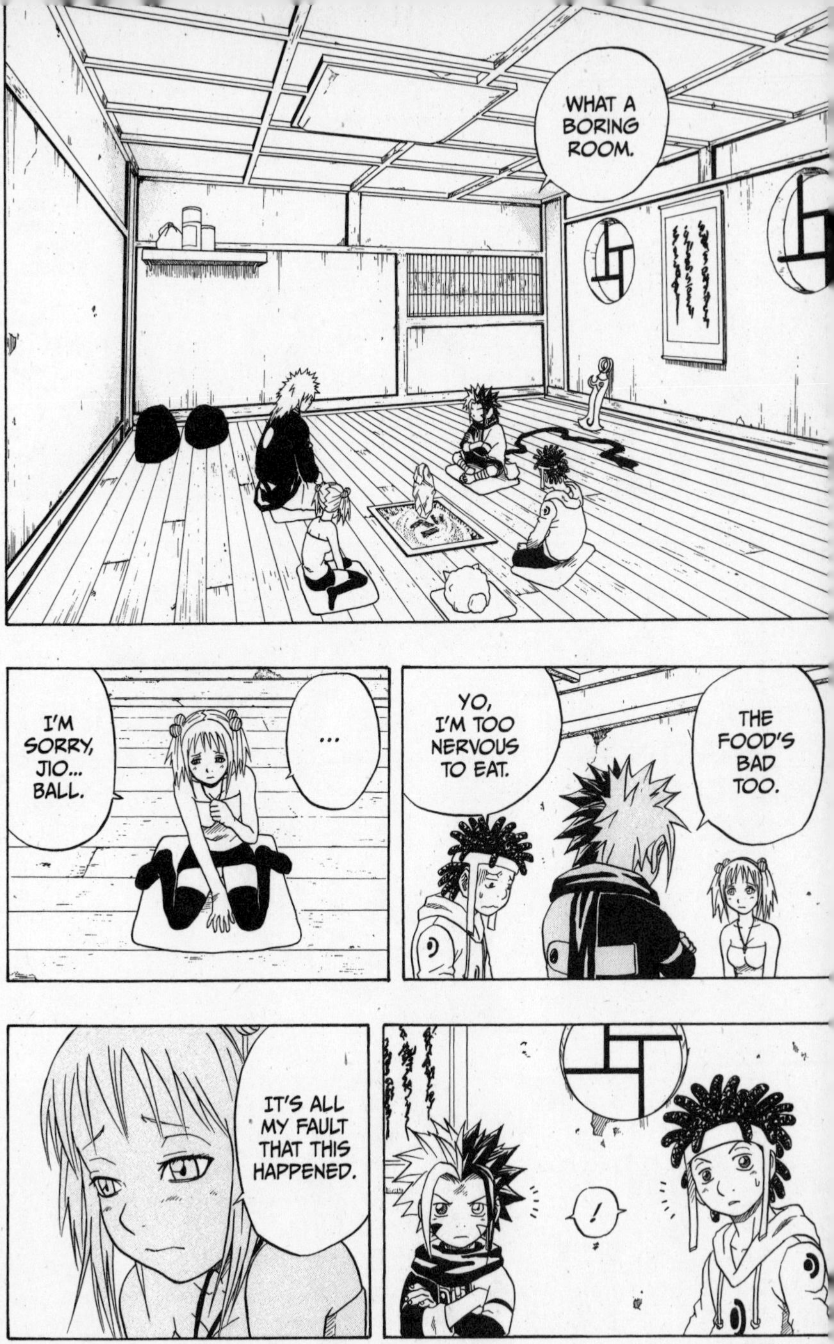
WHAT A BORING ROOM.
THE FOOD'S BAD TOO.
YO, I'M TOO NERVOUS TO EAT.
...
I'M SORRY, JIO... BALL.
!
IT'S ALL MY FAULT THAT THIS HAPPENED.

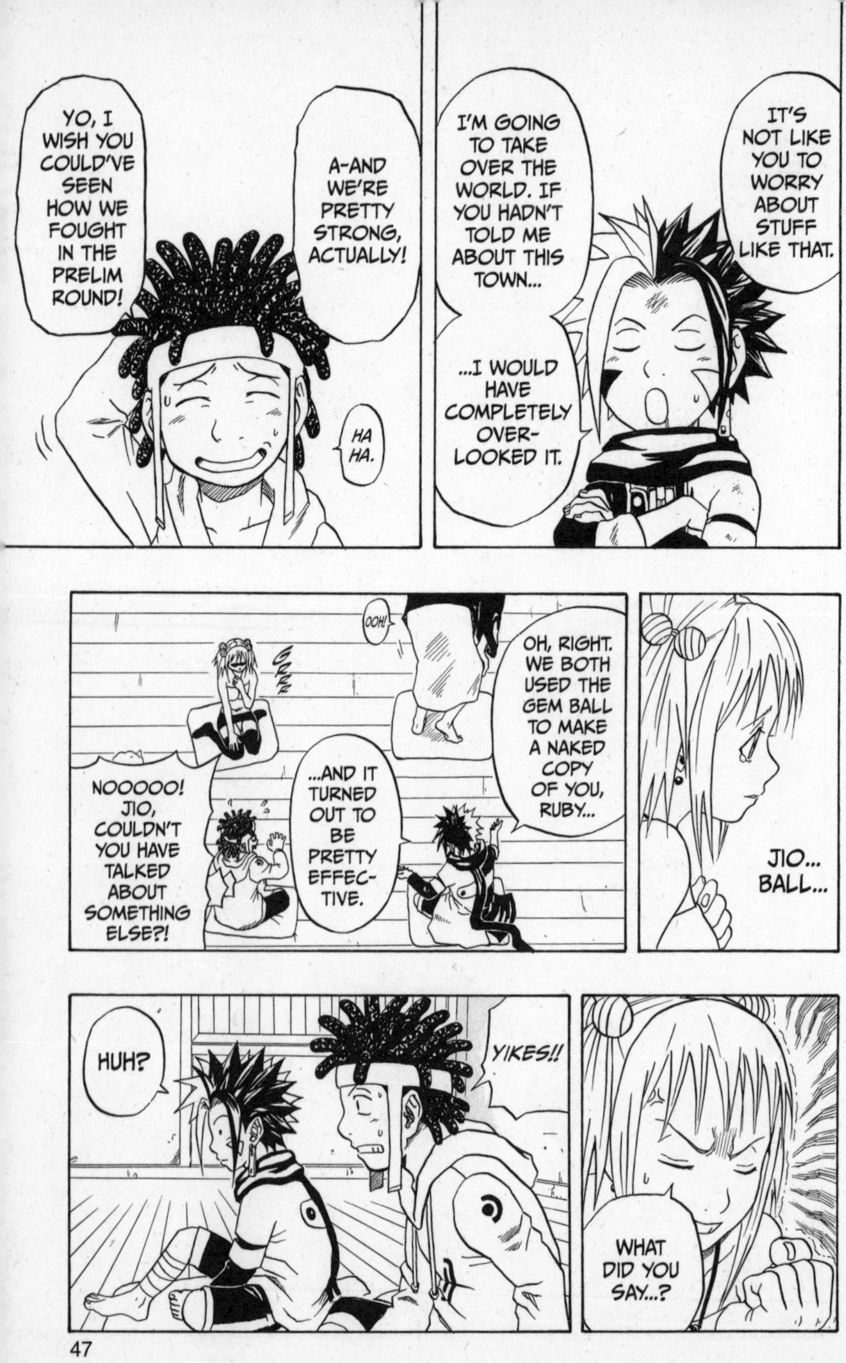
IT'S NOT LIKE YOU TO WORRY ABOUT STUFF LIKE THAT.
I'M GOING TO TAKE OVER THE WORLD. IF YOU HADN'T TOLD ME ABOUT THIS TOWN...
...I WOULD HAVE COMPLETELY OVER-LOOKED IT.
A-AND WE'RE PRETTY STRONG, ACTUALLY!
YO, I WISH YOU COULD'VE SEEN HOW WE FOUGHT IN THE PRELIM ROUND!
HA HA.
JIO... BALL...
OOH!
OH, RIGHT. WE BOTH USED THE GEM BALL TO MAKE A NAKED COPY OF YOU, RUBY...
...AND IT TURNED OUT TO BE PRETTY EFFEC-TIVE.
NOOOOO! JIO, COULDN'T YOU HAVE TALKED ABOUT SOMETHING ELSE?!
WHAT DID YOU SAY...?
YIKES!!
HUH?

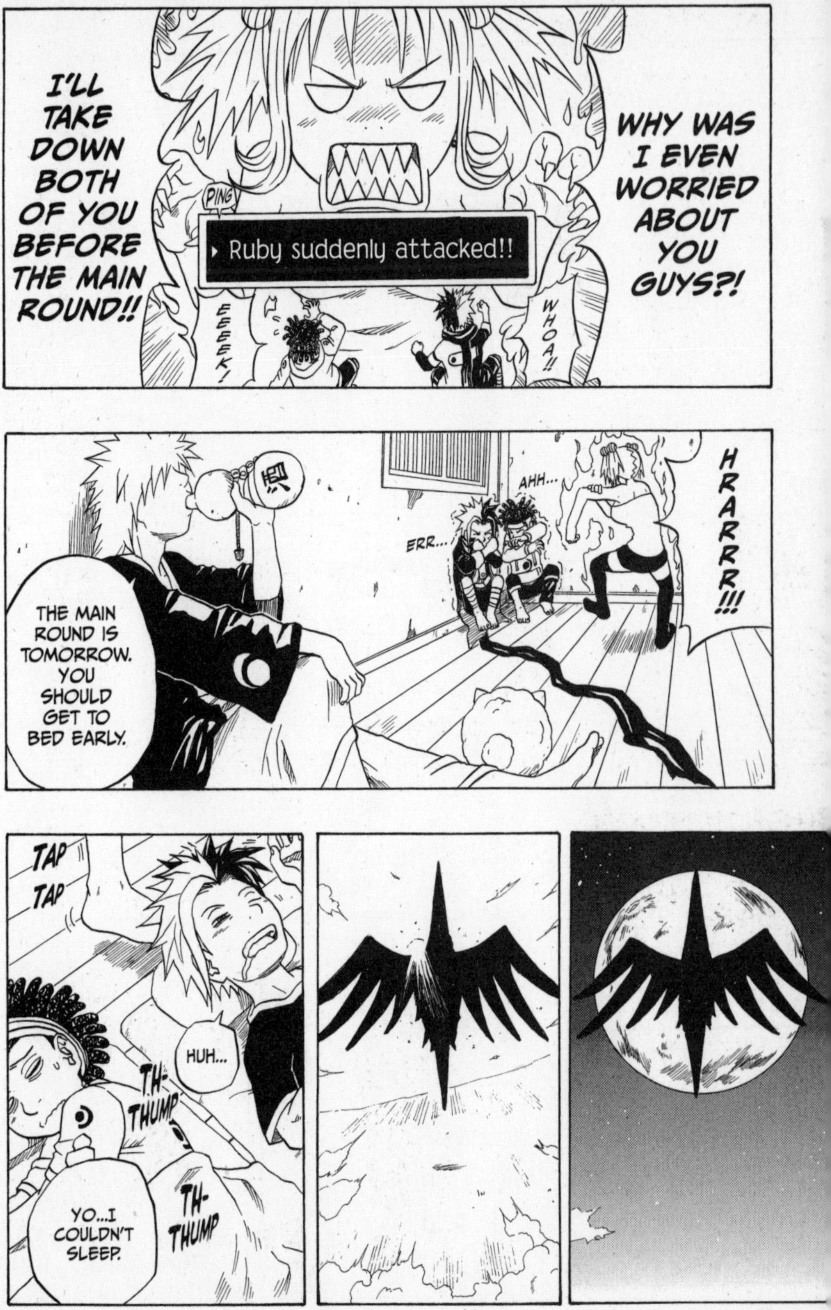
WHY WAS I EVEN WORRIED ABOUT YOU GUYS?!
PING
Ruby suddenly attacked!!
WHOA!!
EEEEK!
I'LL TAKE DOWN BOTH OF YOU BEFORE THE MAIN ROUND!!
HRARRR!!!
AHH...
ERR...
THE MAIN ROUND IS TOMORROW. YOU SHOULD GET TO BED EARLY.
TAP TAP
HUH...
TH-THUMP
TH-THUMP
YO...I COULDN'T SLEEP.

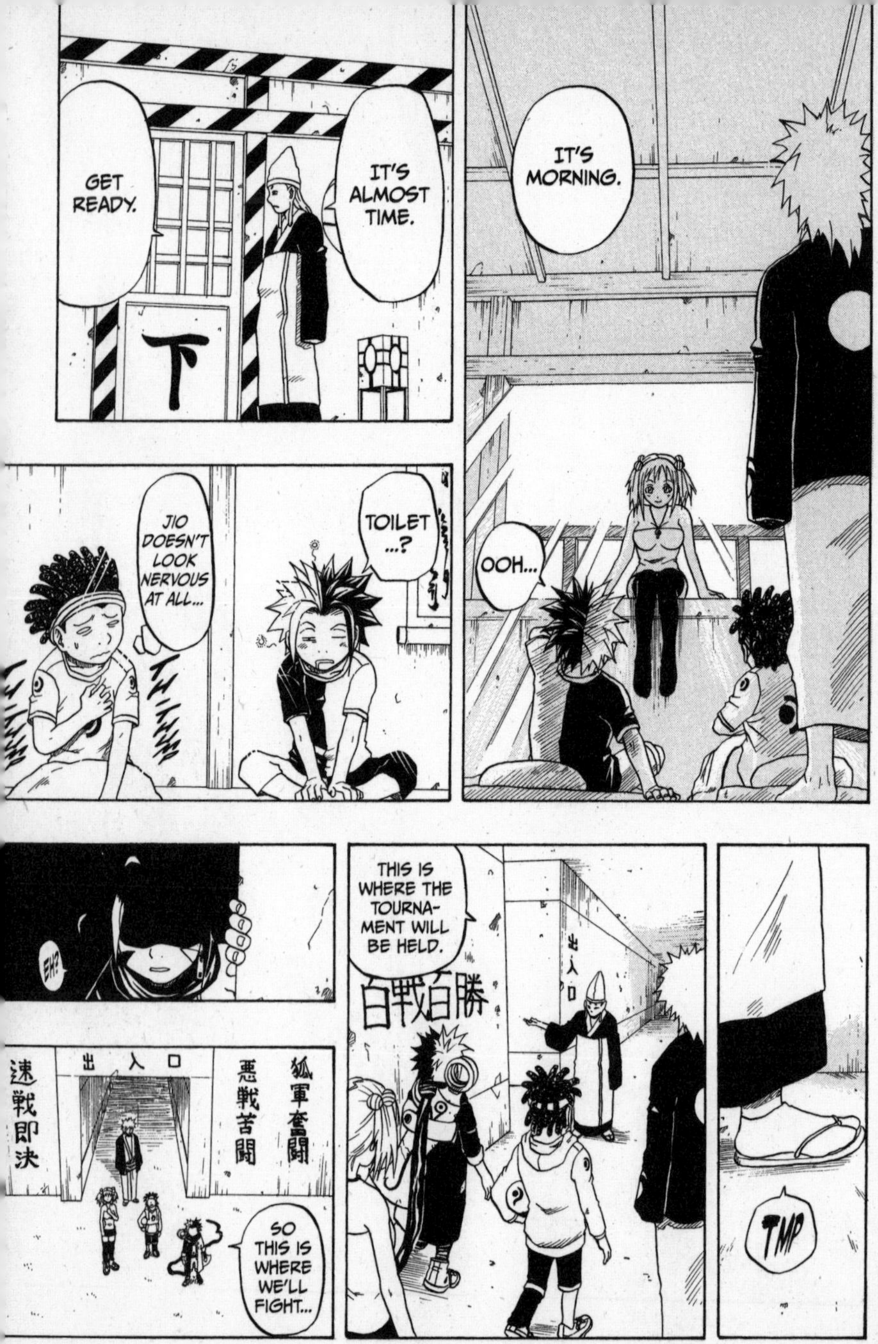

IT'S MORNING.
OOH...
IT'S ALMOST TIME.
GET READY.
TOILET ...?
JIO DOESN'T LOOK NERVOUS AT ALL...
TMP
THIS IS WHERE THE TOURNA-MENT WILL BE HELD.
百戦百勝
出入口
EH?
狐軍奮闘
悪戦苦闘
速戦即決
出入口
SO THIS IS WHERE WE'LL FIGHT...

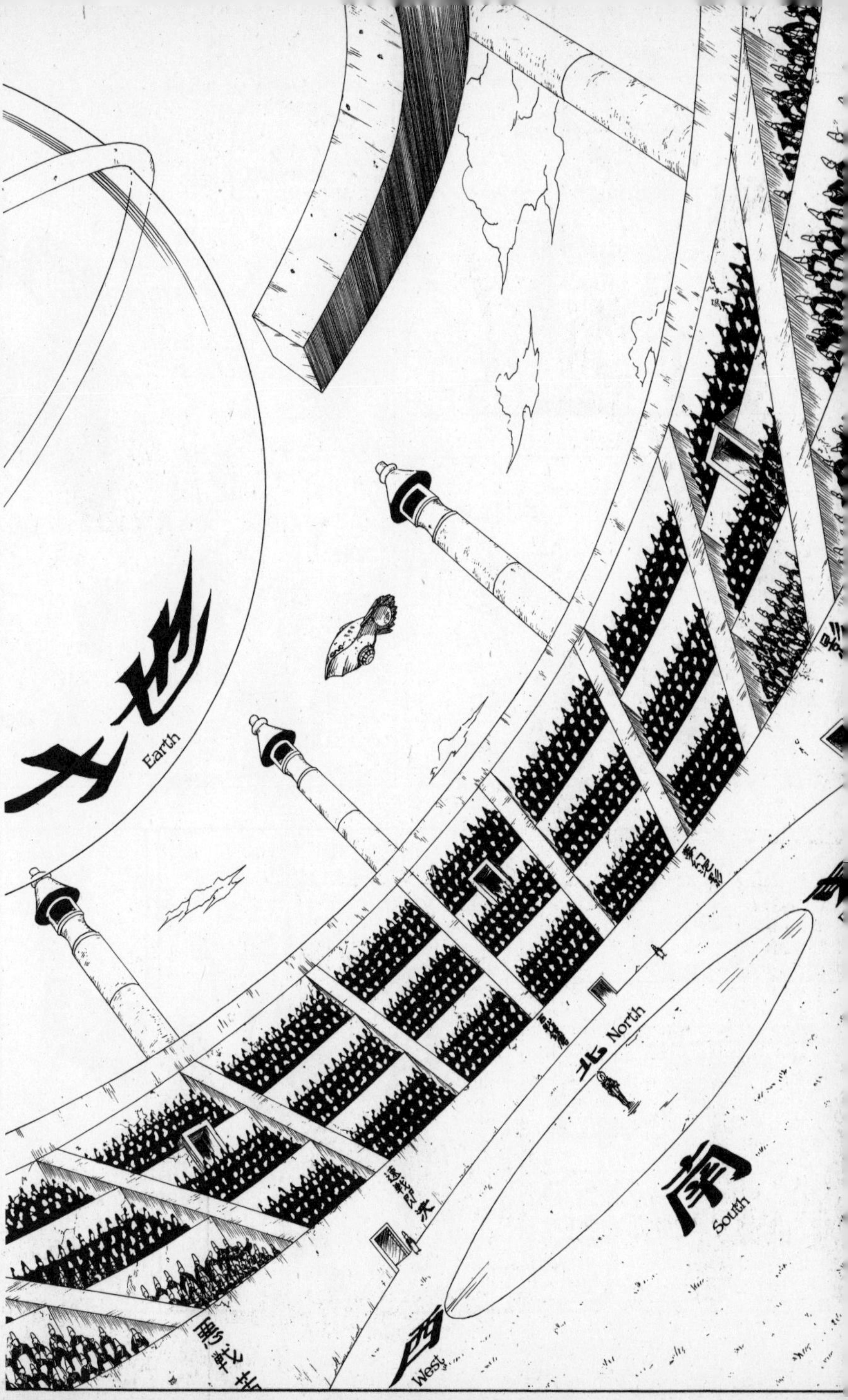
Earth
北
North
南
South
西
West

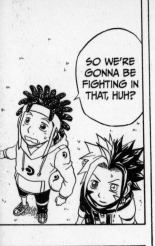

SO WE'RE GONNA BE FIGHTING IN THAT, HUH?

LOOKS LIKE THE GRAVITY IN THERE IS REGULATED. I SEE...IT'S A 360-DEGREE BATTLE RING.

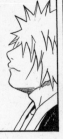

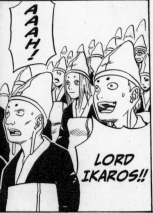

AAAH!

LORD IKAROS!!

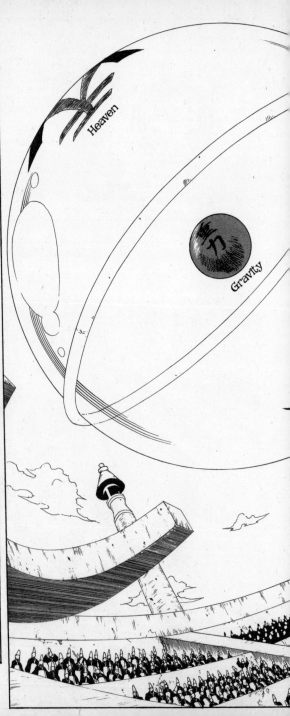

Heaven

Gravity

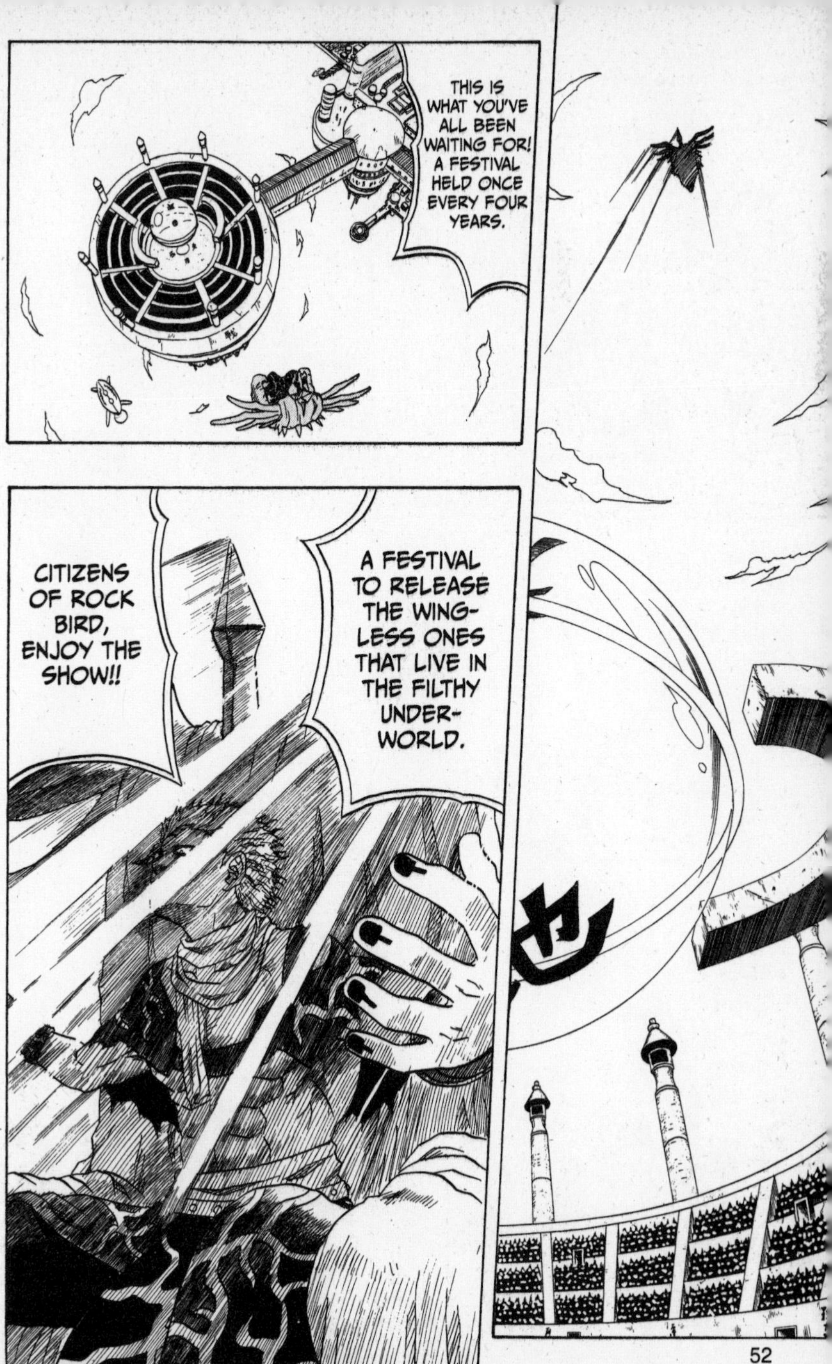
THIS IS WHAT YOU'VE ALL BEEN WAITING FOR! A FESTIVAL HELD ONCE EVERY FOUR YEARS.
A FESTIVAL TO RELEASE THE WING-LESS ONES THAT LIVE IN THE FILTHY UNDER-WORLD.
CITIZENS OF ROCK BIRD, ENJOY THE SHOW!!

Chapter 34
The Main Round Begins

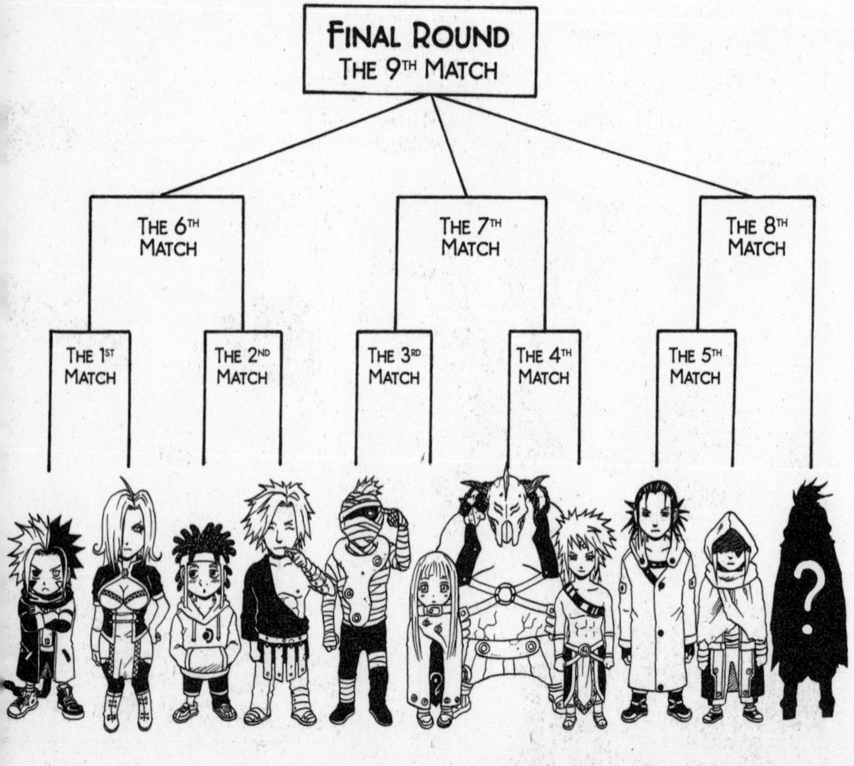
Final Round
The 9th Match
The 6th Match
The 7th Match
The 8th Match
The 1st Match
The 2nd Match
The 3rd Match
The 4th Match
The 5th Match
?

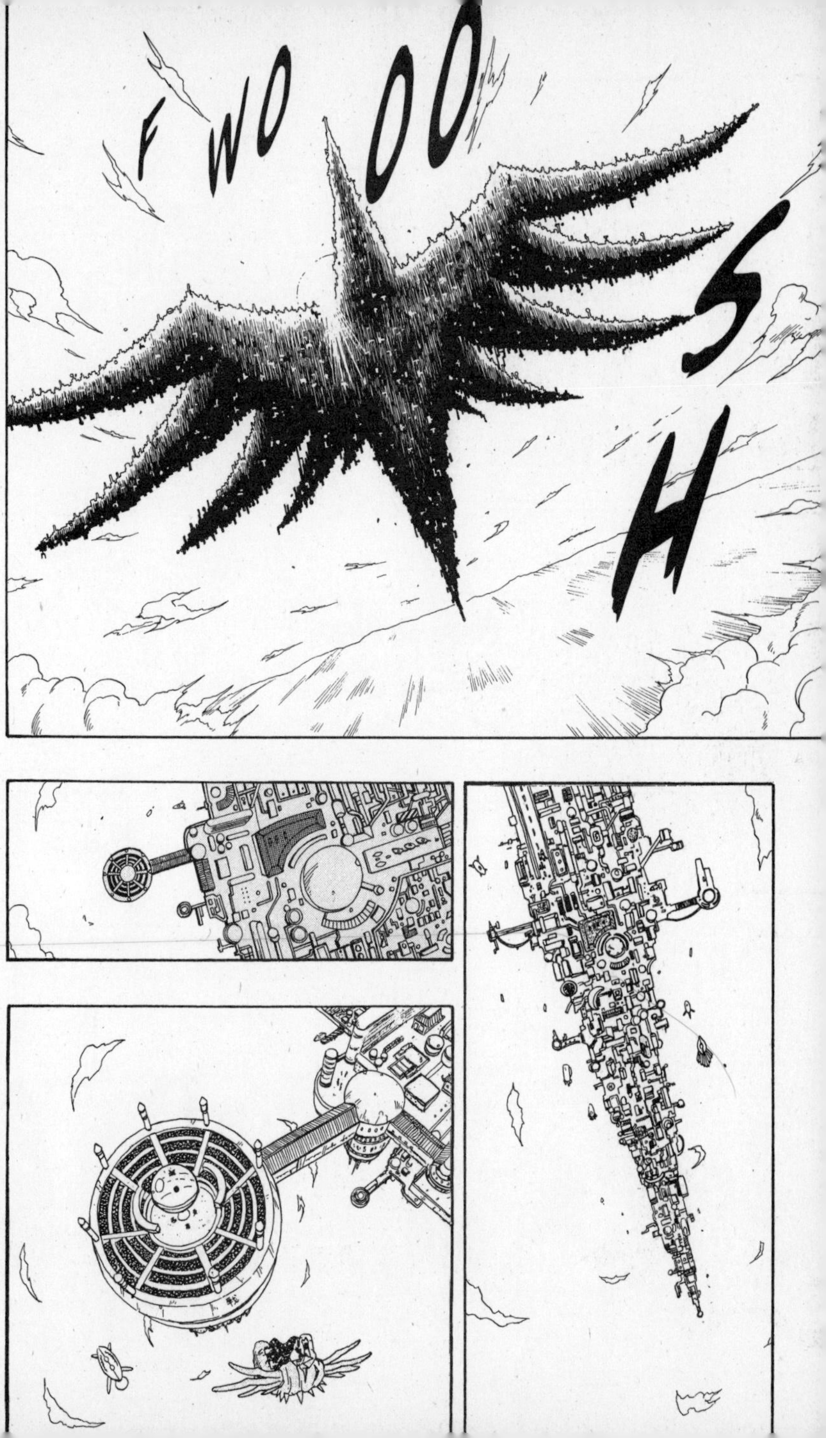
FWOOOSH

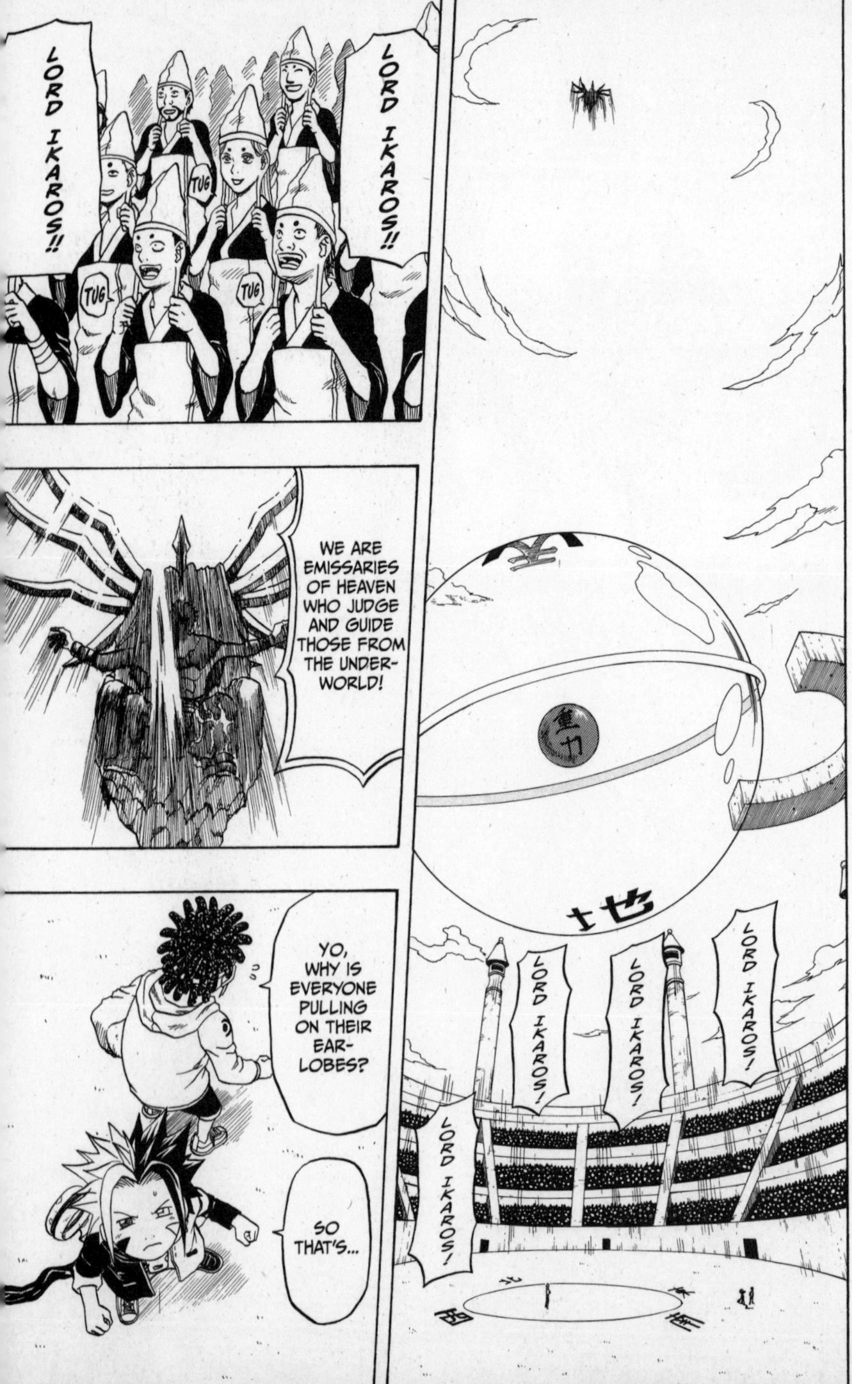
LORD IKAROS!
LORD IKAROS!
LORD IKAROS!
LORD IKAROS!
LORD IKAROS!!
LORD IKAROS!!
TUG
TUG
TUG
WE ARE EMISSARIES OF HEAVEN WHO JUDGE AND GUIDE THOSE FROM THE UNDER-WORLD!
YO, WHY IS EVERYONE PULLING ON THEIR EAR-LOBES?
SO THAT'S...

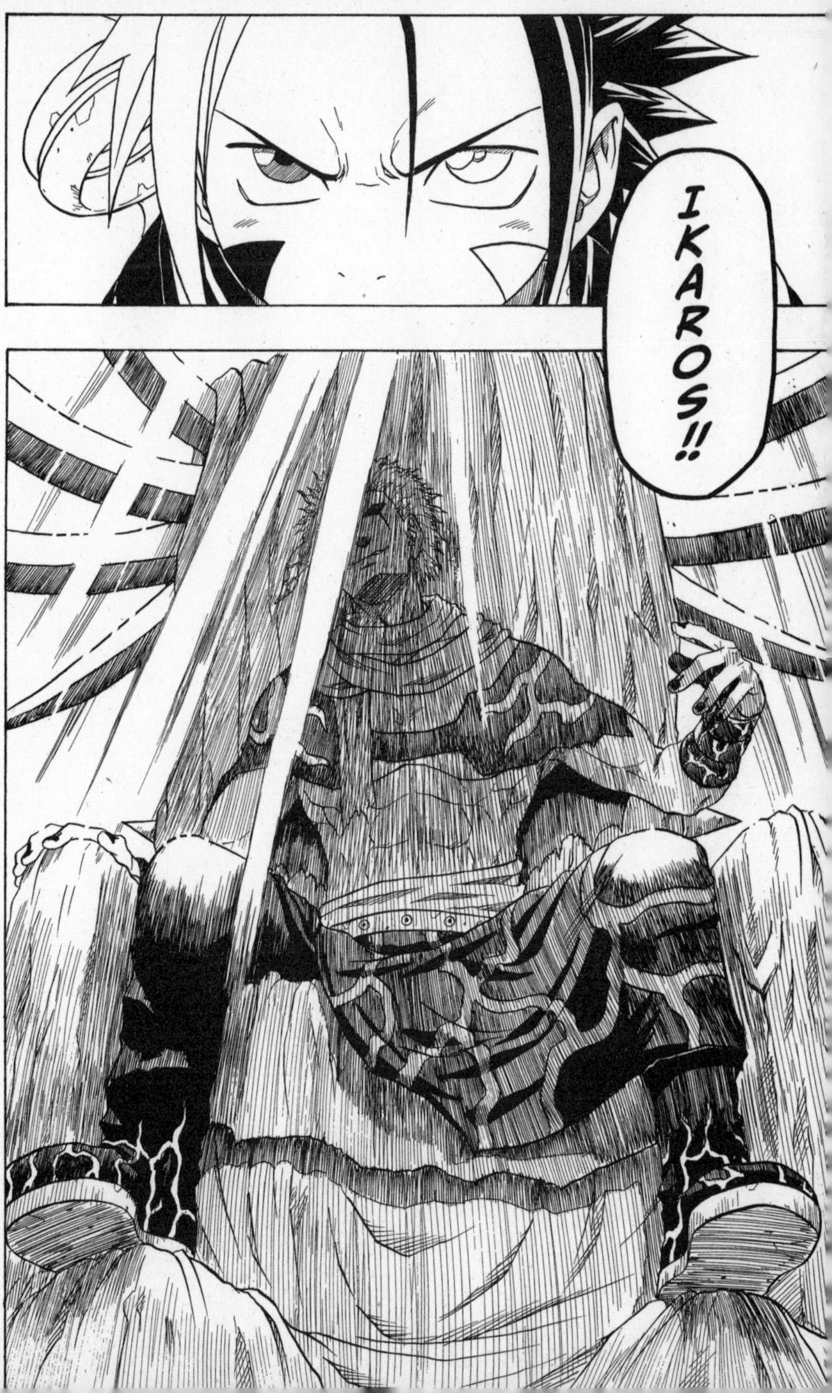
IKAROS!!

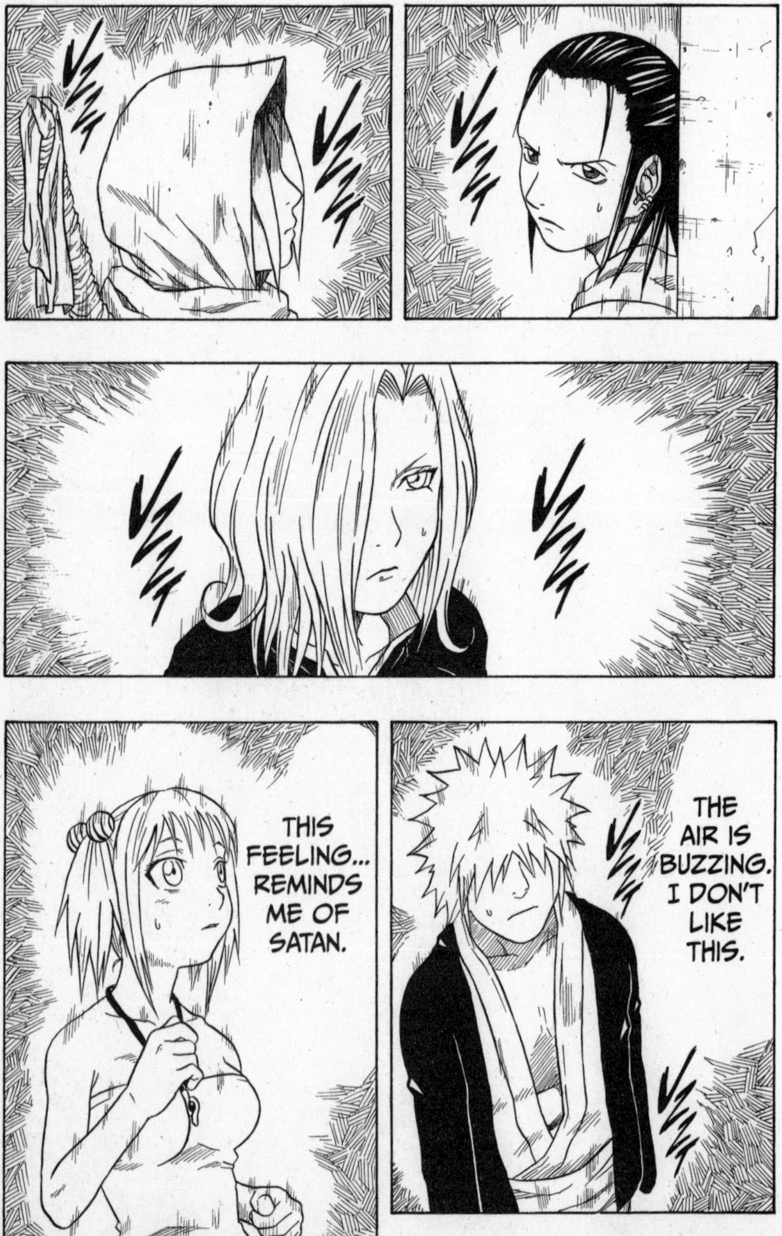
THE AIR IS BUZZING. I DON'T LIKE THIS.
THIS FEELING... REMINDS ME OF SATAN.

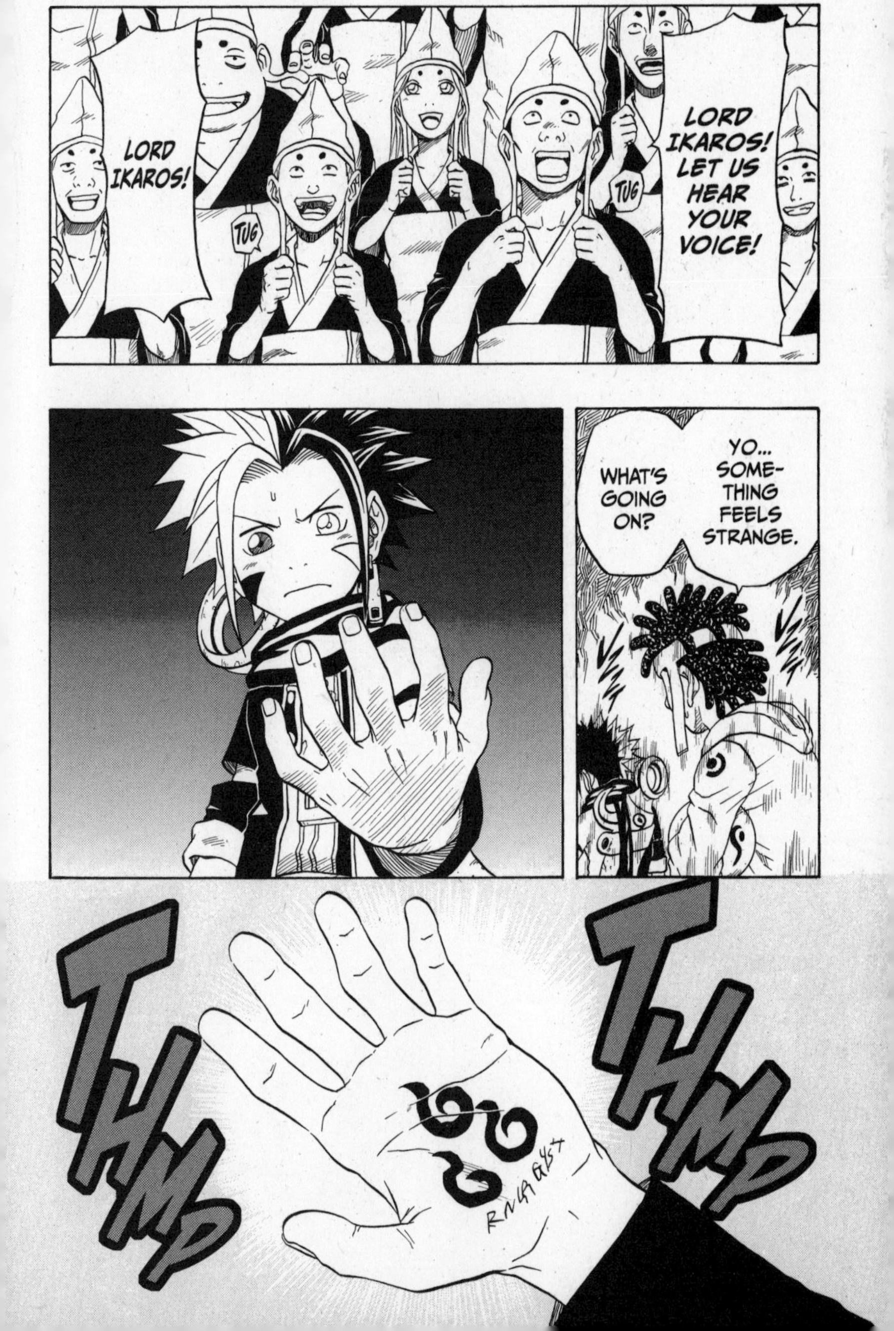
LORD IKAROS! LET US HEAR YOUR VOICE!
TUG
TUG
LORD IKAROS!
YO... SOMETHING FEELS STRANGE.
WHAT'S GOING ON?
THUMP
THUMP

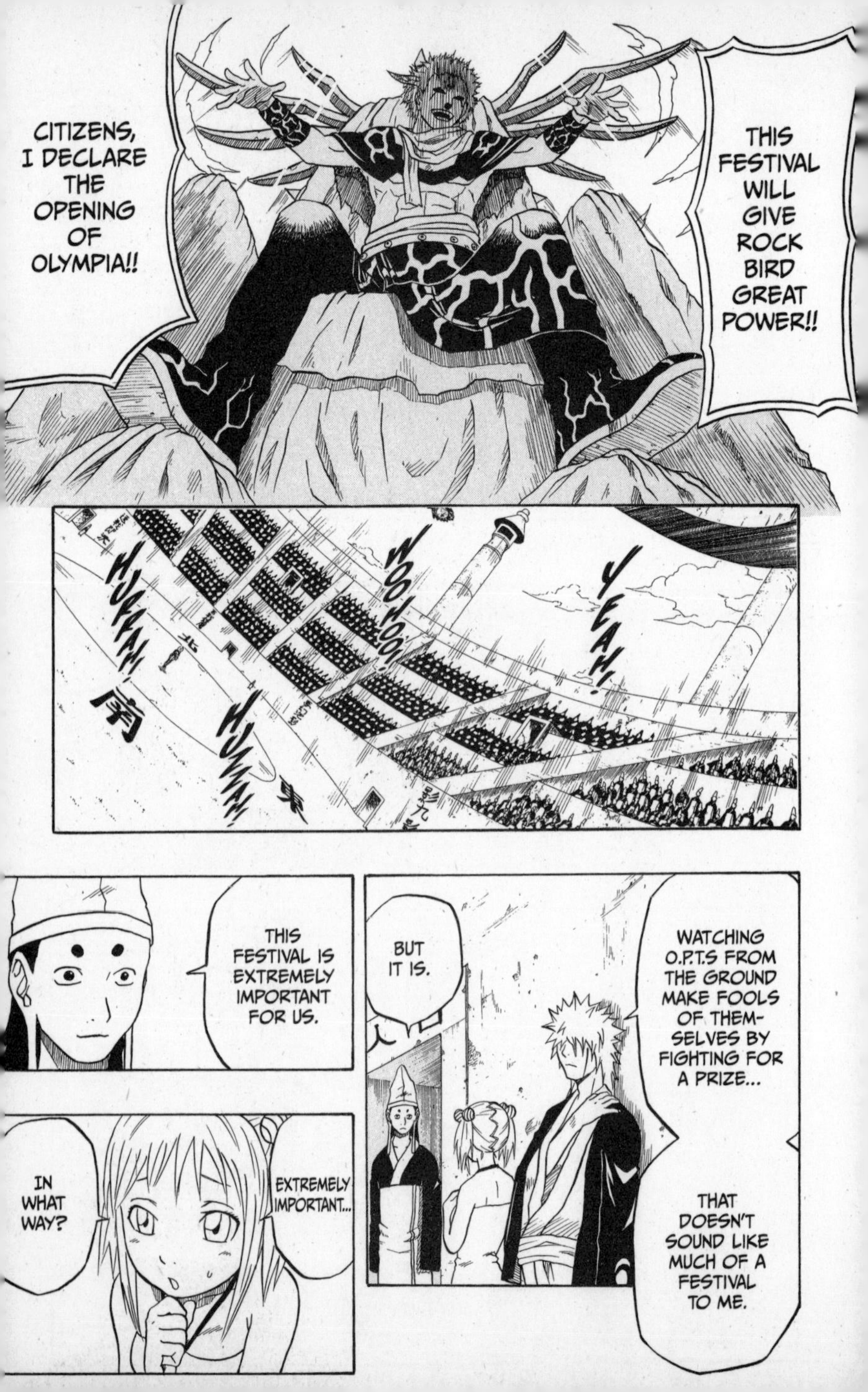
THIS FESTIVAL WILL GIVE ROCK BIRD GREAT POWER!!
CITIZENS, I DECLARE THE OPENING OF OLYMPIA!!
YEAH!
WOO HOO!
HURRAH!
HURRAH!
WATCHING O.P.T.S FROM THE GROUND MAKE FOOLS OF THEM-SELVES BY FIGHTING FOR A PRIZE...
THAT DOESN'T SOUND LIKE MUCH OF A FESTIVAL TO ME.
BUT IT IS.
THIS FESTIVAL IS EXTREMELY IMPORTANT FOR US.
EXTREMELY IMPORTANT...
IN WHAT WAY?

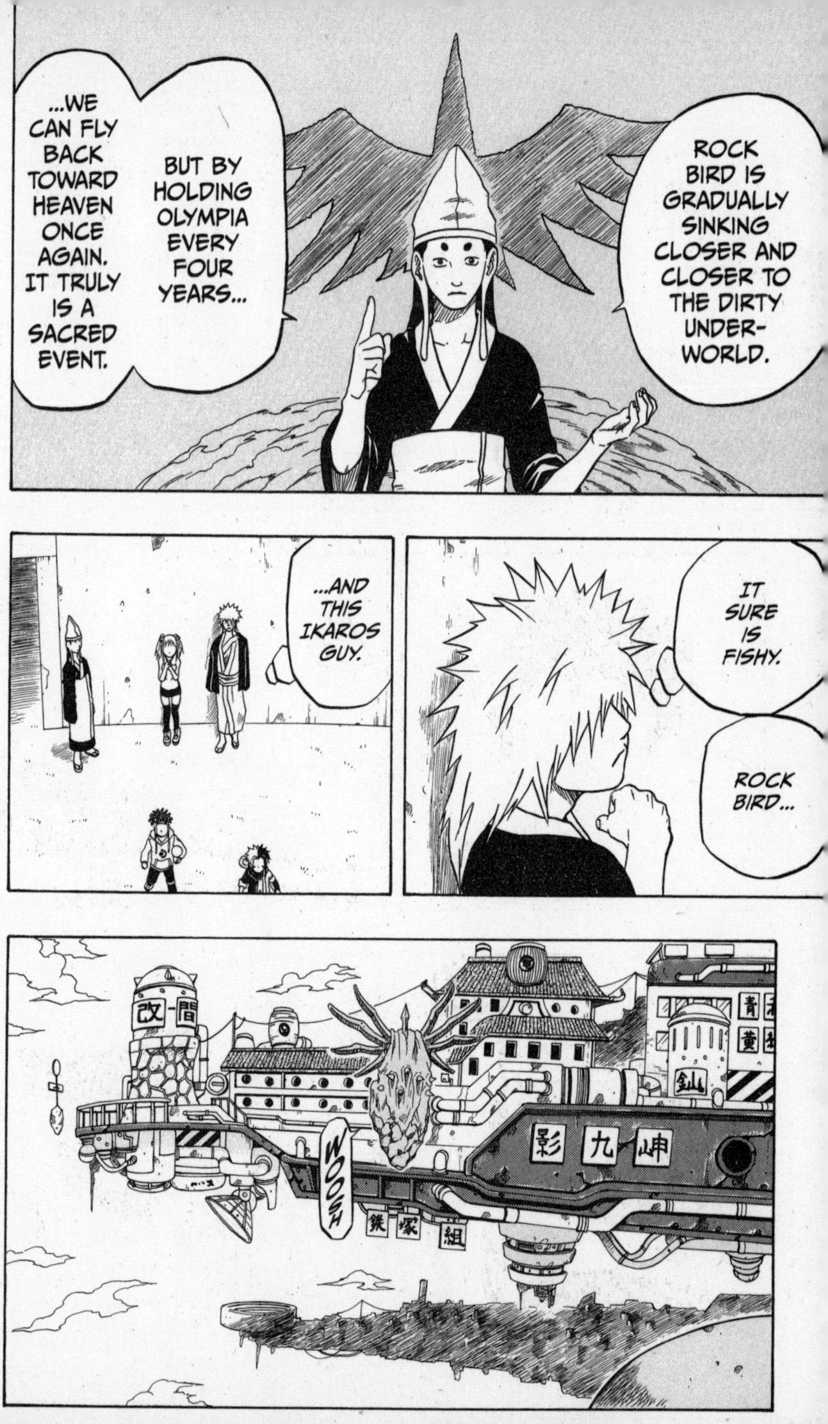
ROCK BIRD IS GRADUALLY SINKING CLOSER AND CLOSER TO THE DIRTY UNDER-WORLD.
BUT BY HOLDING OLYMPIA EVERY FOUR YEARS...
...WE CAN FLY BACK TOWARD HEAVEN ONCE AGAIN. IT TRULY IS A SACRED EVENT.
IT SURE IS FISHY.
ROCK BIRD...
...AND THIS IKAROS GUY.
WOOSH

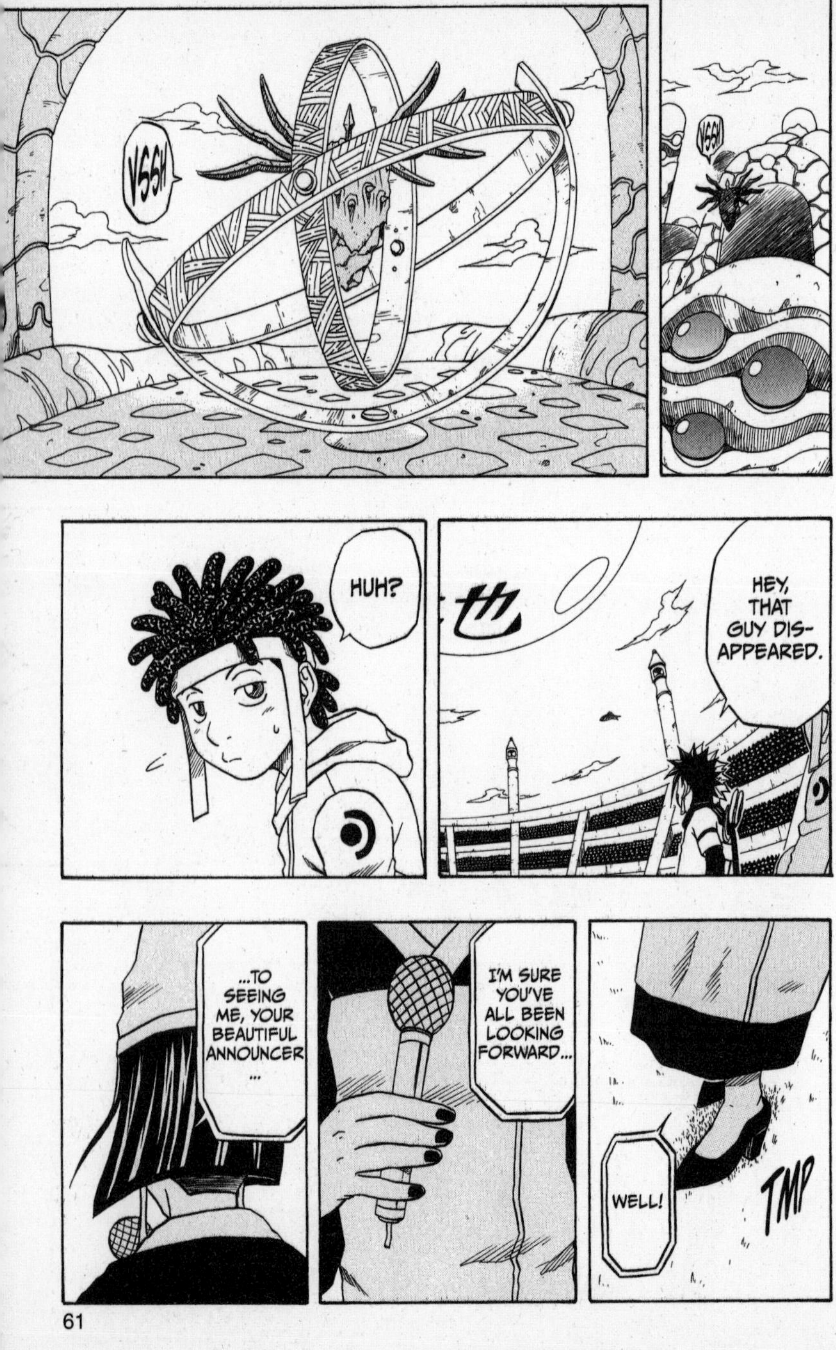

VSSH
VSSH
HEY, THAT GUY DIS-APPEARED.
HUH?
WELL!
TMP
I'M SURE YOU'VE ALL BEEN LOOKING FORWARD...
...TO SEEING ME, YOUR BEAUTIFUL ANNOUNCER ...

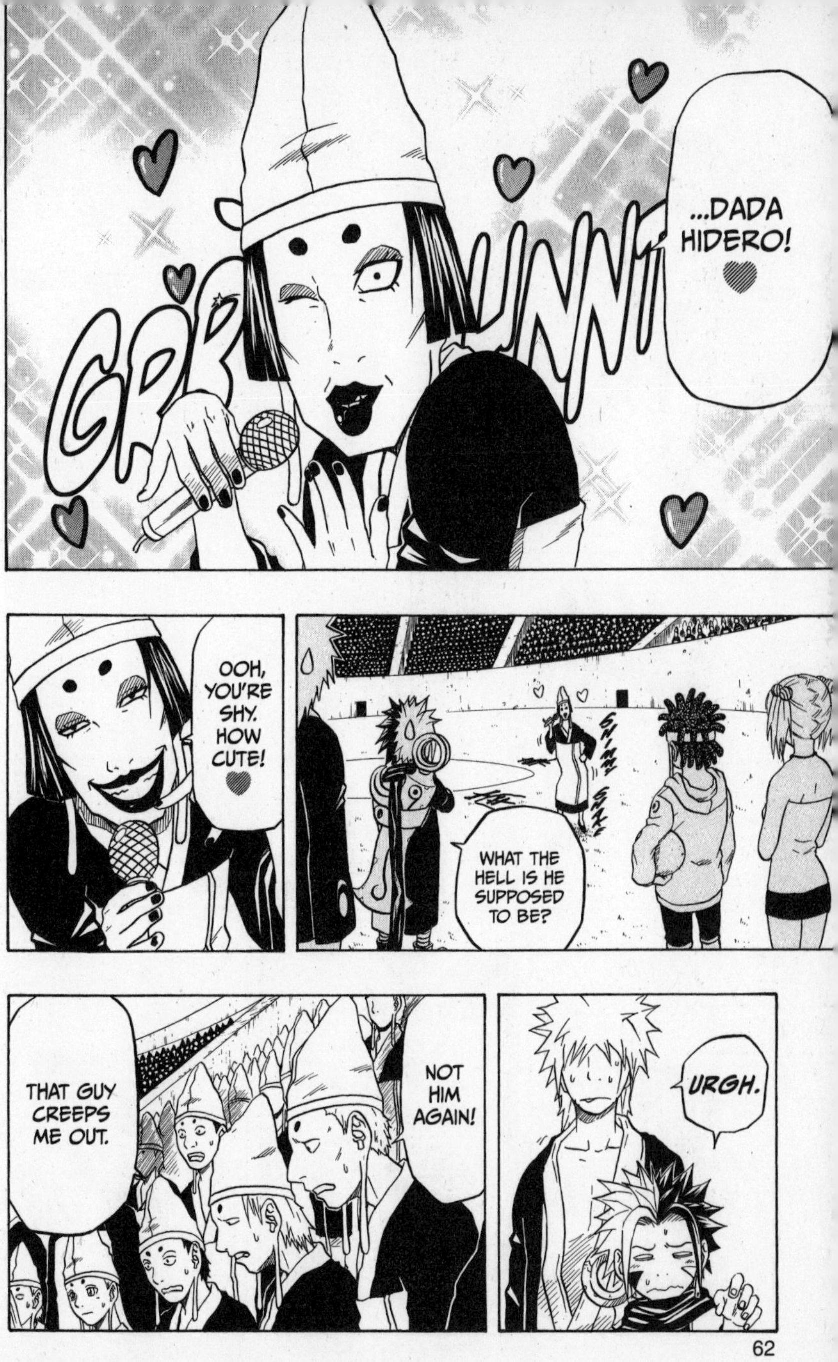
...DADA HIDERO! ♥
WHAT THE HELL IS HE SUPPOSED TO BE?
OOH, YOU'RE SHY. HOW CUTE! ♥
URGH.
NOT HIM AGAIN!
THAT GUY CREEPS ME OUT.

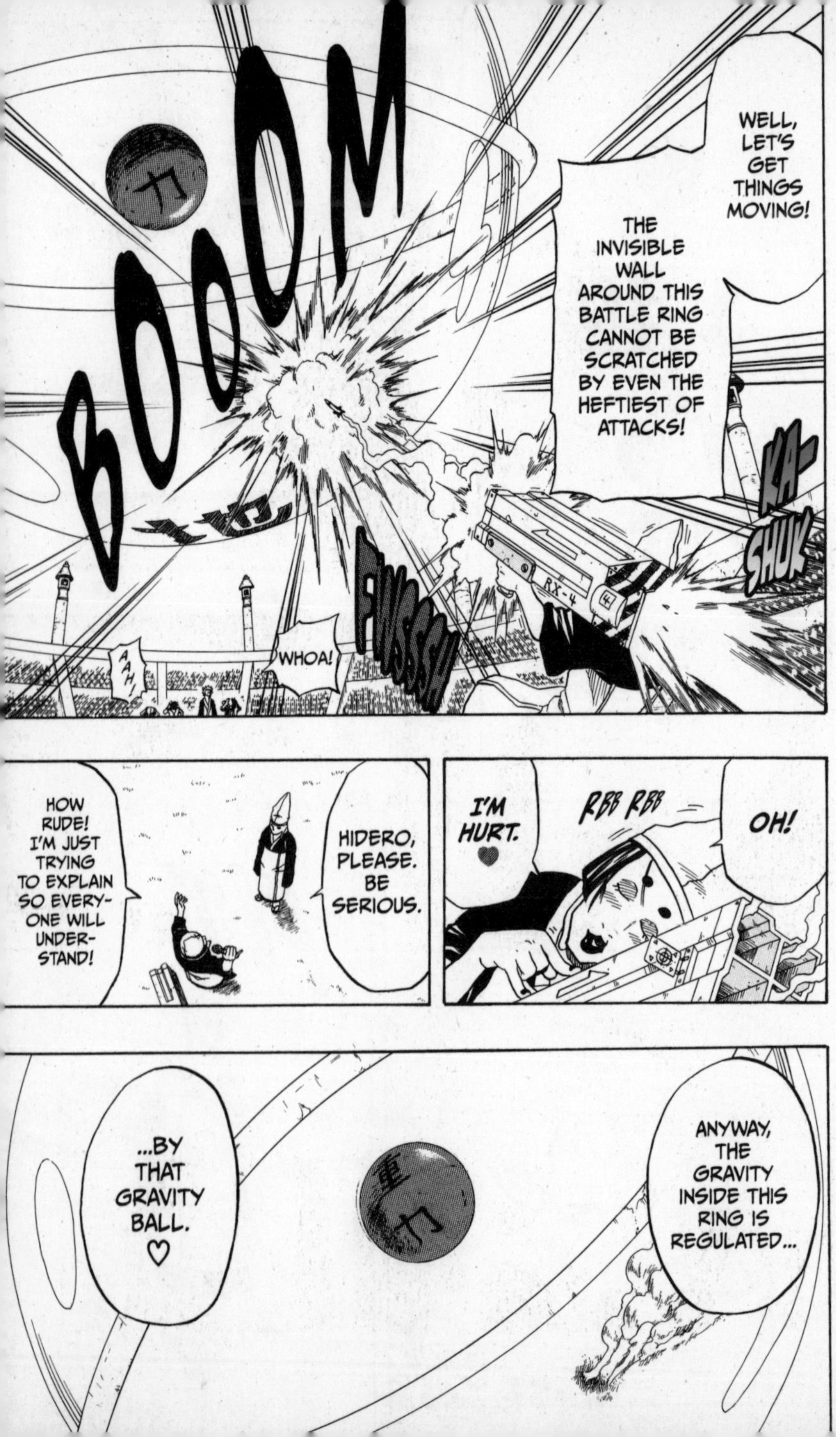
WELL, LET'S GET THINGS MOVING!
THE INVISIBLE WALL AROUND THIS BATTLE RING CANNOT BE SCRATCHED BY EVEN THE HEFTIEST OF ATTACKS!
KA-SHUK
BOOOM
WHOA!
AAH!
OH!
RBB RBB
I'M HURT. ♥
HIDERO, PLEASE. BE SERIOUS.
HOW RUDE! I'M JUST TRYING TO EXPLAIN SO EVERY-ONE WILL UNDER-STAND!
ANYWAY, THE GRAVITY INSIDE THIS RING IS REGULATED...
...BY THAT GRAVITY BALL. ♡

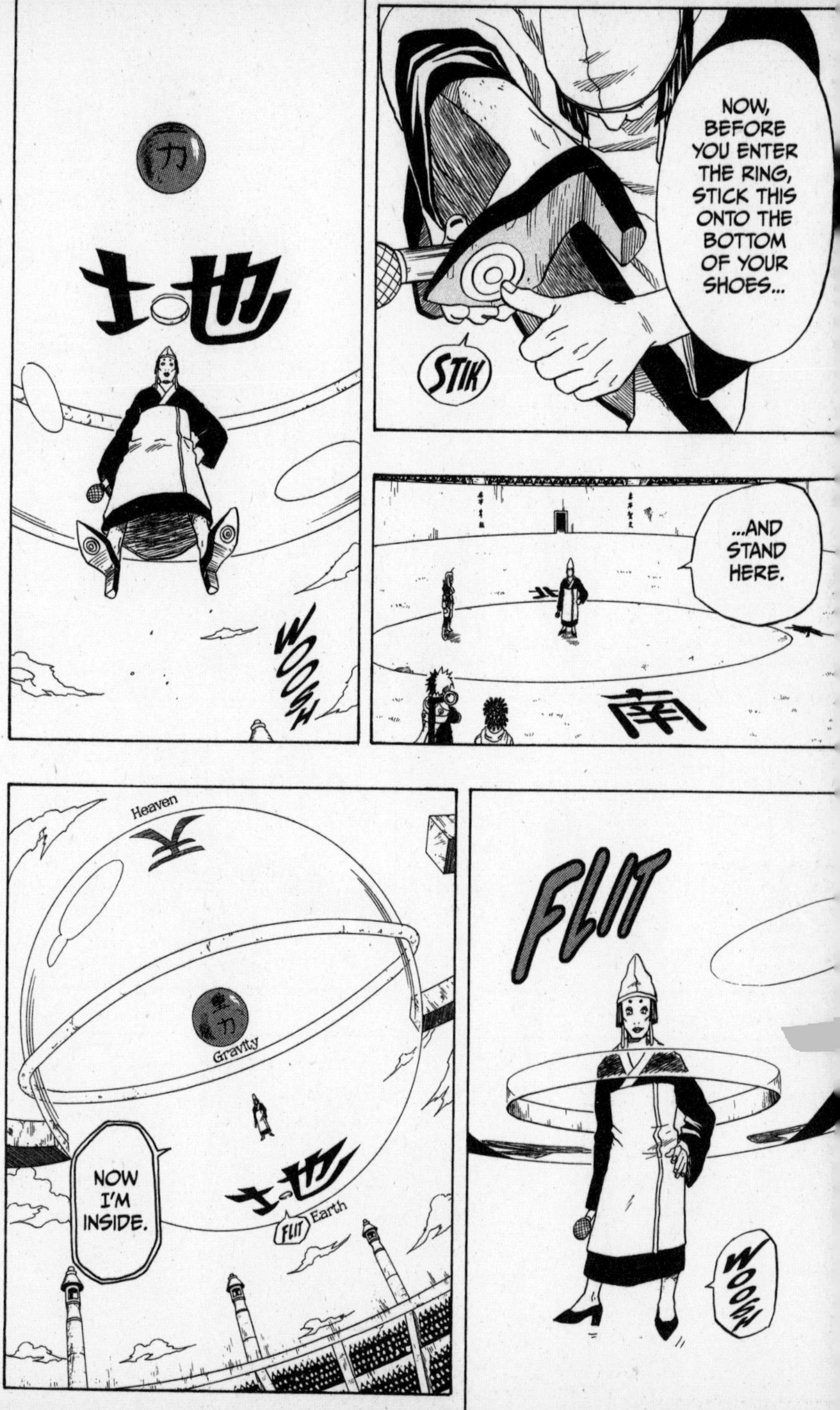
NOW, BEFORE YOU ENTER THE RING, STICK THIS ONTO THE BOTTOM OF YOUR SHOES...
STIK
...AND STAND HERE.
WOOSH
FLIT
WOOSH
Heaven
Gravity
NOW I'M INSIDE.
FLIT
Earth

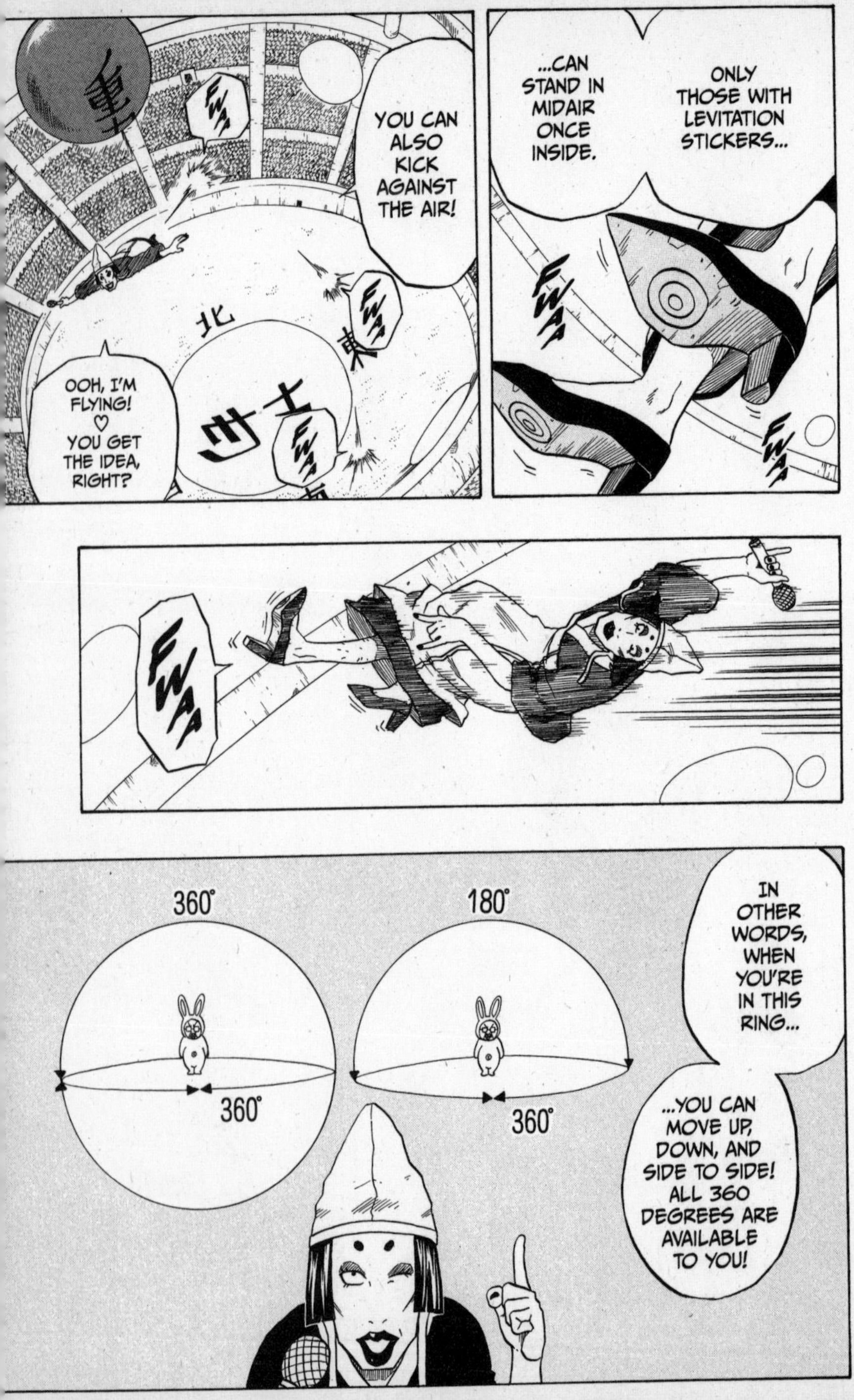
ONLY THOSE WITH LEVITATION STICKERS...
...CAN STAND IN MIDAIR ONCE INSIDE.
FWAP
FWAP
YOU CAN ALSO KICK AGAINST THE AIR!
FWAP
北
東
FWAP
FWAP
OOH, I'M FLYING! ♡ YOU GET THE IDEA, RIGHT?
FWAP
IN OTHER WORDS, WHEN YOU'RE IN THIS RING...
...YOU CAN MOVE UP, DOWN, AND SIDE TO SIDE! ALL 360 DEGREES ARE AVAILABLE TO YOU!
180°
360°
360°
360°

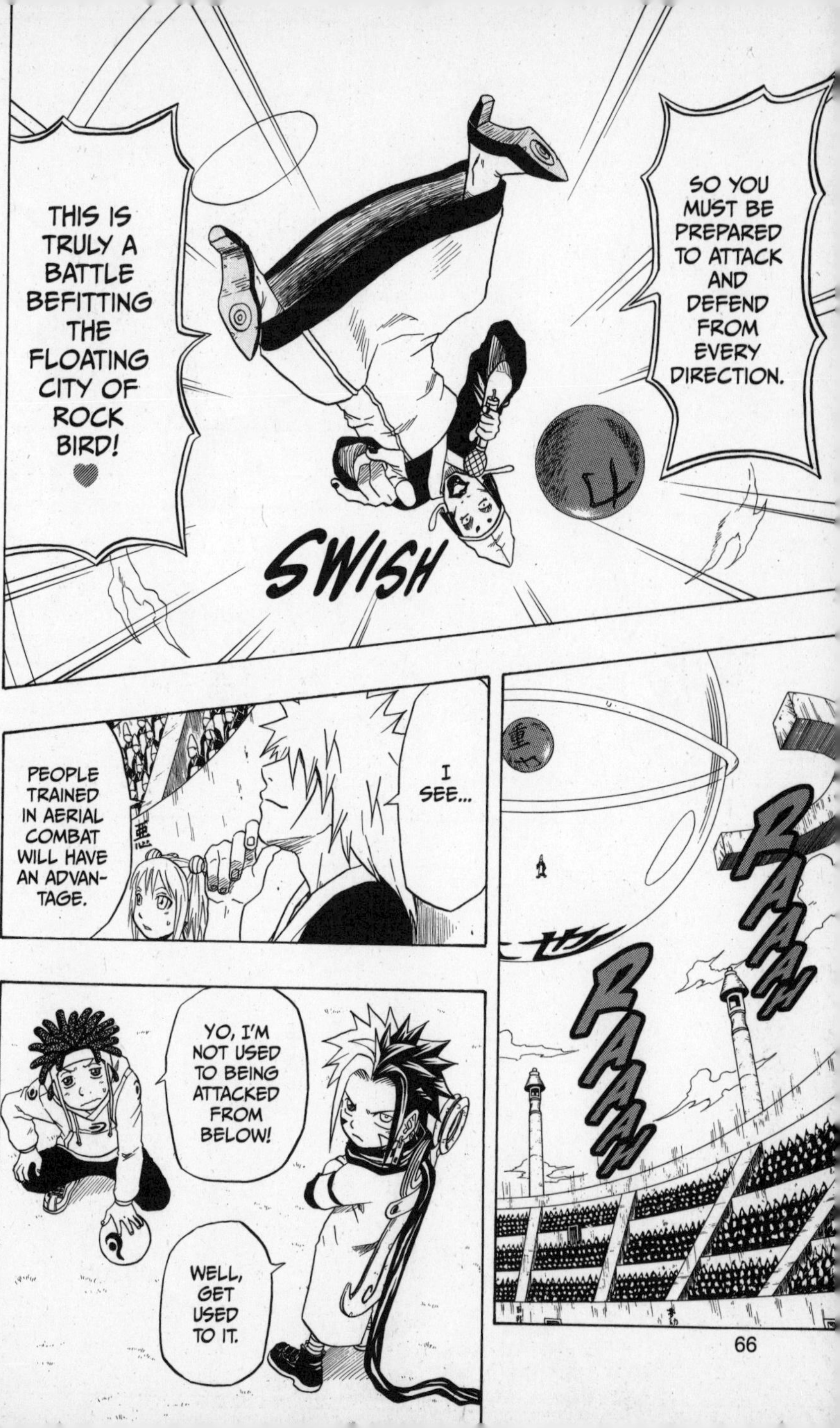
SO YOU MUST BE PREPARED TO ATTACK AND DEFEND FROM EVERY DIRECTION.
THIS IS TRULY A BATTLE BEFITTING THE FLOATING CITY OF ROCK BIRD! ♥
SWISH
RAAAH
RAAAH
I SEE...
PEOPLE TRAINED IN AERIAL COMBAT WILL HAVE AN ADVANTAGE.
YO, I'M NOT USED TO BEING ATTACKED FROM BELOW!
WELL, GET USED TO IT.

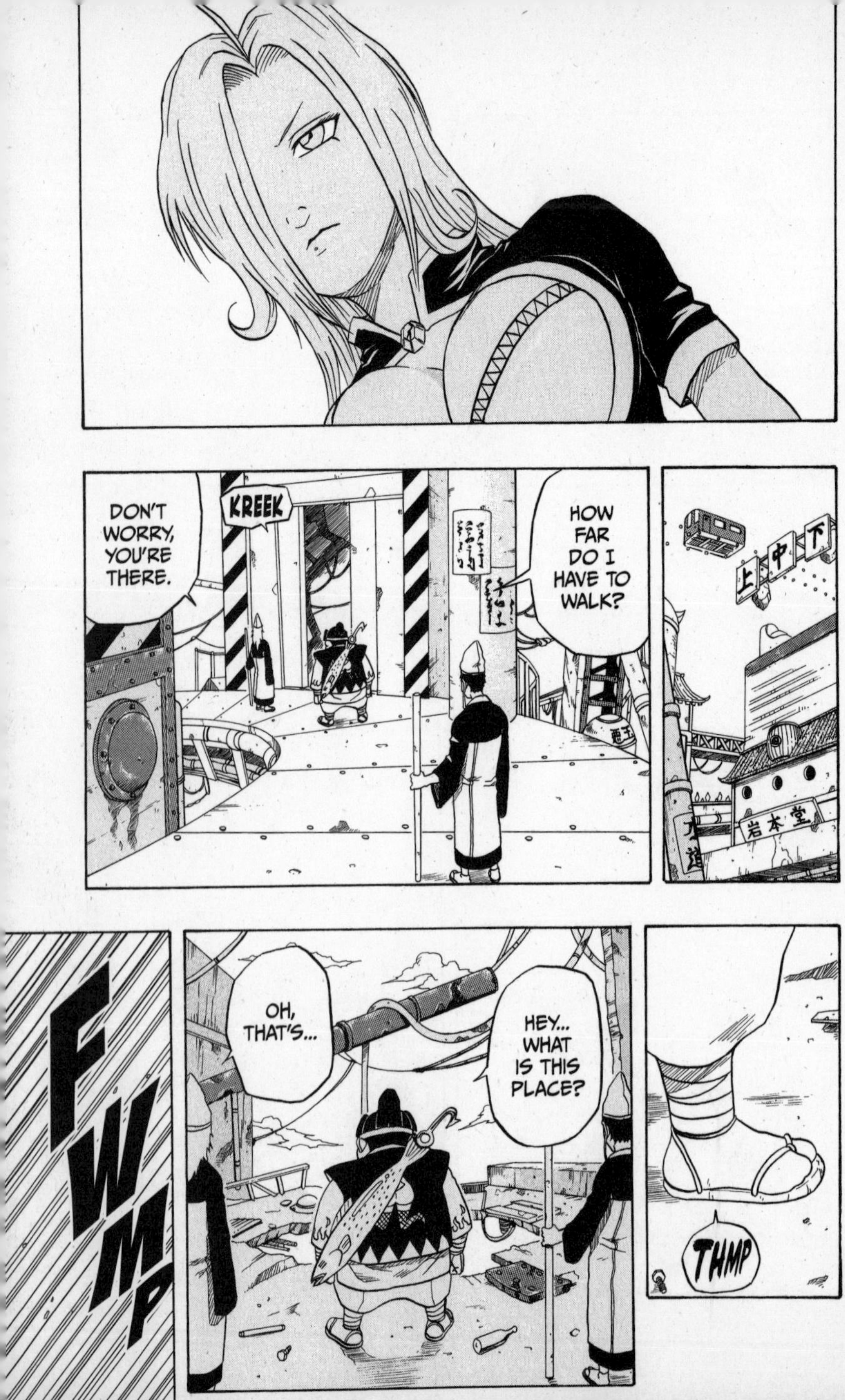

上
中
下
岩本堂
HOW FAR DO I HAVE TO WALK?
KREEK
DON'T WORRY, YOU'RE THERE.
THMP
HEY... WHAT IS THIS PLACE?
OH, THAT'S...
FWMP

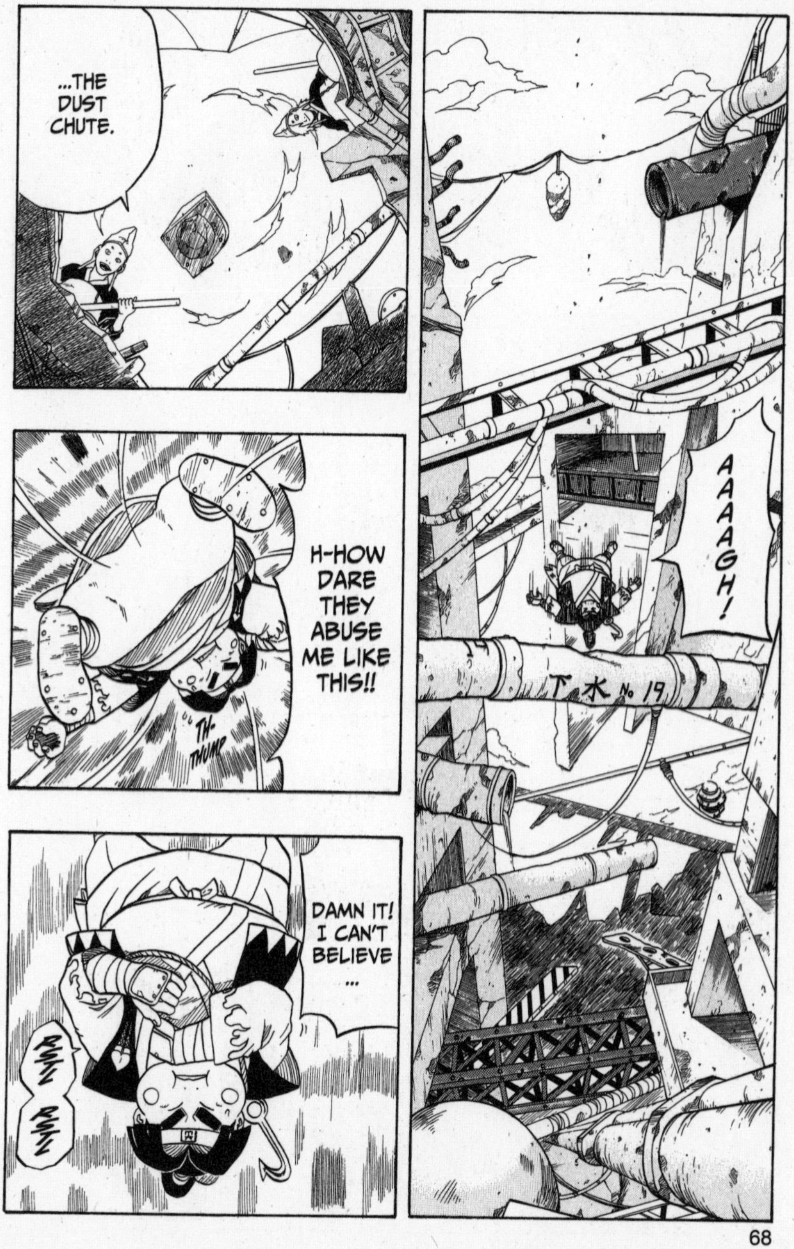
AAAAGH!
下水 No. 19
...THE DUST CHUTE.
H-HOW DARE THEY ABUSE ME LIKE THIS!!
TH-THUMP
DAMN IT! I CAN'T BELIEVE ...

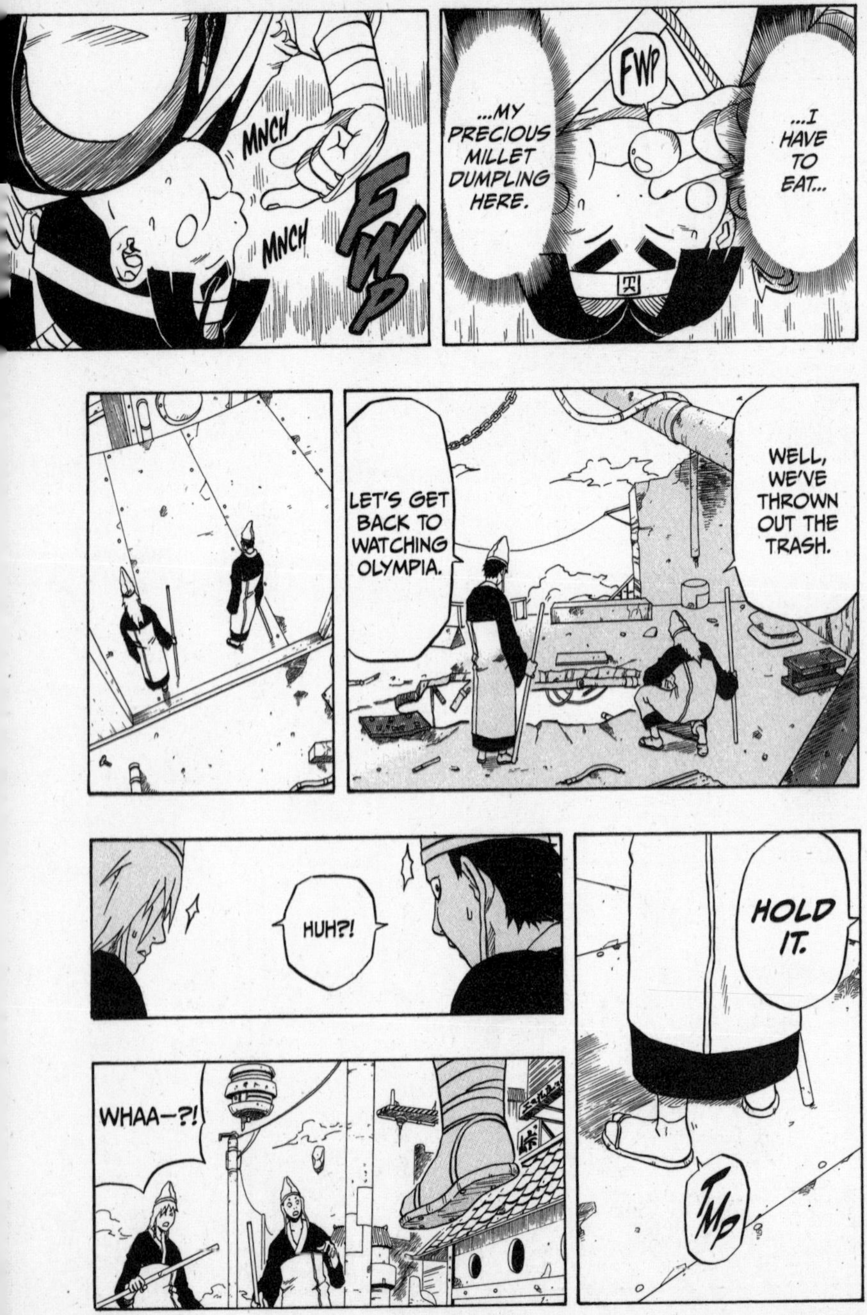
...I HAVE TO EAT...
FWP
...MY PRECIOUS MILLET DUMPLING HERE.
FWP
MNCH
MNCH
WELL, WE'VE THROWN OUT THE TRASH.
LET'S GET BACK TO WATCHING OLYMPIA.
HOLD IT.
TMP
HUH?!
WHAA-?!

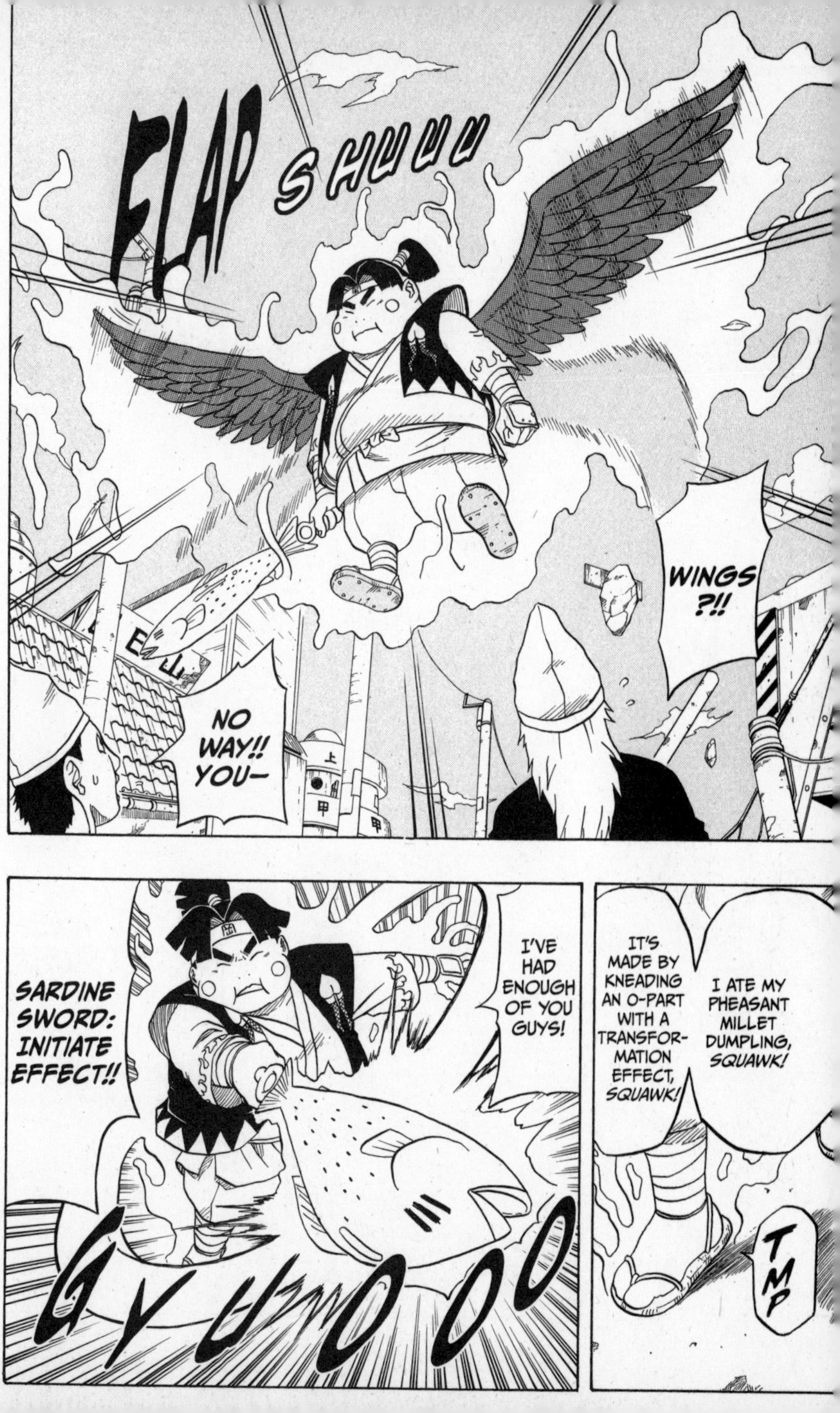
FLAP
SHUUU
WINGS ?!!
NO WAY!! YOU–
I ATE MY PHEASANT MILLET DUMPLING, SQUAWK!
IT'S MADE BY KNEADING AN O-PART WITH A TRANSFORMATION EFFECT, SQUAWK!
TMP
I'VE HAD ENOUGH OF YOU GUYS!
SARDINE SWORD: INITIATE EFFECT!!
GYUNOOO

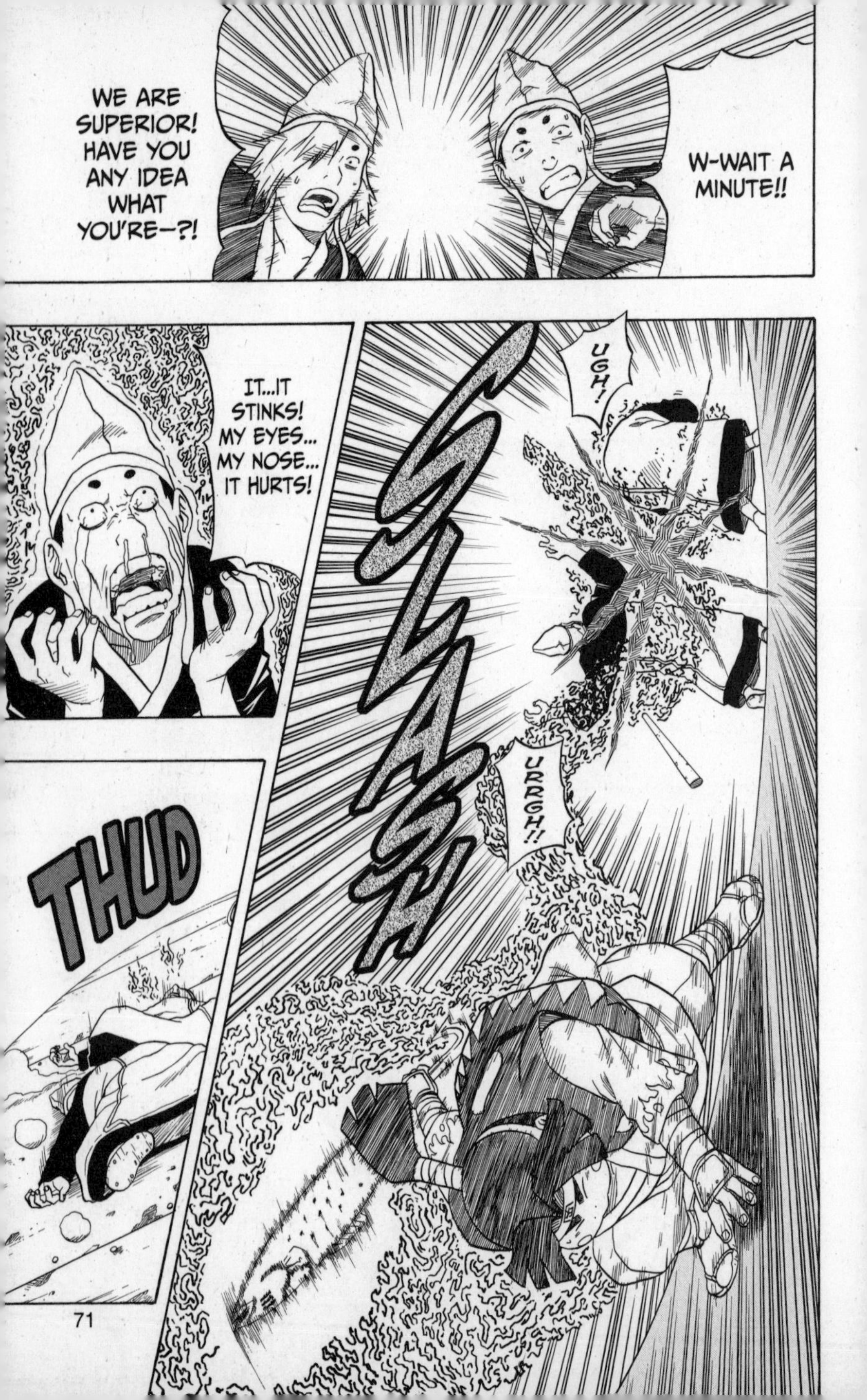
W-WAIT A MINUTE!!
WE ARE SUPERIOR! HAVE YOU ANY IDEA WHAT YOU'RE--?!
UGH!
SLASH
URRGH!!
IT...IT STINKS! MY EYES... MY NOSE... IT HURTS!
THUD

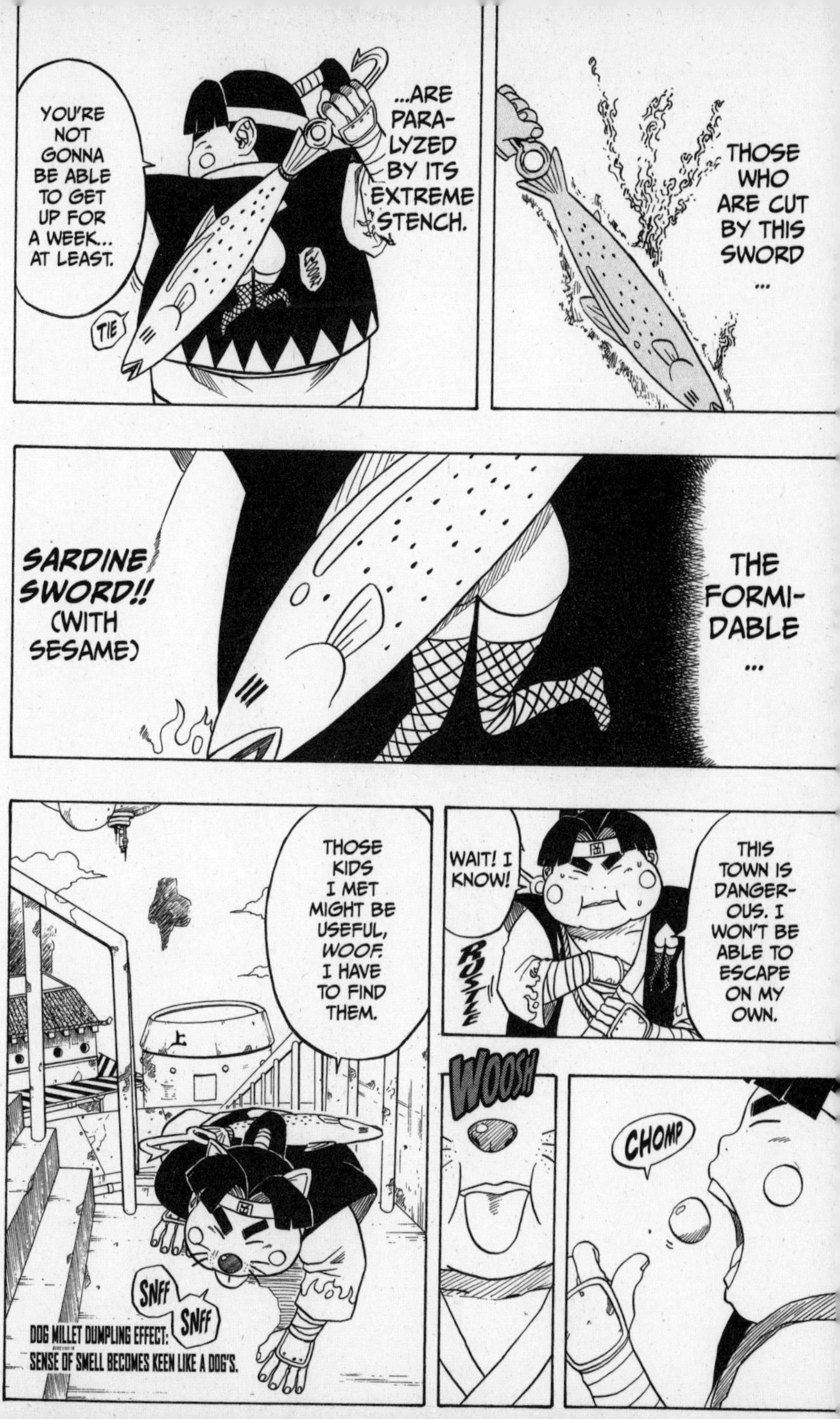
THOSE WHO ARE CUT BY THIS SWORD ...
...ARE PARALYZED BY ITS EXTREME STENCH.
YOU'RE NOT GONNA BE ABLE TO GET UP FOR A WEEK... AT LEAST.
TIE
THE FORMIDABLE ...
SARDINE SWORD!! (WITH SESAME)
THIS TOWN IS DANGEROUS. I WON'T BE ABLE TO ESCAPE ON MY OWN.
WAIT! I KNOW!
RUSTLE
CHOMP
WOOSH
THOSE KIDS I MET MIGHT BE USEFUL, WOOF. I HAVE TO FIND THEM.
SNFF
SNFF
DOG MILLET DUMPLING EFFECT:
SENSE OF SMELL BECOMES KEEN LIKE A DOG'S.

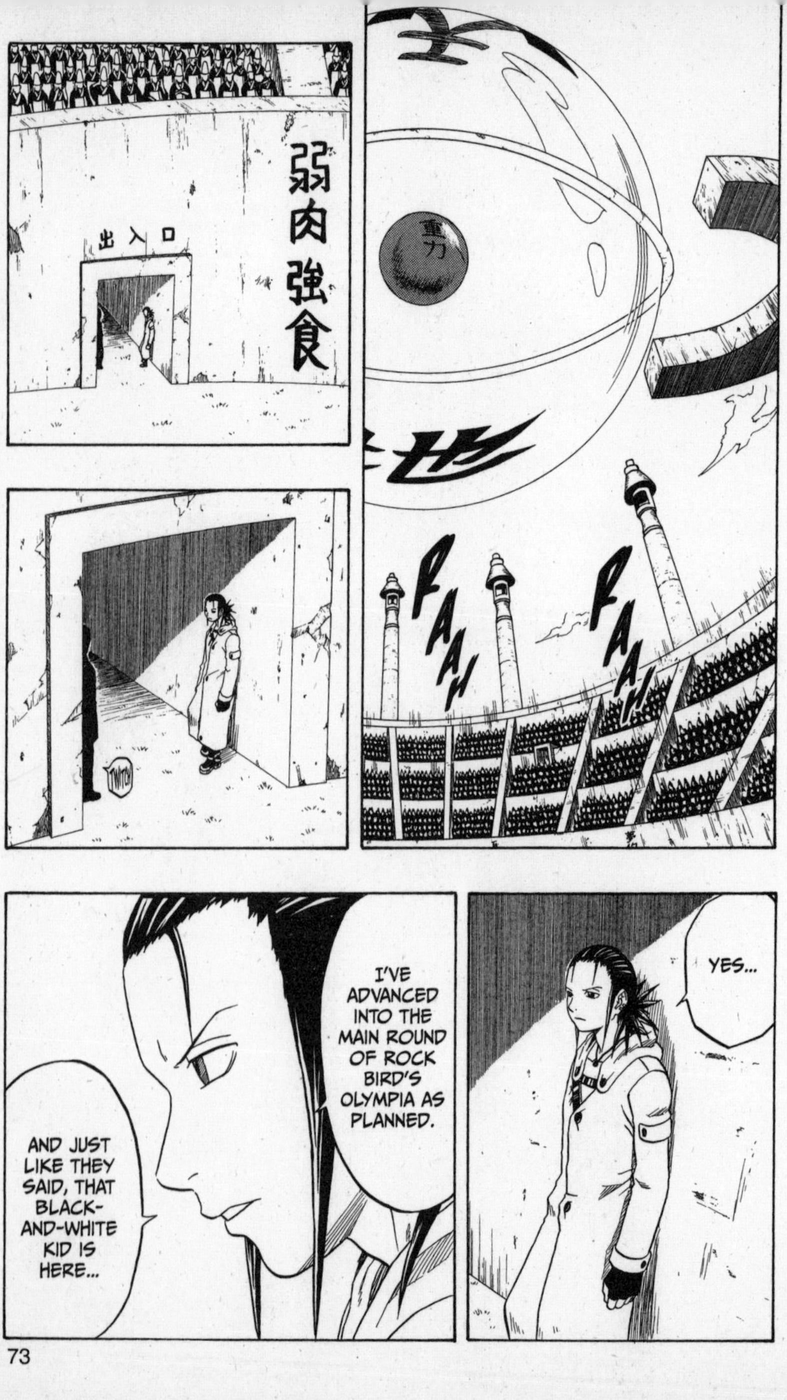
重力
PAAH
PAAH
弱肉強食
出入口
TWITCH
YES...
I'VE ADVANCED INTO THE MAIN ROUND OF ROCK BIRD'S OLYMPIA AS PLANNED.
AND JUST LIKE THEY SAID, THAT BLACK-AND-WHITE KID IS HERE...

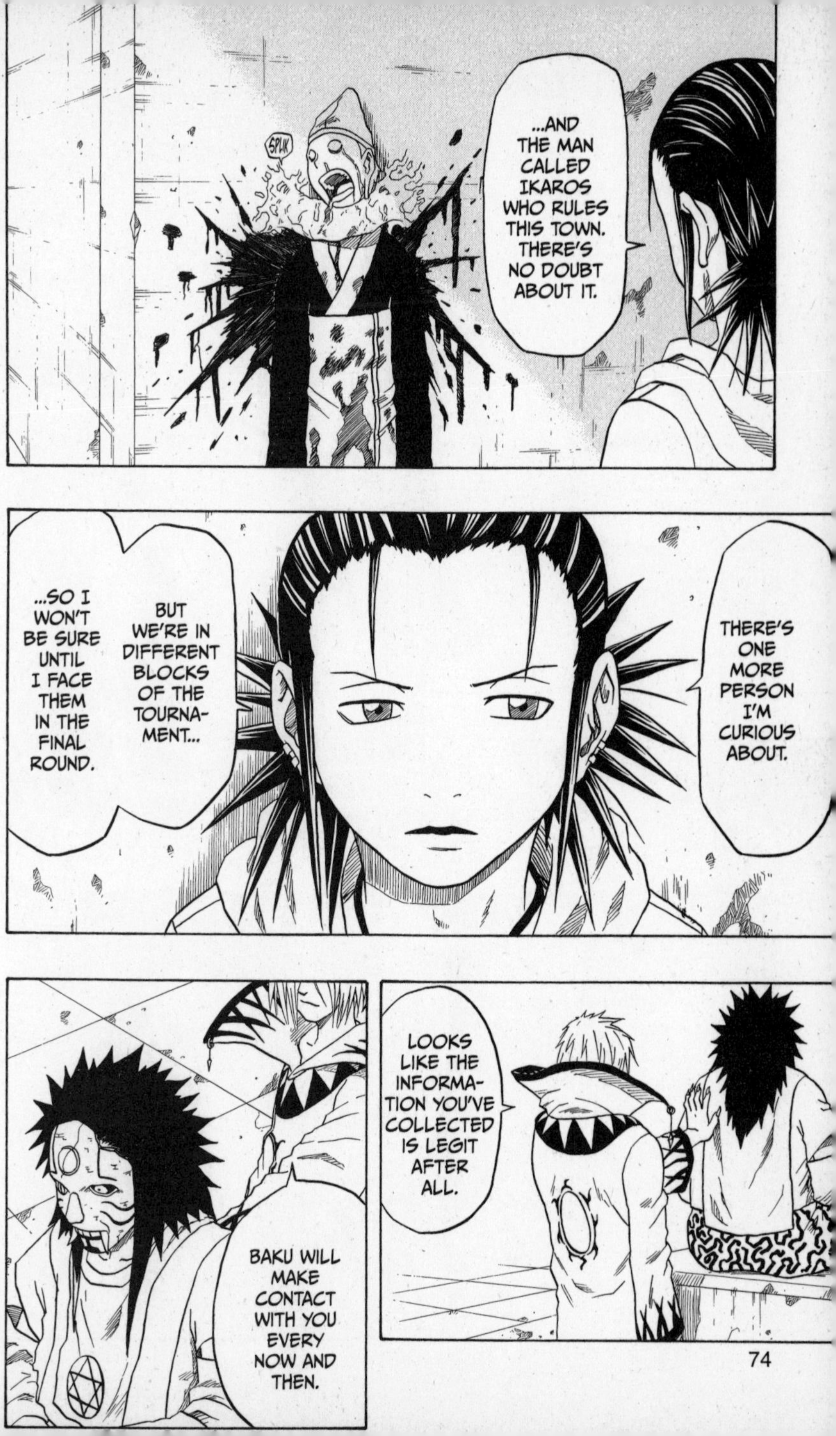
SPLUK
...AND THE MAN CALLED IKAROS WHO RULES THIS TOWN. THERE'S NO DOUBT ABOUT IT.
THERE'S ONE MORE PERSON I'M CURIOUS ABOUT.
BUT WE'RE IN DIFFERENT BLOCKS OF THE TOURNA-MENT...
...SO I WON'T BE SURE UNTIL I FACE THEM IN THE FINAL ROUND.
LOOKS LIKE THE INFORMA-TION YOU'VE COLLECTED IS LEGIT AFTER ALL.
BAKU WILL MAKE CONTACT WITH YOU EVERY NOW AND THEN.

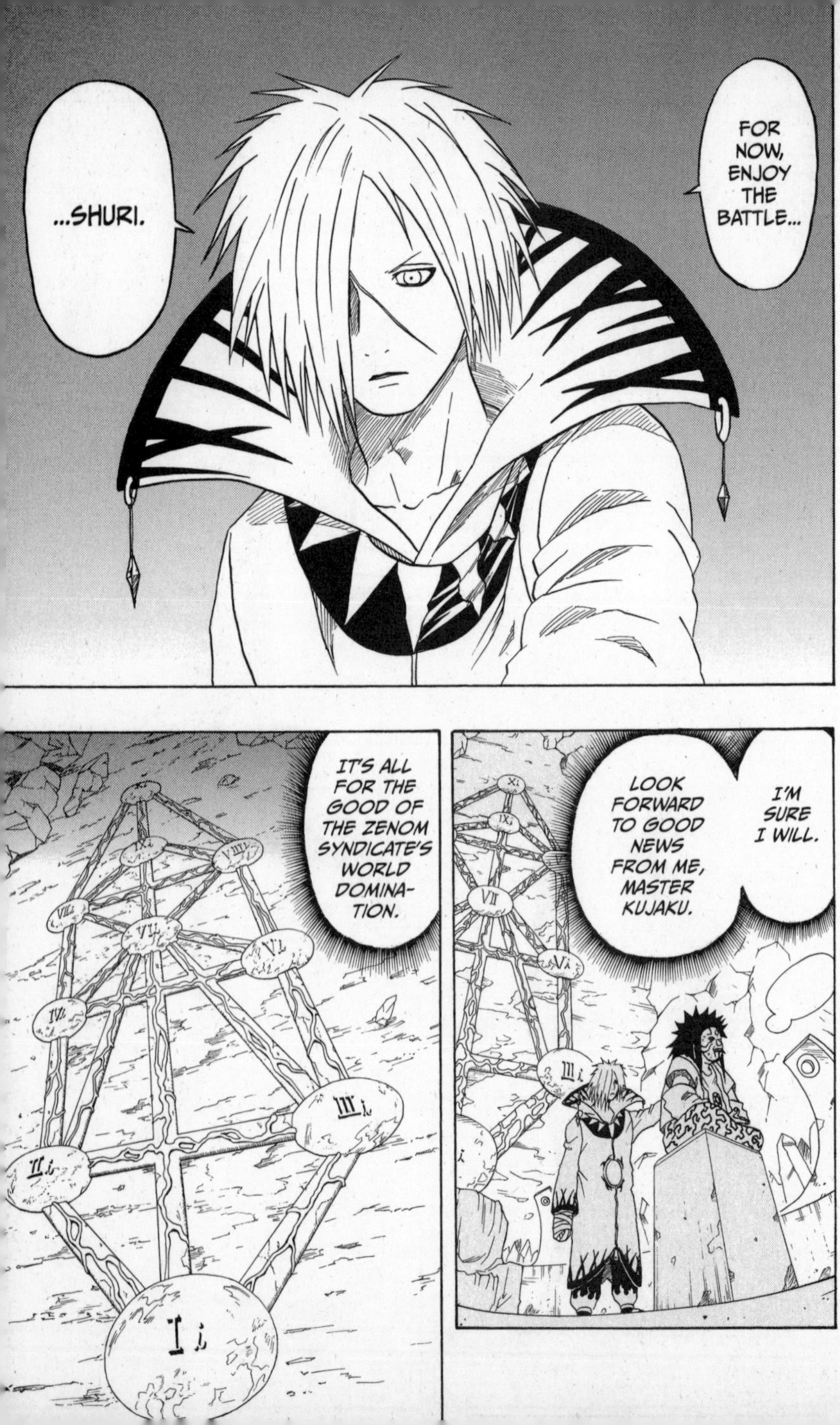
FOR NOW, ENJOY THE BATTLE...
...SHURI.
I'M SURE I WILL.
LOOK FORWARD TO GOOD NEWS FROM ME, MASTER KUJAKU.
IT'S ALL FOR THE GOOD OF THE ZENOM SYNDICATE'S WORLD DOMINA-TION.

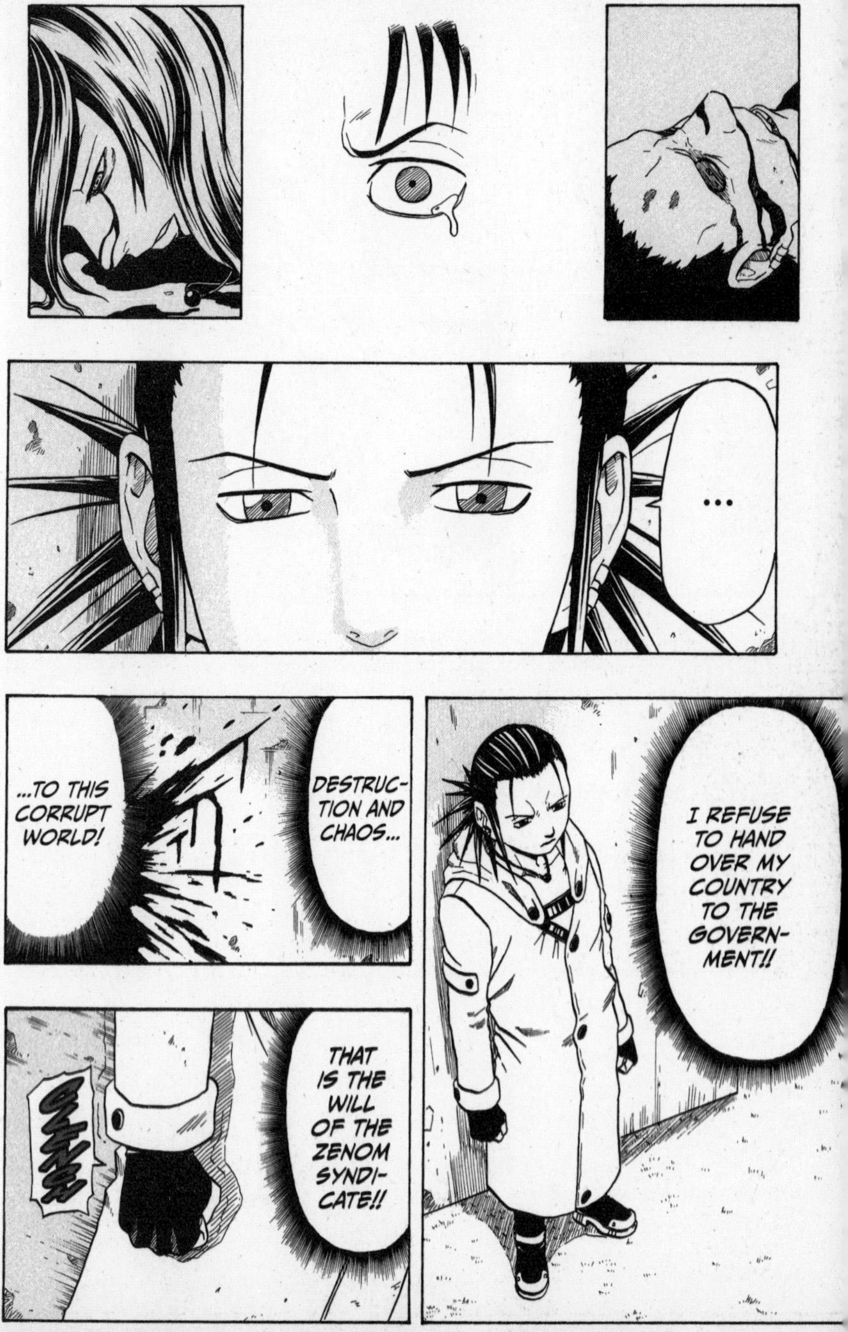
...
I REFUSE TO HAND OVER MY COUNTRY TO THE GOVERN-MENT!!
DESTRUC-TION AND CHAOS...
...TO THIS CORRUPT WORLD!
THAT IS THE WILL OF THE ZENOM SYNDI-CATE!!

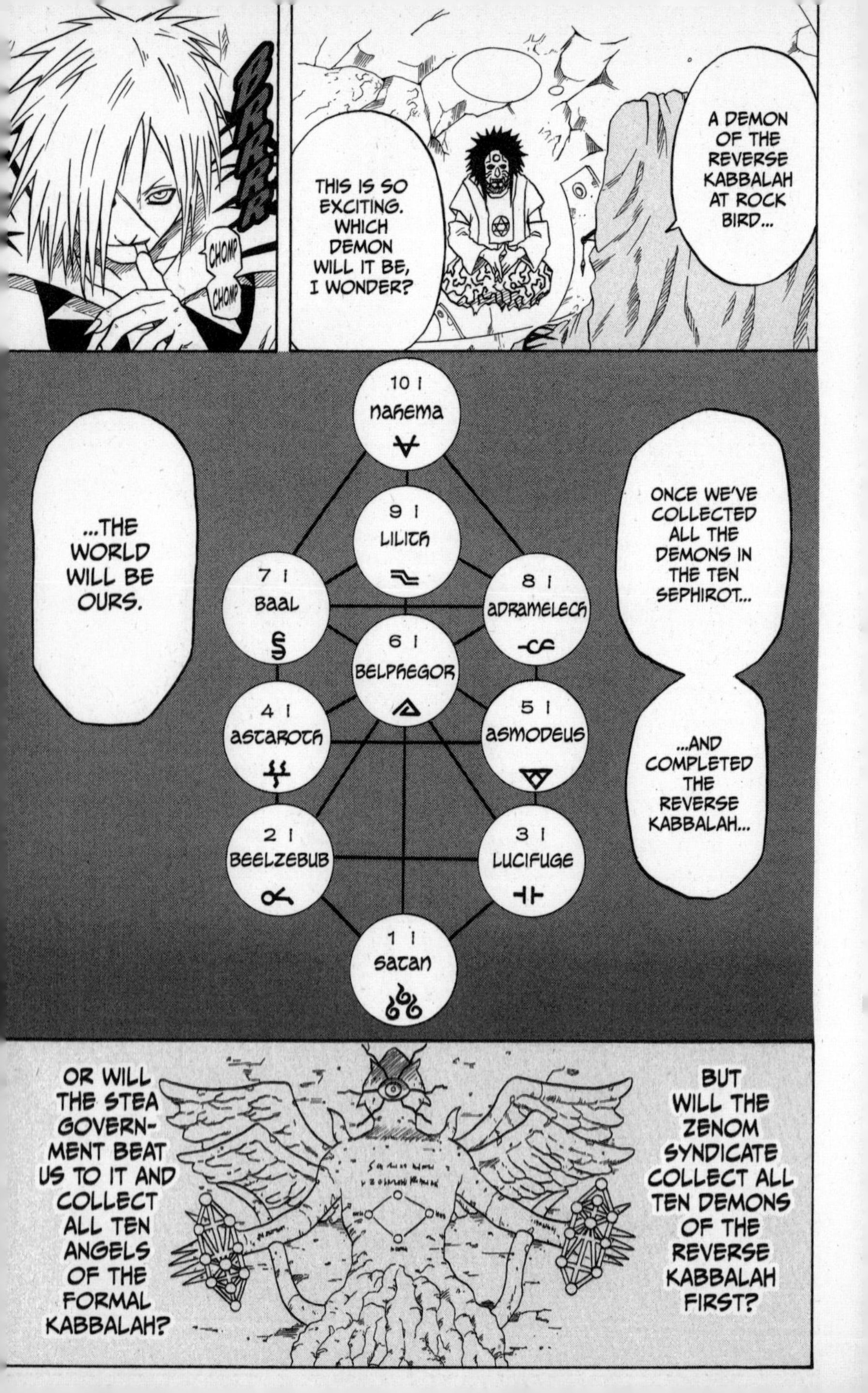
A DEMON OF THE REVERSE KABBALAH AT ROCK BIRD...
THIS IS SO EXCITING. WHICH DEMON WILL IT BE, I WONDER?
CHOMP
CHOMP
ONCE WE'VE COLLECTED ALL THE DEMONS IN THE TEN SEPHIROT...
...AND COMPLETED THE REVERSE KABBALAH...
...THE WORLD WILL BE OURS.
10 | NAHEMA
9 | LILITH
8 | ADRAMELECH
7 | BAAL
6 | BELPHEGOR
5 | ASMODEUS
4 | ASTAROTH
3 | LUCIFUGE
2 | BEELZEBUB
1 | SATAN
BUT WILL THE ZENOM SYNDICATE COLLECT ALL TEN DEMONS OF THE REVERSE KABBALAH FIRST?
OR WILL THE STEA GOVERNMENT BEAT US TO IT AND COLLECT ALL TEN ANGELS OF THE FORMAL KABBALAH?

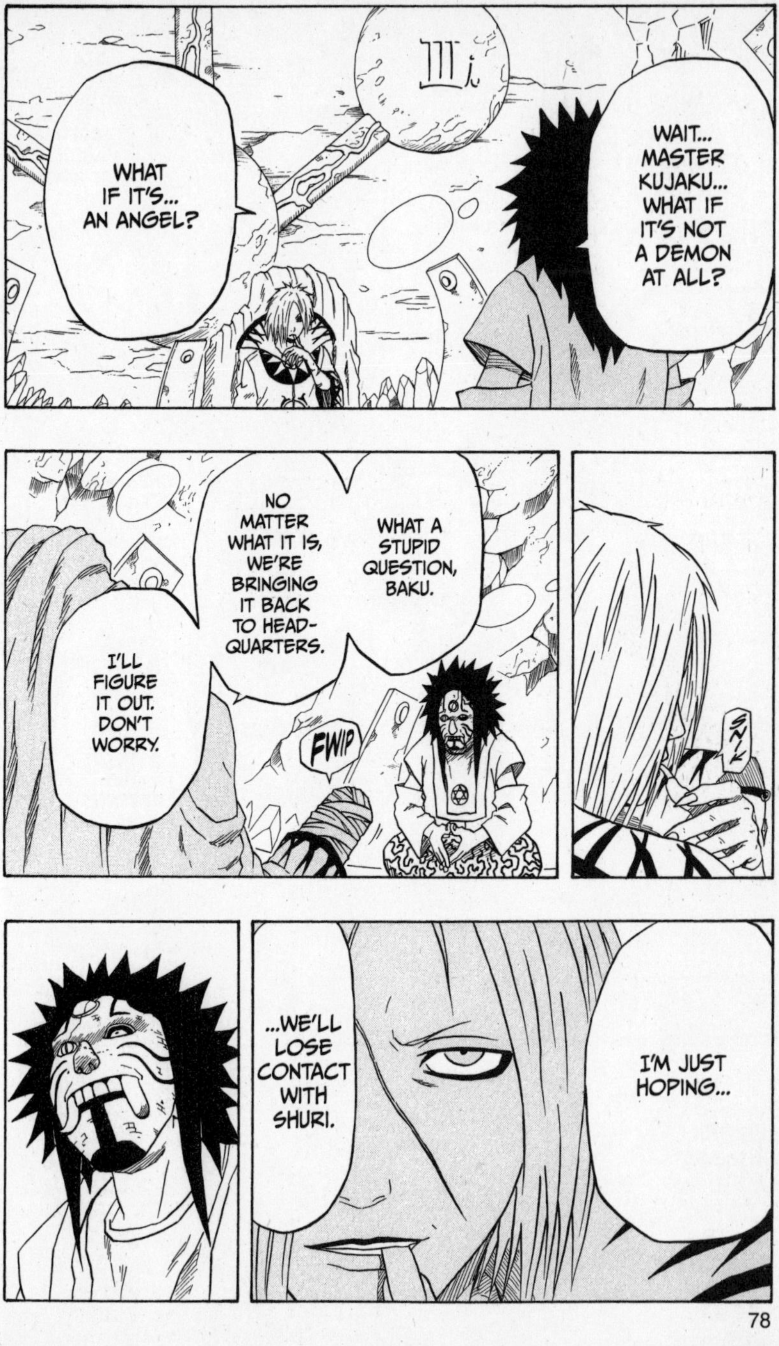
WAIT... MASTER KUJAKU... WHAT IF IT'S NOT A DEMON AT ALL?
WHAT IF IT'S... AN ANGEL?
SNIK
WHAT A STUPID QUESTION, BAKU.
NO MATTER WHAT IT IS, WE'RE BRINGING IT BACK TO HEAD-QUARTERS.
FWIP
I'LL FIGURE IT OUT. DON'T WORRY.
I'M JUST HOPING...
...WE'LL LOSE CONTACT WITH SHURI.

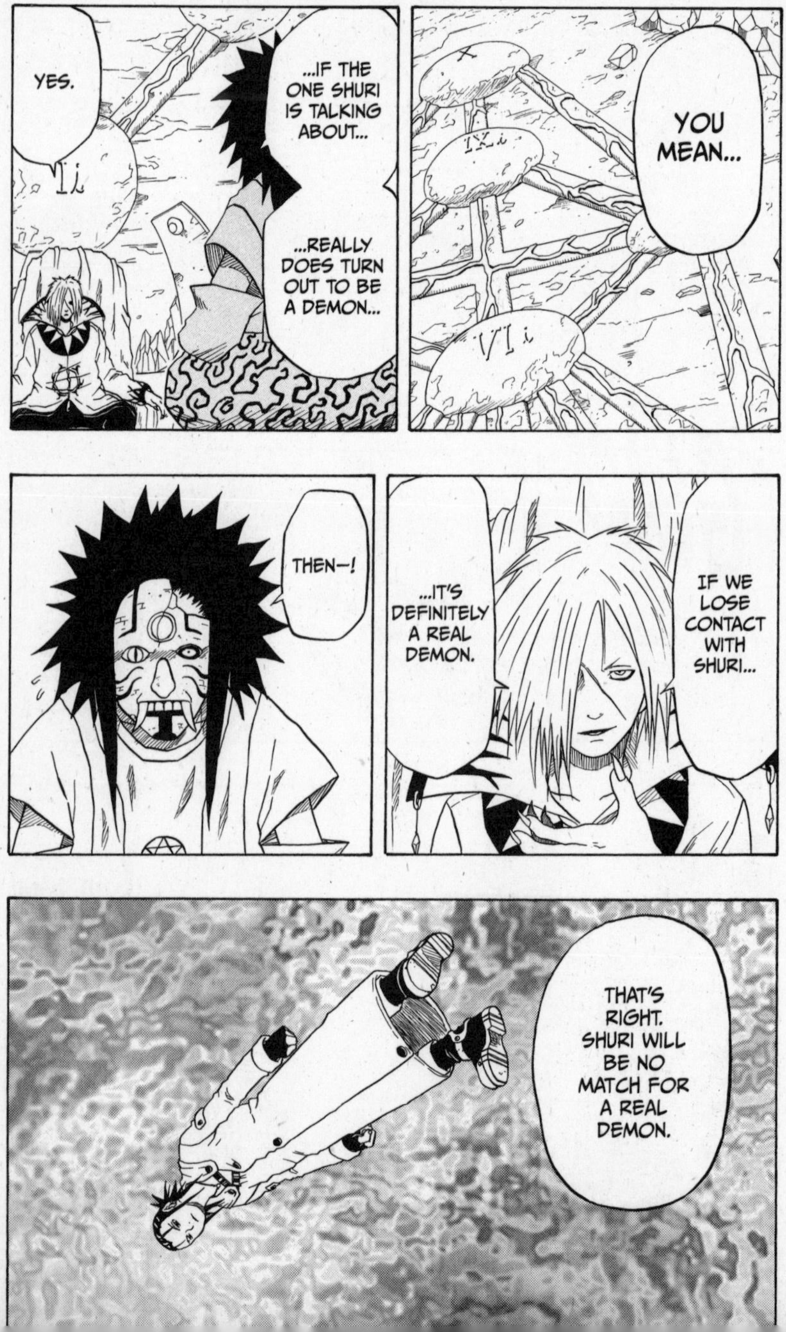

YOU MEAN...
...IF THE ONE SHURI IS TALKING ABOUT...
...REALLY DOES TURN OUT TO BE A DEMON...
YES.
IF WE LOSE CONTACT WITH SHURI...
...IT'S DEFINITELY A REAL DEMON.
THEN—!
THAT'S RIGHT. SHURI WILL BE NO MATCH FOR A REAL DEMON.

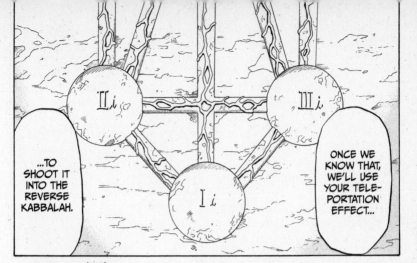

ONCE WE KNOW THAT, WE'LL USE YOUR TELE-PORTATION EFFECT...
...TO SHOOT IT INTO THE REVERSE KABBALAH.
BUT...YOU REALLY MEAN TO TURN YOUR BACK ON SHURI?
UNLIKE WISE, HE'S ALWAYS ACTED ON BEHALF OF THE SYNDICATE.
GLARE
WATCH IT, BAKU.
I DON'T LIKE YOUR TONE.

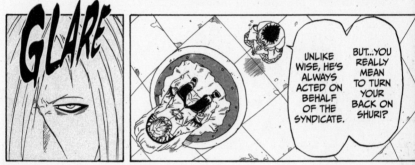

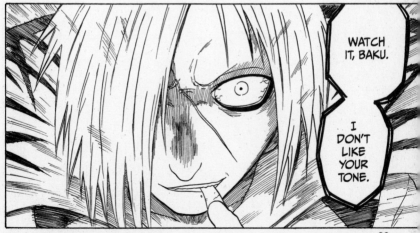

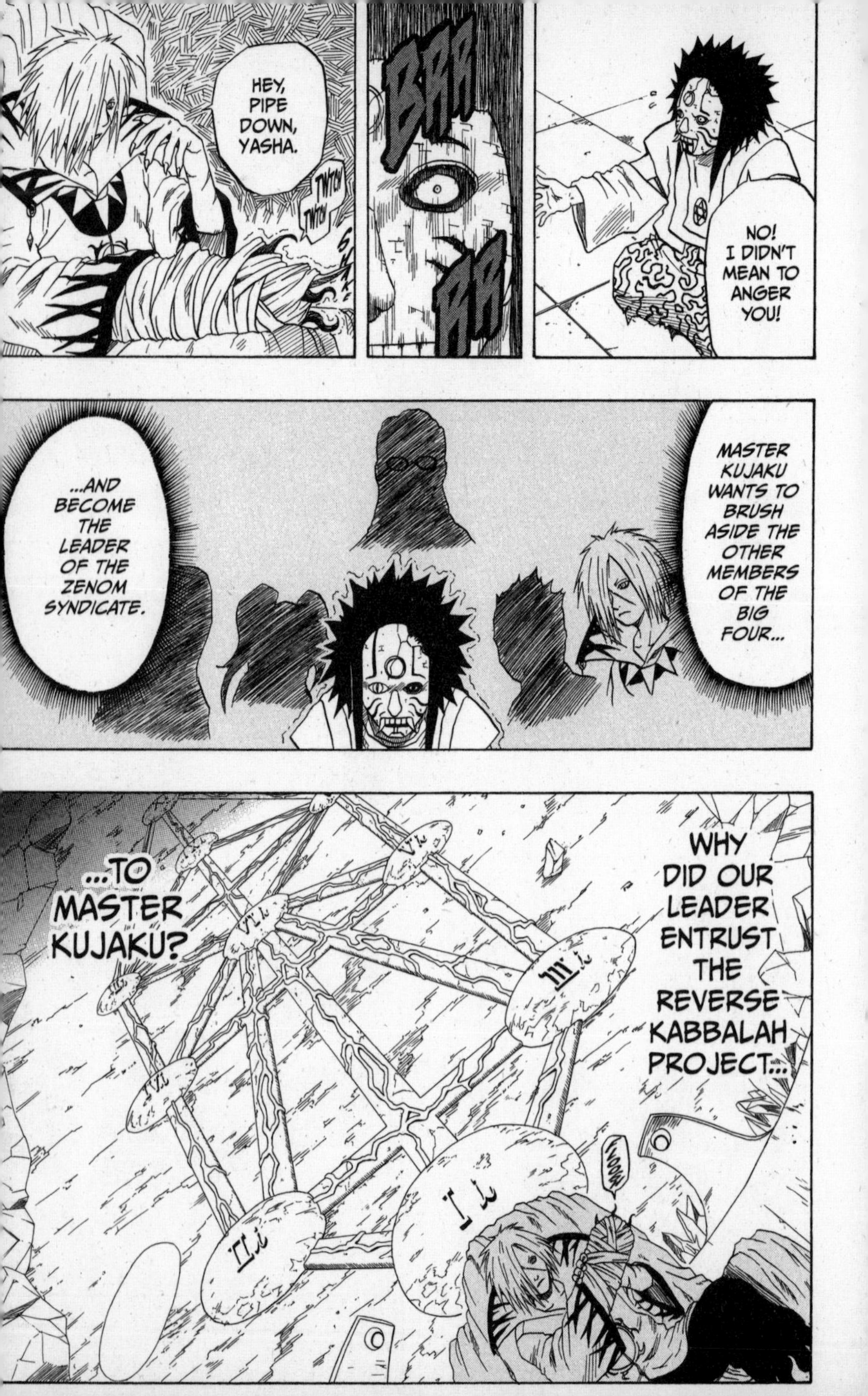
NO! I DIDN'T MEAN TO ANGER YOU!
BRR
RR
HEY, PIPE DOWN, YASHA.
TWITCH TWITCH
MASTER KUJAKU WANTS TO BRUSH ASIDE THE OTHER MEMBERS OF THE BIG FOUR...
...AND BECOME THE LEADER OF THE ZENOM SYNDICATE.
WHY DID OUR LEADER ENTRUST THE REVERSE KABBALAH PROJECT...
...TO MASTER KUJAKU?

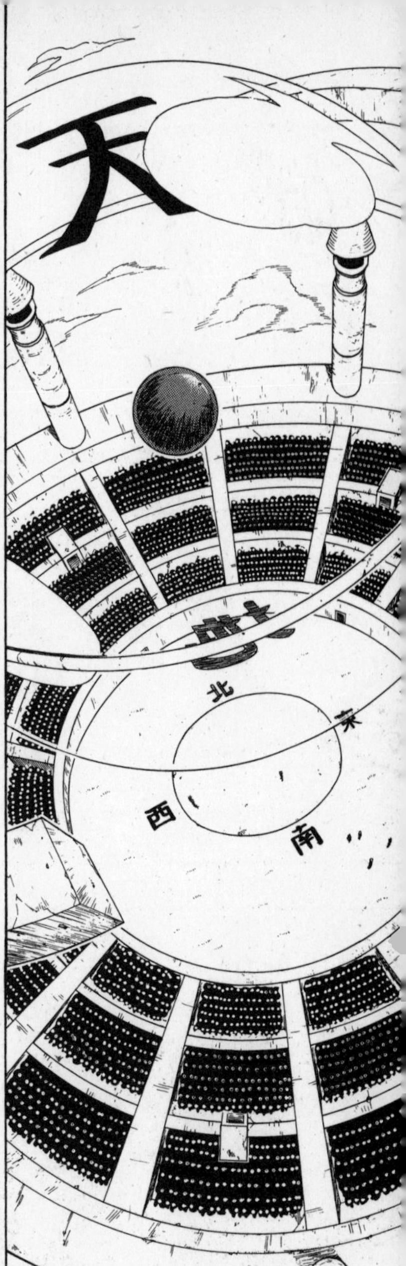
天
北
東
西
南

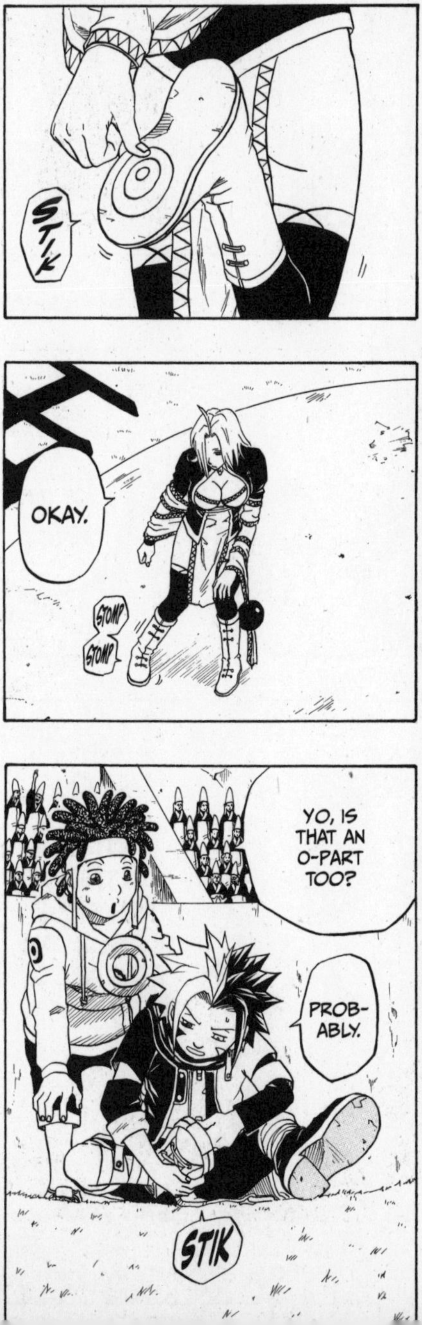
STIK
OKAY.
STOMP
STOMP
YO, IS THAT AN O-PART TOO?
PROB-ABLY.
STIK

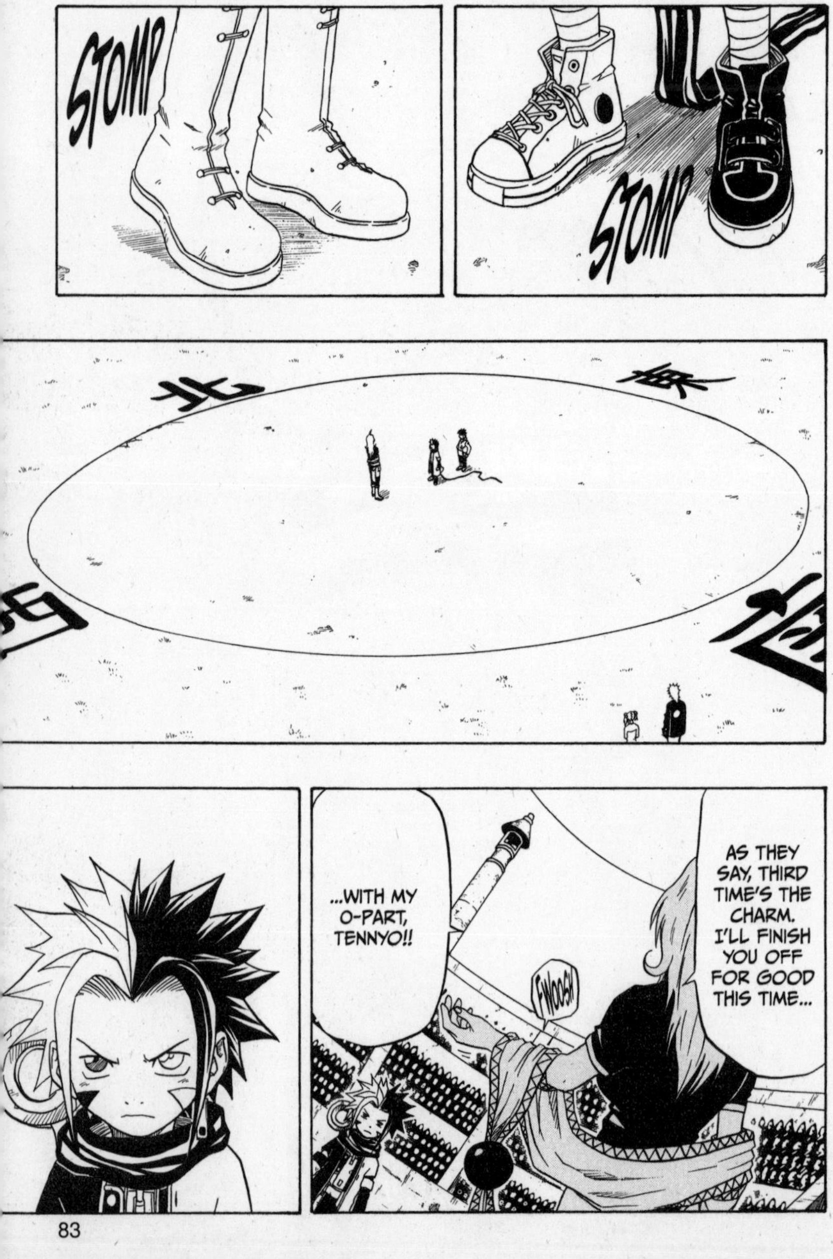
STOMP
STOMP
AS THEY SAY, THIRD TIME'S THE CHARM. I'LL FINISH YOU OFF FOR GOOD THIS TIME...
SWOOSH
...WITH MY O-PART, TENNYO!!

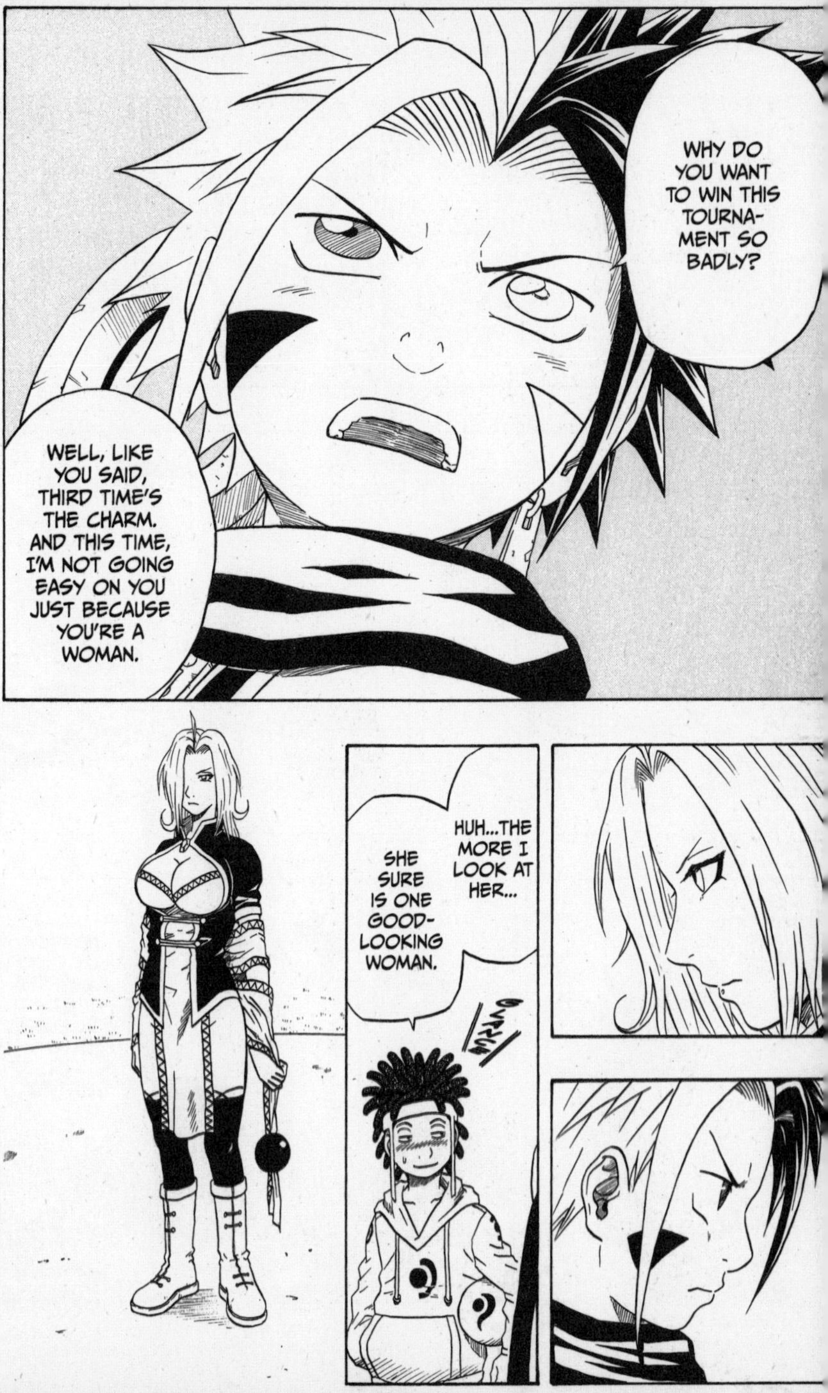
WHY DO YOU WANT TO WIN THIS TOURNAMENT SO BADLY?
WELL, LIKE YOU SAID, THIRD TIME'S THE CHARM. AND THIS TIME, I'M NOT GOING EASY ON YOU JUST BECAUSE YOU'RE A WOMAN.
HUH...THE MORE I LOOK AT HER...
SHE SURE IS ONE GOOD-LOOKING WOMAN.

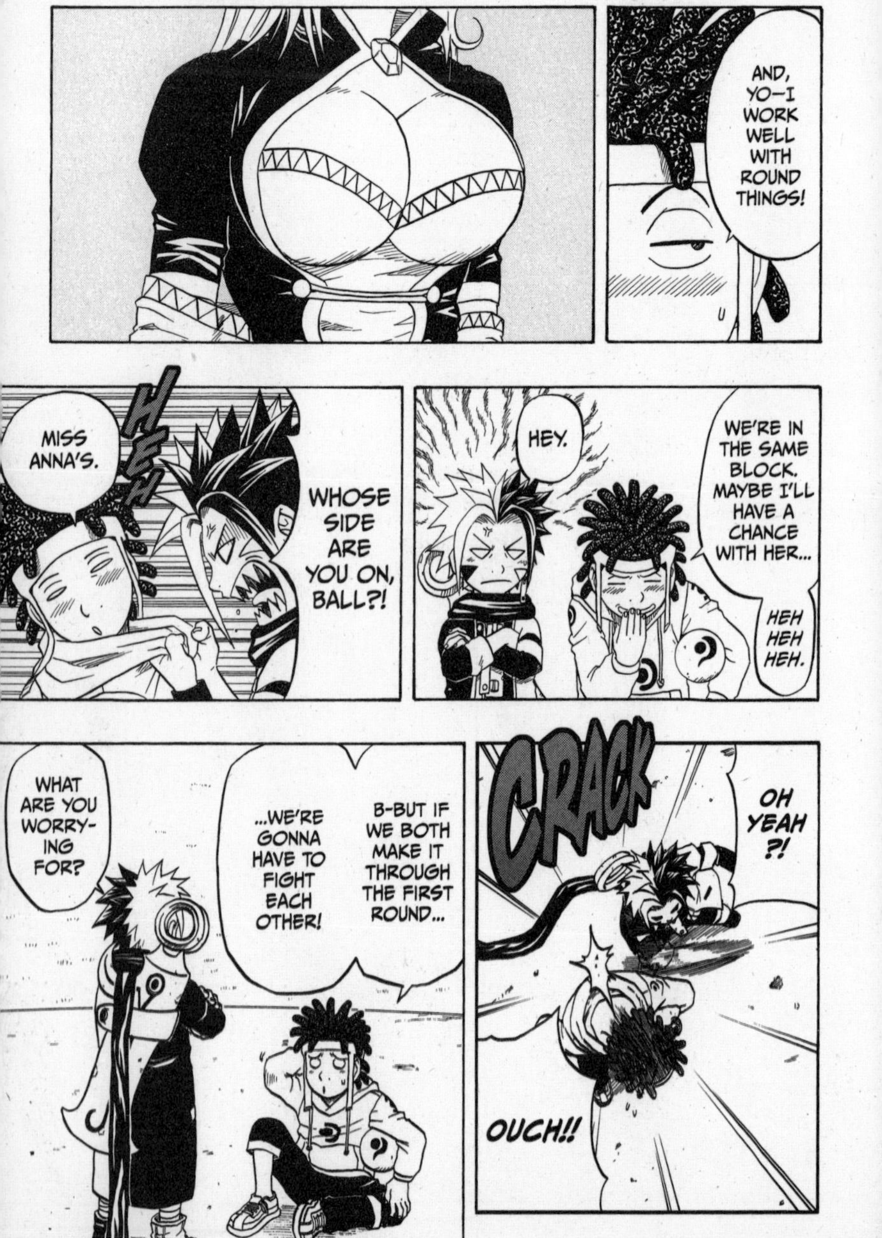
AND, YO—I WORK WELL WITH ROUND THINGS!
WE'RE IN THE SAME BLOCK. MAYBE I'LL HAVE A CHANCE WITH HER...
HEH HEH HEH.
HEY.
WHOSE SIDE ARE YOU ON, BALL?!
HEH
MISS ANNA'S.
OH YEAH?!
CRACK
OUCH!!
B-BUT IF WE BOTH MAKE IT THROUGH THE FIRST ROUND...
...WE'RE GONNA HAVE TO FIGHT EACH OTHER!
WHAT ARE YOU WORRYING FOR?

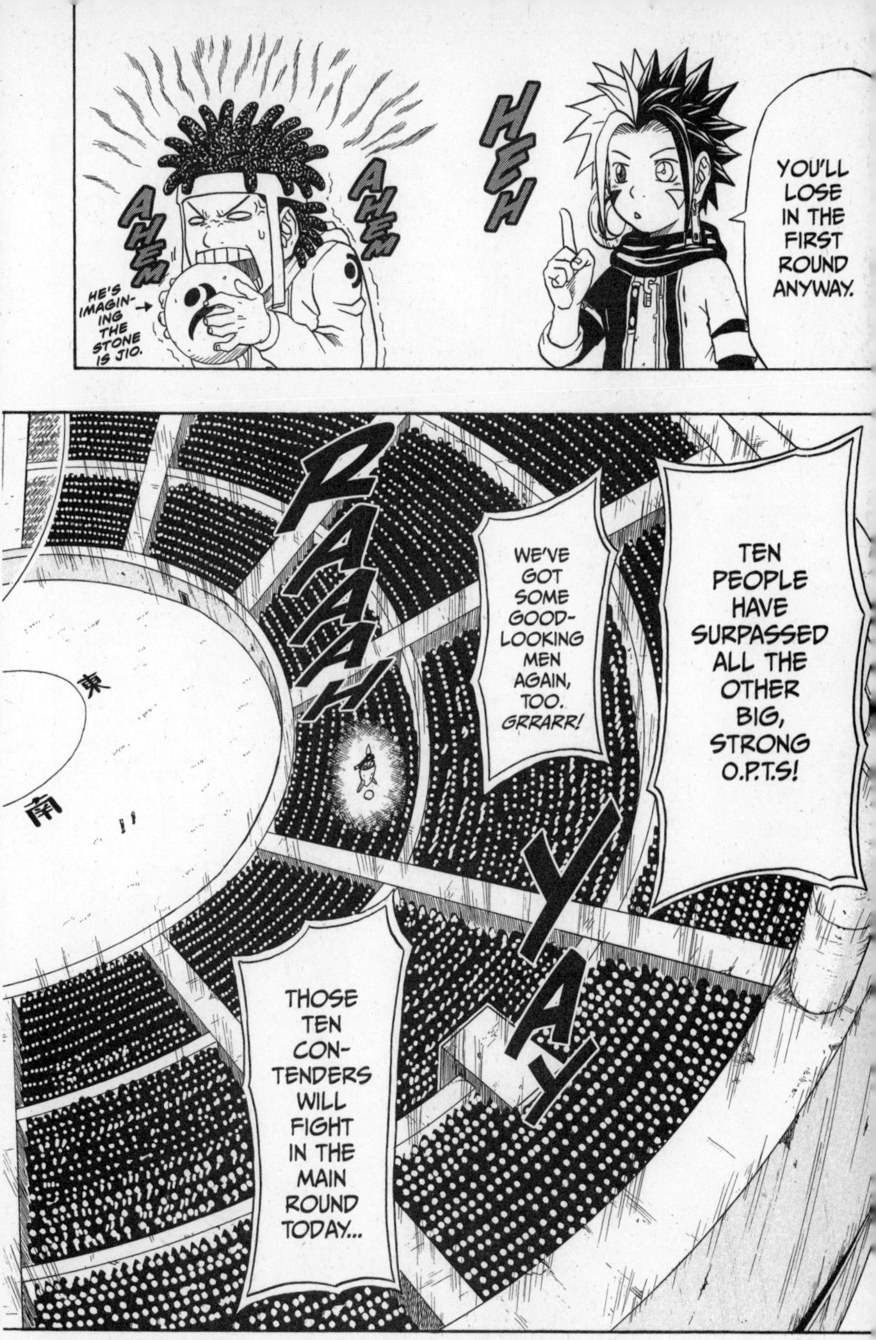
YOU'LL LOSE IN THE FIRST ROUND ANYWAY.
HEH
AHEM
AHEM
HE'S IMAGINING THE STONE IS JIO.
TEN PEOPLE HAVE SURPASSED ALL THE OTHER BIG, STRONG O.P.T.S!
WE'VE GOT SOME GOOD-LOOKING MEN AGAIN, TOO. GRRARR!
RAAAH
YAY
東
南
THOSE TEN CON-TENDERS WILL FIGHT IN THE MAIN ROUND TODAY...

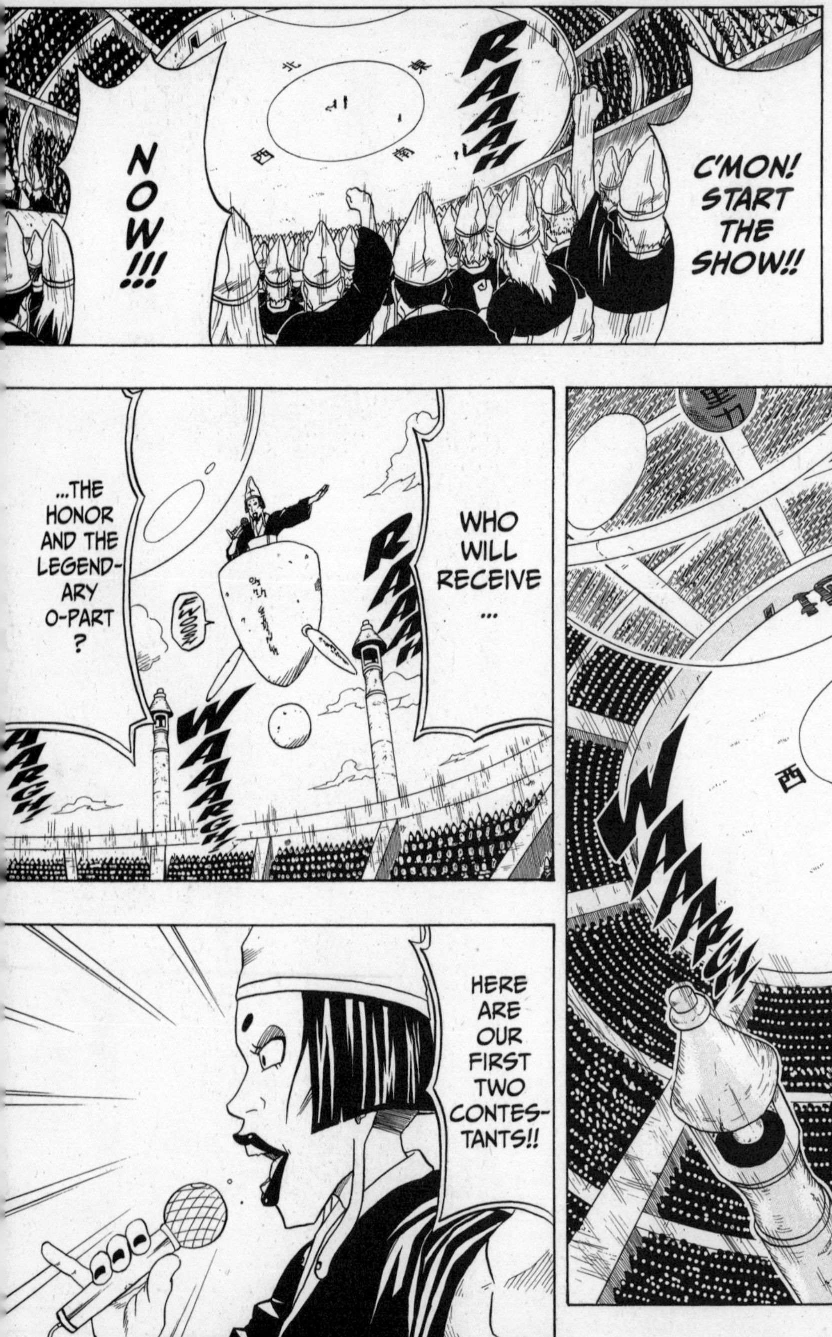
C'MON! START THE SHOW!!
RAAAH
NOW!!!
WAAARGH!!
WHO WILL RECEIVE ...
RAAAH
...THE HONOR AND THE LEGEND-ARY O-PART ?
WAAARGH!
WAAARGH!
HERE ARE OUR FIRST TWO CONTES-TANTS!!

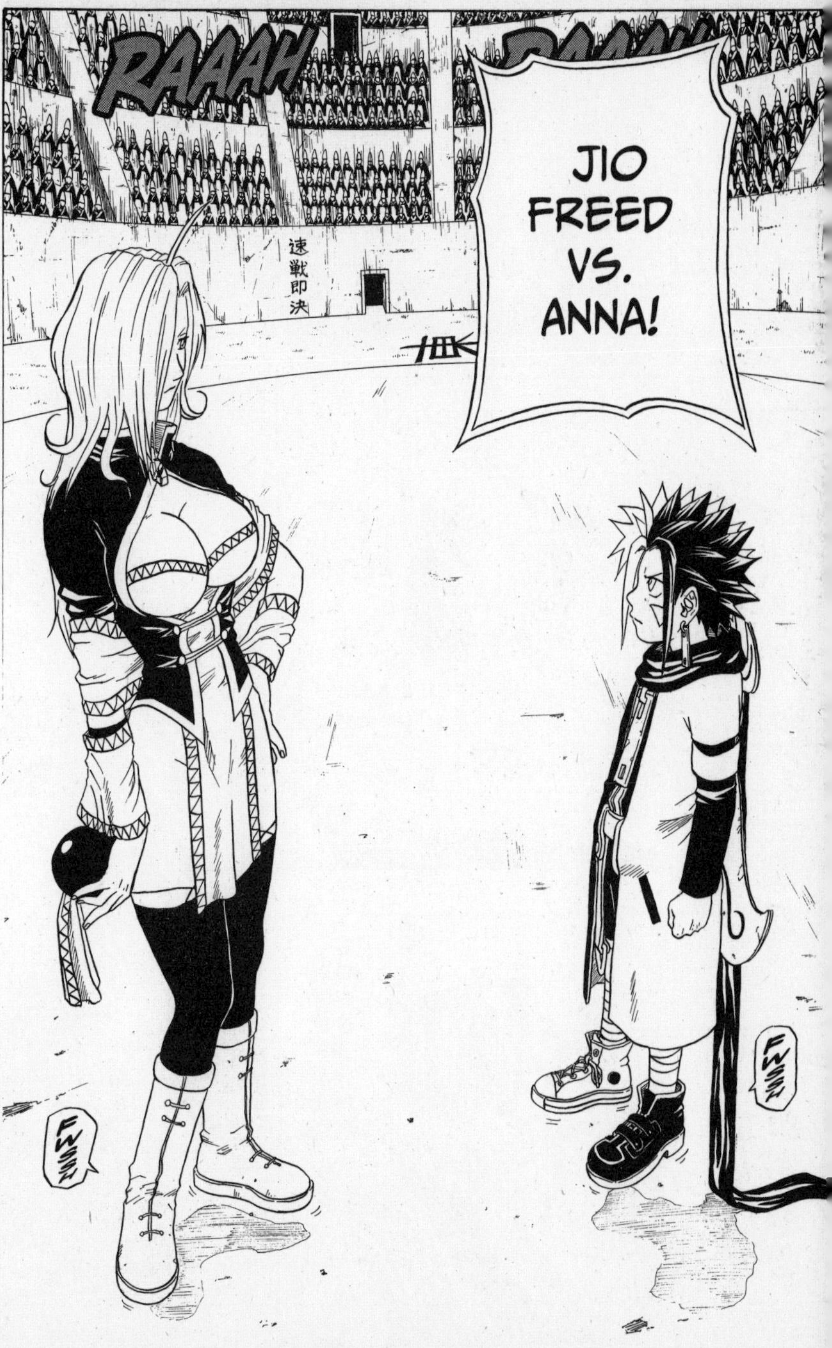
JIO FREED VS. ANNA!
RAAAH
速戦即決
FWSSH
FWSSH

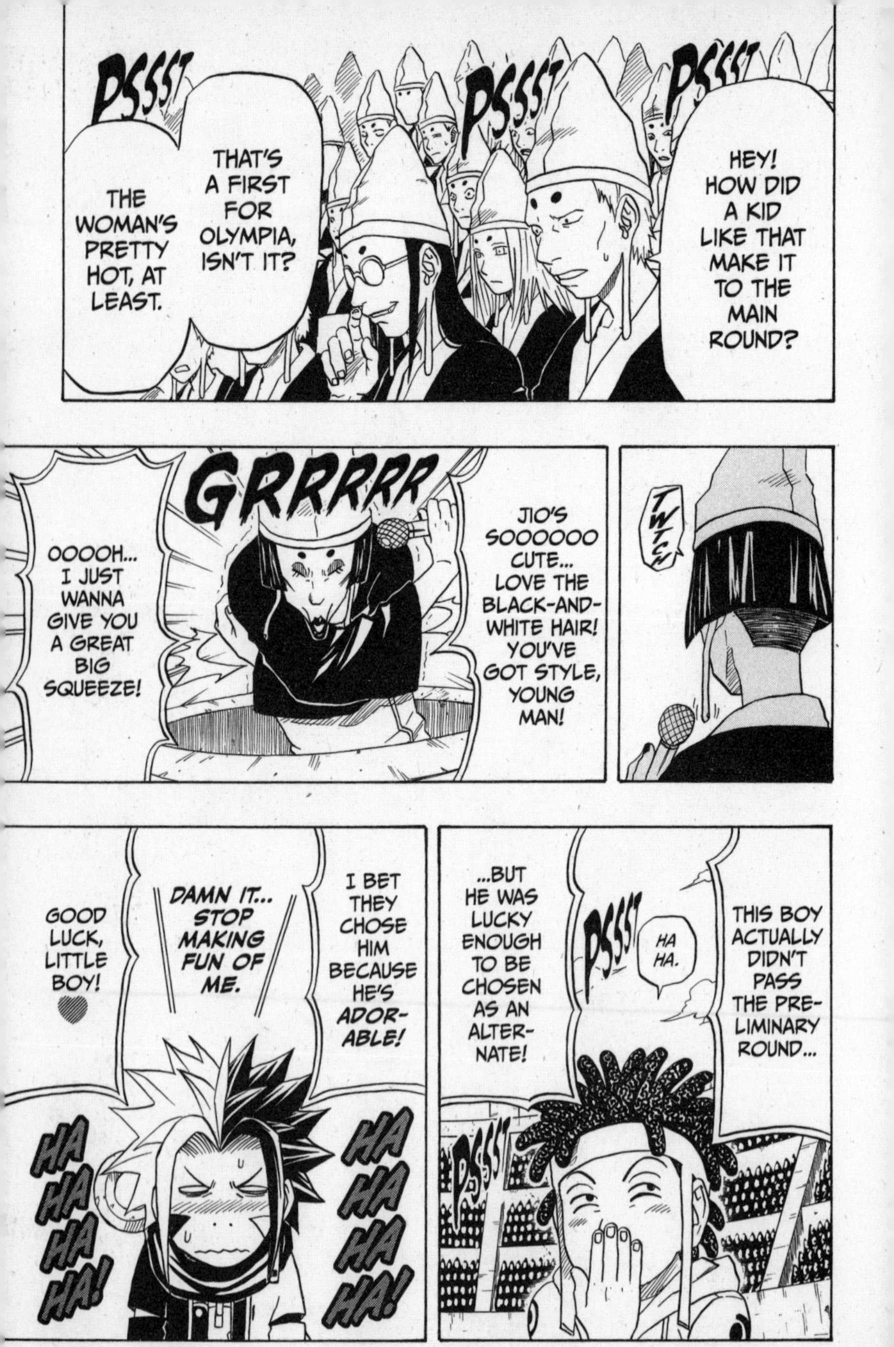
PSSST
HEY! HOW DID A KID LIKE THAT MAKE IT TO THE MAIN ROUND?
PSSST
THAT'S A FIRST FOR OLYMPIA, ISN'T IT?
THE WOMAN'S PRETTY HOT, AT LEAST.
PSSST
TWITCH
JIO'S SOOOOOO CUTE... LOVE THE BLACK-AND-WHITE HAIR! YOU'VE GOT STYLE, YOUNG MAN!
GRRRRR
OOOOH... I JUST WANNA GIVE YOU A GREAT BIG SQUEEZE!
THIS BOY ACTUALLY DIDN'T PASS THE PRELIMINARY ROUND...
HA HA.
PSSST
...BUT HE WAS LUCKY ENOUGH TO BE CHOSEN AS AN ALTERNATE!
PSSST
I BET THEY CHOSE HIM BECAUSE HE'S *ADORABLE!*
DAMN IT... STOP MAKING FUN OF ME.
GOOD LUCK, LITTLE BOY!
HA HA HA HA HA!
HA HA HA HA HA!

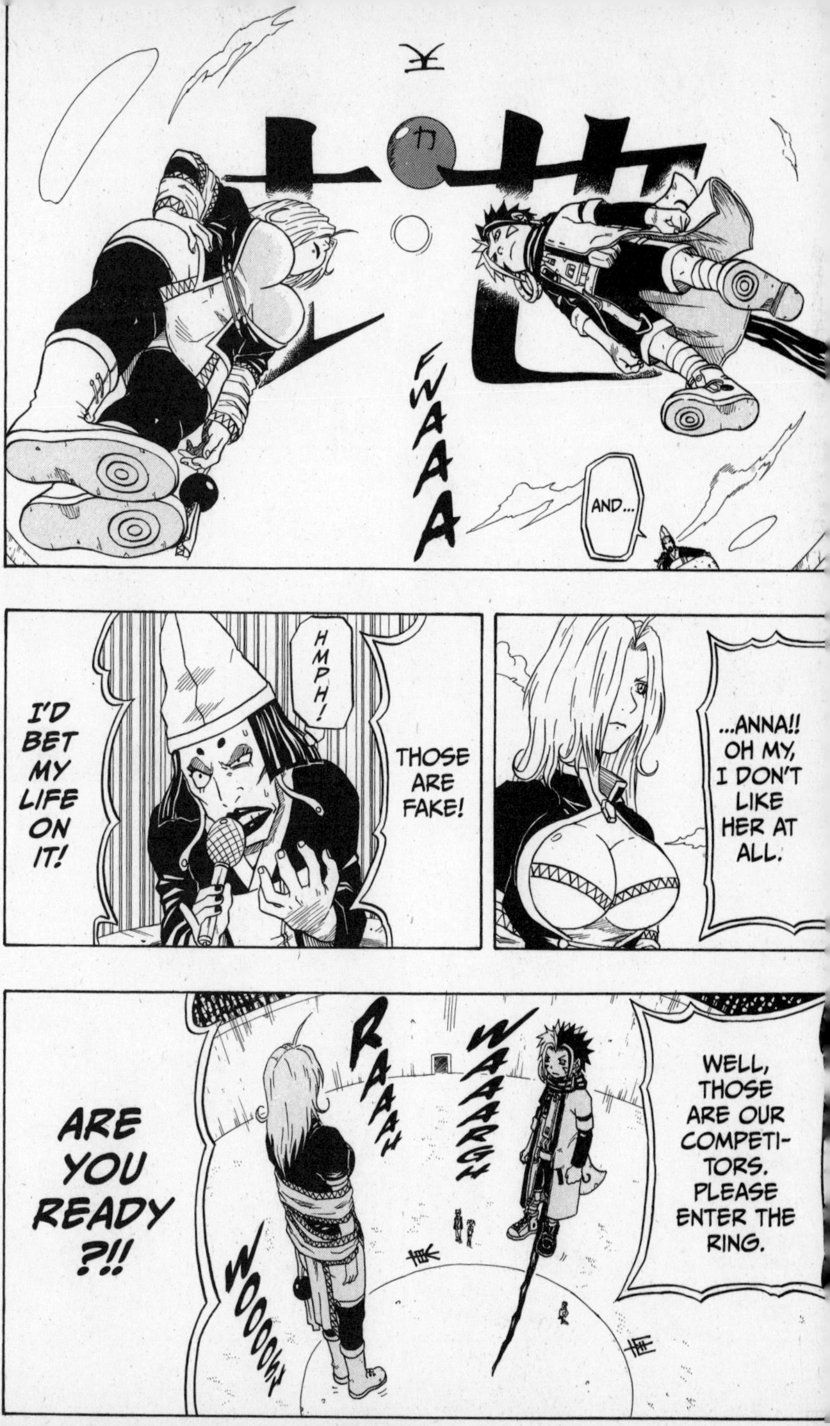
FWAAAA
AND...
...ANNA!! OH MY, I DON'T LIKE HER AT ALL.
HMPH!
THOSE ARE FAKE!
I'D BET MY LIFE ON IT!
WELL, THOSE ARE OUR COMPETI-TORS. PLEASE ENTER THE RING.
WAAAARGH
RAAAAH
ARE YOU READY ?!!
WOOOOW

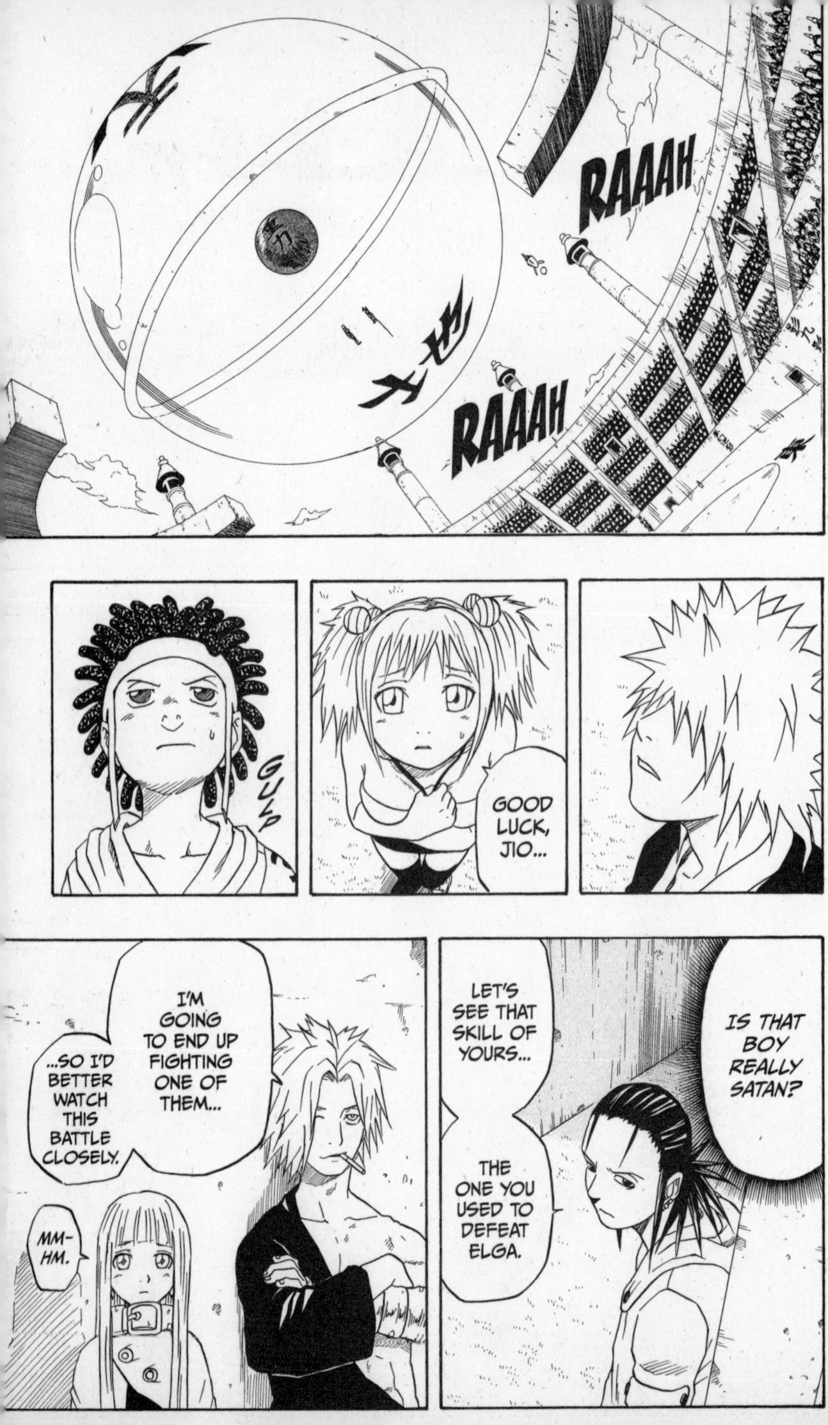
RAAAH
RAAAH
GOOD LUCK, JIO...
GULP
IS THAT BOY REALLY SATAN?
LET'S SEE THAT SKILL OF YOURS...
THE ONE YOU USED TO DEFEAT ELGA.
I'M GOING TO END UP FIGHTING ONE OF THEM...
...SO I'D BETTER WATCH THIS BATTLE CLOSELY.
MM-HM.

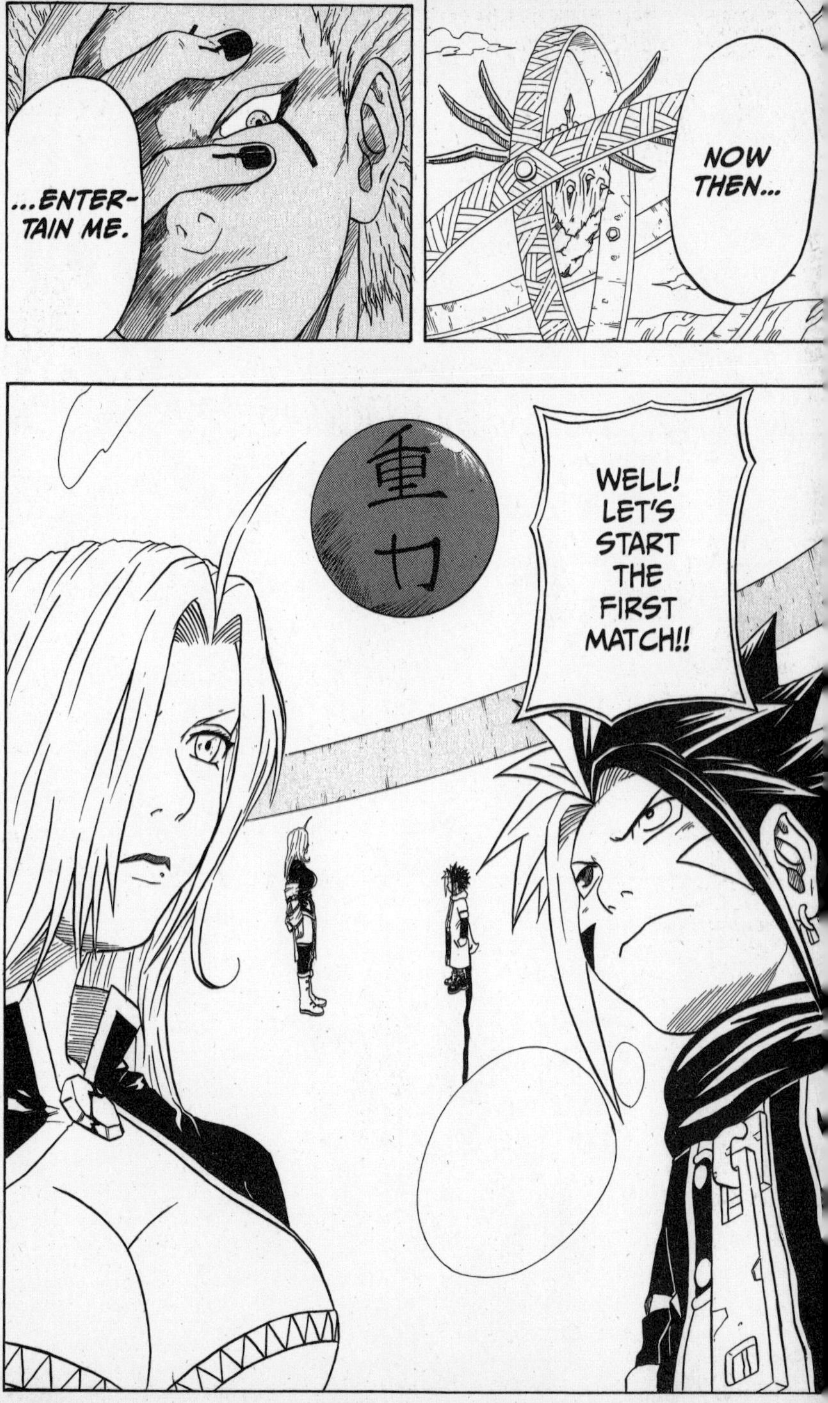
NOW THEN...
...ENTER-TAIN ME.
WELL! LET'S START THE FIRST MATCH!!
重力

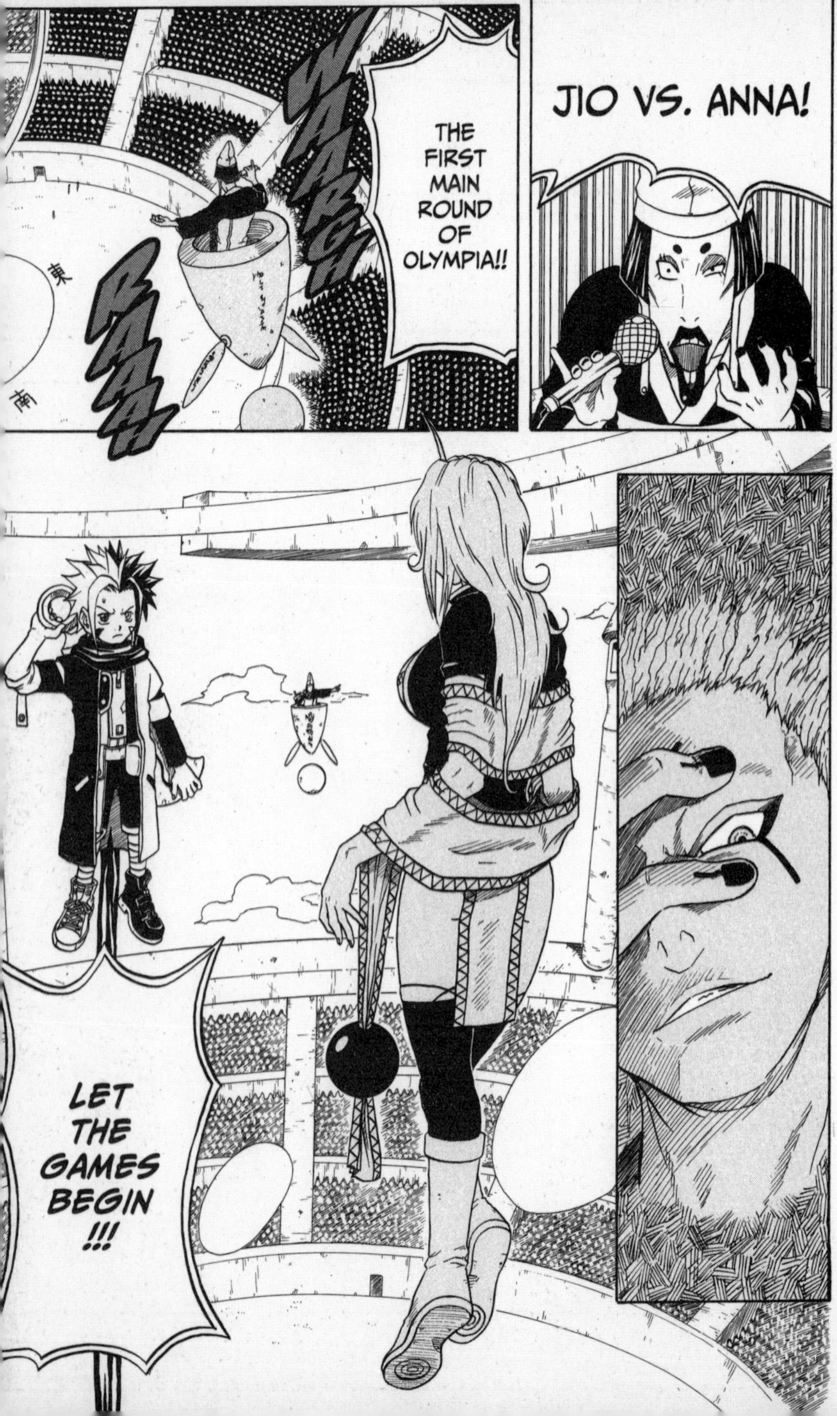
JIO VS. ANNA!
THE FIRST MAIN ROUND OF OLYMPIA!!
WAAAGH
WAAAAH
東
南
LET THE GAMES BEGIN!!!

CHAPTER 35: THE PROMISE

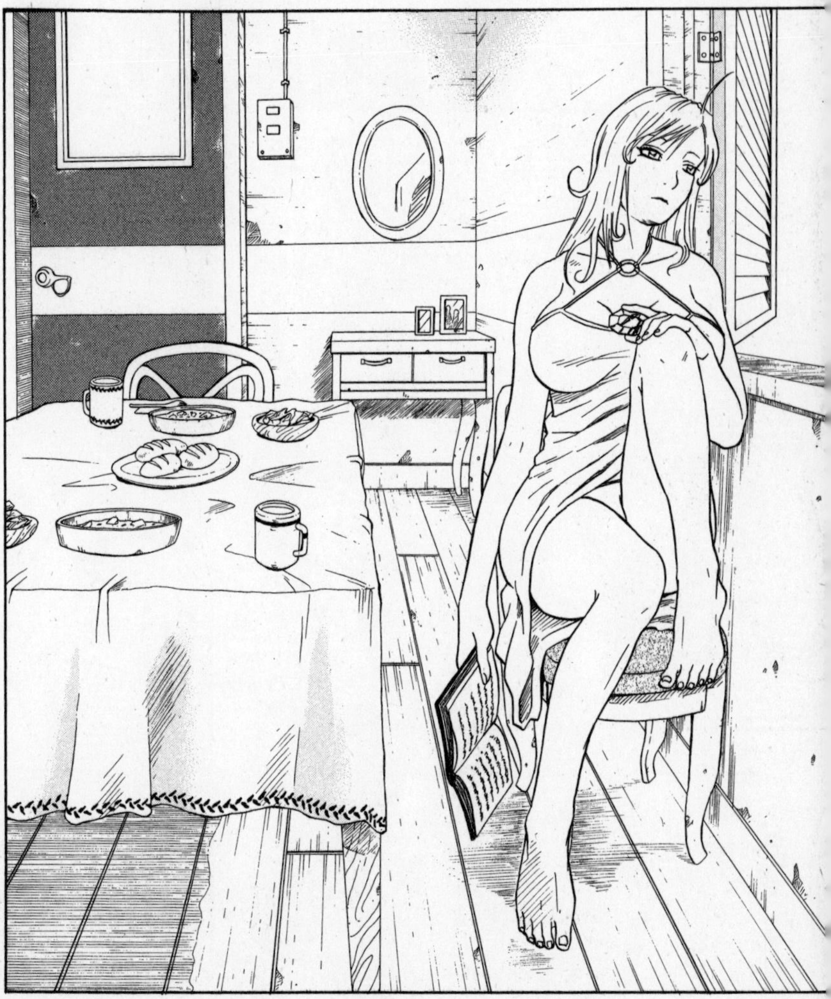

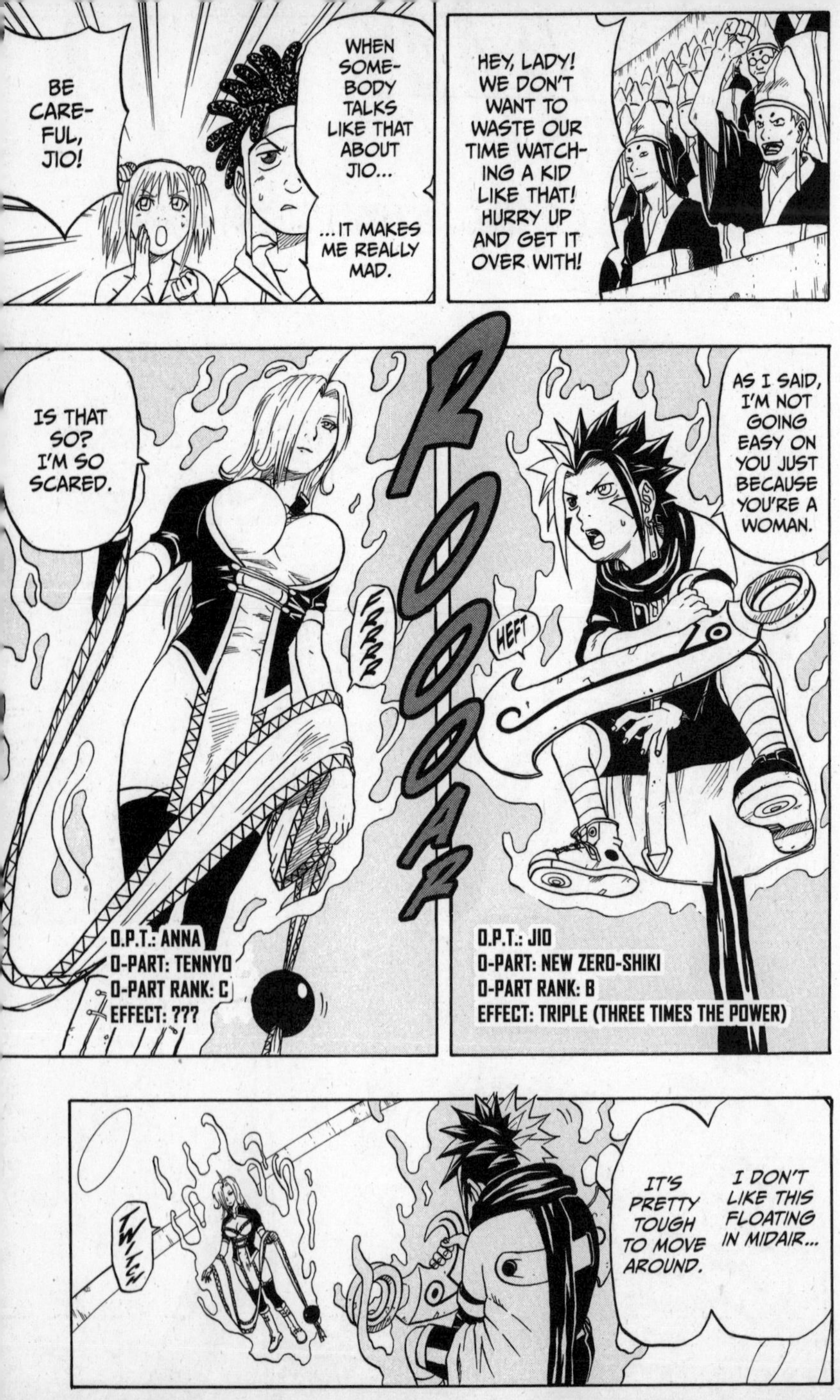
HEY, LADY! WE DON'T WANT TO WASTE OUR TIME WATCHING A KID LIKE THAT! HURRY UP AND GET IT OVER WITH!
WHEN SOMEBODY TALKS LIKE THAT ABOUT JIO...
...IT MAKES ME REALLY MAD.
BE CAREFUL, JIO!
AS I SAID, I'M NOT GOING EASY ON YOU JUST BECAUSE YOU'RE A WOMAN.
HEFT
ROOOOAR
O.P.T.: JIO
O-PART: NEW ZERO-SHIKI
O-PART RANK: B
EFFECT: TRIPLE (THREE TIMES THE POWER)
IS THAT SO? I'M SO SCARED.
O.P.T.: ANNA
O-PART: TENNYO
O-PART RANK: C
EFFECT: ???
I DON'T LIKE THIS FLOATING IN MIDAIR...
IT'S PRETTY TOUGH TO MOVE AROUND.
TWITCH

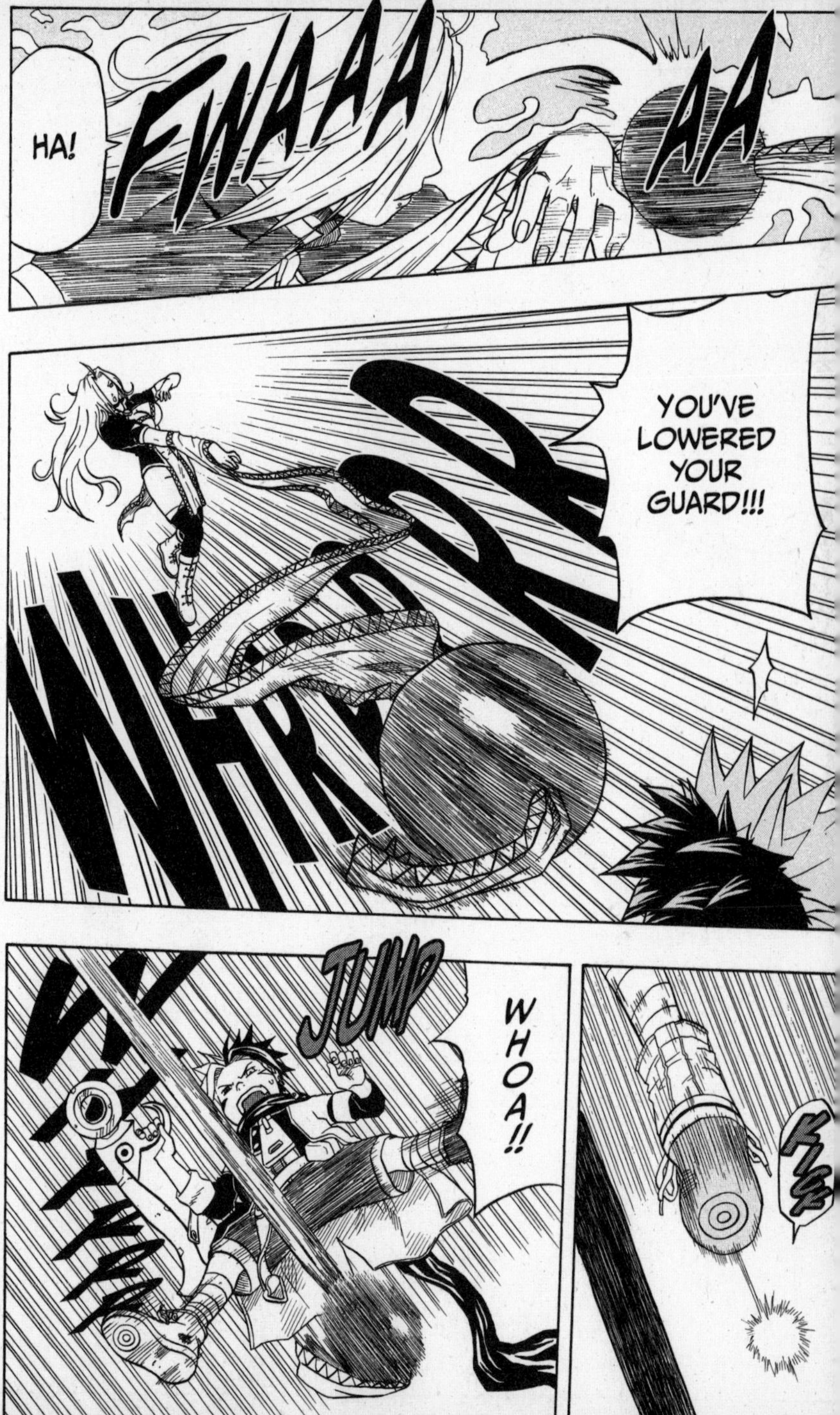
FWAAAAA
HA!
YOU'VE LOWERED YOUR GUARD!!!
WHHRRP
JUMP
WHOA!!
KWW

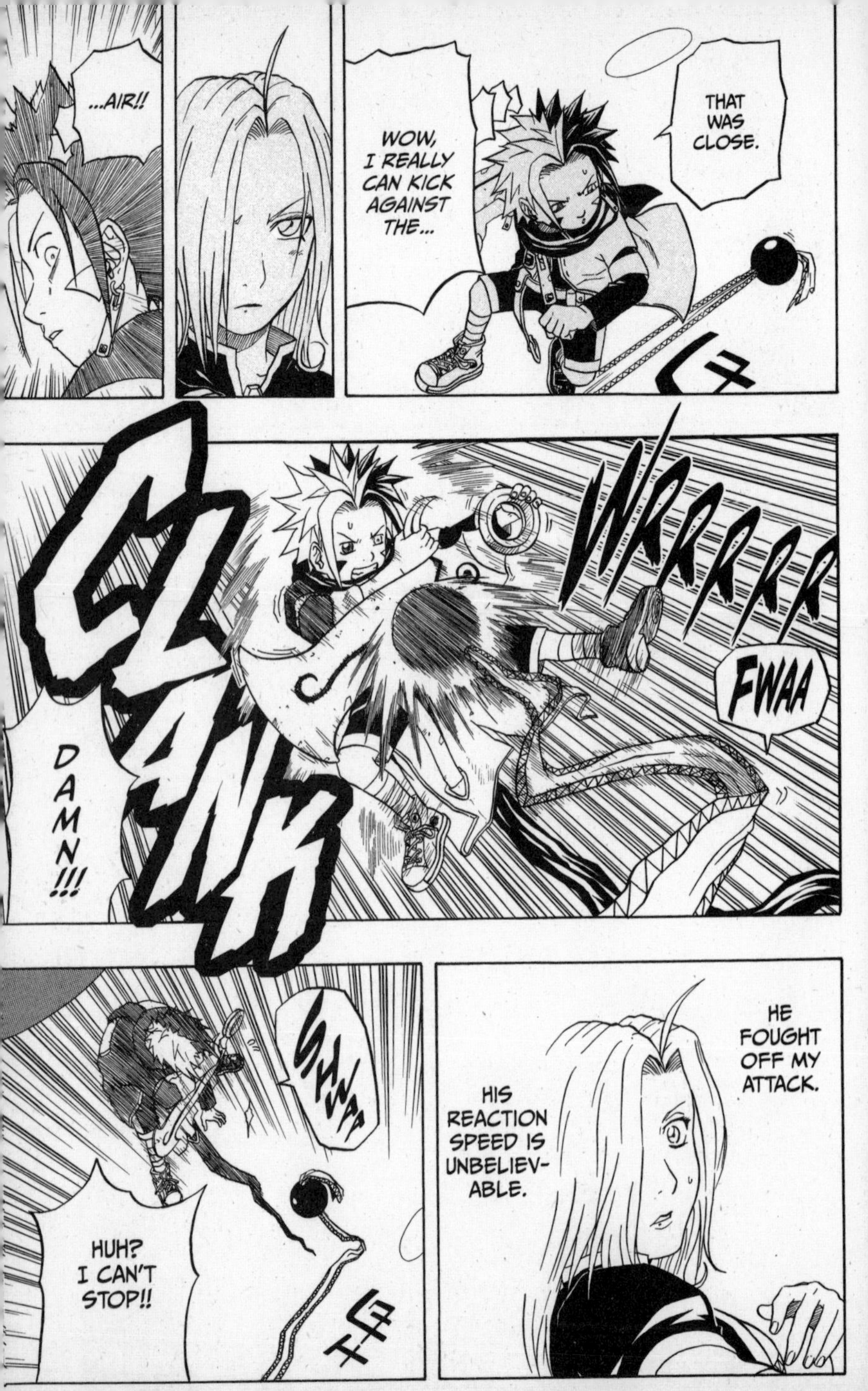
THAT WAS CLOSE.
WOW, I REALLY CAN KICK AGAINST THE...
...AIR!!
WRRRRRR
FWAA
CLANK
DAMN!!!
HE FOUGHT OFF MY ATTACK.
HIS REACTION SPEED IS UNBELIEV-ABLE.
SHWAA
HUH? I CAN'T STOP!!

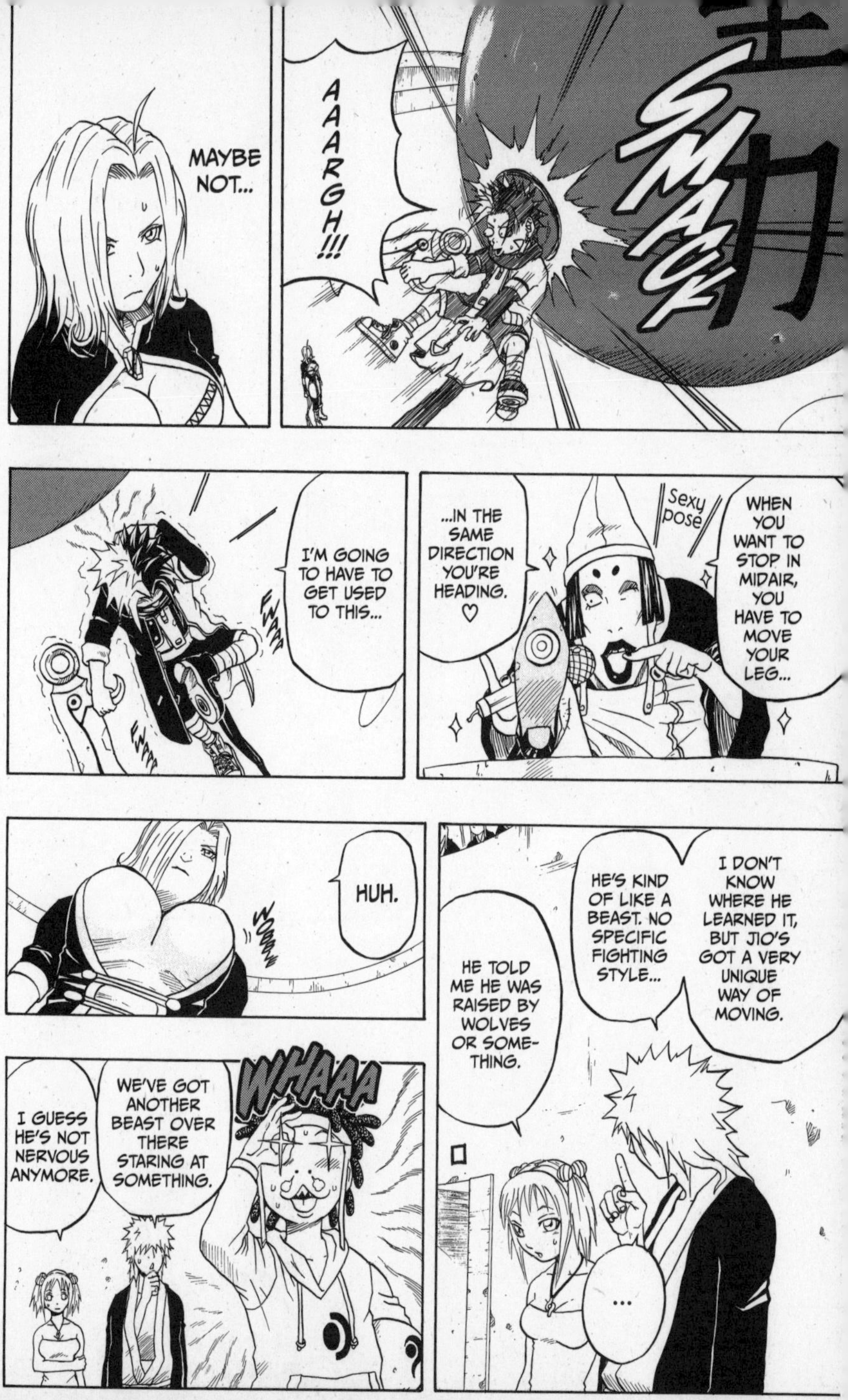
SMACK
AAAARGH!!!
MAYBE NOT...
Sexy pose
WHEN YOU WANT TO STOP IN MIDAIR, YOU HAVE TO MOVE YOUR LEG...
...IN THE SAME DIRECTION YOU'RE HEADING. ♡
I'M GOING TO HAVE TO GET USED TO THIS...
I DON'T KNOW WHERE HE LEARNED IT, BUT JIO'S GOT A VERY UNIQUE WAY OF MOVING.
HE'S KIND OF LIKE A BEAST. NO SPECIFIC FIGHTING STYLE...
HE TOLD ME HE WAS RAISED BY WOLVES OR SOME-THING.
...
HUH.
WHAAAA
WE'VE GOT ANOTHER BEAST OVER THERE STARING AT SOMETHING.
I GUESS HE'S NOT NERVOUS ANYMORE.

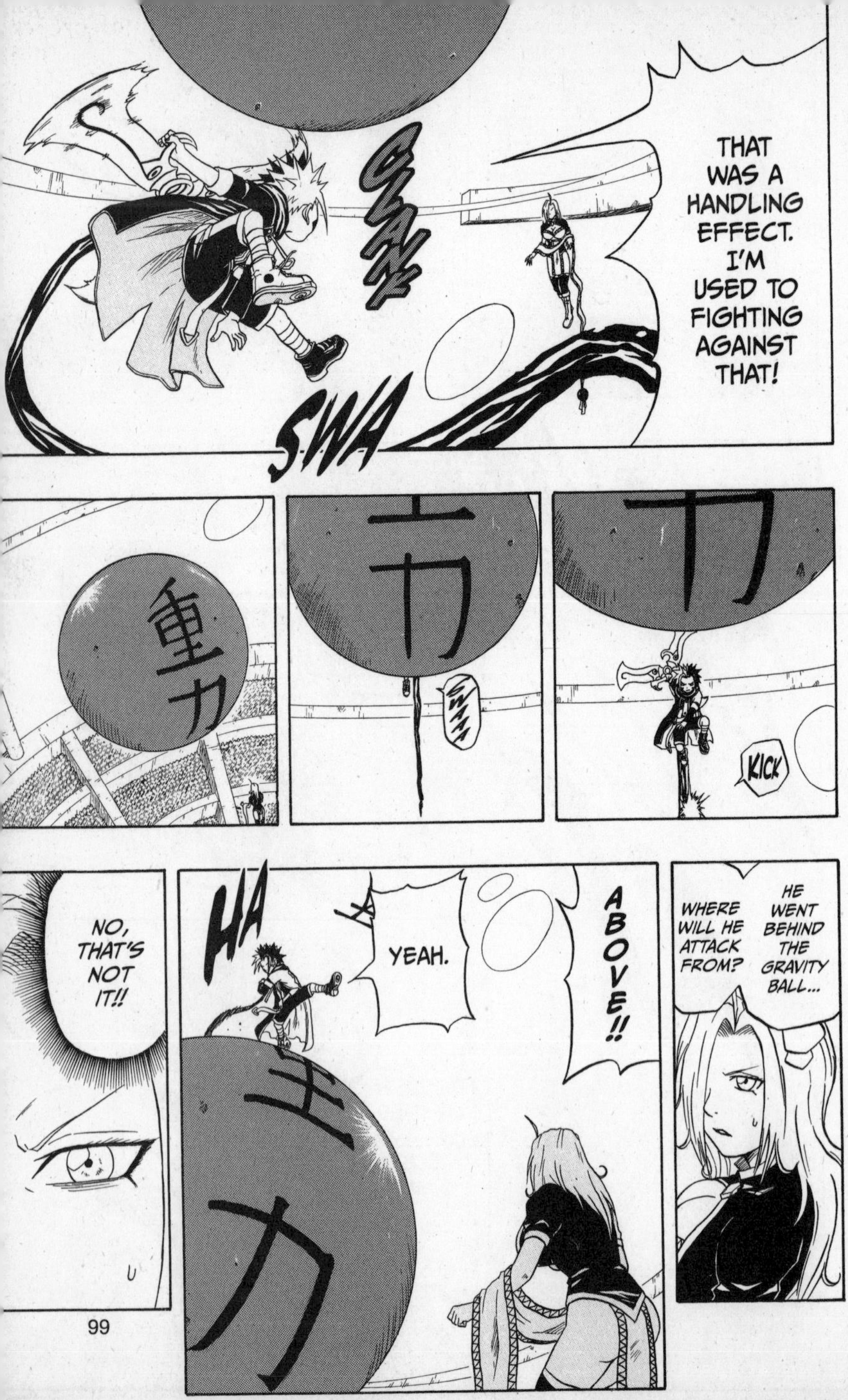
THAT WAS A HANDLING EFFECT. I'M USED TO FIGHTING AGAINST THAT!
SWA
KICK
重力
HE WENT BEHIND THE GRAVITY BALL...
WHERE WILL HE ATTACK FROM?
ABOVE!!
YEAH.
HA
NO, THAT'S NOT IT!!

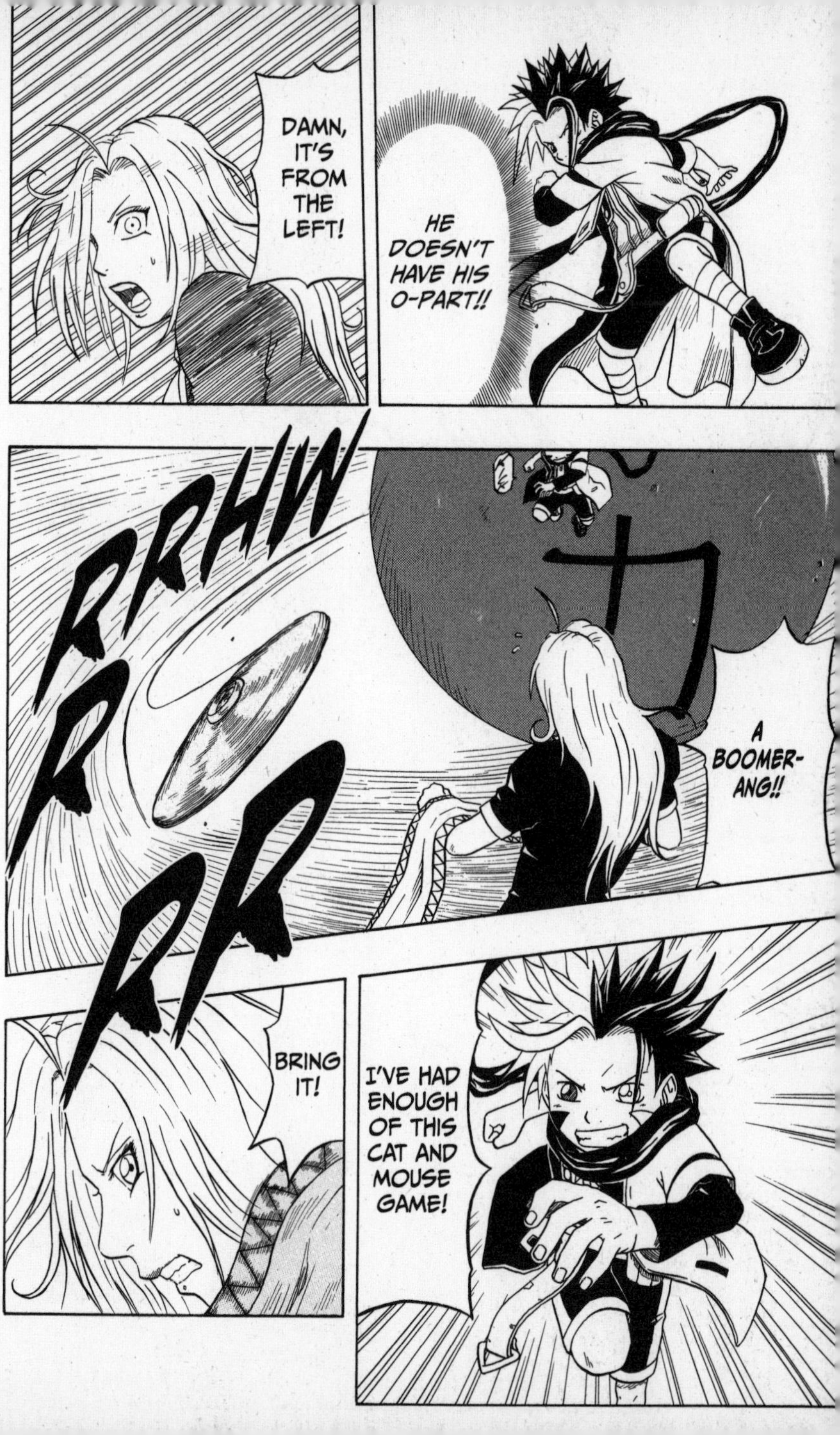
HE DOESN'T HAVE HIS O-PART!!
DAMN, IT'S FROM THE LEFT!
A BOOMER-ANG!!
RRHW
RRRRR
I'VE HAD ENOUGH OF THIS CAT AND MOUSE GAME!
BRING IT!

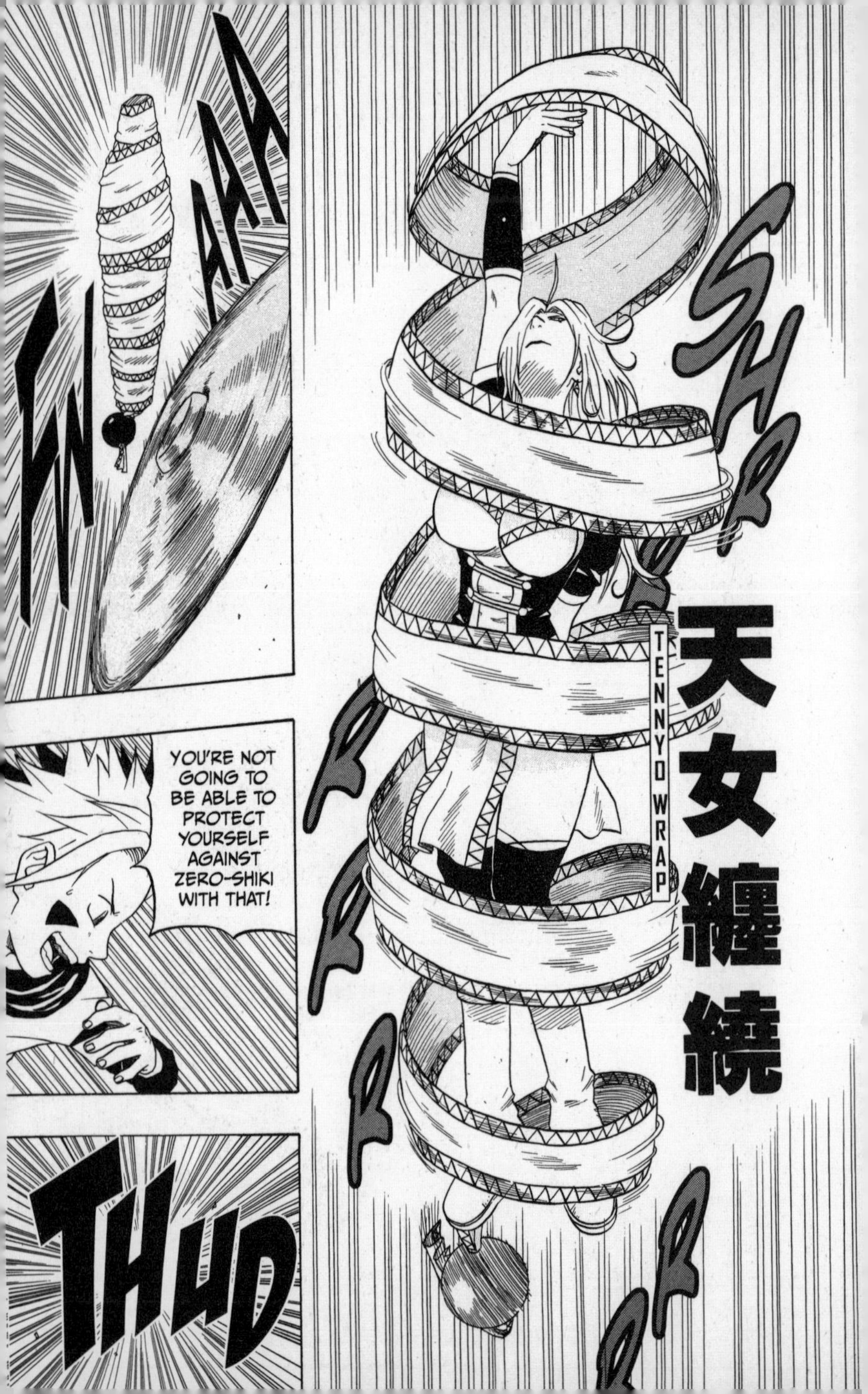
天女纏繞
TENNYO WRAP
YOU'RE NOT GOING TO BE ABLE TO PROTECT YOURSELF AGAINST ZERO-SHIKI WITH THAT!
THUD

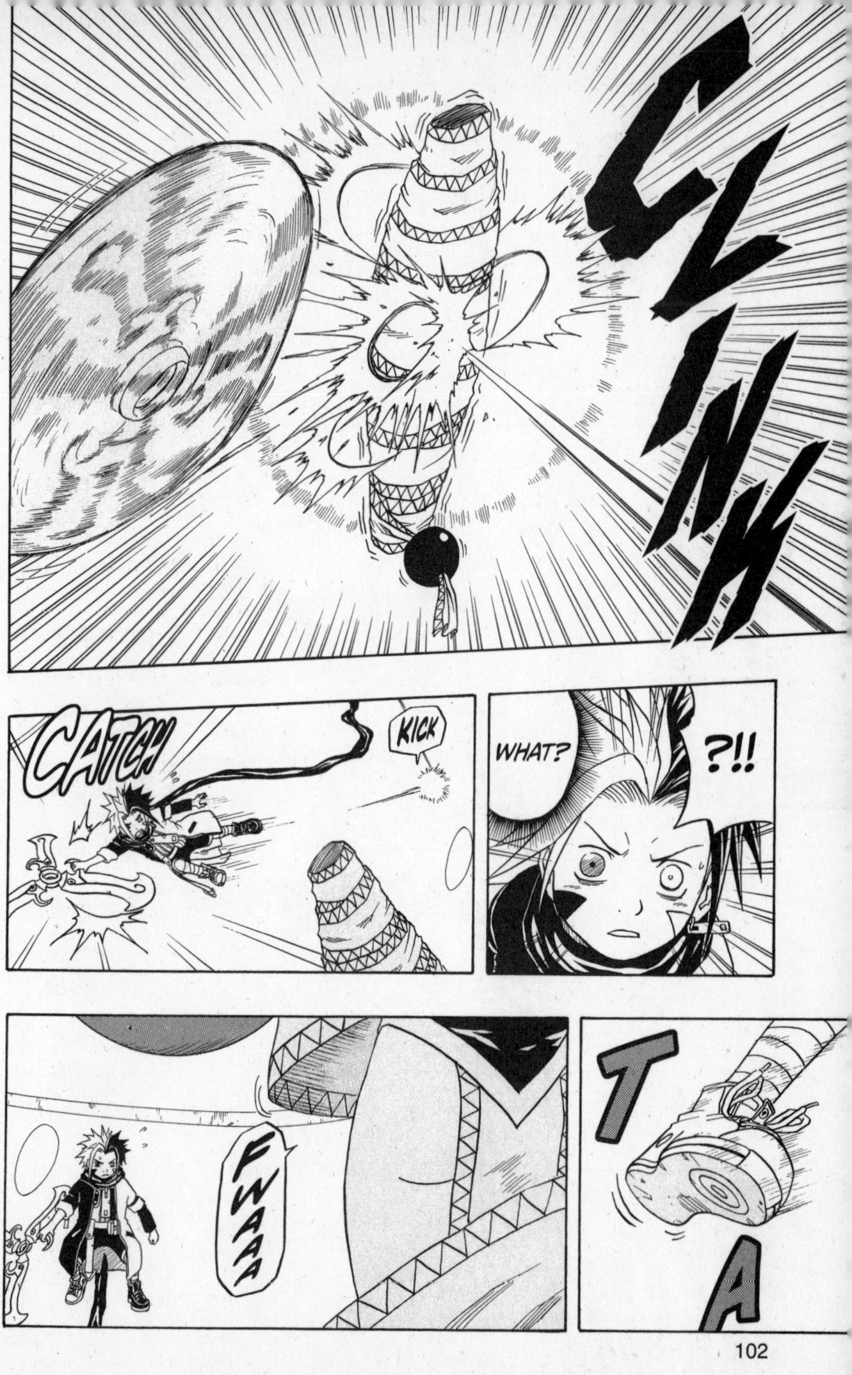
CLINK
?!!
WHAT?
KICK
CATCH
TA
FWAAA

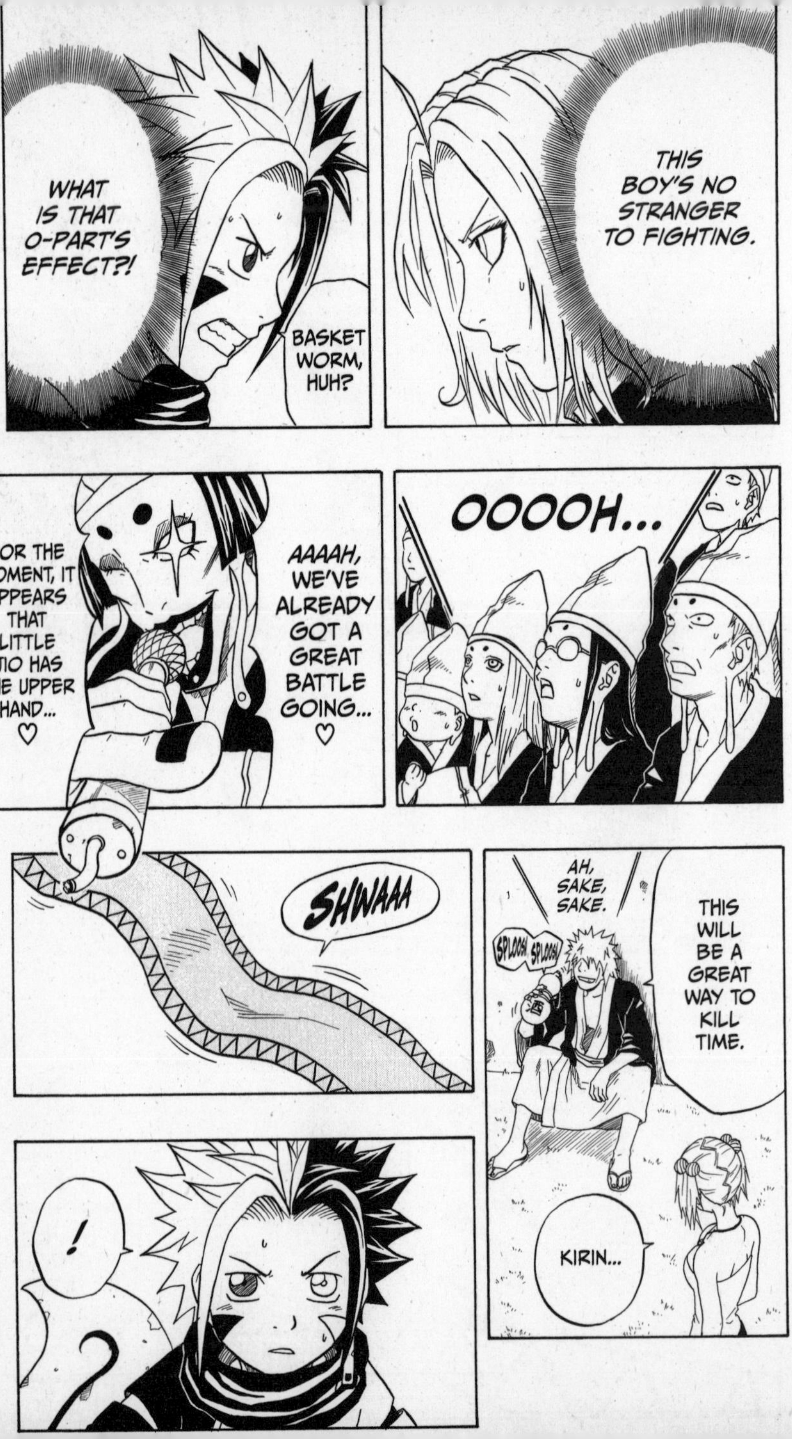
THIS BOY'S NO STRANGER TO FIGHTING.
WHAT IS THAT O-PART'S EFFECT?!
BASKET WORM, HUH?
OOOOH...
AAAAH, WE'VE ALREADY GOT A GREAT BATTLE GOING... ♡
FOR THE MOMENT, IT APPEARS THAT LITTLE JIO HAS THE UPPER HAND... ♡
AH, SAKE, SAKE.
SPLOOSH
SPLOOSH
THIS WILL BE A GREAT WAY TO KILL TIME.
KIRIN...
SHWAAA
!

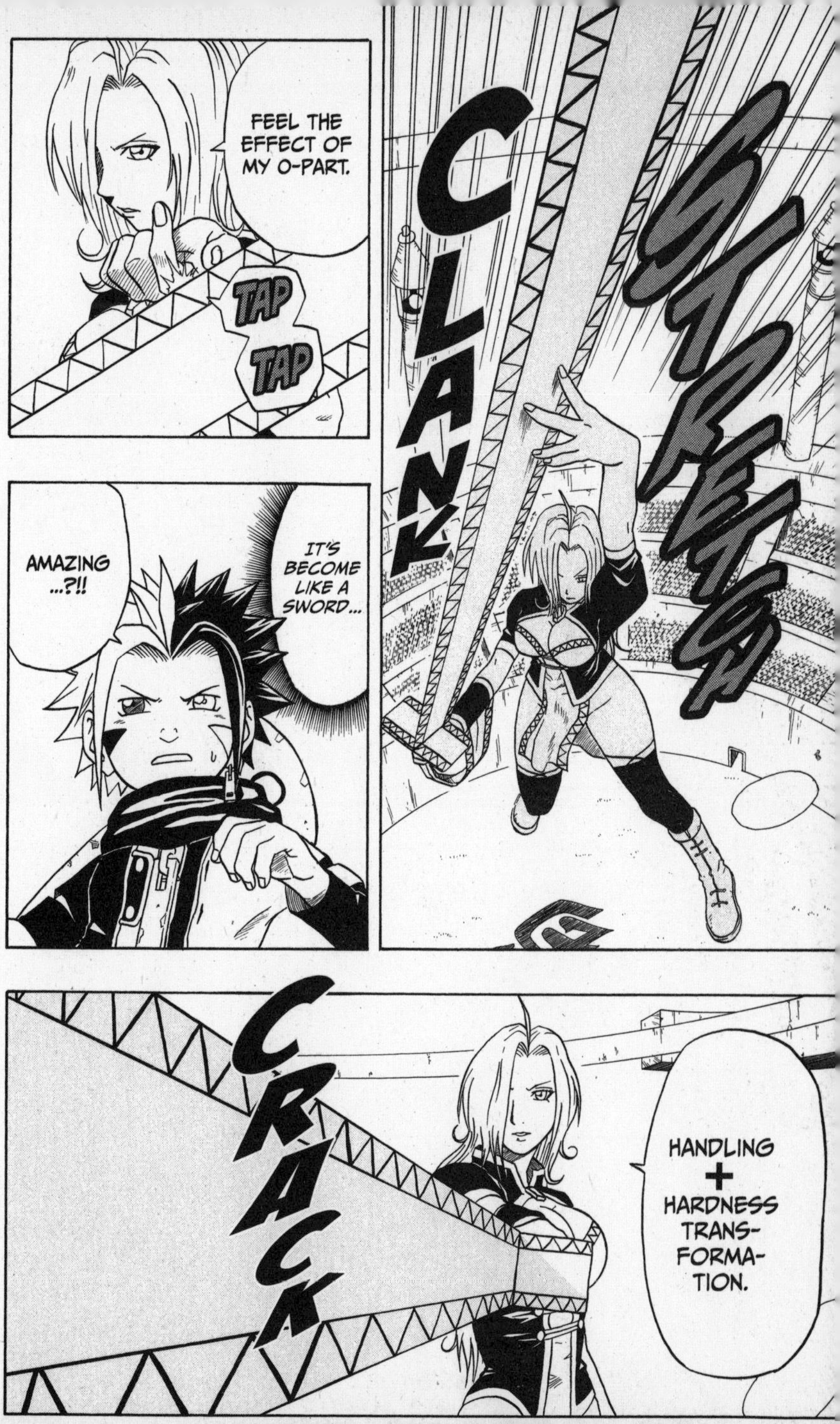
CLANK
FEEL THE EFFECT OF MY O-PART.
TAP
TAP
IT'S BECOME LIKE A SWORD...
AMAZING ...?!!
CRACK
HANDLING + HARDNESS TRANSFORMATION.

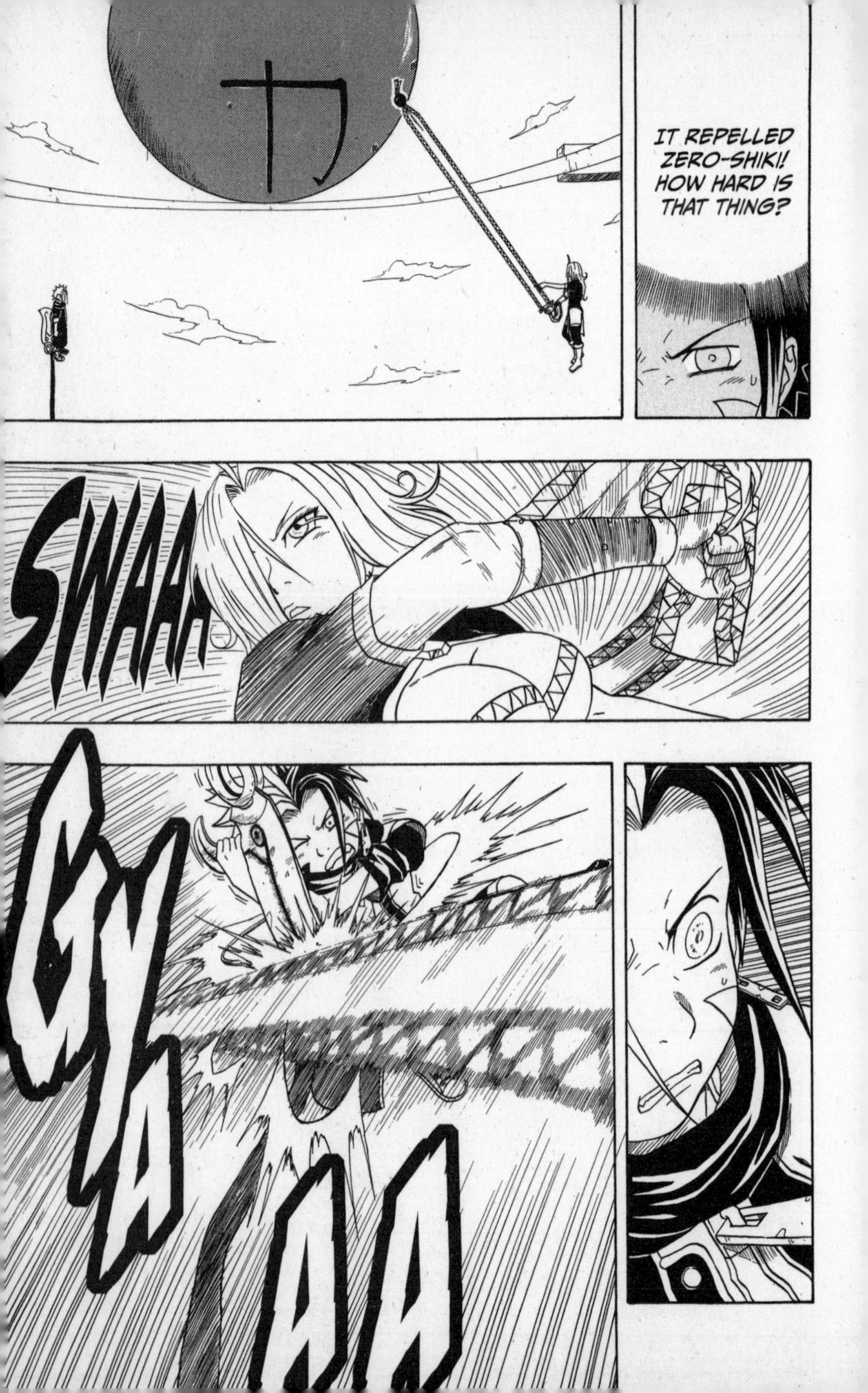
IT REPELLED ZERO-SHIKI! HOW HARD IS THAT THING?
SWAA
GYAAA

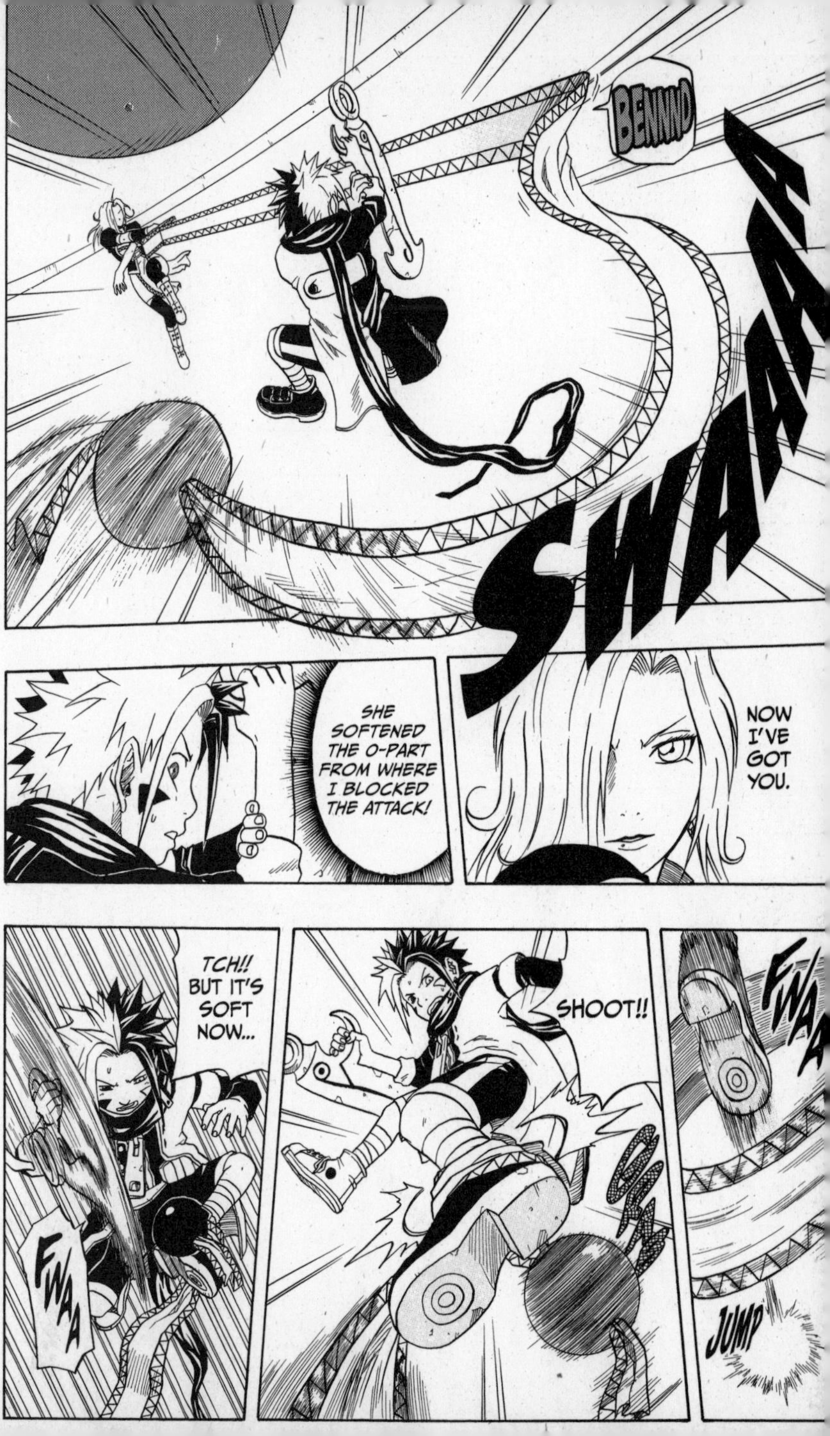
BENNND
SWAAAA
NOW I'VE GOT YOU.
SHE SOFTENED THE O-PART FROM WHERE I BLOCKED THE ATTACK!
FWAA
JUMP
SHOOT!!
TCH!! BUT IT'S SOFT NOW...
FWAA

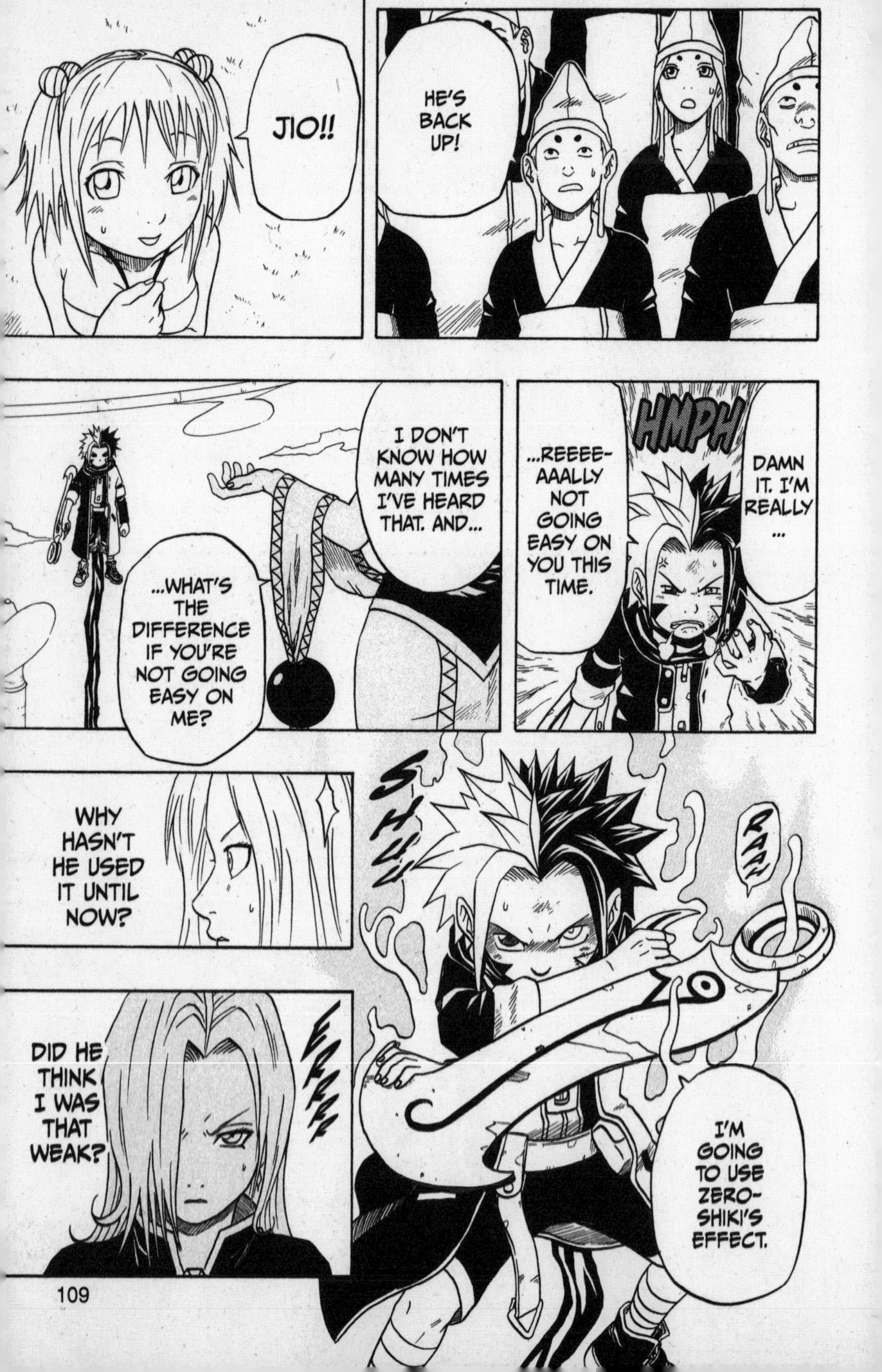
HE'S BACK UP!
JIO!!
HMPH
DAMN IT. I'M REALLY ...
...REEEE-AAALLY NOT GOING EASY ON YOU THIS TIME.
I DON'T KNOW HOW MANY TIMES I'VE HEARD THAT. AND...
...WHAT'S THE DIFFERENCE IF YOU'RE NOT GOING EASY ON ME?
SHUU
I'M GOING TO USE ZERO-SHIKI'S EFFECT.
WHY HASN'T HE USED IT UNTIL NOW?
DID HE THINK I WAS THAT WEAK?

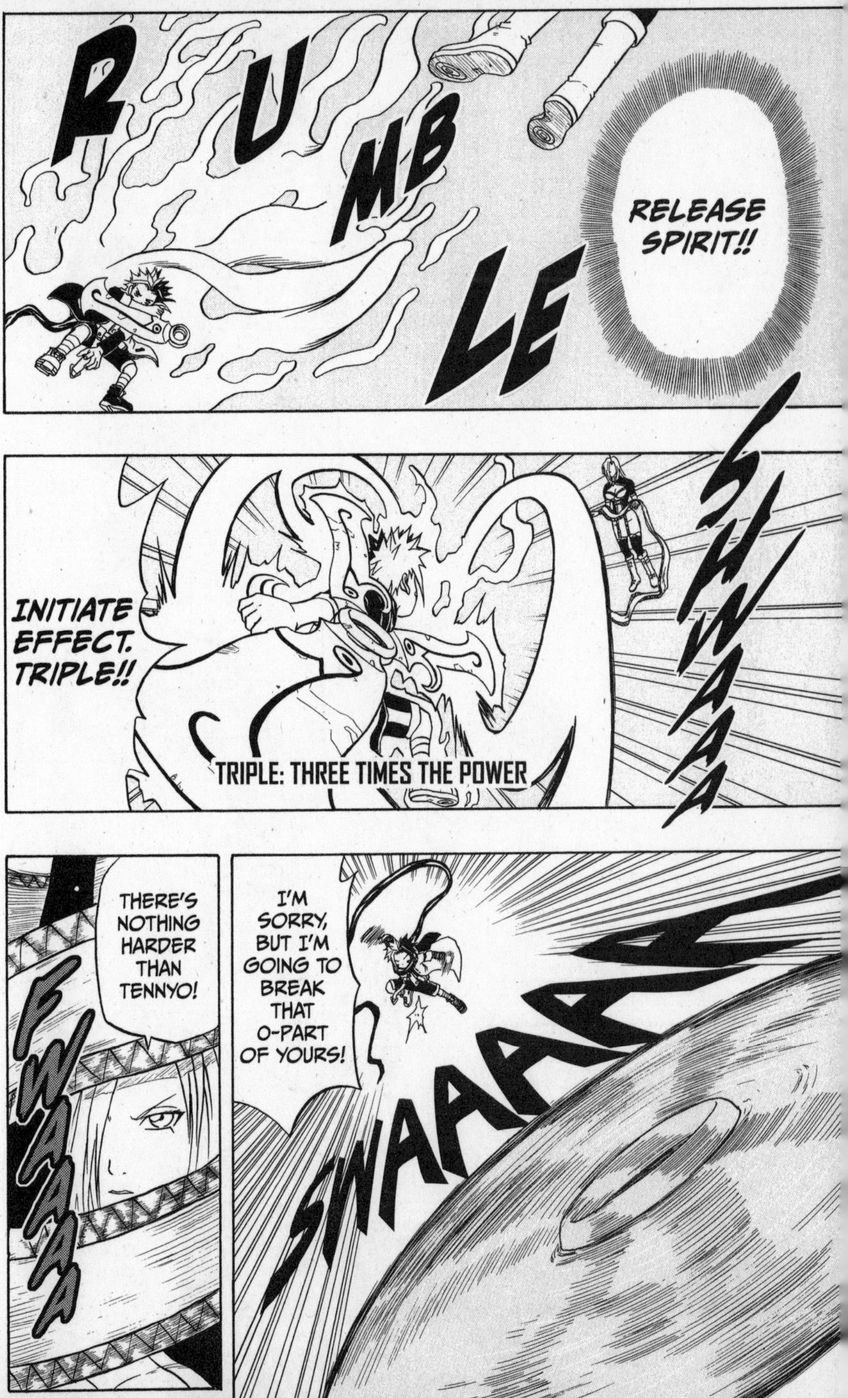
RELEASE SPIRIT!!
RUMBLE
SHWAAAAA
INITIATE EFFECT. TRIPLE!!
TRIPLE: THREE TIMES THE POWER
I'M SORRY, BUT I'M GOING TO BREAK THAT O-PART OF YOURS!
SWAAAAAA
THERE'S NOTHING HARDER THAN TENNYO!
FWAAAAA

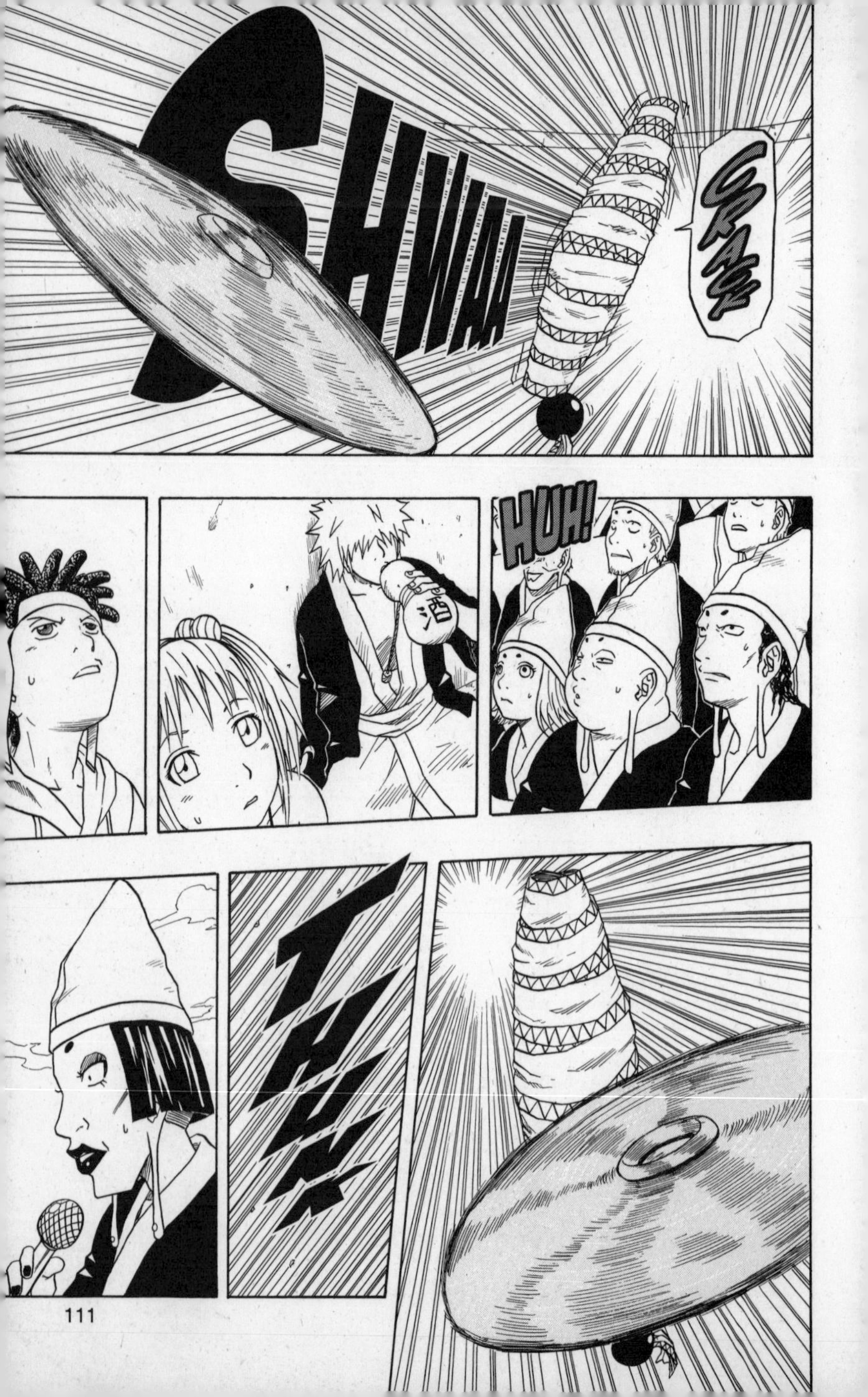
CRACK
SHWAA
HUH!
酒

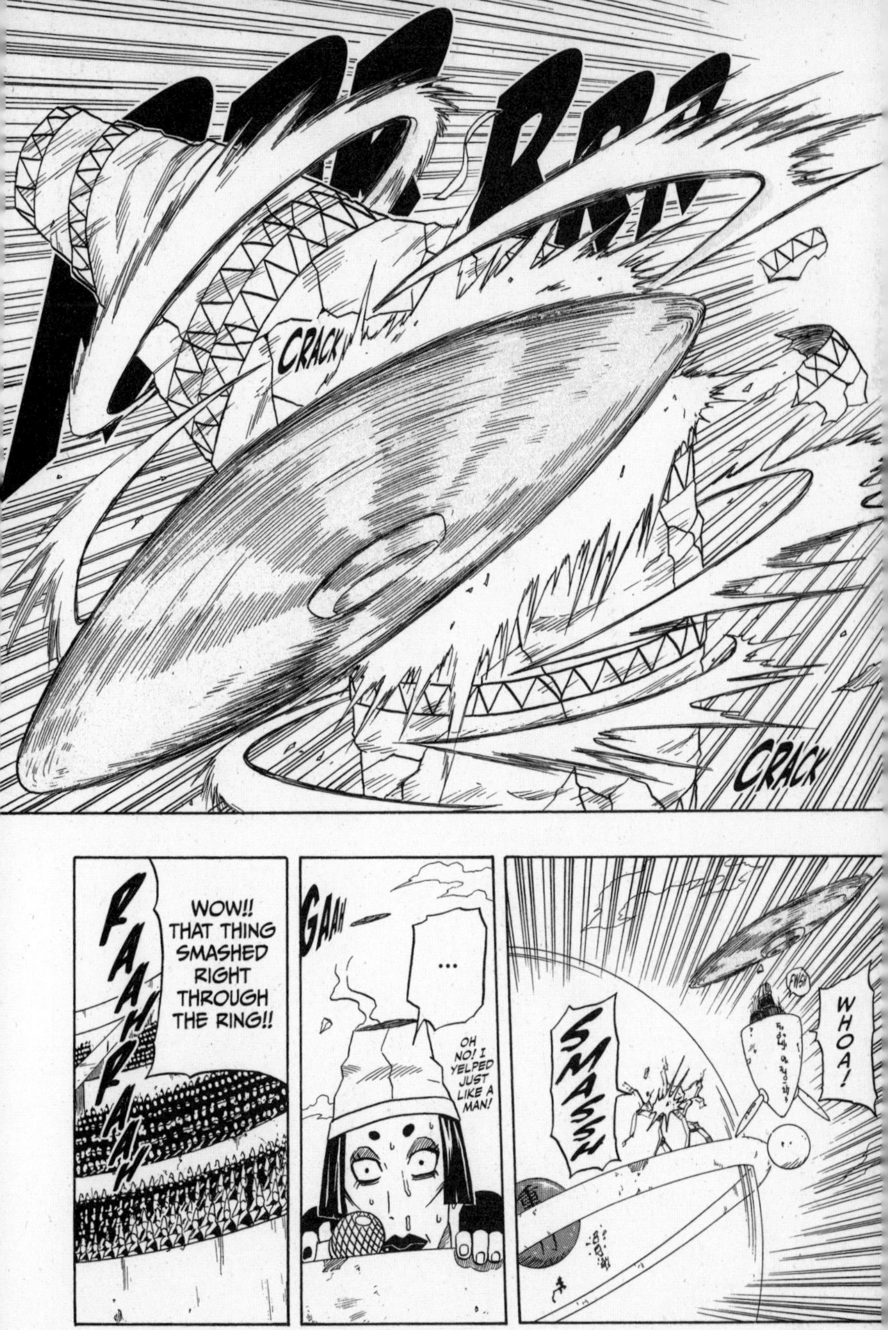
CRACK
CRACK
WHOA!
SMASSH
GAAH
...
OH NO! I YELPED JUST LIKE A MAN!
PAAHPAAH
WOW!! THAT THING SMASHED RIGHT THROUGH THE RING!!

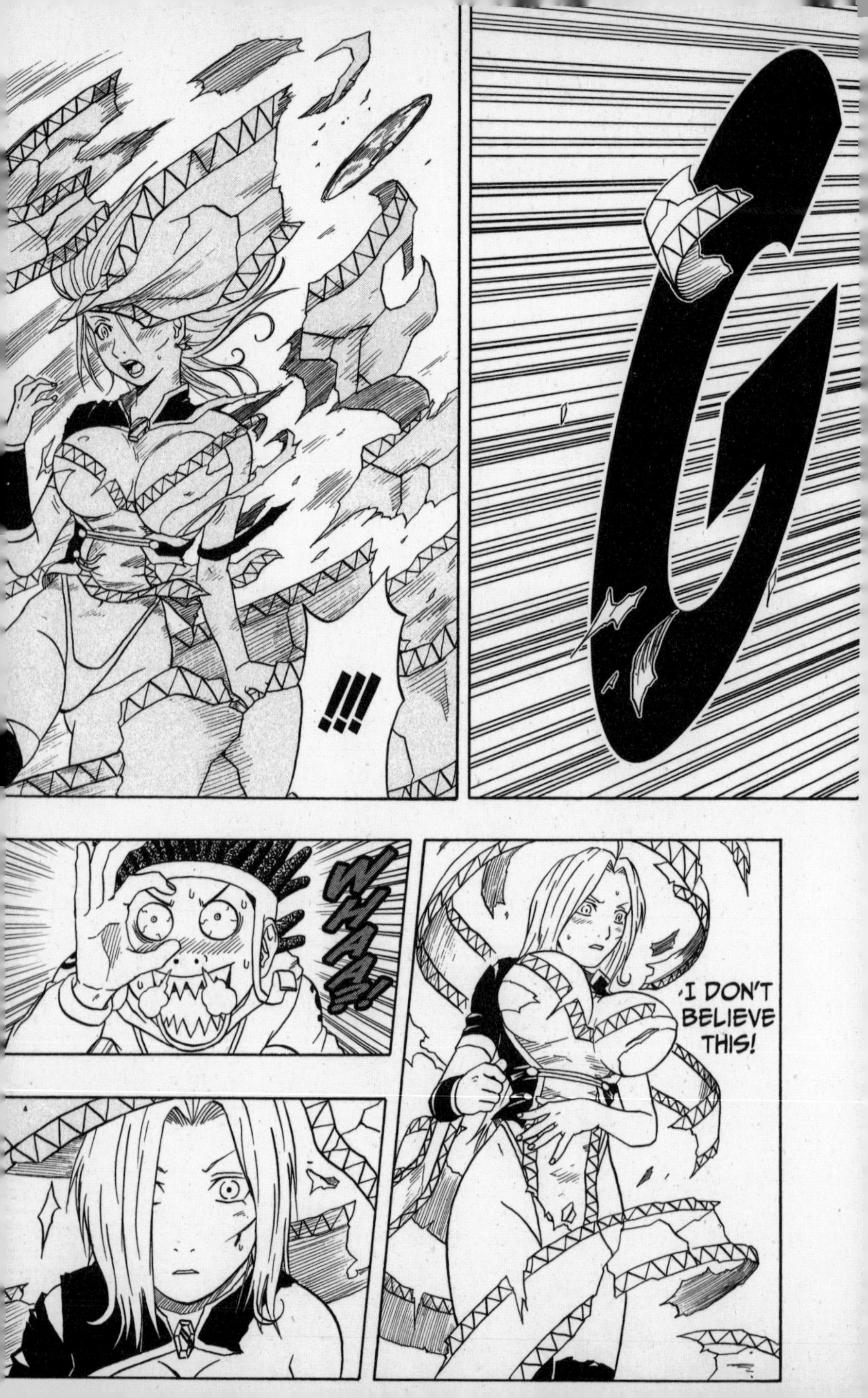
!!!
WHAA!
I DON'T BELIEVE THIS!

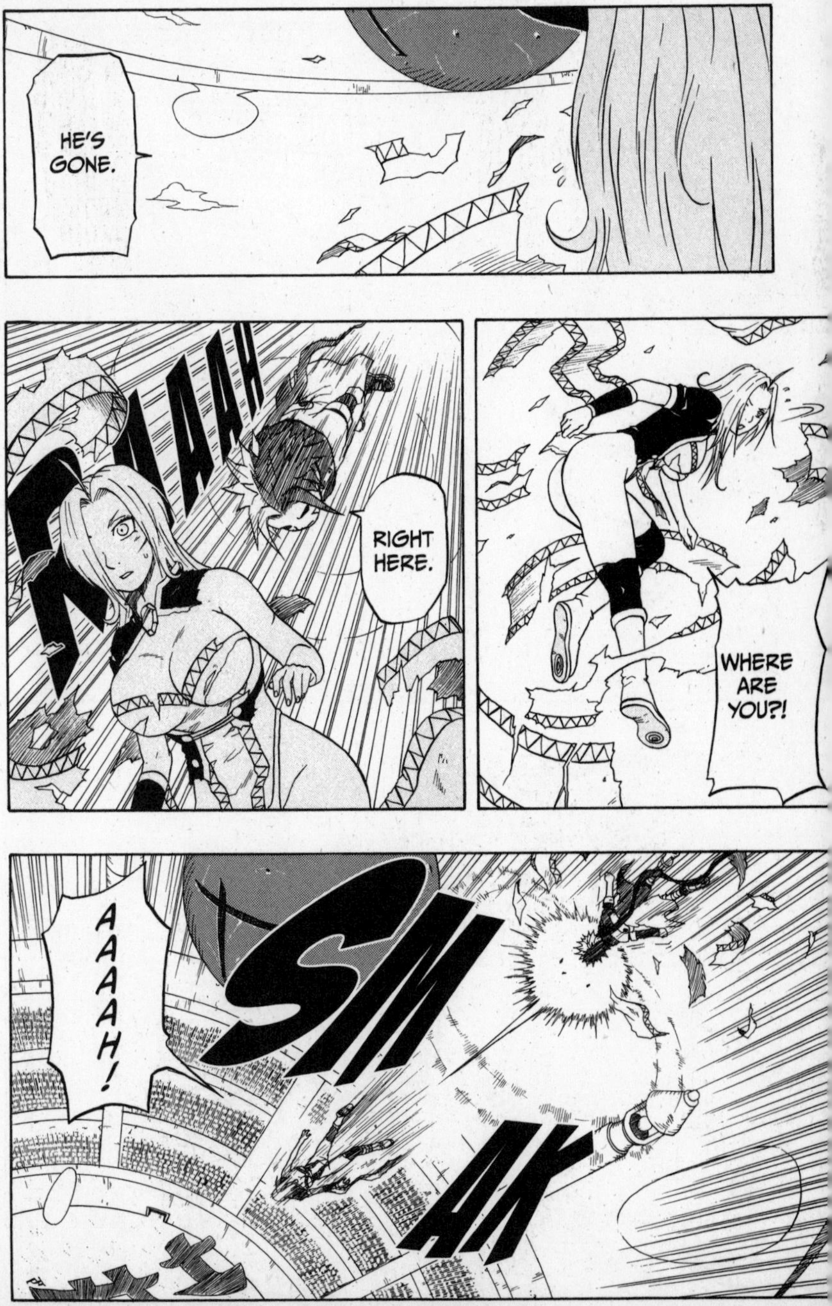
HE'S GONE.
WHERE ARE YOU?!
RIGHT HERE.
AAAAAH!

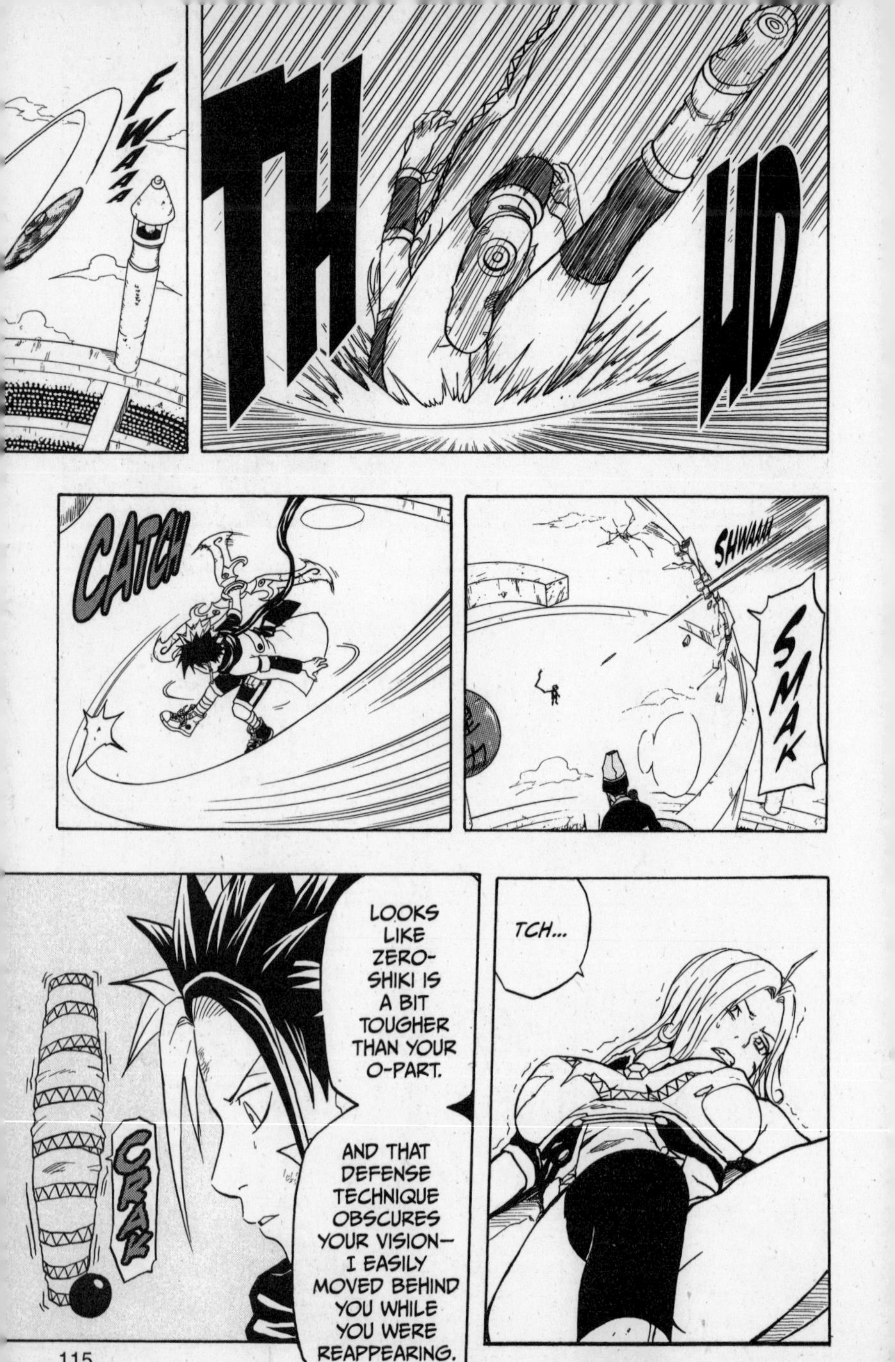
THWD
FWAAA
SHWAAA
SMAK
CATCH
TCH...
LOOKS LIKE ZERO-SHIKI IS A BIT TOUGHER THAN YOUR O-PART.
AND THAT DEFENSE TECHNIQUE OBSCURES YOUR VISION—I EASILY MOVED BEHIND YOU WHILE YOU WERE REAPPEARING.
CRAK

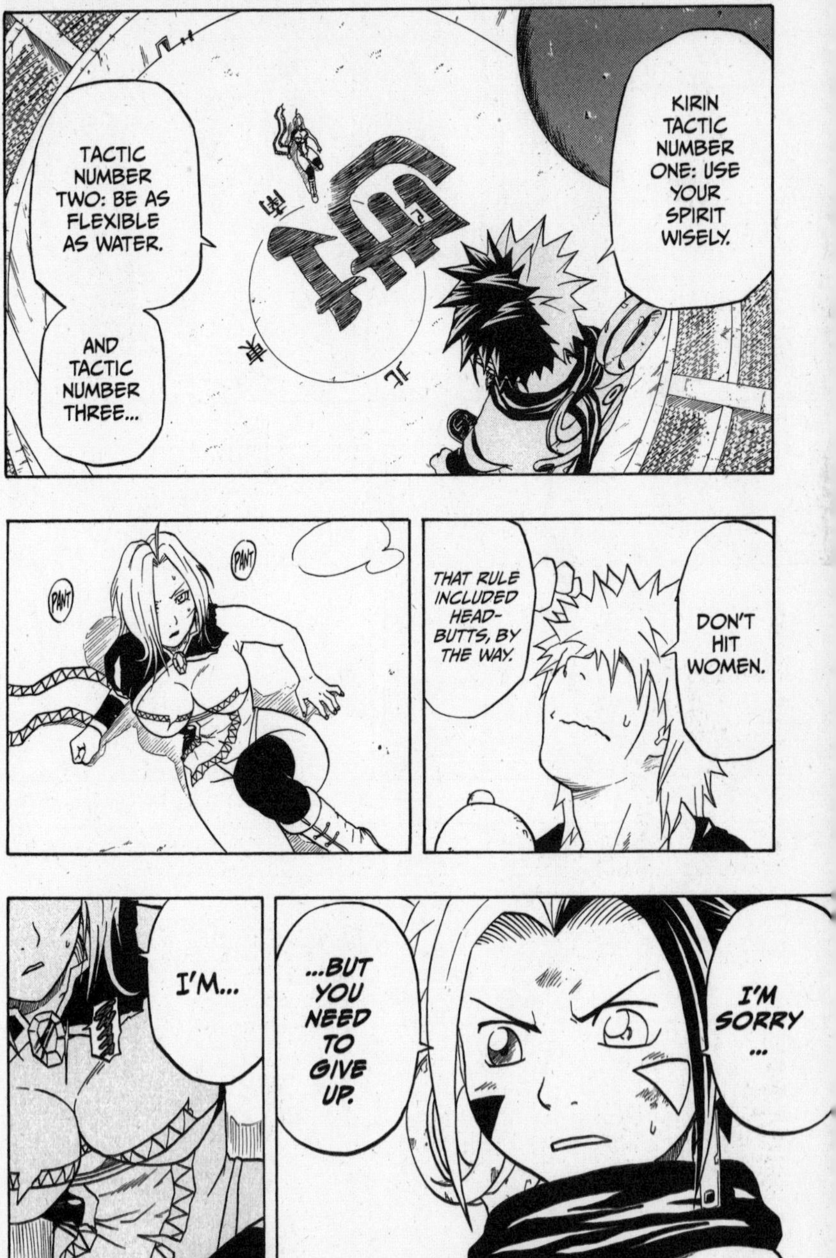
KIRIN TACTIC NUMBER ONE: USE YOUR SPIRIT WISELY.
TACTIC NUMBER TWO: BE AS FLEXIBLE AS WATER.
AND TACTIC NUMBER THREE...
DON'T HIT WOMEN.
THAT RULE INCLUDED HEAD-BUTTS, BY THE WAY.
PANT
PANT
I'M SORRY ...
...BUT YOU NEED TO GIVE UP.
I'M...

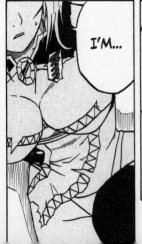

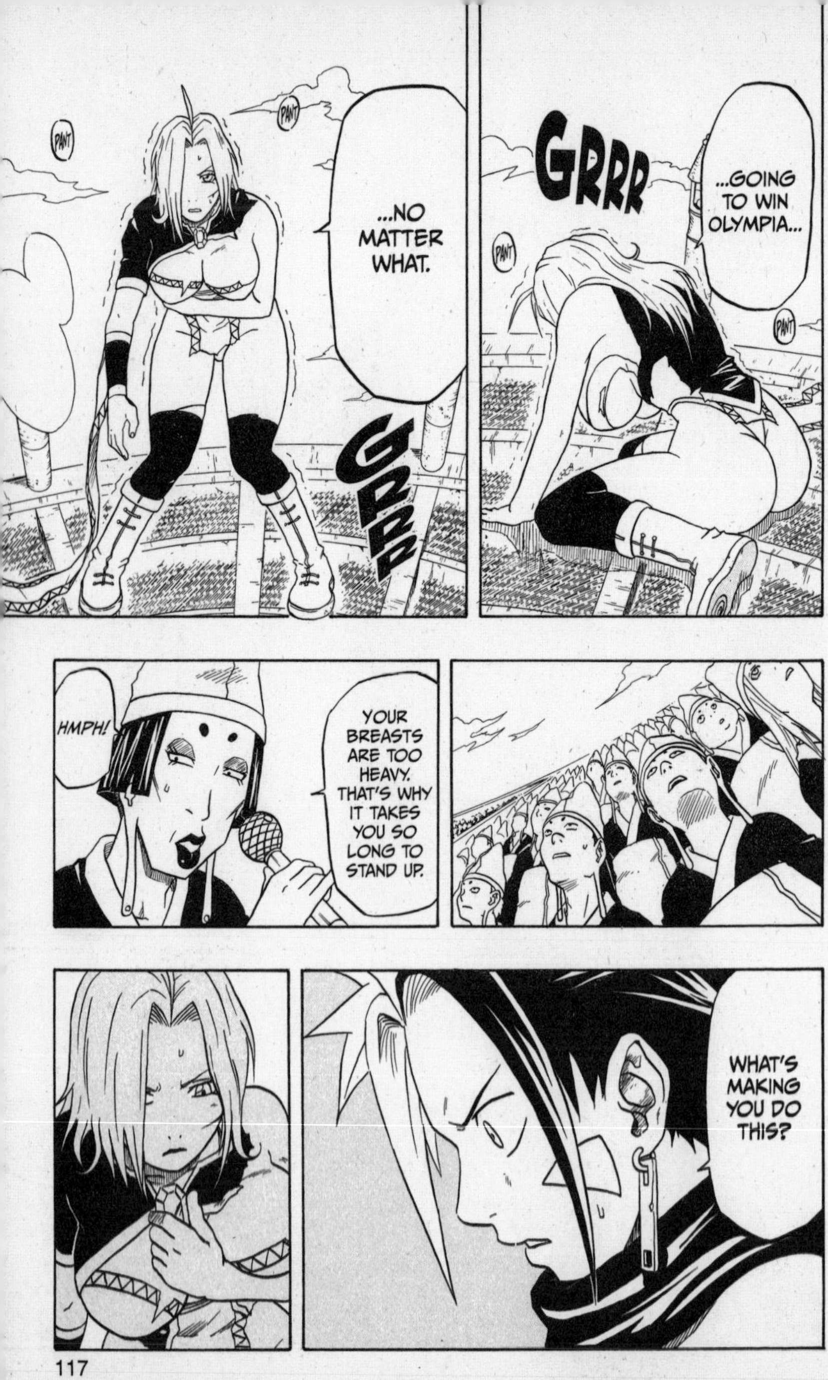
GRRR
PANT
...GOING TO WIN OLYMPIA...
PANT
PANT
PANT
...NO MATTER WHAT.
GRRR
YOUR BREASTS ARE TOO HEAVY. THAT'S WHY IT TAKES YOU SO LONG TO STAND UP.
HMPH!
WHAT'S MAKING YOU DO THIS?

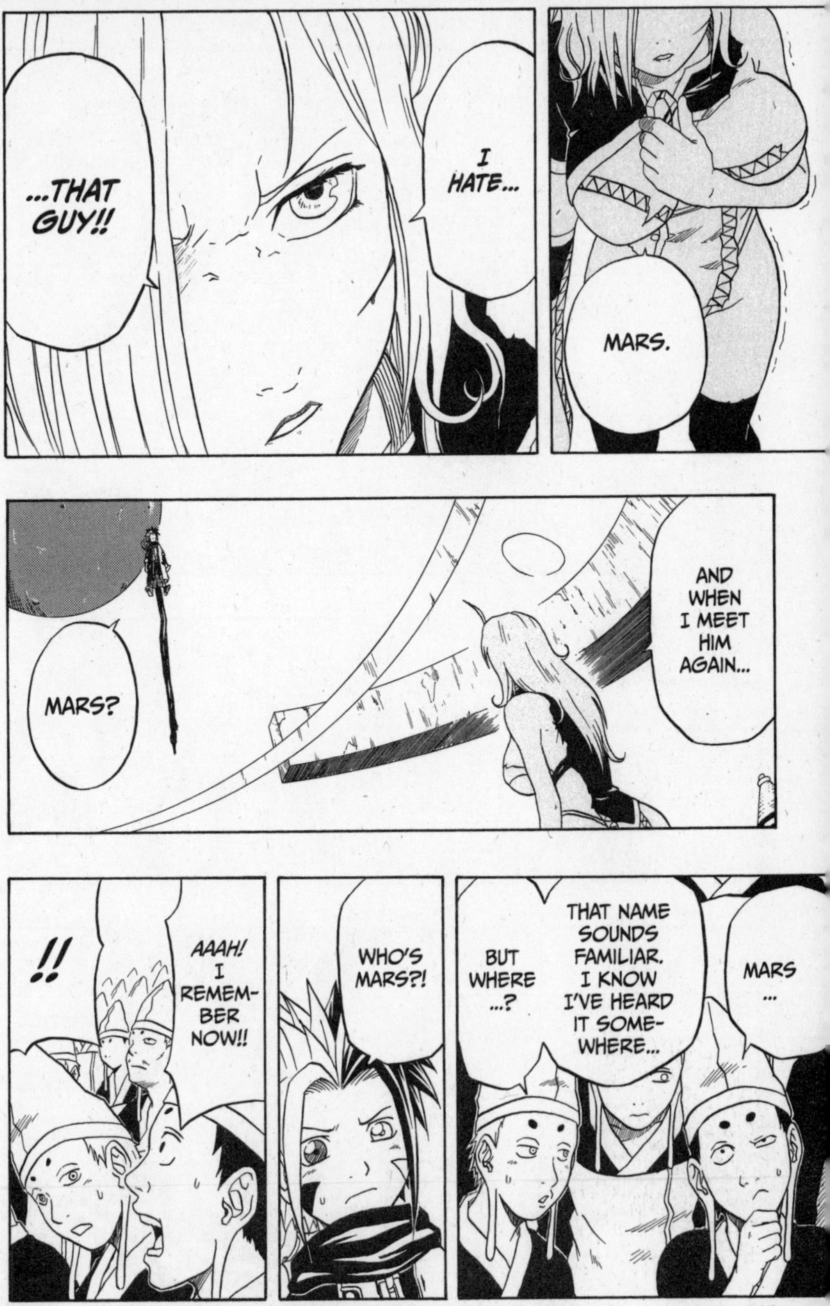
MARS.
I HATE...
...THAT GUY!!
AND WHEN I MEET HIM AGAIN...
MARS?
MARS ...
THAT NAME SOUNDS FAMILIAR. I KNOW I'VE HEARD IT SOME-WHERE...
BUT WHERE ...?
WHO'S MARS?!
AAAH! I REMEM-BER NOW!!
!!

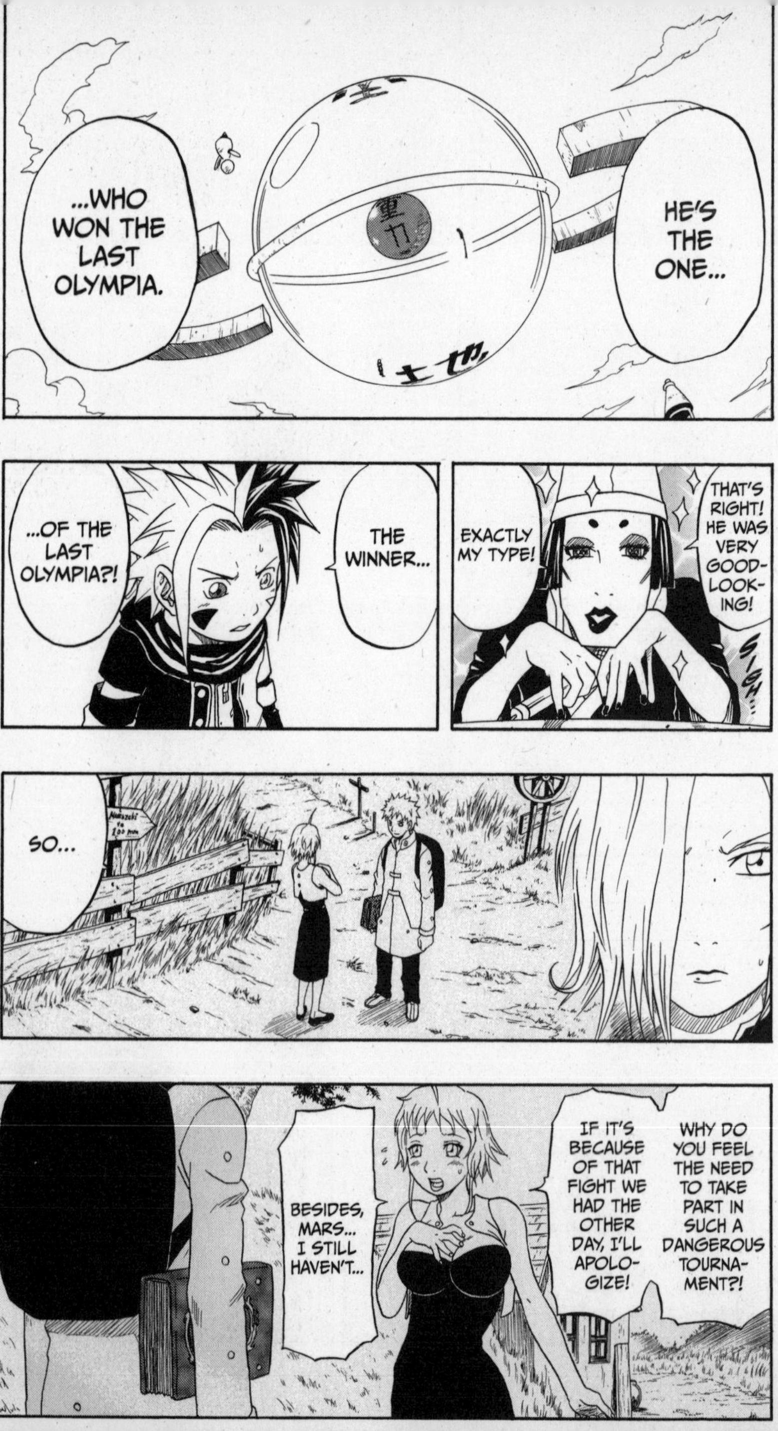
HE'S THE ONE...
...WHO WON THE LAST OLYMPIA.
THAT'S RIGHT! HE WAS VERY GOOD-LOOKING!
EXACTLY MY TYPE!
SIGH...
THE WINNER...
...OF THE LAST OLYMPIA?!
SO...
WHY DO YOU FEEL THE NEED TO TAKE PART IN SUCH A DANGEROUS TOURNAMENT?!
IF IT'S BECAUSE OF THAT FIGHT WE HAD THE OTHER DAY, I'LL APOLOGIZE!
BESIDES, MARS... I STILL HAVEN'T...

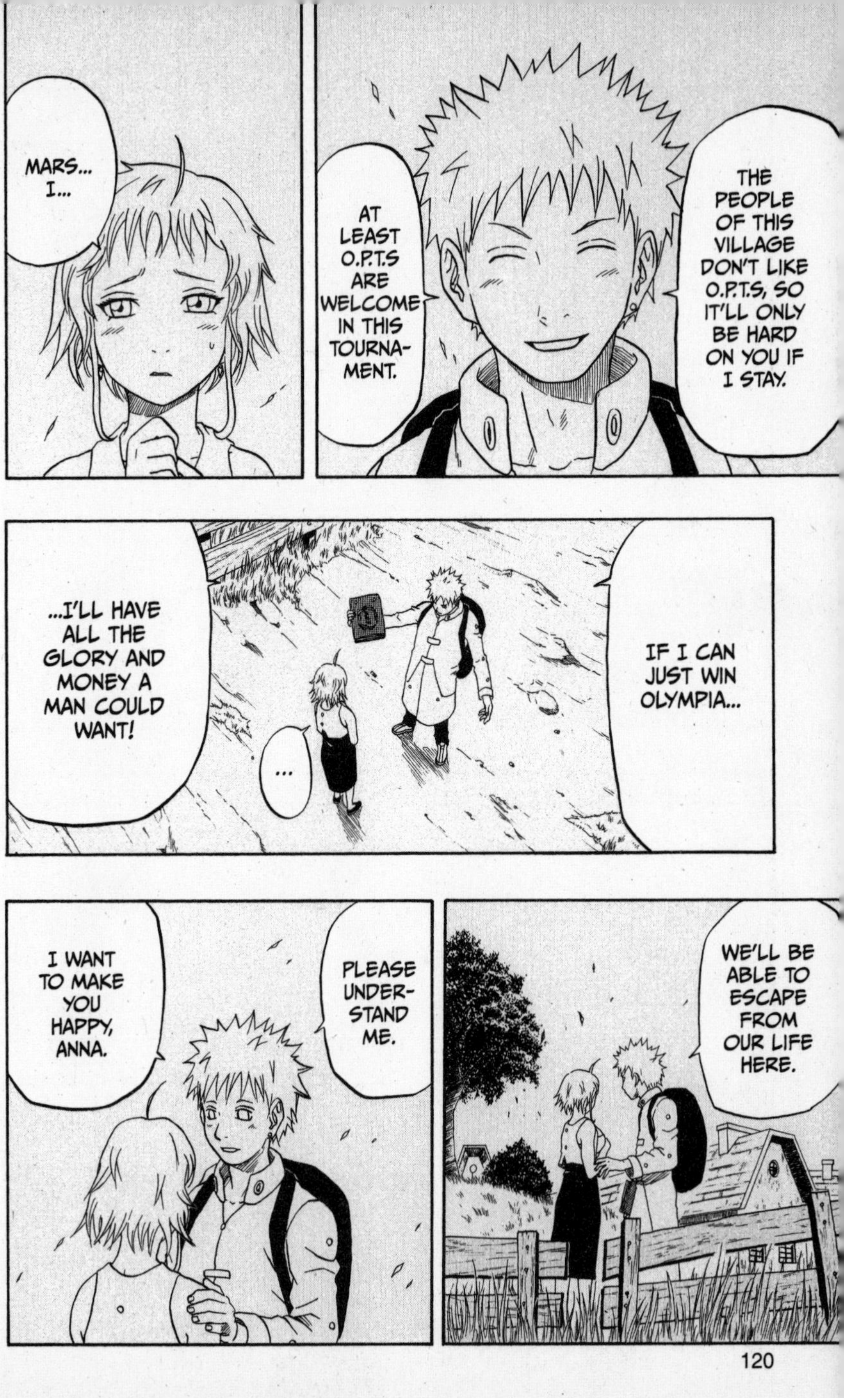
THE PEOPLE OF THIS VILLAGE DON'T LIKE O.P.T.S, SO IT'LL ONLY BE HARD ON YOU IF I STAY.
AT LEAST O.P.T.S ARE WELCOME IN THIS TOURNA-MENT.
MARS... I...
IF I CAN JUST WIN OLYMPIA...
...I'LL HAVE ALL THE GLORY AND MONEY A MAN COULD WANT!
...
WE'LL BE ABLE TO ESCAPE FROM OUR LIFE HERE.
PLEASE UNDER-STAND ME.
I WANT TO MAKE YOU HAPPY, ANNA.

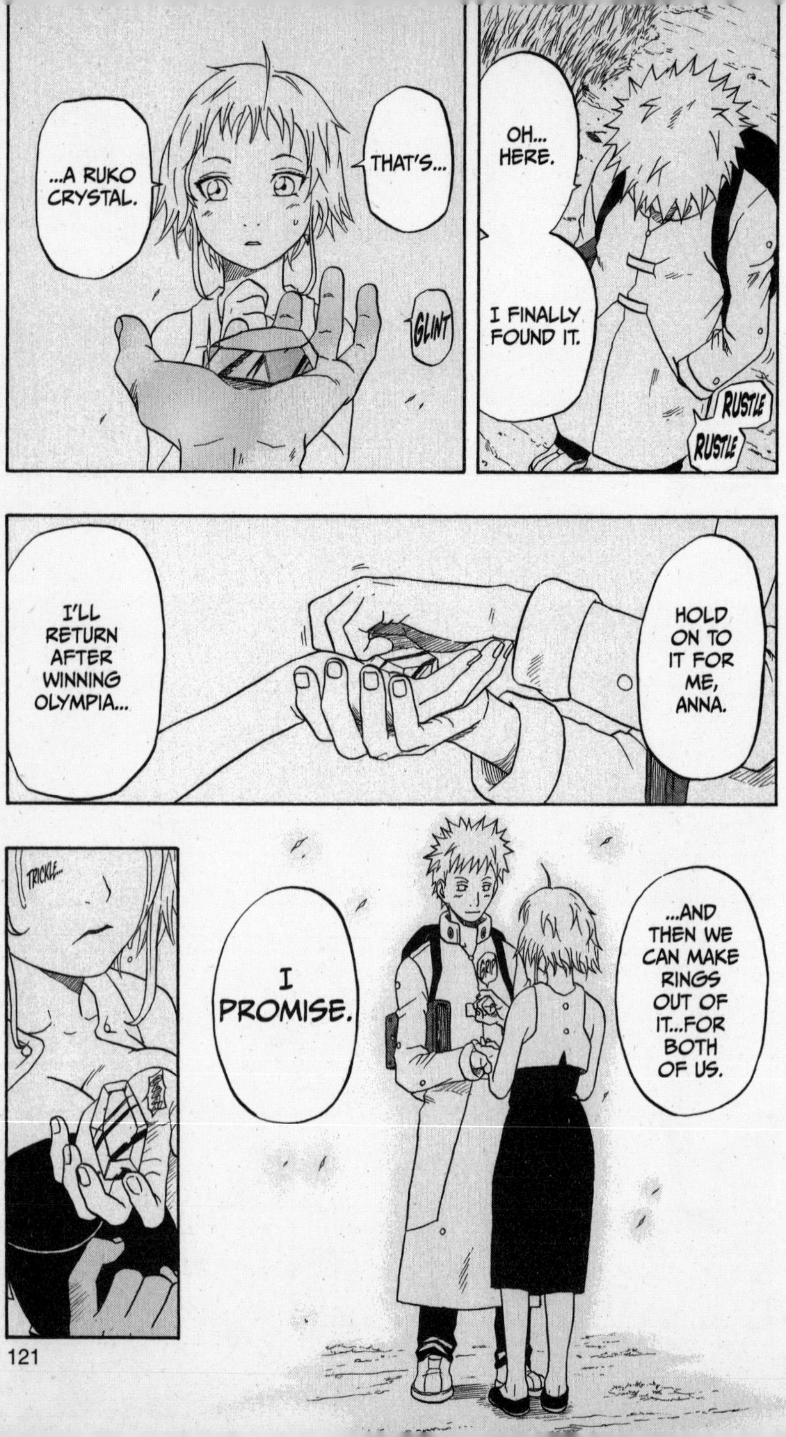
OH... HERE.
I FINALLY FOUND IT.
RUSTLE
RUSTLE
THAT'S...
...A RUKO CRYSTAL.
GLINT
HOLD ON TO IT FOR ME, ANNA.
I'LL RETURN AFTER WINNING OLYMPIA...
...AND THEN WE CAN MAKE RINGS OUT OF IT...FOR BOTH OF US.
GRIP
I PROMISE.
TRICKLE...

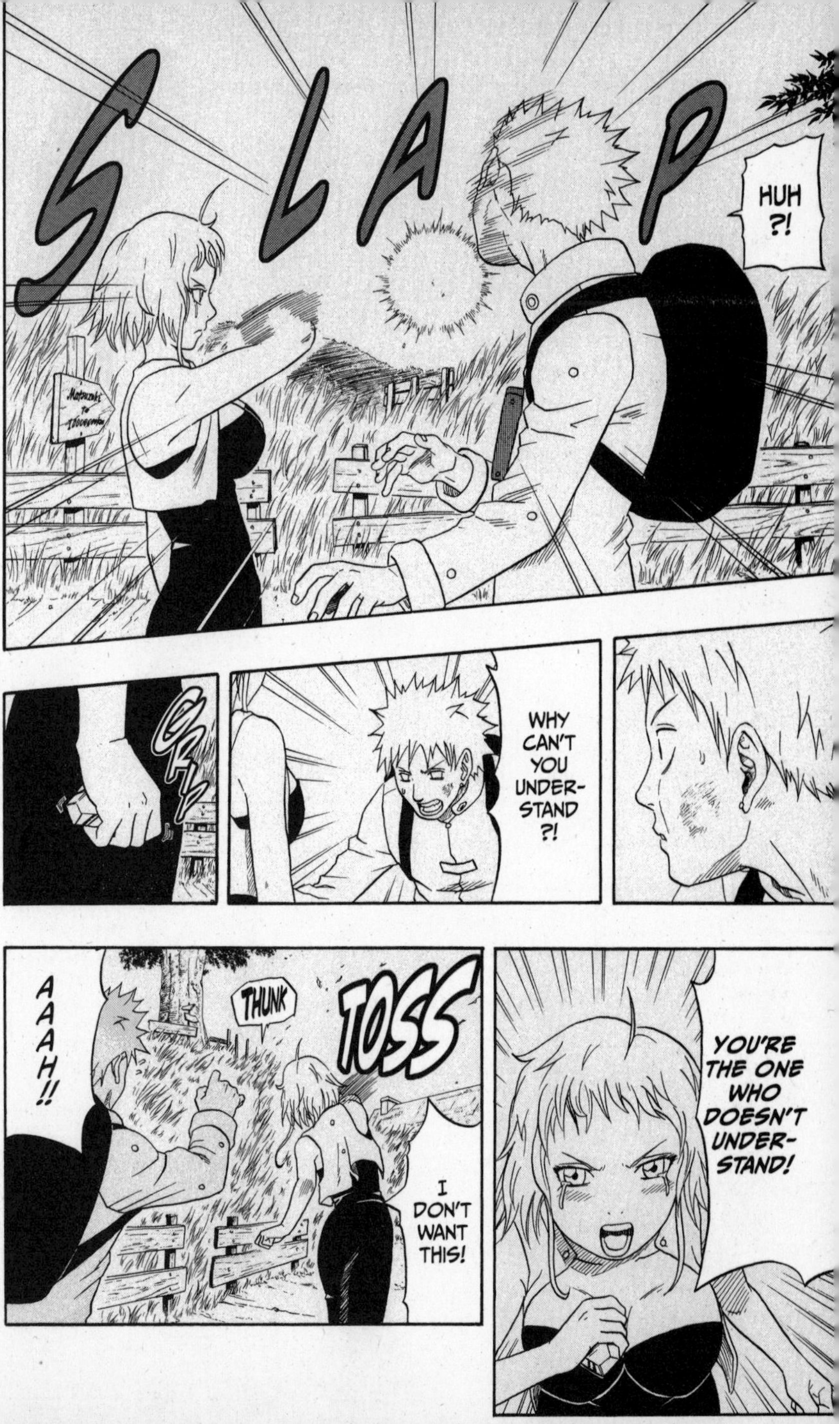
SLAP
HUH?!
WHY CAN'T YOU UNDERSTAND?!
YOU'RE THE ONE WHO DOESN'T UNDERSTAND!
TOSS
THUNK
I DON'T WANT THIS!
AAAAH!!

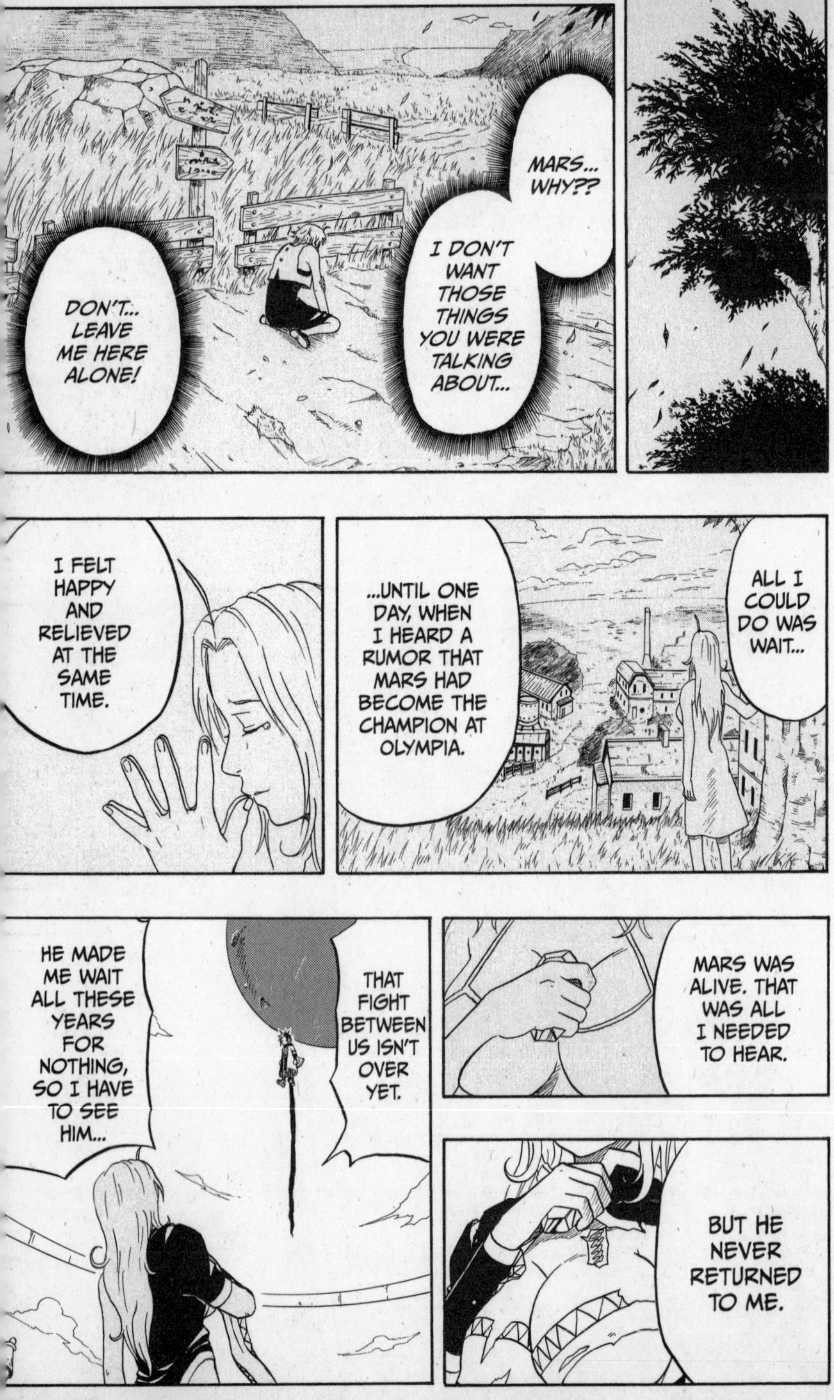
MARS... WHY??
I DON'T WANT THOSE THINGS YOU WERE TALKING ABOUT...
DON'T... LEAVE ME HERE ALONE!
ALL I COULD DO WAS WAIT...
...UNTIL ONE DAY, WHEN I HEARD A RUMOR THAT MARS HAD BECOME THE CHAMPION AT OLYMPIA.
I FELT HAPPY AND RELIEVED AT THE SAME TIME.
MARS WAS ALIVE. THAT WAS ALL I NEEDED TO HEAR.
BUT HE NEVER RETURNED TO ME.
THAT FIGHT BETWEEN US ISN'T OVER YET.
HE MADE ME WAIT ALL THESE YEARS FOR NOTHING, SO I HAVE TO SEE HIM...

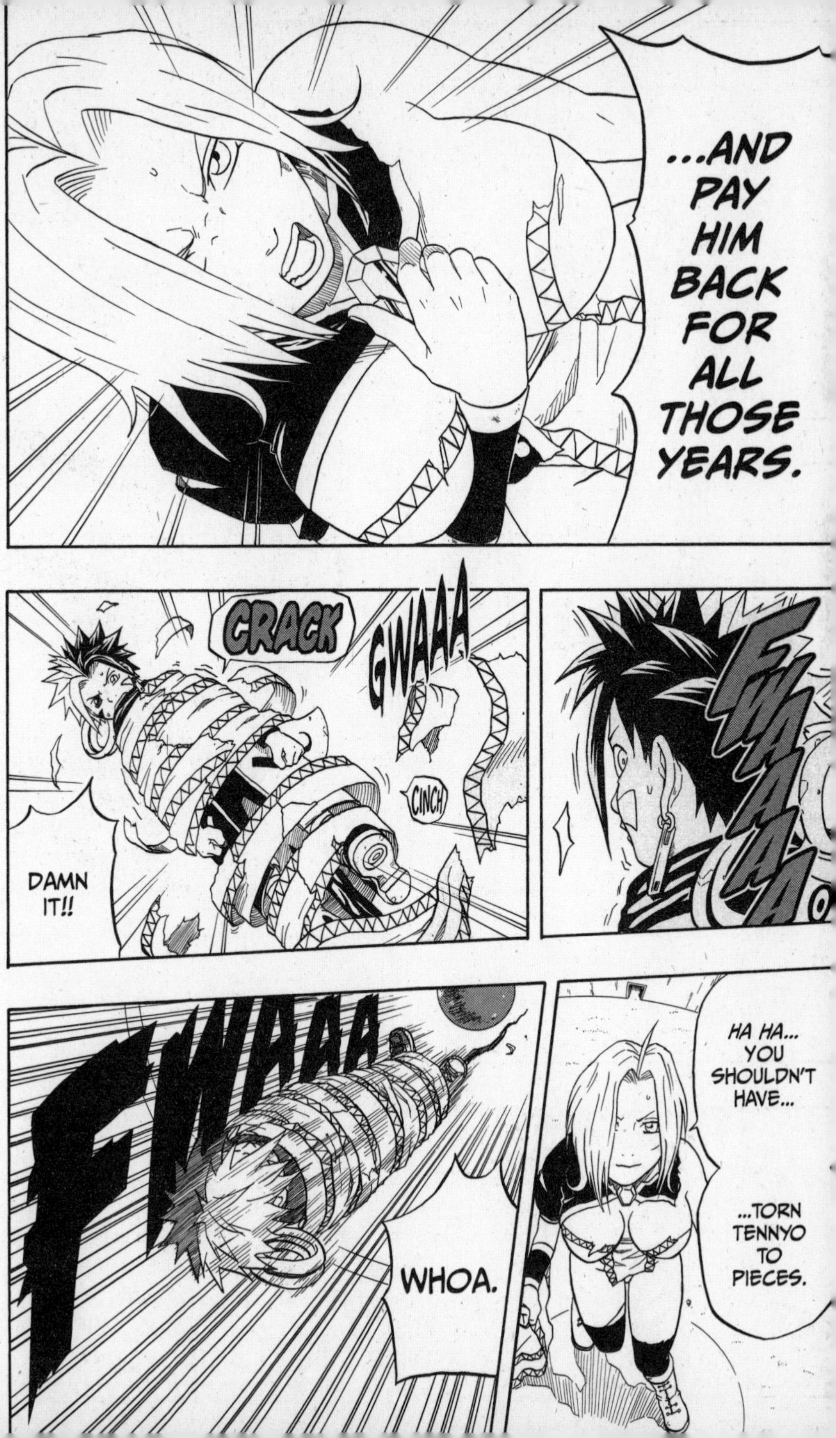
...AND PAY HIM BACK FOR ALL THOSE YEARS.
GWAAA
CRACK
CINCH
DAMN IT!!
HA HA... YOU SHOULDN'T HAVE...
...TORN TENNYO TO PIECES.
WHOA.
FWAAAA

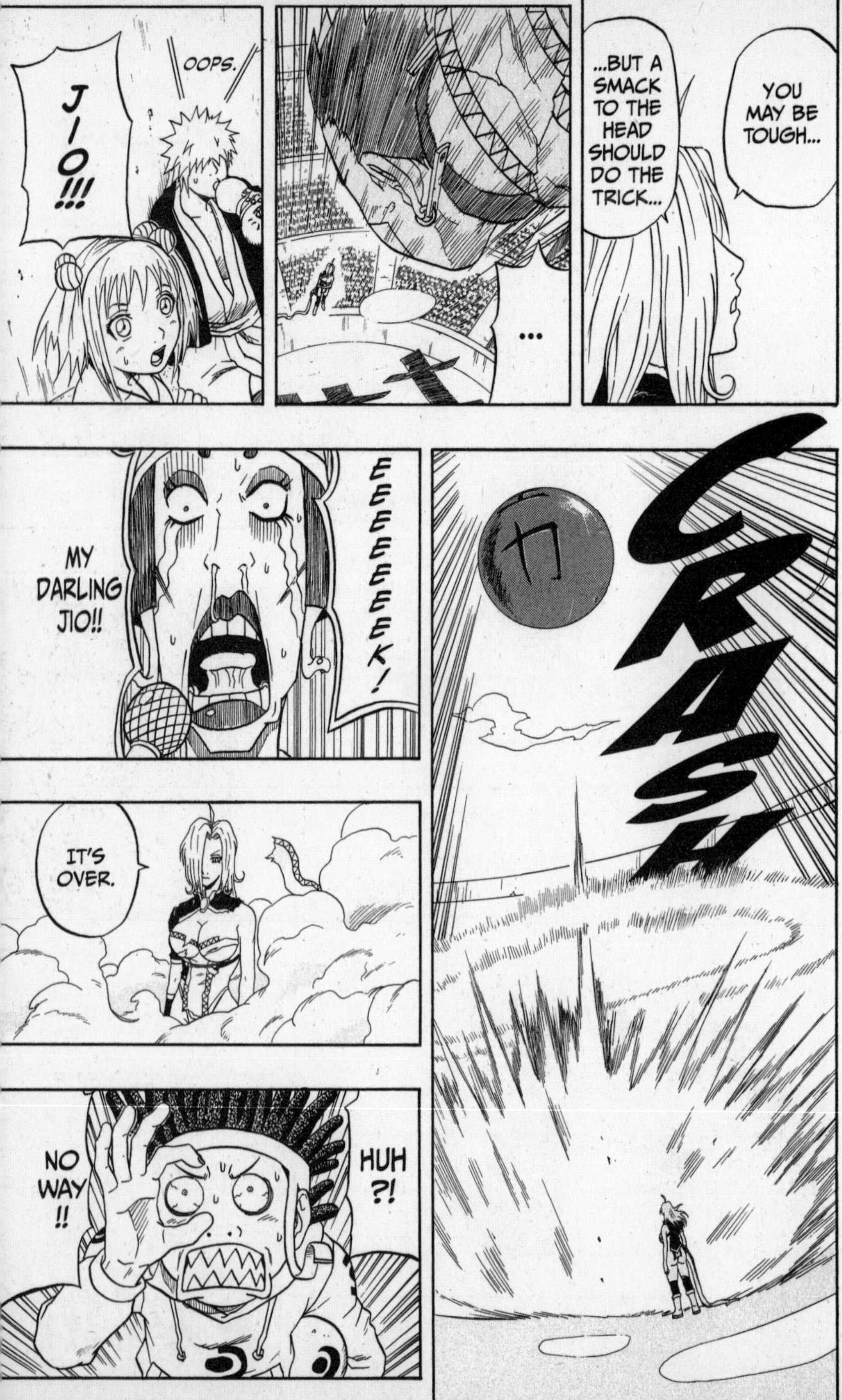
YOU MAY BE TOUGH...
...BUT A SMACK TO THE HEAD SHOULD DO THE TRICK...
...
OOPS.
JIO!!!
CRASH
EEEEEEEEK!
MY DARLING JIO!!
IT'S OVER.
HUH?!
NO WAY!!

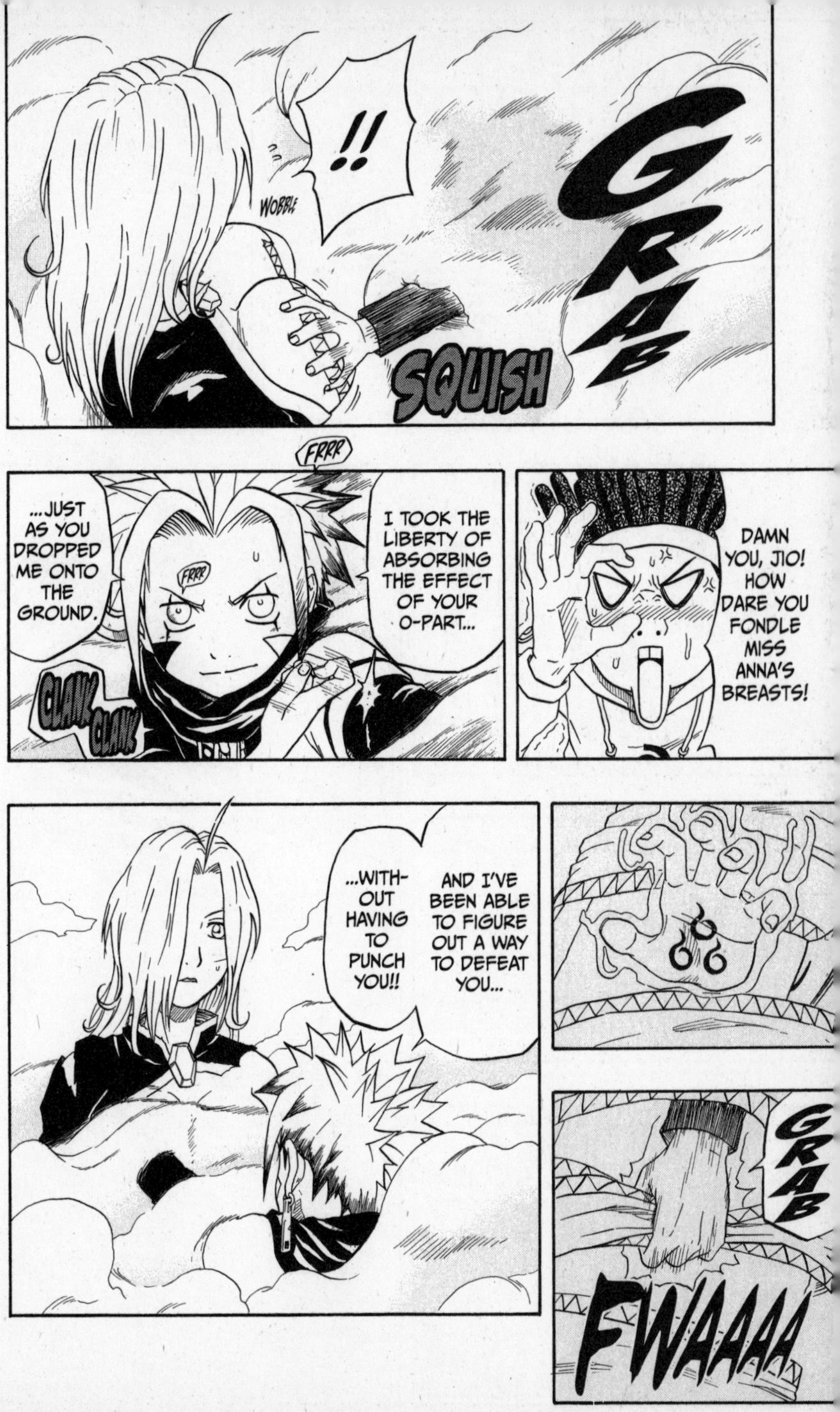
GRAB
!!
WOBBLE
SQUISH
DAMN YOU, JIO! HOW DARE YOU FONDLE MISS ANNA'S BREASTS!
FRRR
FRRR
I TOOK THE LIBERTY OF ABSORBING THE EFFECT OF YOUR O-PART...
...JUST AS YOU DROPPED ME ONTO THE GROUND.
CLANK CLANK
GRAB
FWAAAA
AND I'VE BEEN ABLE TO FIGURE OUT A WAY TO DEFEAT YOU...
...WITH-OUT HAVING TO PUNCH YOU!!

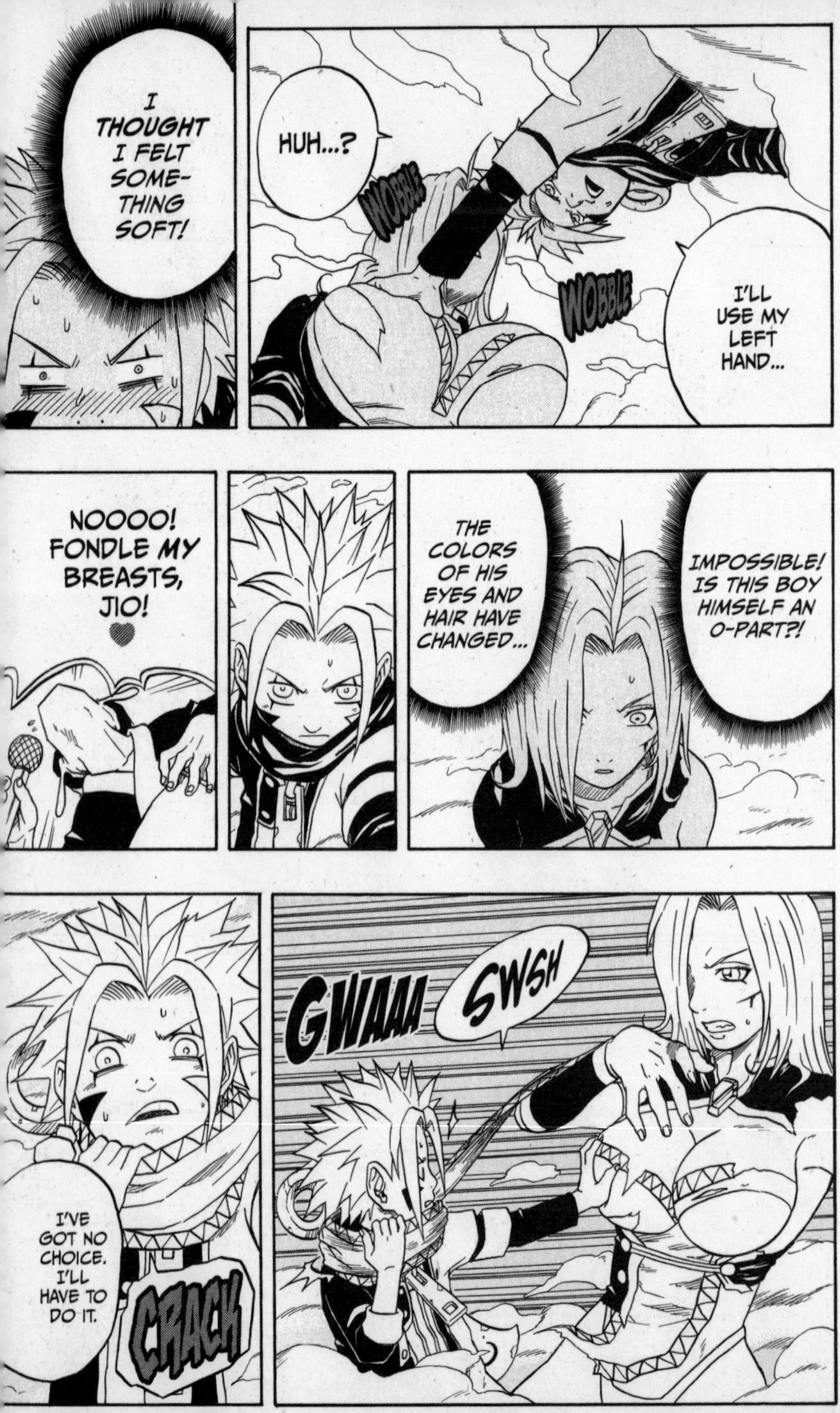
I'LL USE MY LEFT HAND...
HUH...?
WOBBLE
WOBBLE
I THOUGHT I FELT SOME-THING SOFT!
THE COLORS OF HIS EYES AND HAIR HAVE CHANGED...
IMPOSSIBLE! IS THIS BOY HIMSELF AN O-PART?!
NOOOO! FONDLE MY BREASTS, JIO!
SWSH
GWAAA
I'VE GOT NO CHOICE. I'LL HAVE TO DO IT.
CRACK

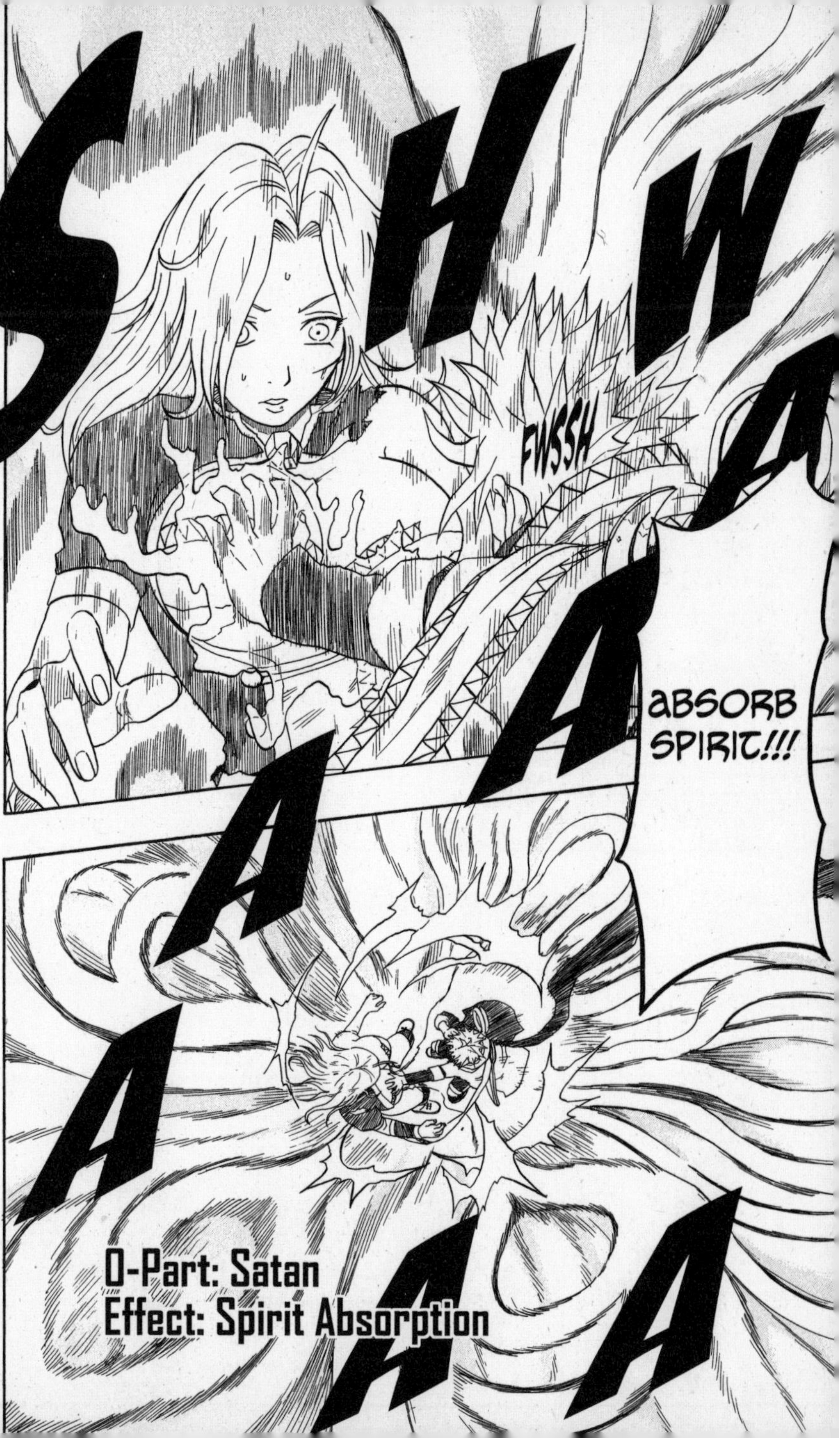
SHWAAAAAAAA
FWSSH
ABSORB SPIRIT!!!
O-Part: Satan
Effect: Spirit Absorption

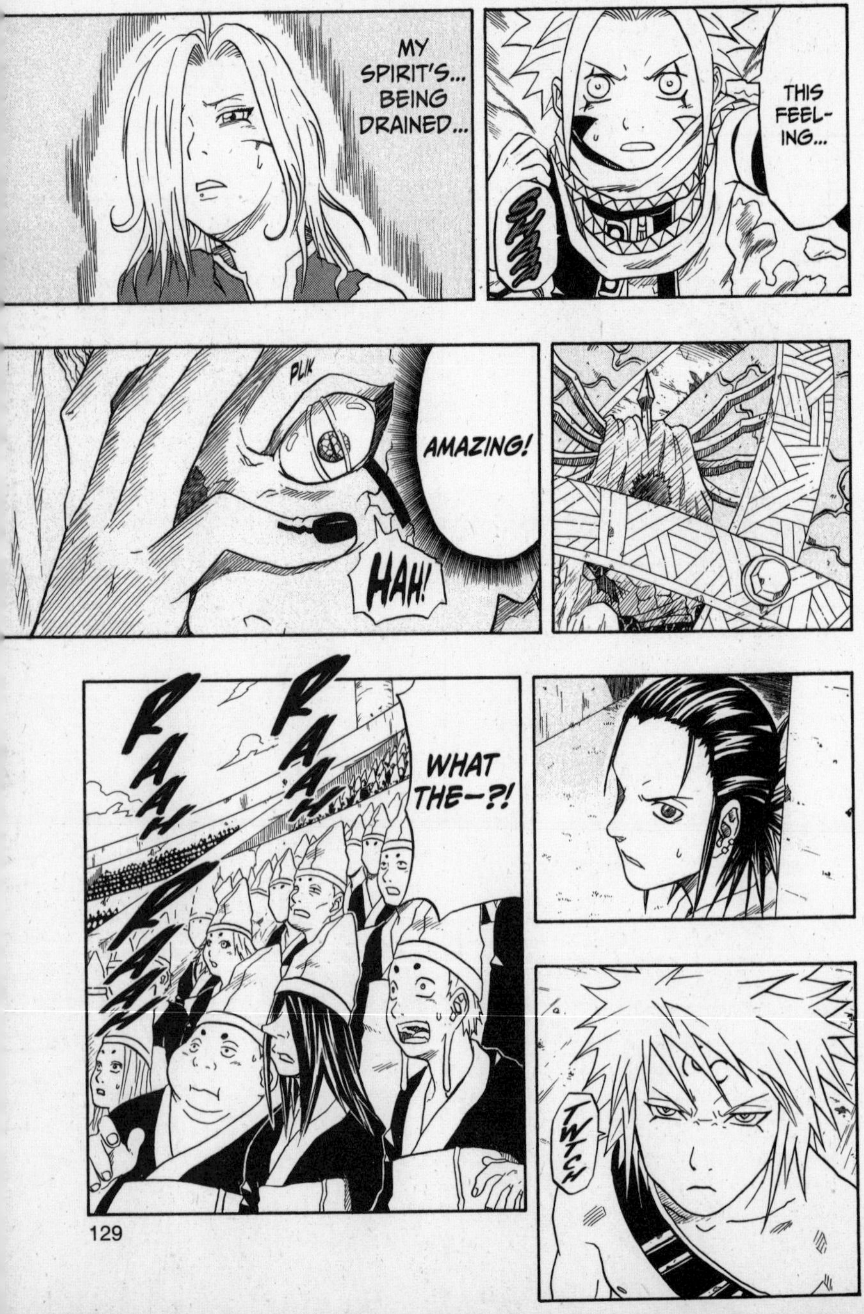
THIS FEEL-ING...
MY SPIRIT'S... BEING DRAINED...
PLIK
AMAZING!
HAH!
TWTCH
WHAT THE--?!

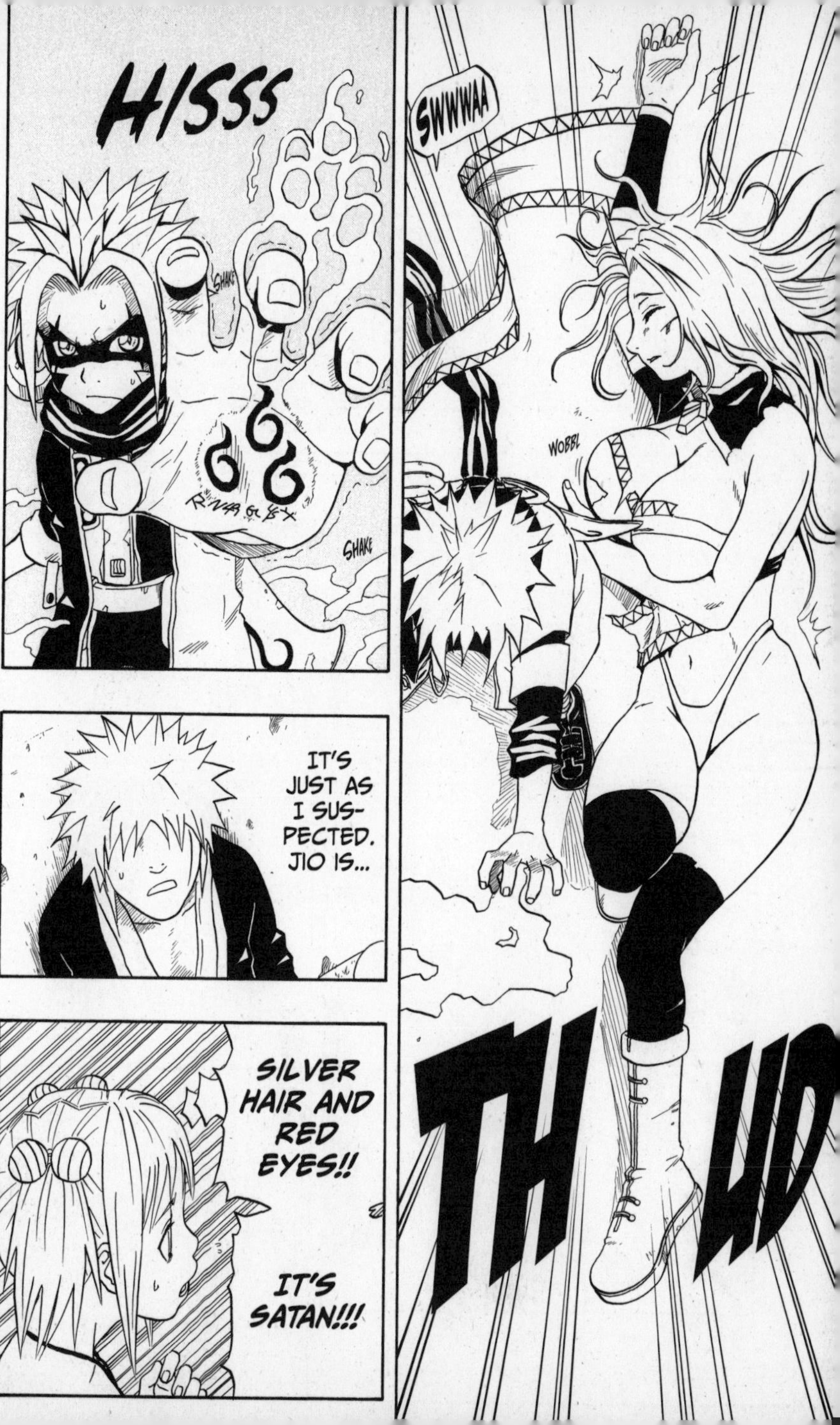
SWWWAA
WOBBL
THUD
HISSS
SHAKE
SHAKE
IT'S JUST AS I SUSPECTED. JIO IS...
SILVER HAIR AND RED EYES!!
IT'S SATAN!!!

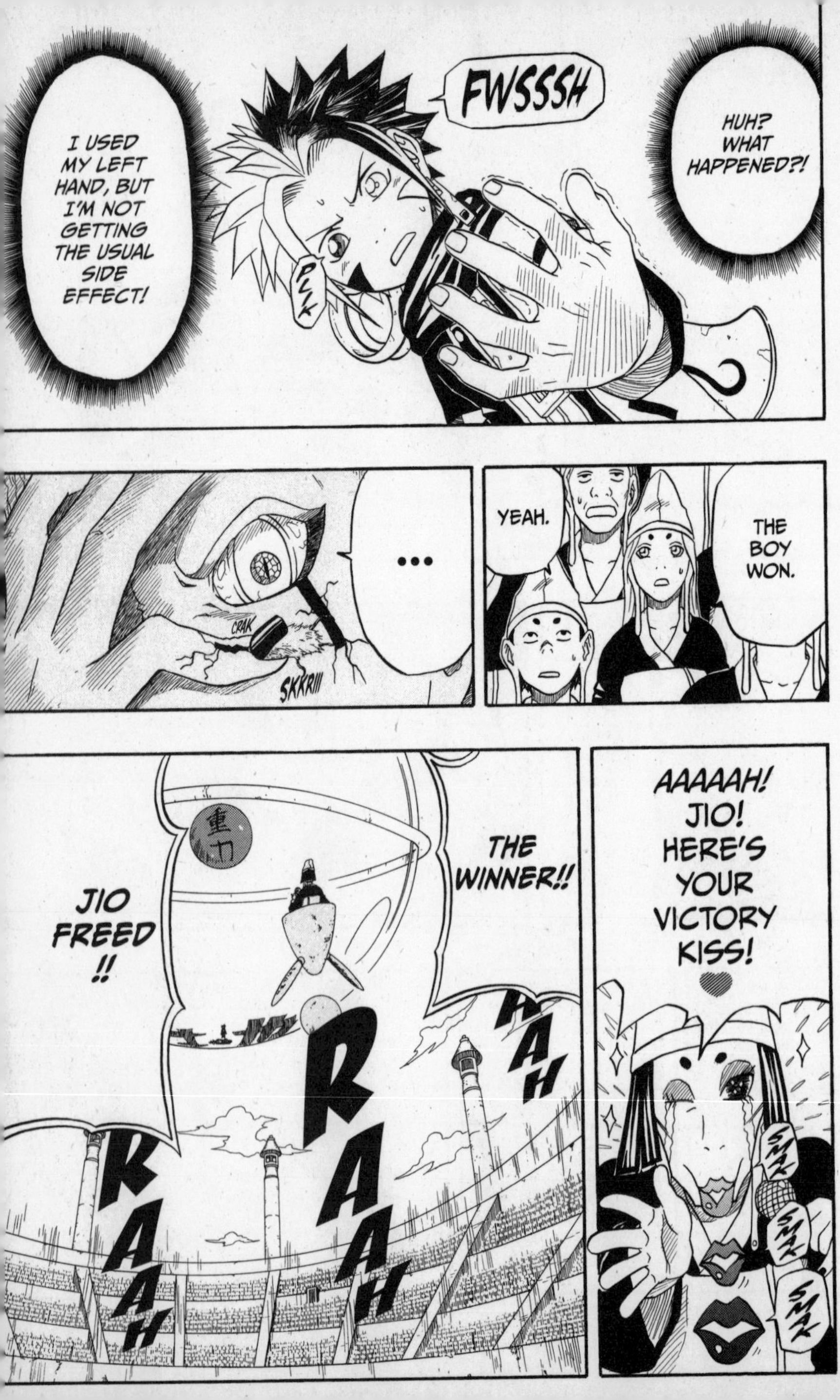
HUH? WHAT HAPPENED?!
FWSSSH
I USED MY LEFT HAND, BUT I'M NOT GETTING THE USUAL SIDE EFFECT!
PLIK
THE BOY WON.
YEAH.
...
CRAK
SKKRIII
AAAAAH! JIO! HERE'S YOUR VICTORY KISS!
SMAK
SMAK
SMAK
THE WINNER!!
JIO FREED!!
RAAH
RAAH
RAAH

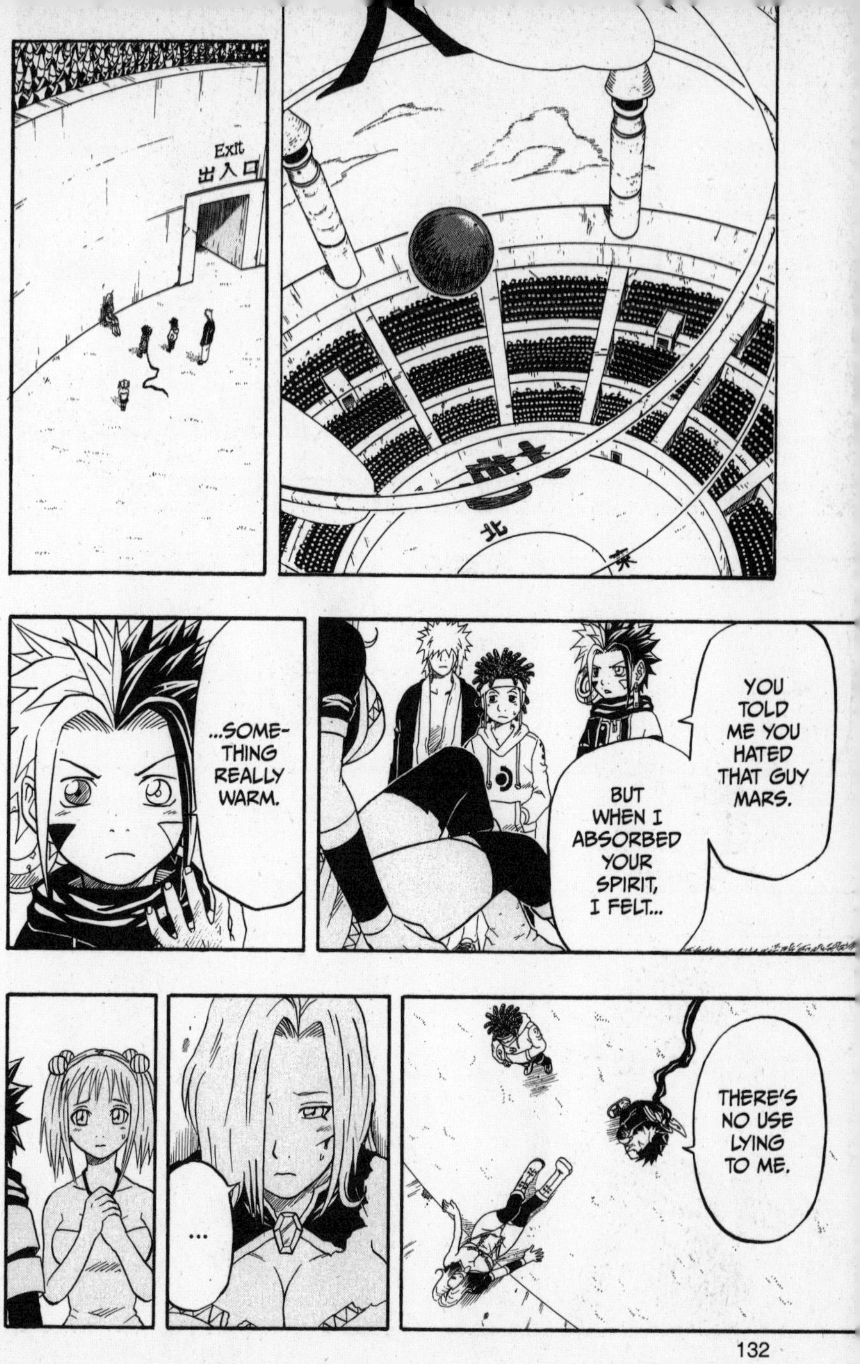
Exit
出入口
YOU TOLD ME YOU HATED THAT GUY MARS.
BUT WHEN I ABSORBED YOUR SPIRIT, I FELT...
...SOME-THING REALLY WARM.
THERE'S NO USE LYING TO ME.
...

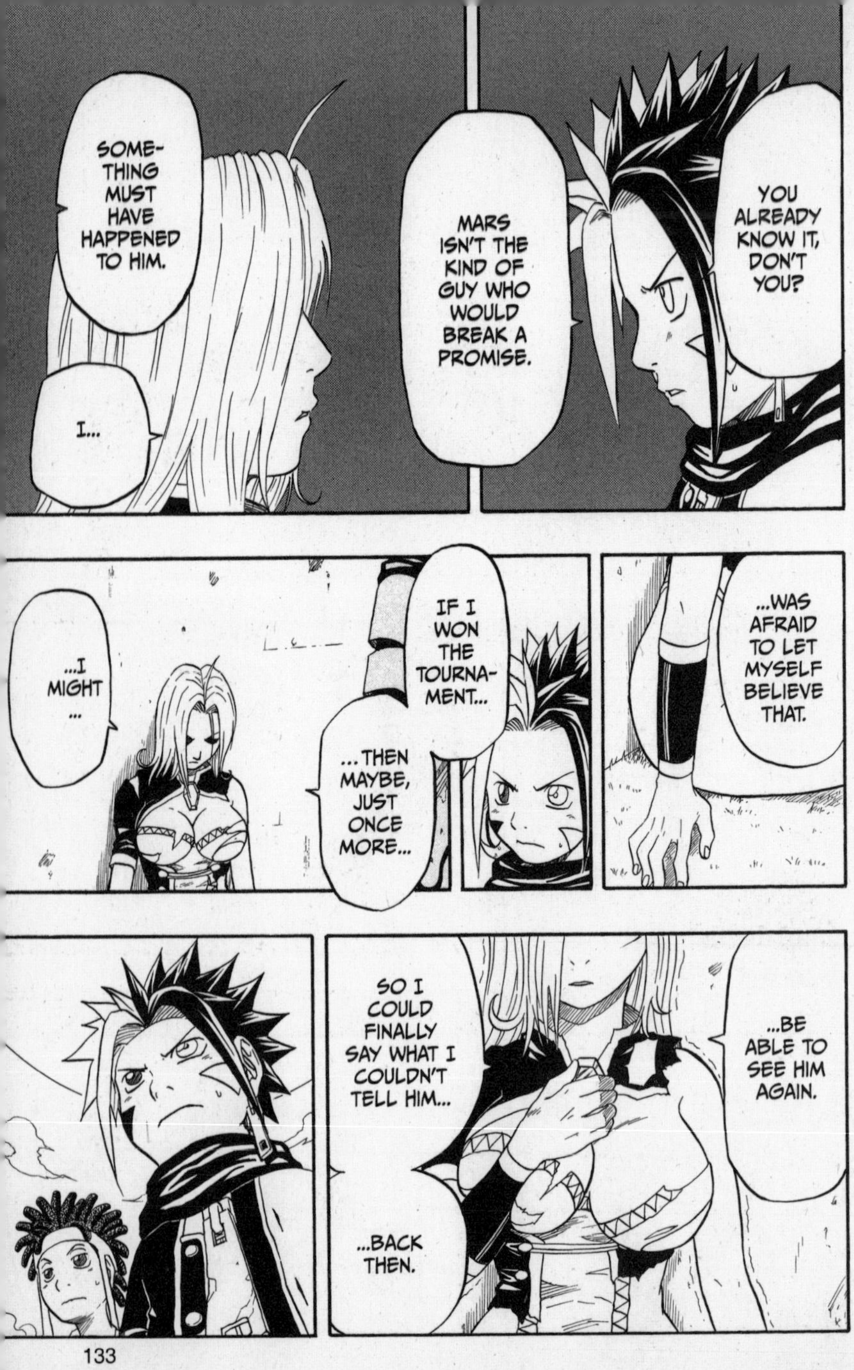
YOU ALREADY KNOW IT, DON'T YOU?
MARS ISN'T THE KIND OF GUY WHO WOULD BREAK A PROMISE.
SOMETHING MUST HAVE HAPPENED TO HIM.
I...
...WAS AFRAID TO LET MYSELF BELIEVE THAT.
IF I WON THE TOURNAMENT...
...THEN MAYBE, JUST ONCE MORE...
...I MIGHT ...
...BE ABLE TO SEE HIM AGAIN.
SO I COULD FINALLY SAY WHAT I COULDN'T TELL HIM...
...BACK THEN.

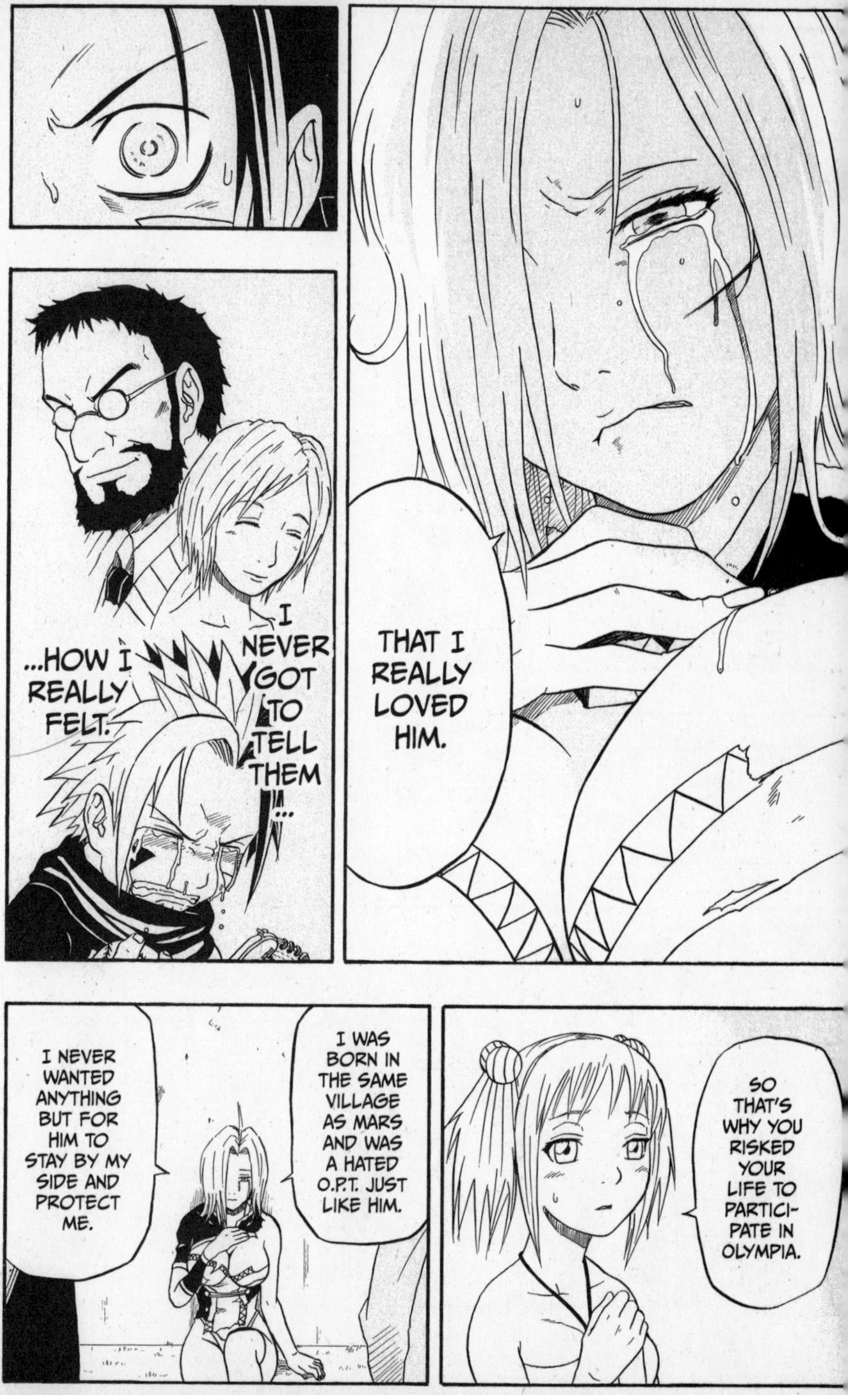
THAT I REALLY LOVED HIM.
I NEVER GOT TO TELL THEM...
...HOW I REALLY FELT.
SO THAT'S WHY YOU RISKED YOUR LIFE TO PARTICI-PATE IN OLYMPIA.
I WAS BORN IN THE SAME VILLAGE AS MARS AND WAS A HATED O.P.T. JUST LIKE HIM.
I NEVER WANTED ANYTHING BUT FOR HIM TO STAY BY MY SIDE AND PROTECT ME.

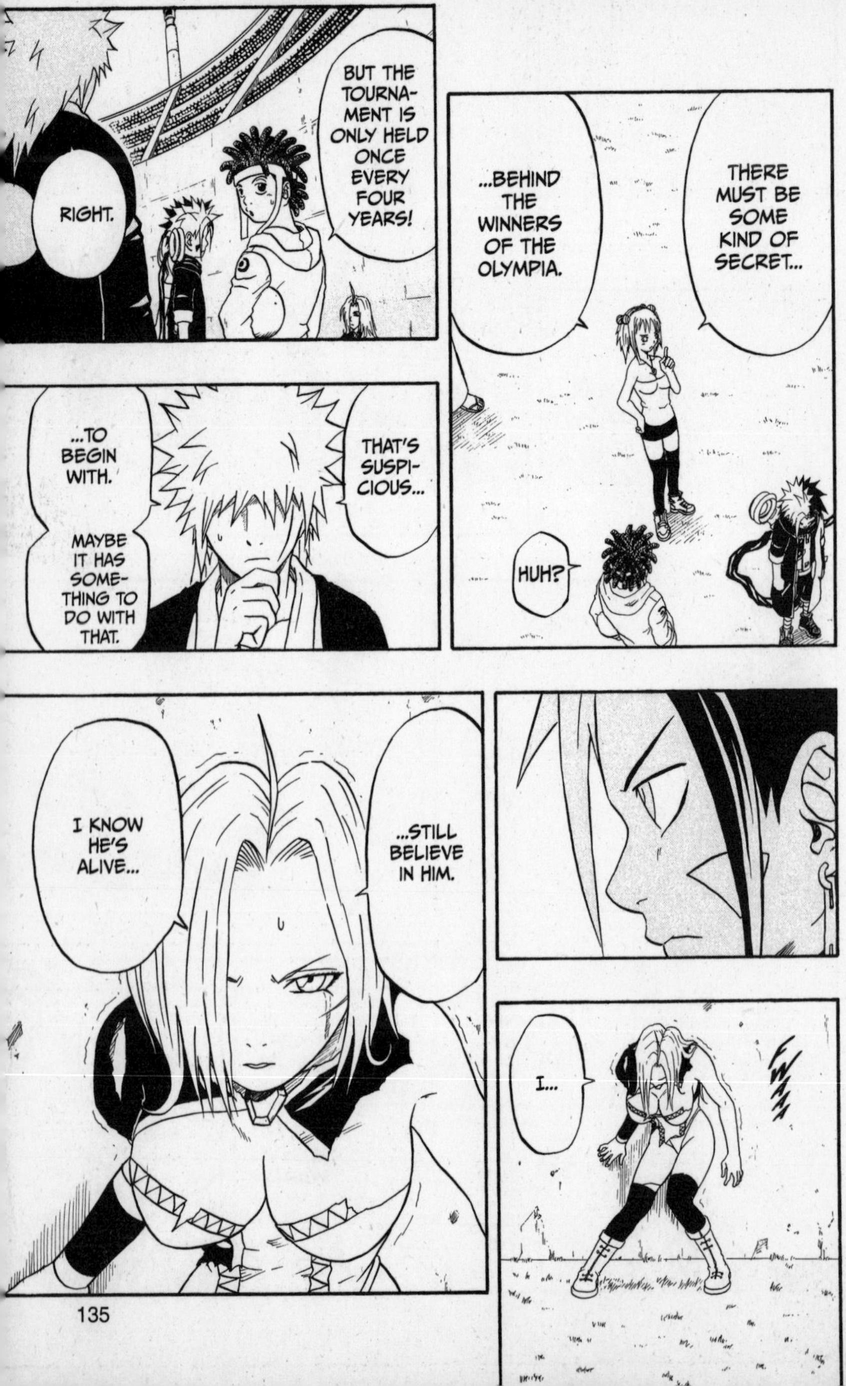
THERE MUST BE SOME KIND OF SECRET...
...BEHIND THE WINNERS OF THE OLYMPIA.
HUH?
BUT THE TOURNAMENT IS ONLY HELD ONCE EVERY FOUR YEARS!
RIGHT.
THAT'S SUSPICIOUS...
...TO BEGIN WITH.
MAYBE IT HAS SOMETHING TO DO WITH THAT.
I...
FWAAA
...STILL BELIEVE IN HIM.
I KNOW HE'S ALIVE...

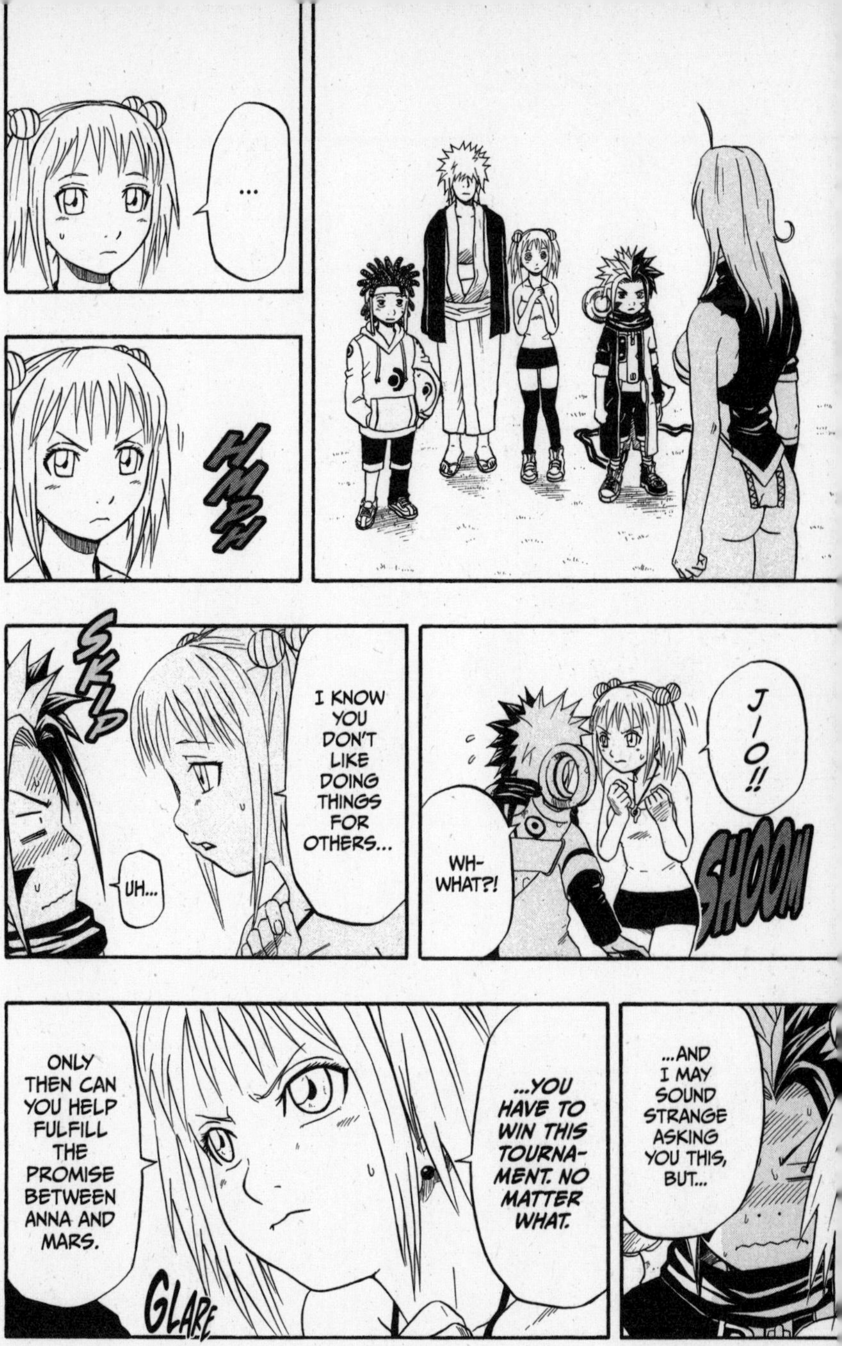
...
HMPH
JIO!!
SHOOM
WH-WHAT?!
SKIP
I KNOW YOU DON'T LIKE DOING THINGS FOR OTHERS...
UH...
...AND I MAY SOUND STRANGE ASKING YOU THIS, BUT...
...YOU HAVE TO WIN THIS TOURNAMENT. NO MATTER WHAT.
ONLY THEN CAN YOU HELP FULFILL THE PROMISE BETWEEN ANNA AND MARS.
GLARE

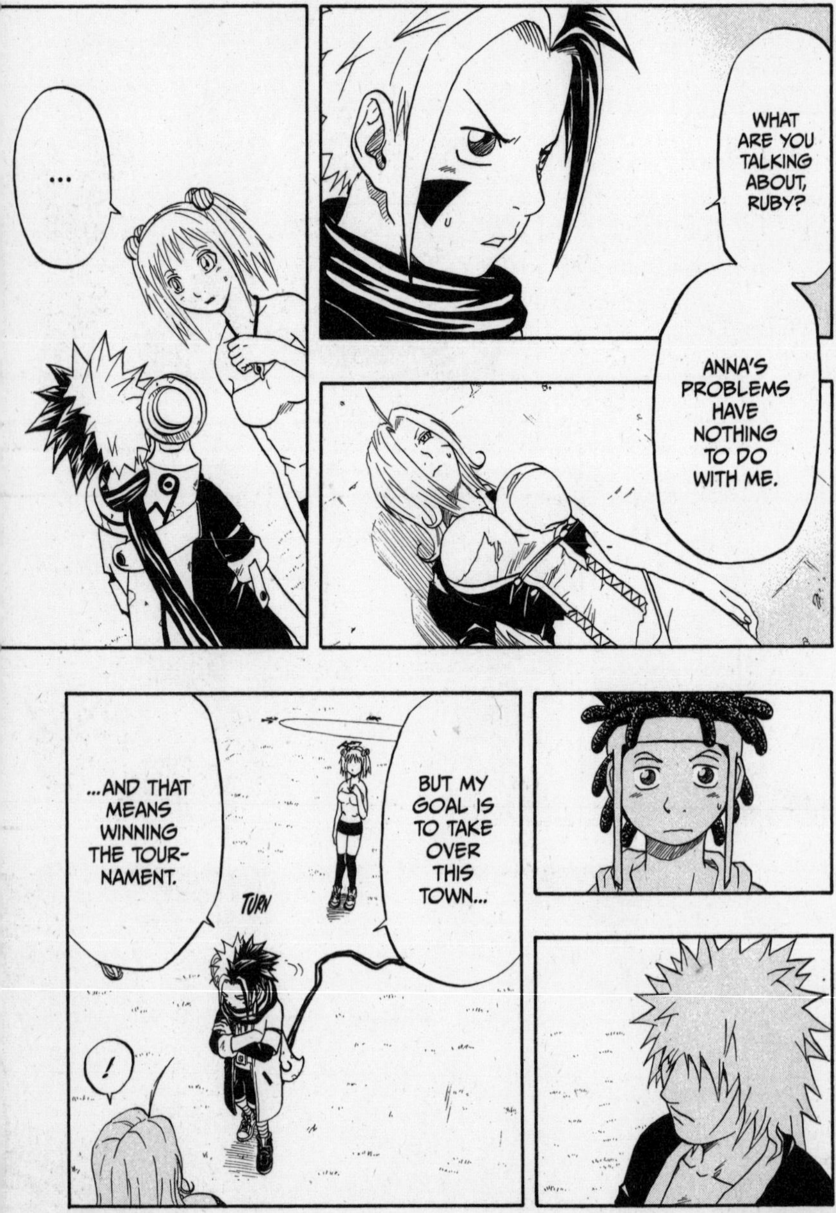
WHAT ARE YOU TALKING ABOUT, RUBY?
ANNA'S PROBLEMS HAVE NOTHING TO DO WITH ME.
...
BUT MY GOAL IS TO TAKE OVER THIS TOWN...
...AND THAT MEANS WINNING THE TOURNAMENT.
TURN
!

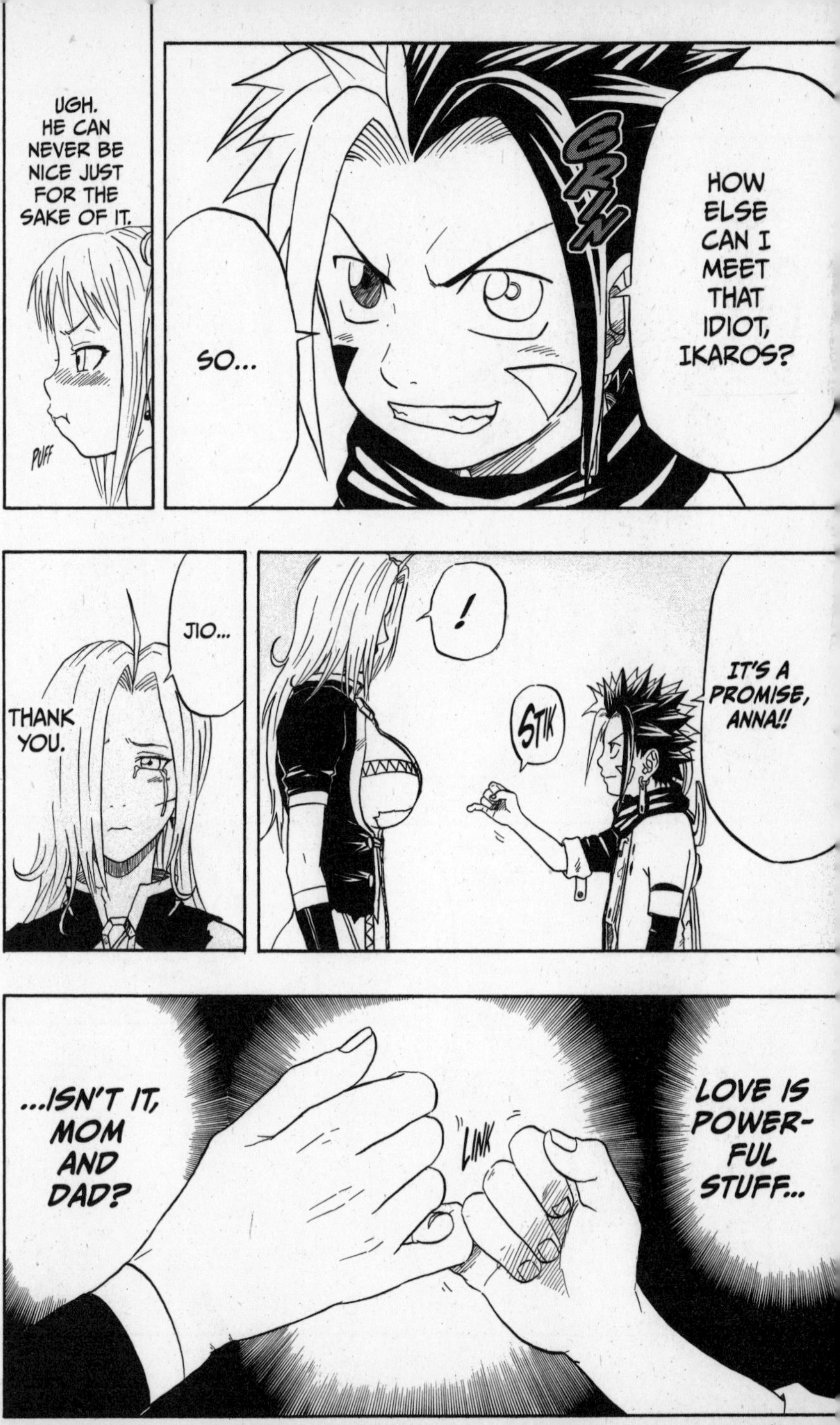
HOW ELSE CAN I MEET THAT IDIOT, IKAROS?
GRIN
SO...
UGH. HE CAN NEVER BE NICE JUST FOR THE SAKE OF IT.
PUFF
IT'S A PROMISE, ANNA!!
STIK
!
JIO...
THANK YOU.
LOVE IS POWER-FUL STUFF...
LINK
...ISN'T IT, MOM AND DAD?

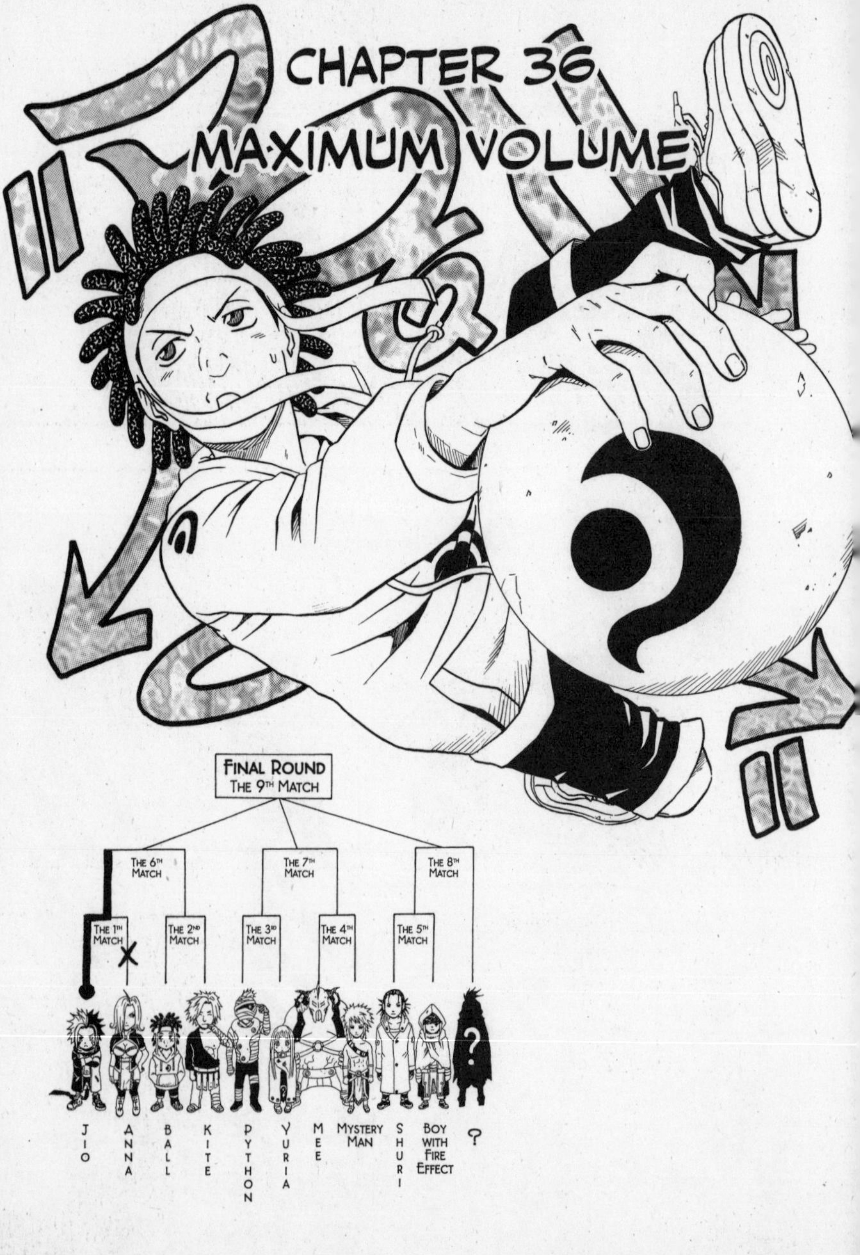
CHAPTER 36
MAXIMUM VOLUME
FINAL ROUND
THE 9TH MATCH
THE 6TH MATCH
THE 7TH MATCH
THE 8TH MATCH
THE 1TH MATCH
THE 2ND MATCH
THE 3RD MATCH
THE 4TH MATCH
THE 5TH MATCH
JIO
ANNA
BALL
KITE
PYTHON
YURIA
MEE
MYSTERY MAN
SHURI
BOY WITH FIRE EFFECT
?

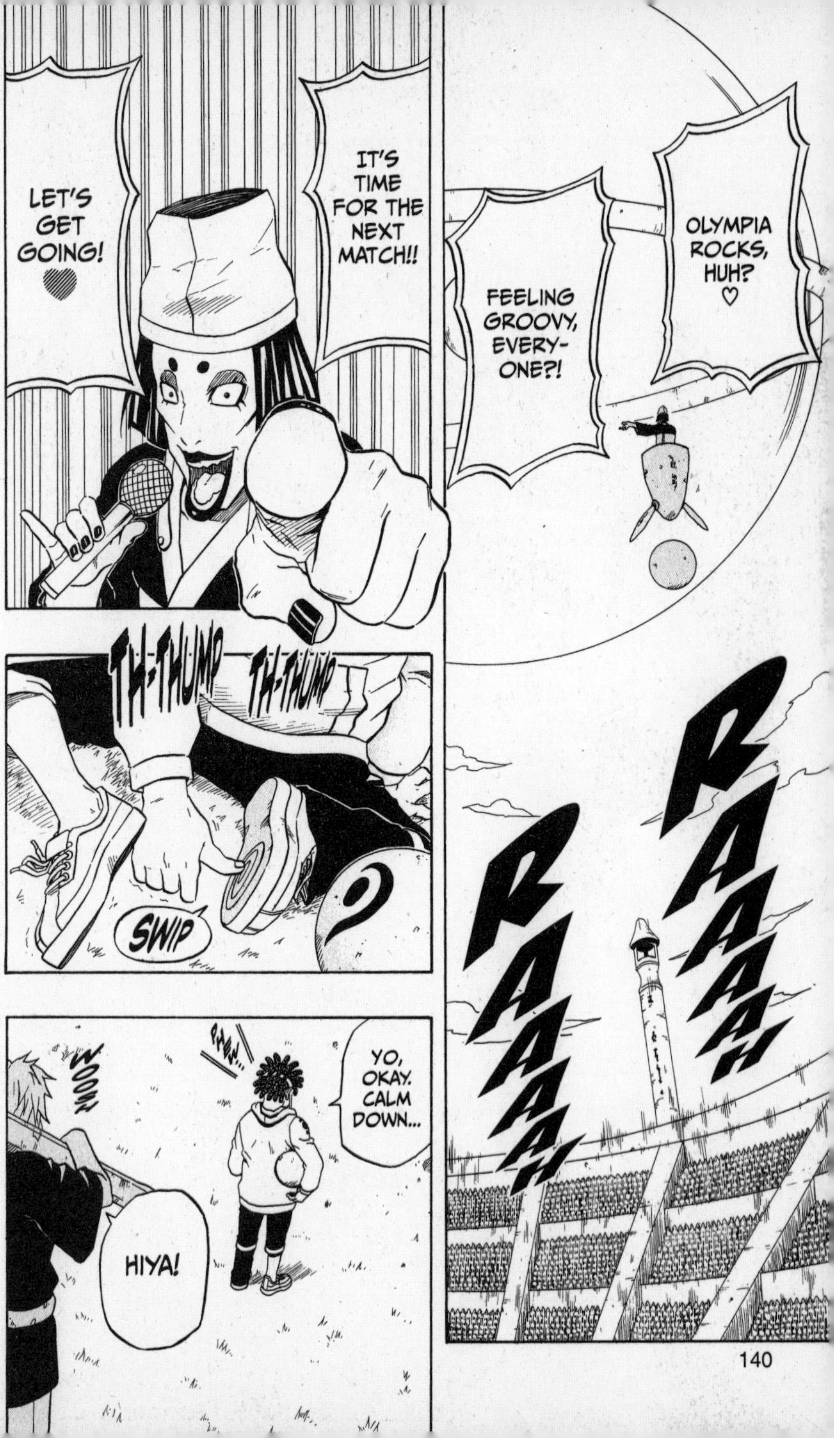
OLYMPIA ROCKS, HUH? ♡
FEELING GROOVY, EVERYONE?!
RAAAAH
RAAAAAH
IT'S TIME FOR THE NEXT MATCH!!
LET'S GET GOING! ♥
TH-THUMP
TH-THUMP
SWIP
YO, OKAY. CALM DOWN...
HIYA!

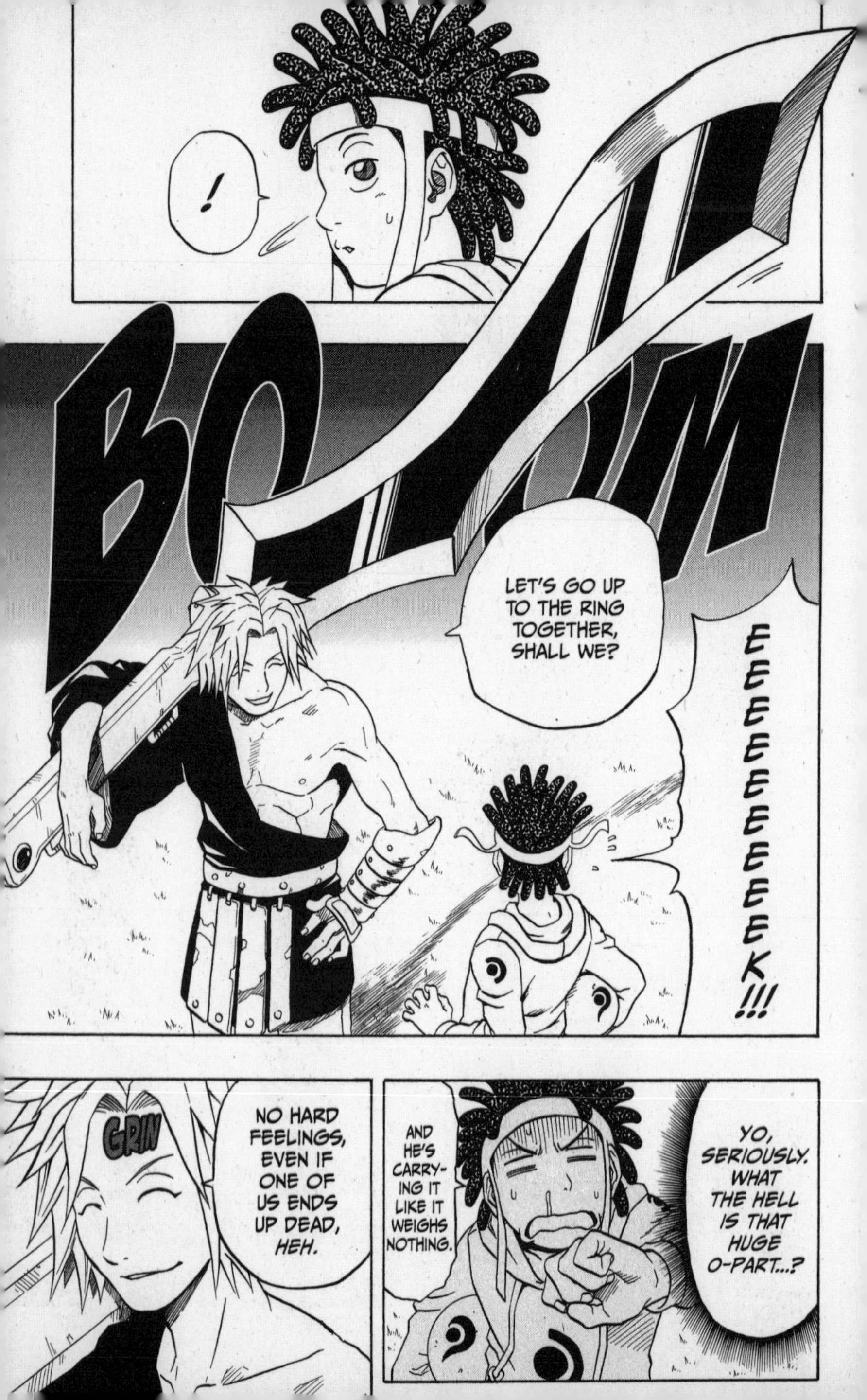
!
BOOM
LET'S GO UP TO THE RING TOGETHER, SHALL WE?
EEEEEEEEEEK!!!
YO, SERIOUSLY. WHAT THE HELL IS THAT HUGE O-PART...?
AND HE'S CARRYING IT LIKE IT WEIGHS NOTHING.
GRIN
NO HARD FEELINGS, EVEN IF ONE OF US ENDS UP DEAD, HEH.

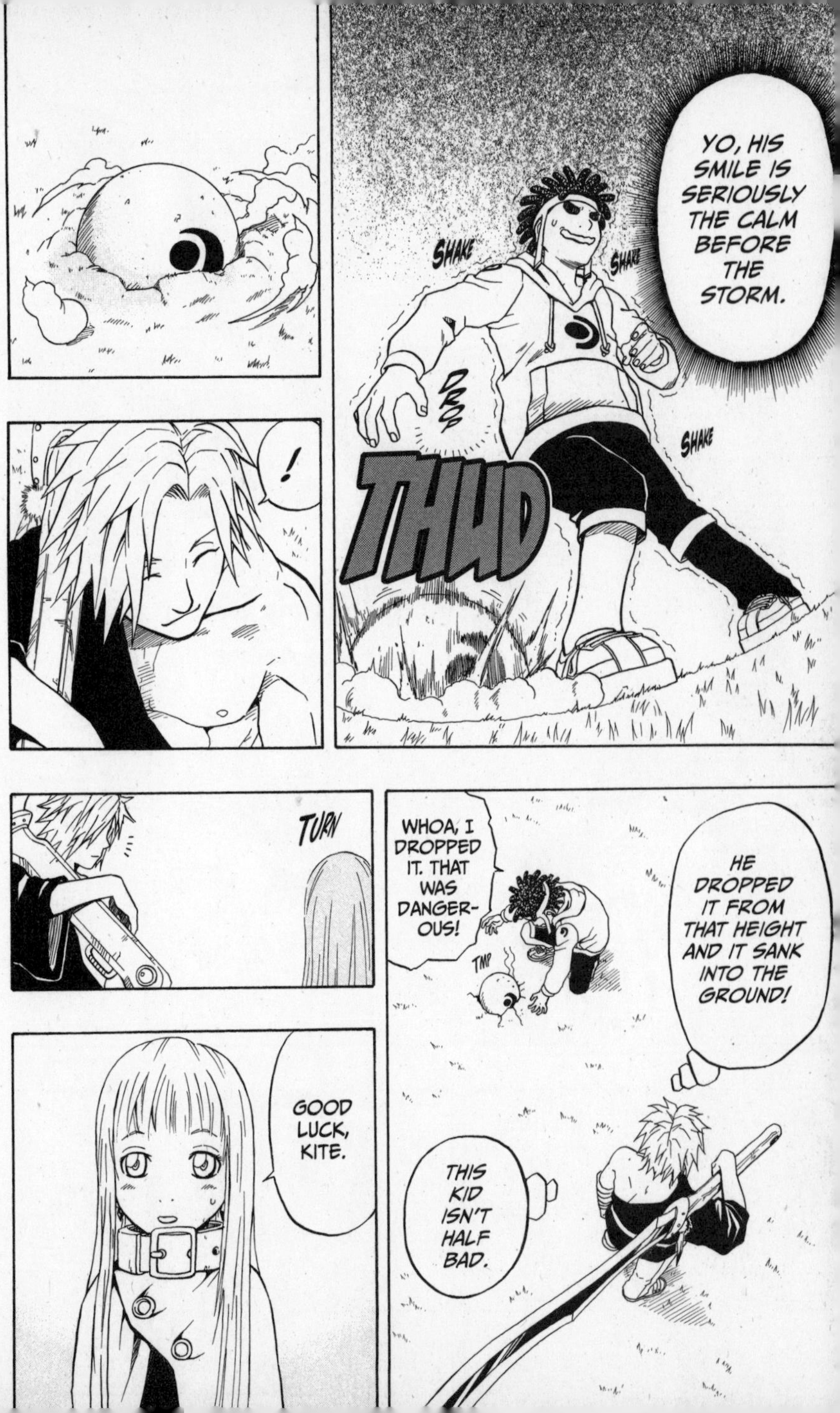
YO, HIS SMILE IS SERIOUSLY THE CALM BEFORE THE STORM.
SHAKE
SHAKE
DROP
THUD
SHAKE
!
WHOA, I DROPPED IT. THAT WAS DANGER-OUS!
HE DROPPED IT FROM THAT HEIGHT AND IT SANK INTO THE GROUND!
TMP
THIS KID ISN'T HALF BAD.
TURN
GOOD LUCK, KITE.

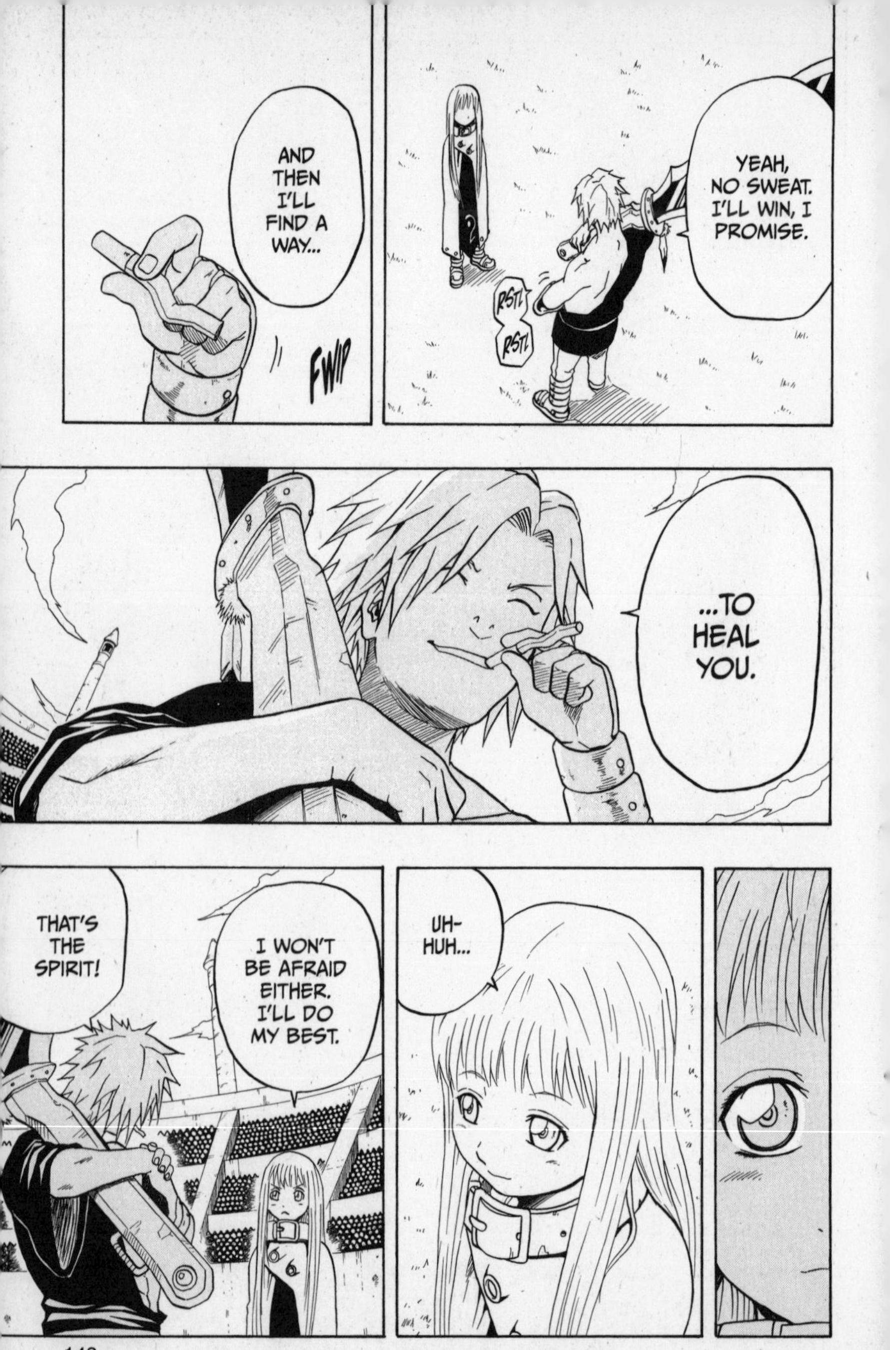
YEAH, NO SWEAT. I'LL WIN, I PROMISE.
RSTL
RSTL
AND THEN I'LL FIND A WAY...
FWIP
...TO HEAL YOU.
UH-HUH...
I WON'T BE AFRAID EITHER. I'LL DO MY BEST.
THAT'S THE SPIRIT!

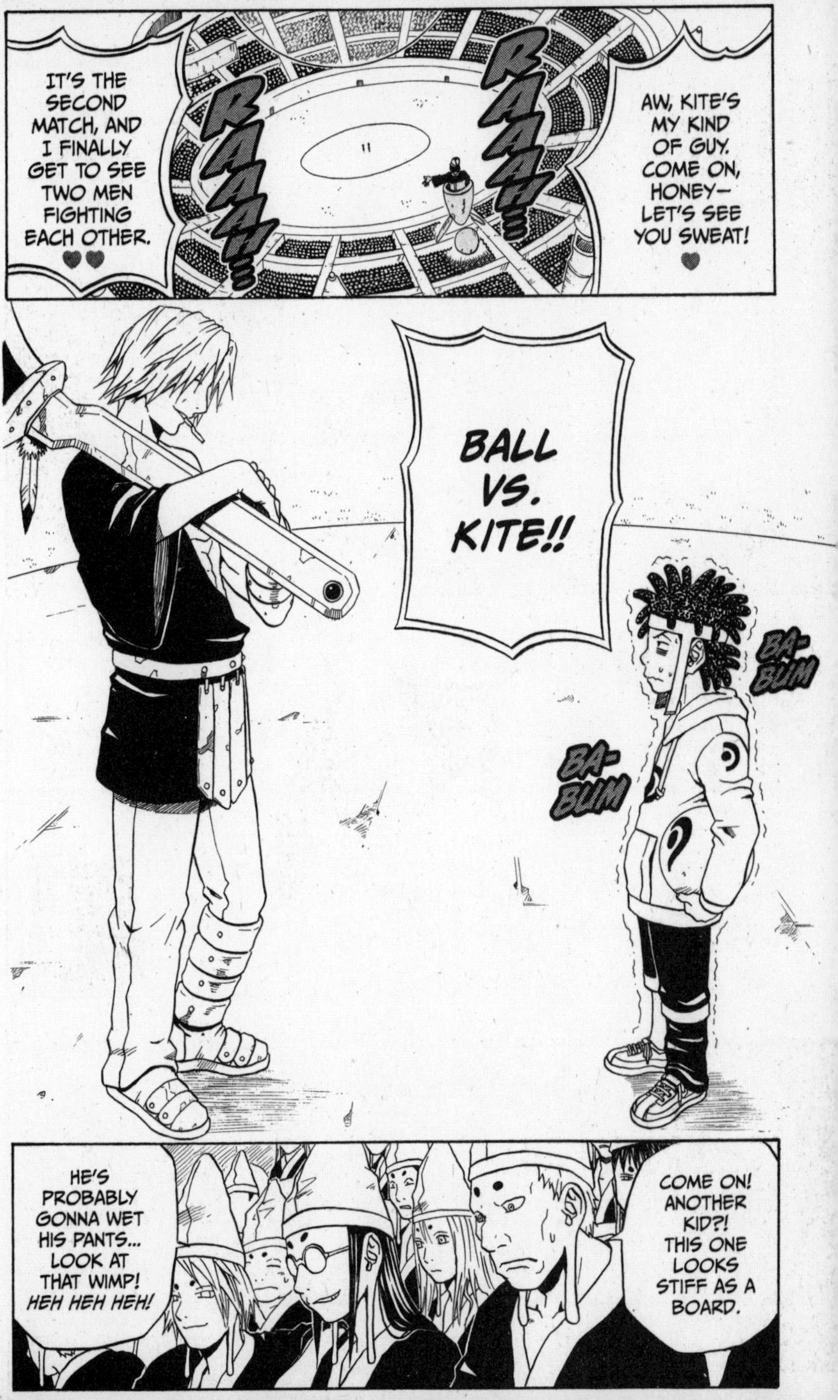
AW, KITE'S MY KIND OF GUY. COME ON, HONEY— LET'S SEE YOU SWEAT! ♥
RAAAAH
RAAAAH
IT'S THE SECOND MATCH, AND I FINALLY GET TO SEE TWO MEN FIGHTING EACH OTHER. ♥♥
BA-BUM
BA-BUM
BALL VS. KITE!!
COME ON! ANOTHER KID?! THIS ONE LOOKS STIFF AS A BOARD.
HE'S PROBABLY GONNA WET HIS PANTS... LOOK AT THAT WIMP! *HEH HEH HEH!*

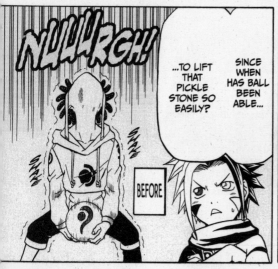

COME TO THINK OF IT...
SINCE WHEN HAS BALL BEEN ABLE...
...TO LIFT THAT PICKLE STONE SO EASILY?
BEFORE
NUUURGH!
SHAKE
SHAKE
NAH, THAT'S THE DIFFERENCE BETWEEN YOU AND HIM, JIO.
OOH.
WHENEVER BALL USES HIS O-PART, HE MAKES USE OF THE MAGNETISM EFFECT...
...AND CHARGES THE LEFT-OVER SPIRIT INSIDE IT!
SO WHEN HE'S WALKING AROUND WITH IT, HE'S USING THE EXTRA SPIRIT HE CHARGED.
BUT HE HAS NO IDEA HE'S DOING IT.

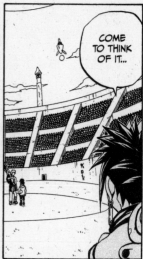

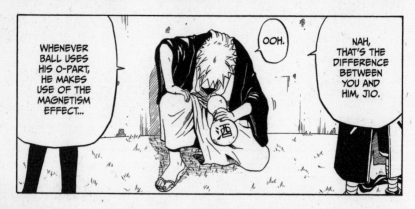

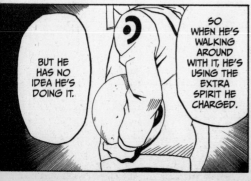

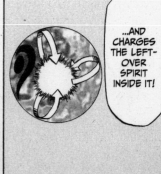

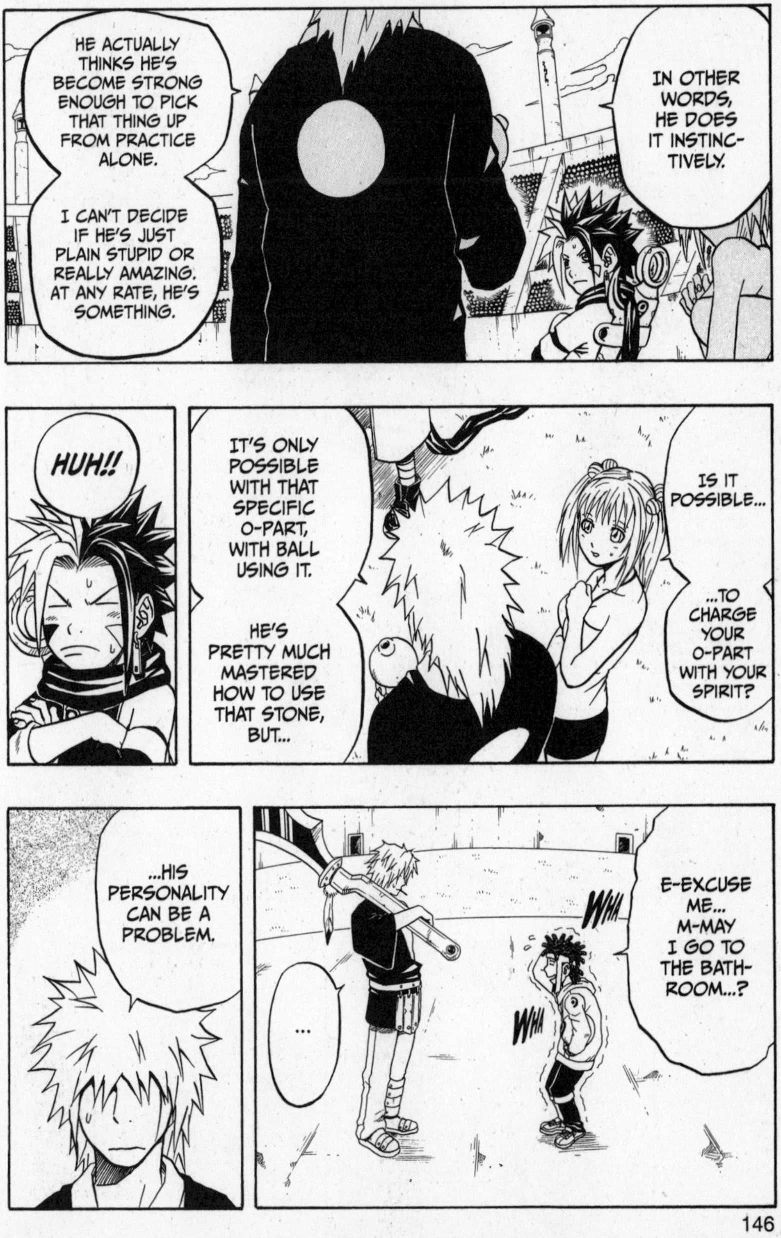
IN OTHER WORDS, HE DOES IT INSTINCTIVELY.
HE ACTUALLY THINKS HE'S BECOME STRONG ENOUGH TO PICK THAT THING UP FROM PRACTICE ALONE.
I CAN'T DECIDE IF HE'S JUST PLAIN STUPID OR REALLY AMAZING. AT ANY RATE, HE'S SOMETHING.
IS IT POSSIBLE...
...TO CHARGE YOUR O-PART WITH YOUR SPIRIT?
IT'S ONLY POSSIBLE WITH THAT SPECIFIC O-PART, WITH BALL USING IT.
HE'S PRETTY MUCH MASTERED HOW TO USE THAT STONE, BUT...
HUH!!
E-EXCUSE ME... M-MAY I GO TO THE BATHROOM...?
WHA
WHA
...
...HIS PERSONALITY CAN BE A PROBLEM.

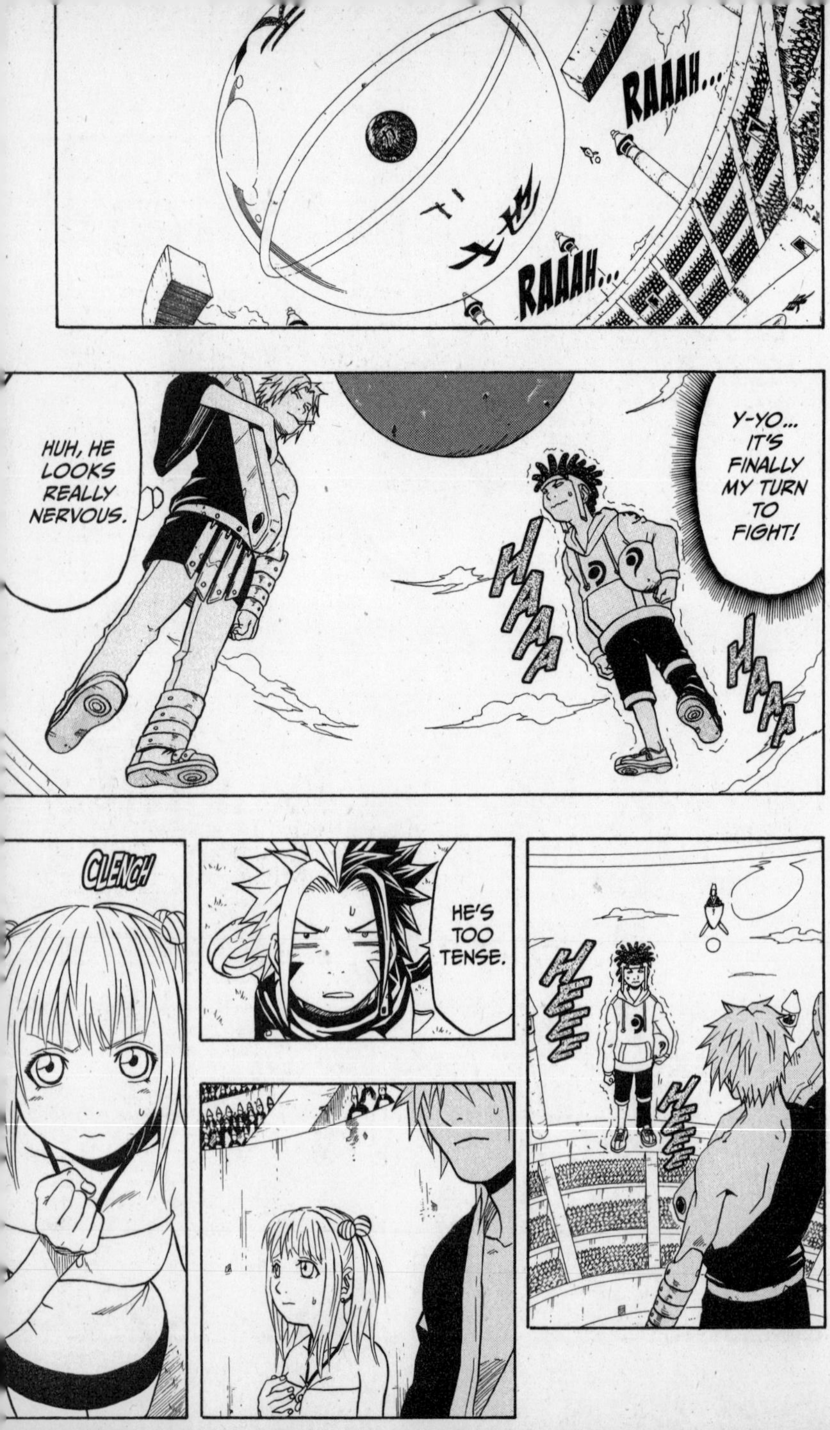
RAAAH...
RAAAH...
Y-YO... IT'S FINALLY MY TURN TO FIGHT!
HUH, HE LOOKS REALLY NERVOUS.
HE'S TOO TENSE.
CLENCH

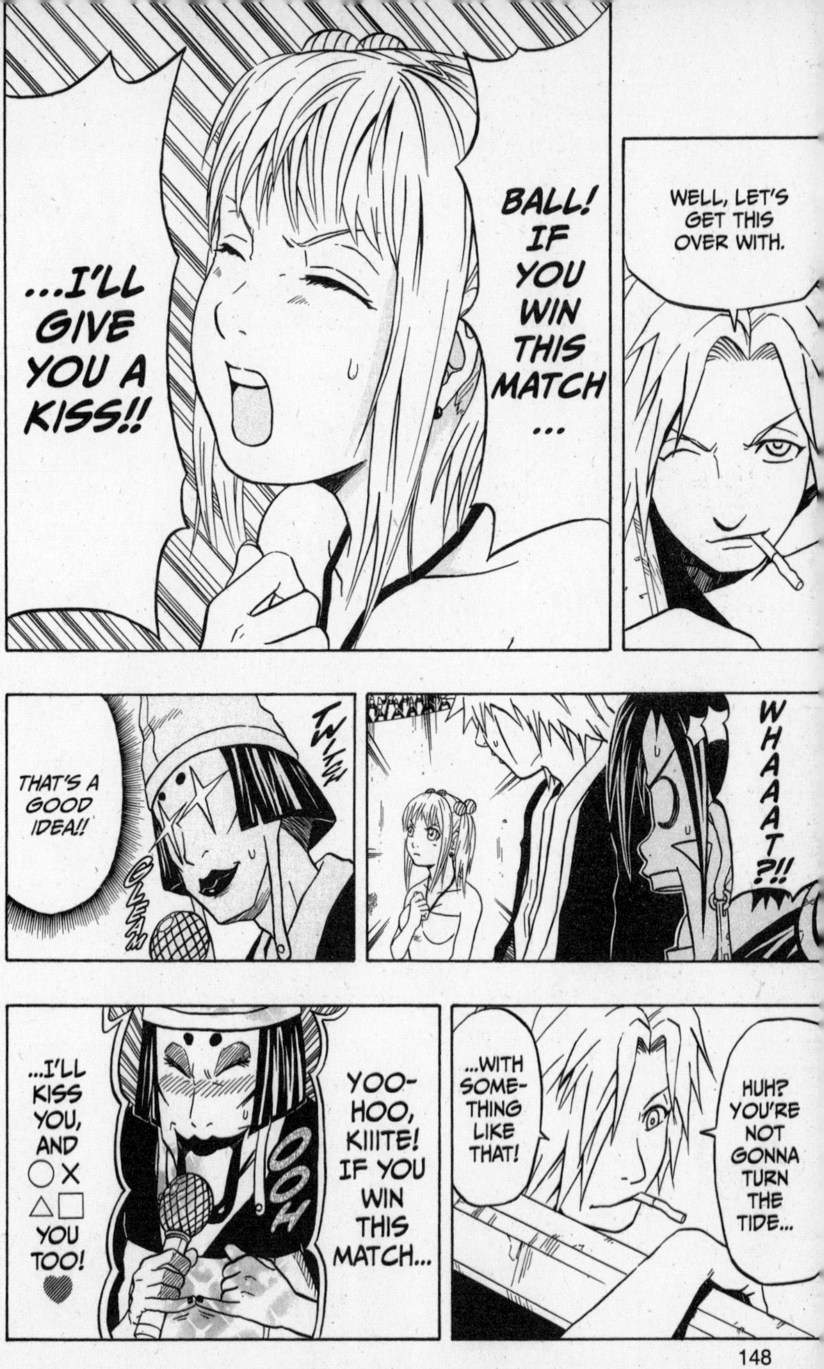
WELL, LET'S GET THIS OVER WITH.
BALL! IF YOU WIN THIS MATCH ...
...I'LL GIVE YOU A KISS!!
WHAAAAT?!!
THAT'S A GOOD IDEA!!
HUH? YOU'RE NOT GONNA TURN THE TIDE...
...WITH SOMETHING LIKE THAT!
YOO-HOO, KIIITE! IF YOU WIN THIS MATCH...
...I'LL KISS YOU, AND ○X △□ YOU TOO! ♥

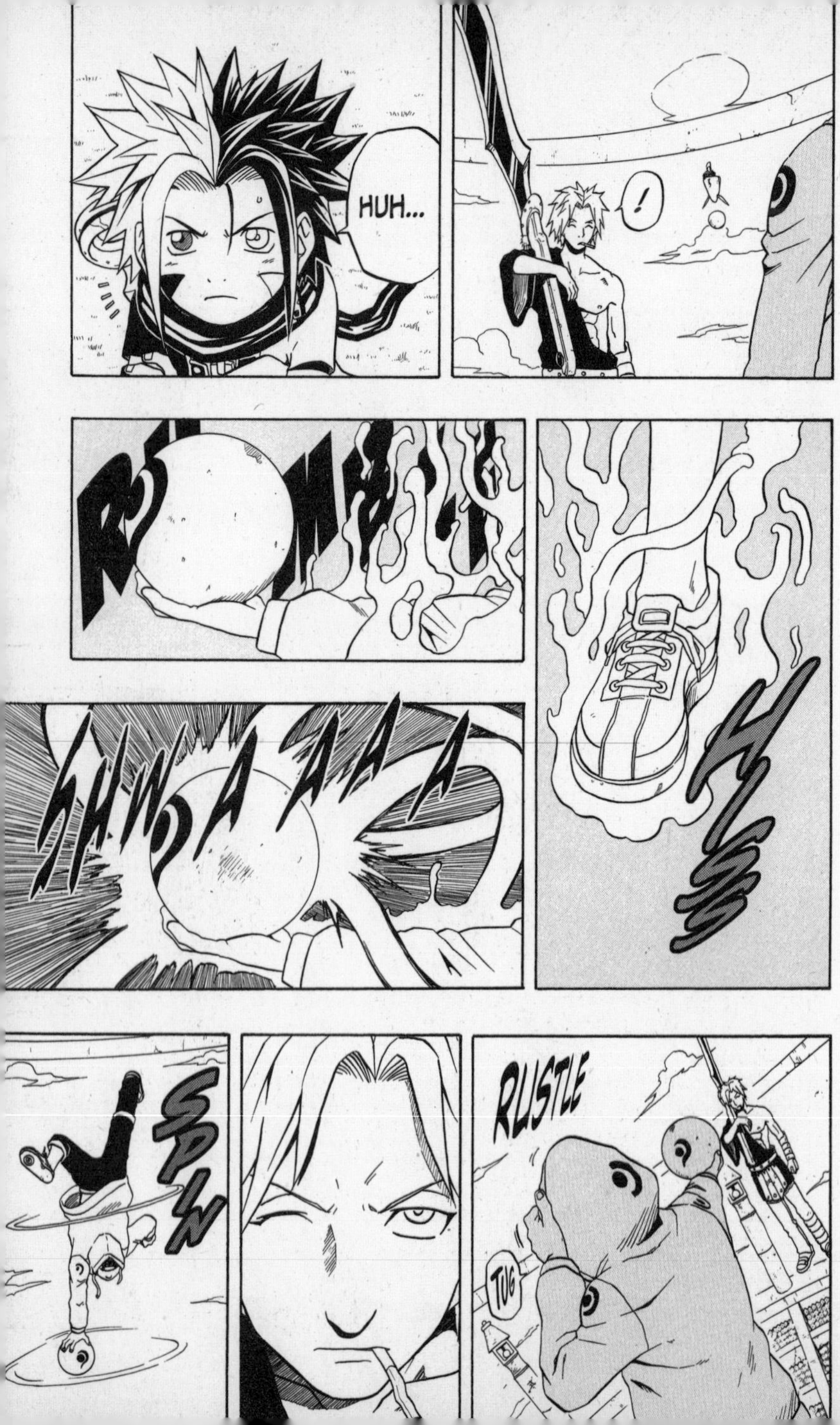
!
HUH...
SHWOAAAA
RUSTLE
TUG
SPIN

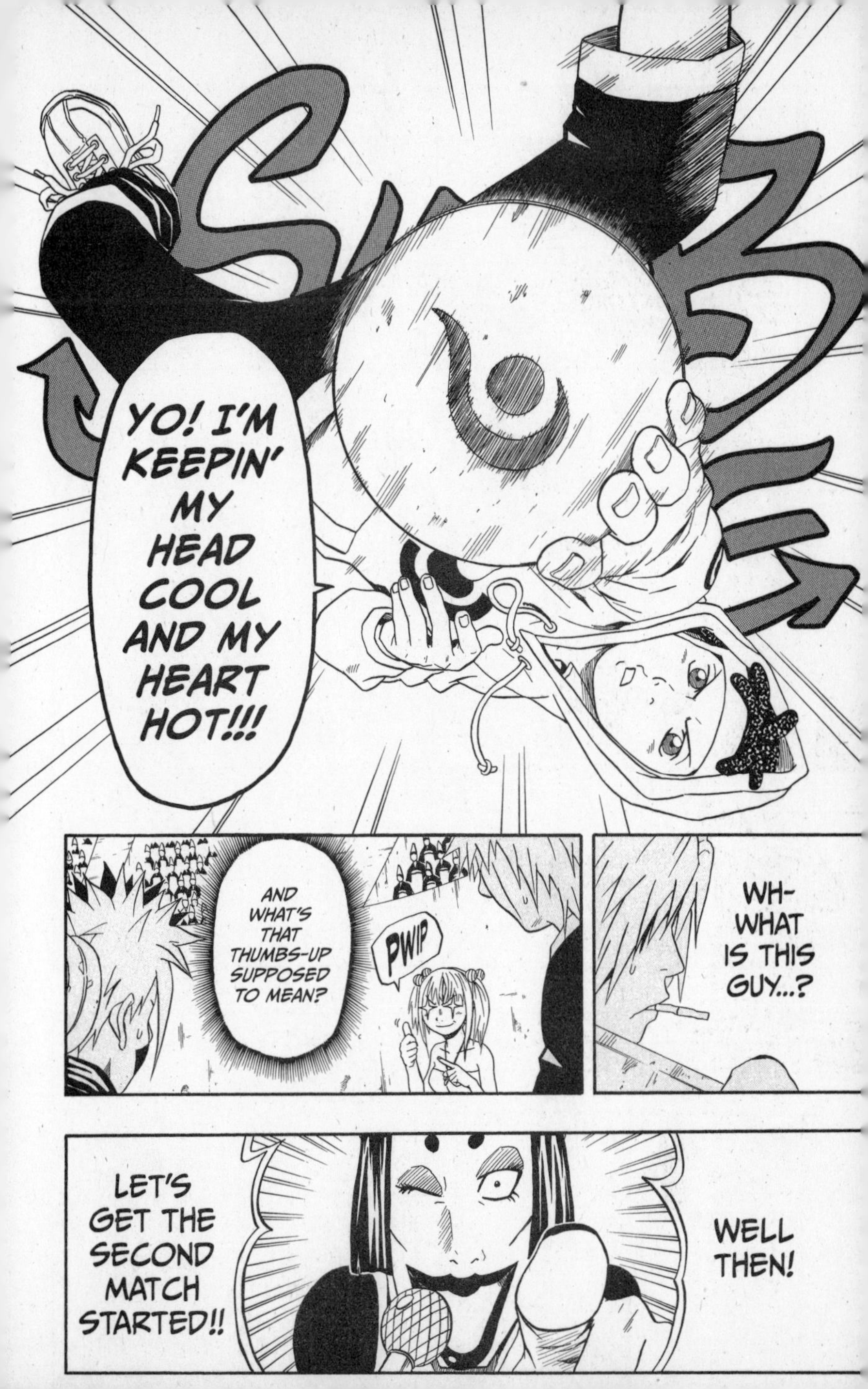
YO! I'M KEEPIN' MY HEAD COOL AND MY HEART HOT!!!
WH-WHAT IS THIS GUY...?
AND WHAT'S THAT THUMBS-UP SUPPOSED TO MEAN?
PWIP
WELL THEN!
LET'S GET THE SECOND MATCH STARTED!!

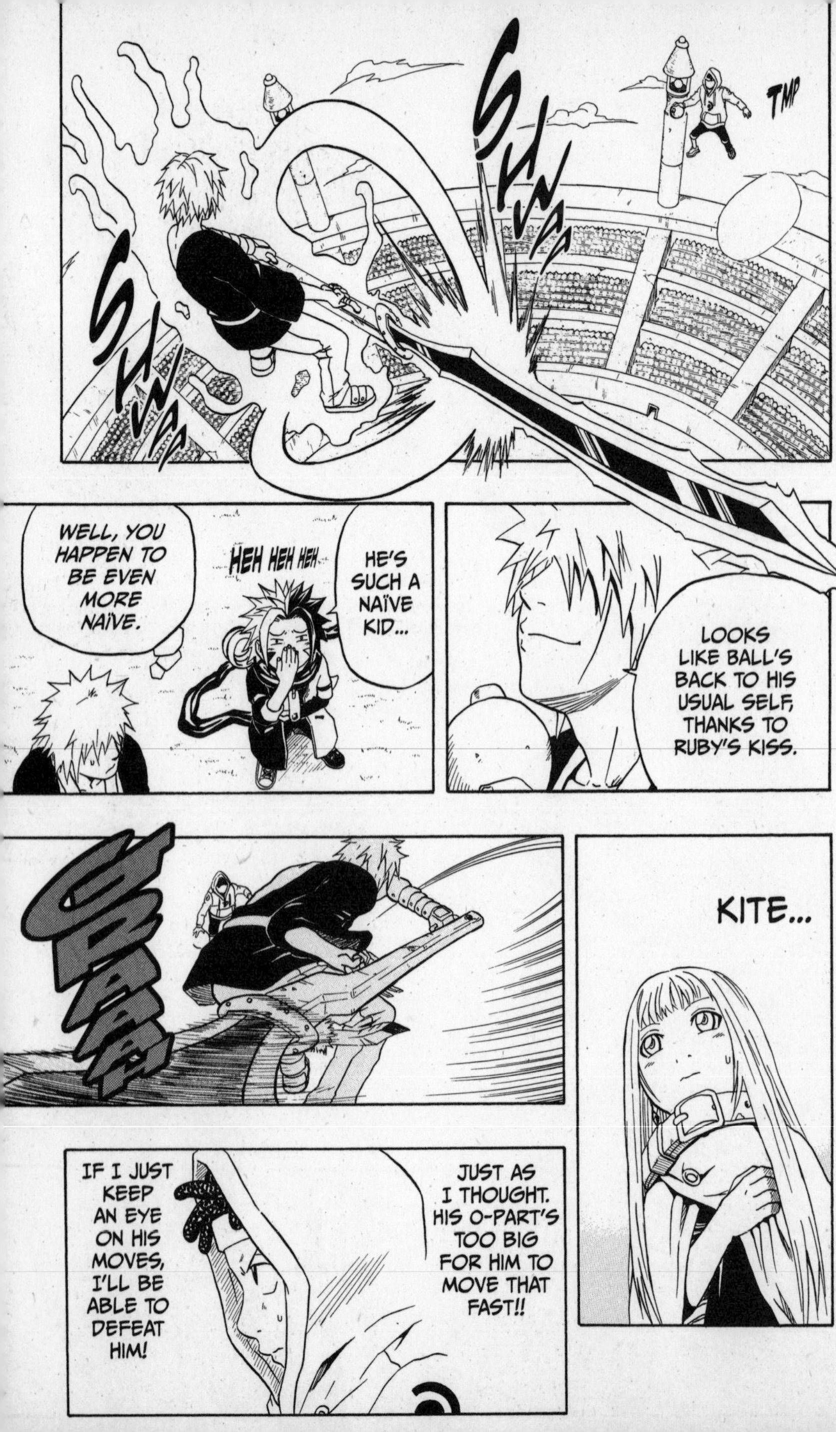
TMP
LOOKS LIKE BALL'S BACK TO HIS USUAL SELF, THANKS TO RUBY'S KISS.
HE'S SUCH A NAÏVE KID...
HEH HEH HEH
WELL, YOU HAPPEN TO BE EVEN MORE NAÏVE.
KITE...
JUST AS I THOUGHT. HIS O-PART'S TOO BIG FOR HIM TO MOVE THAT FAST!!
IF I JUST KEEP AN EYE ON HIS MOVES, I'LL BE ABLE TO DEFEAT HIM!

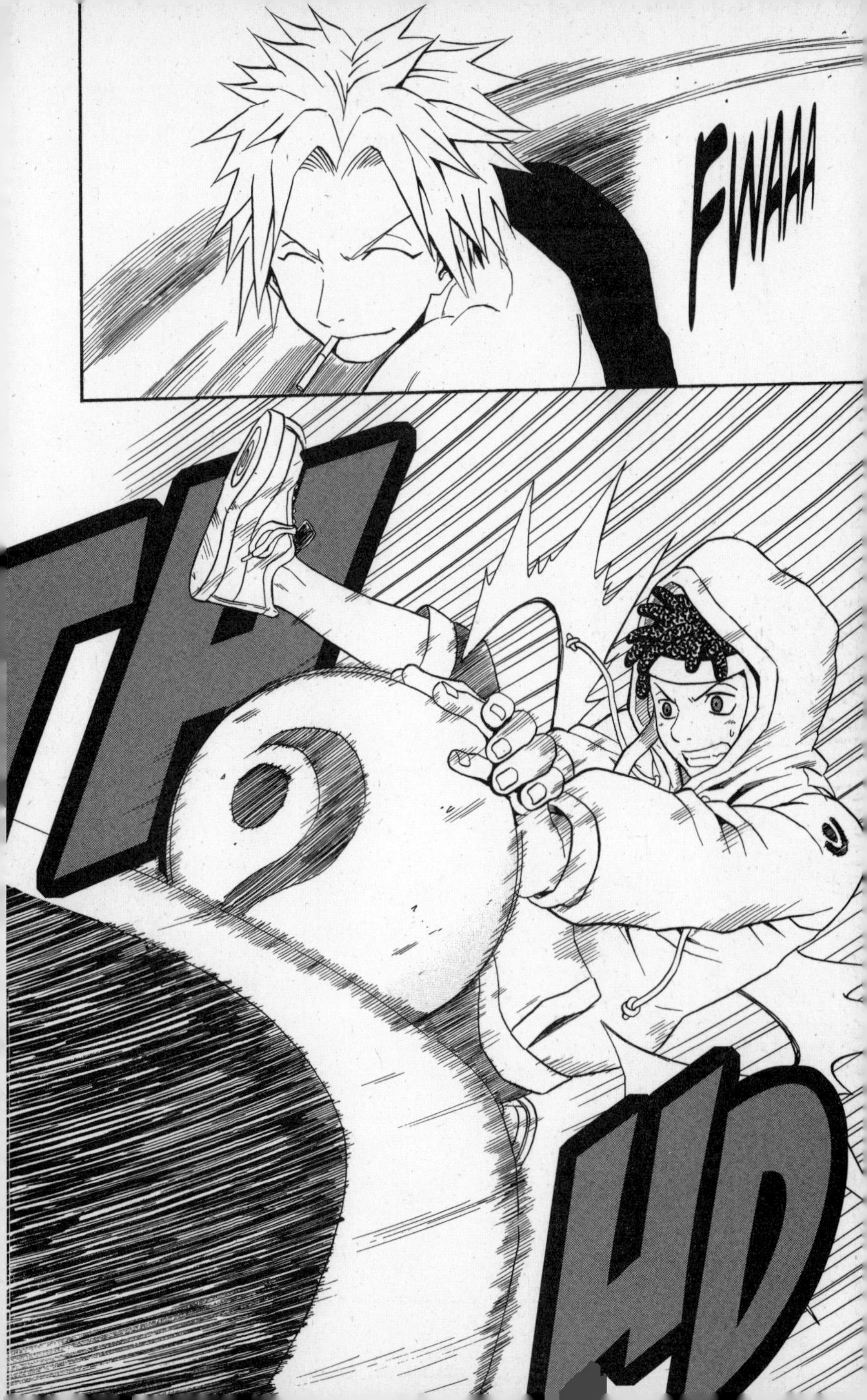
FWAAA

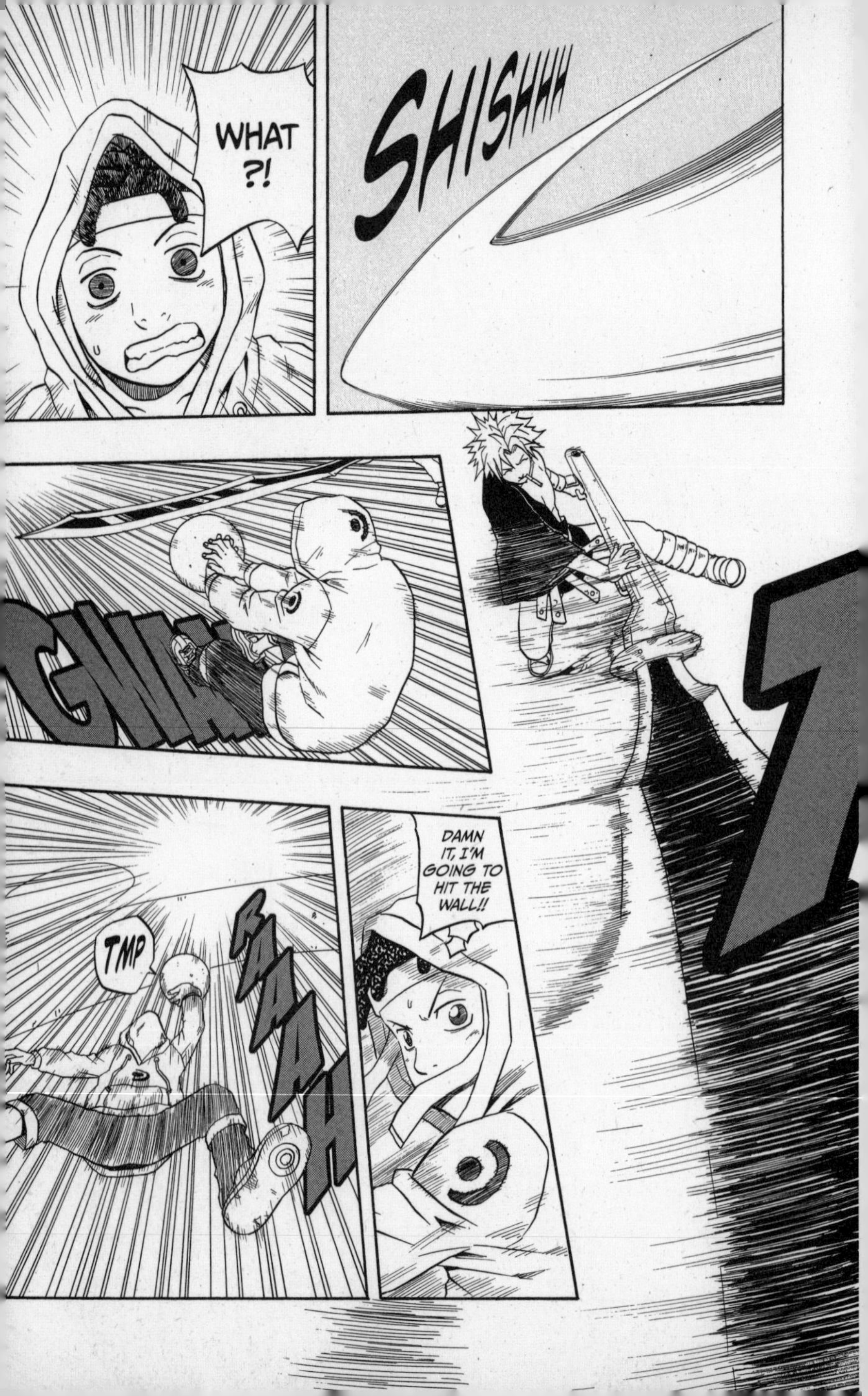
SHISHHH
WHAT ?!
DAMN IT, I'M GOING TO HIT THE WALL!!
TMP
RAAAAH

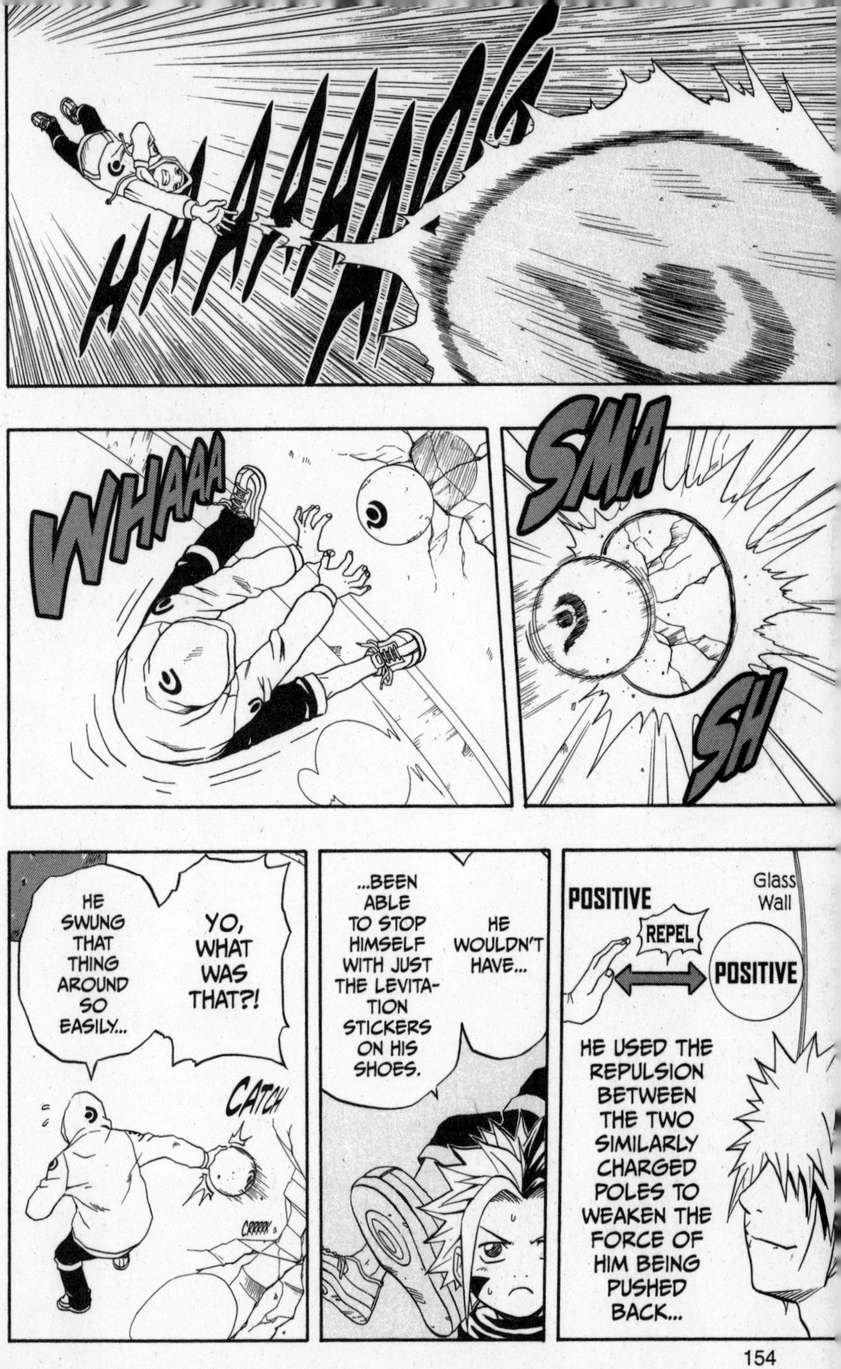
SMA
SH
WHAAA
POSITIVE
Glass Wall
REPEL
POSITIVE
HE USED THE REPULSION BETWEEN THE TWO SIMILARLY CHARGED POLES TO WEAKEN THE FORCE OF HIM BEING PUSHED BACK...
HE WOULDN'T HAVE...
...BEEN ABLE TO STOP HIMSELF WITH JUST THE LEVITA-TION STICKERS ON HIS SHOES.
YO, WHAT WAS THAT?!
HE SWUNG THAT THING AROUND SO EASILY...
CATCH
CRRRK

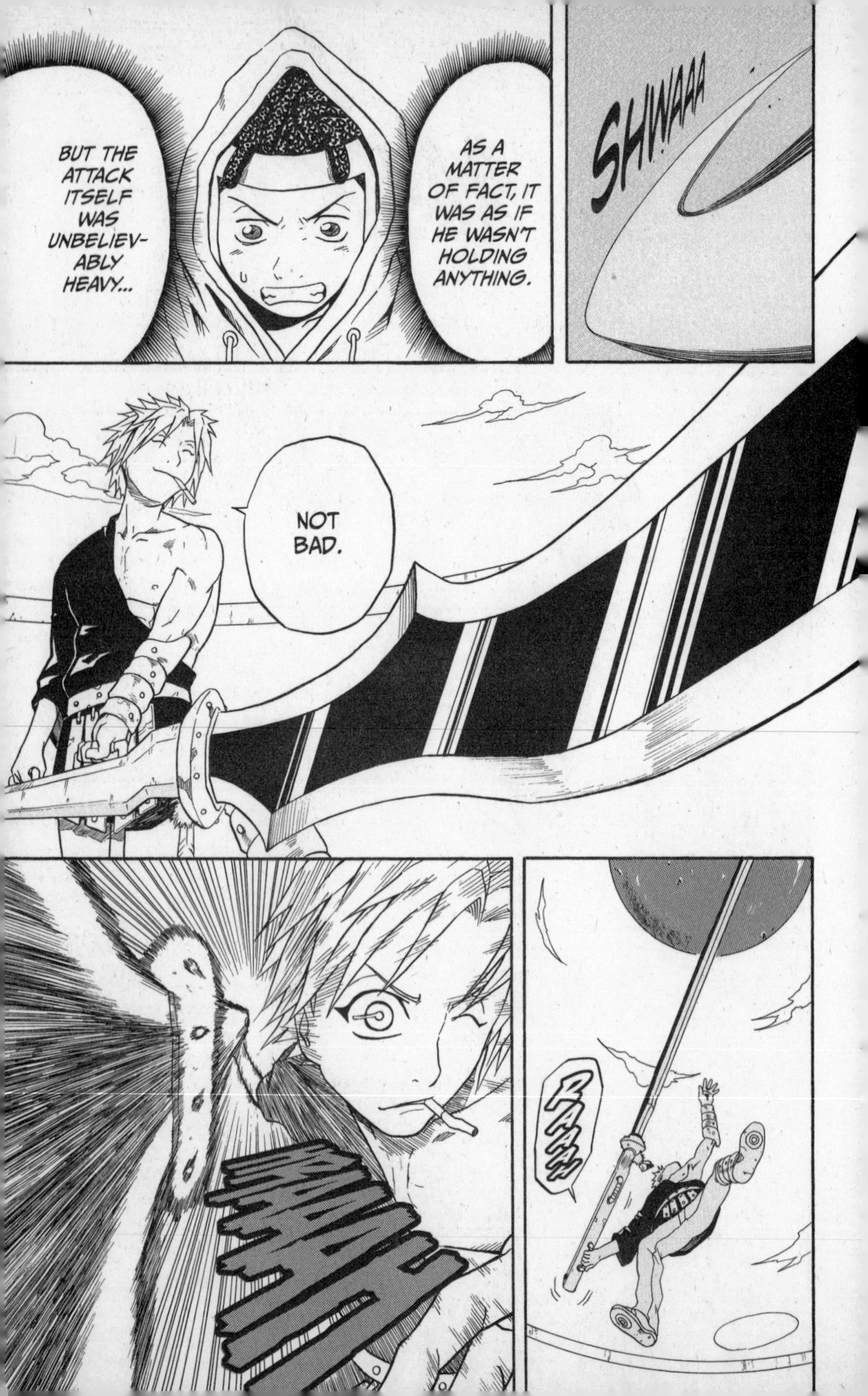
SHWAAA
AS A MATTER OF FACT, IT WAS AS IF HE WASN'T HOLDING ANYTHING.
BUT THE ATTACK ITSELF WAS UNBELIEV-ABLY HEAVY...
NOT BAD.

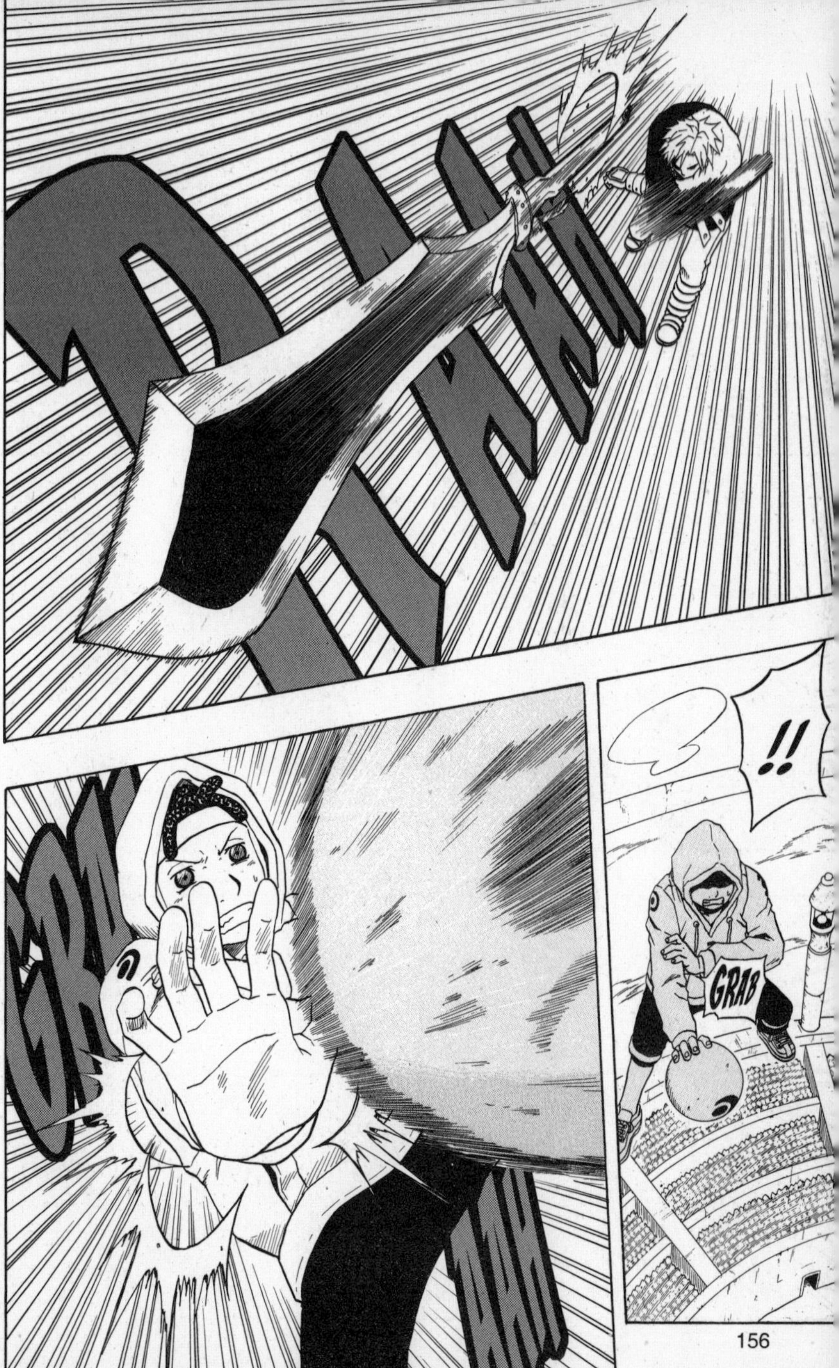
!!
GRAB

FWAAAAA
CLANK
FOR REAL?!
THUD
STAB

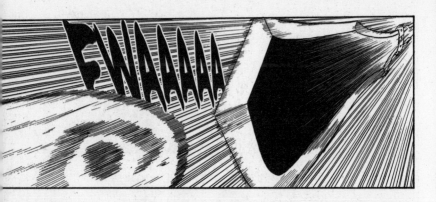

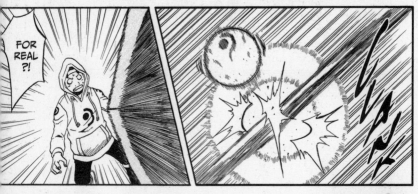

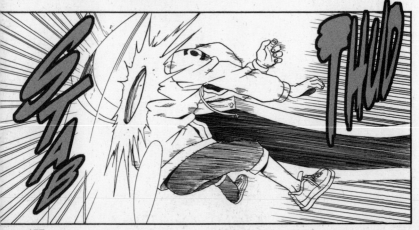

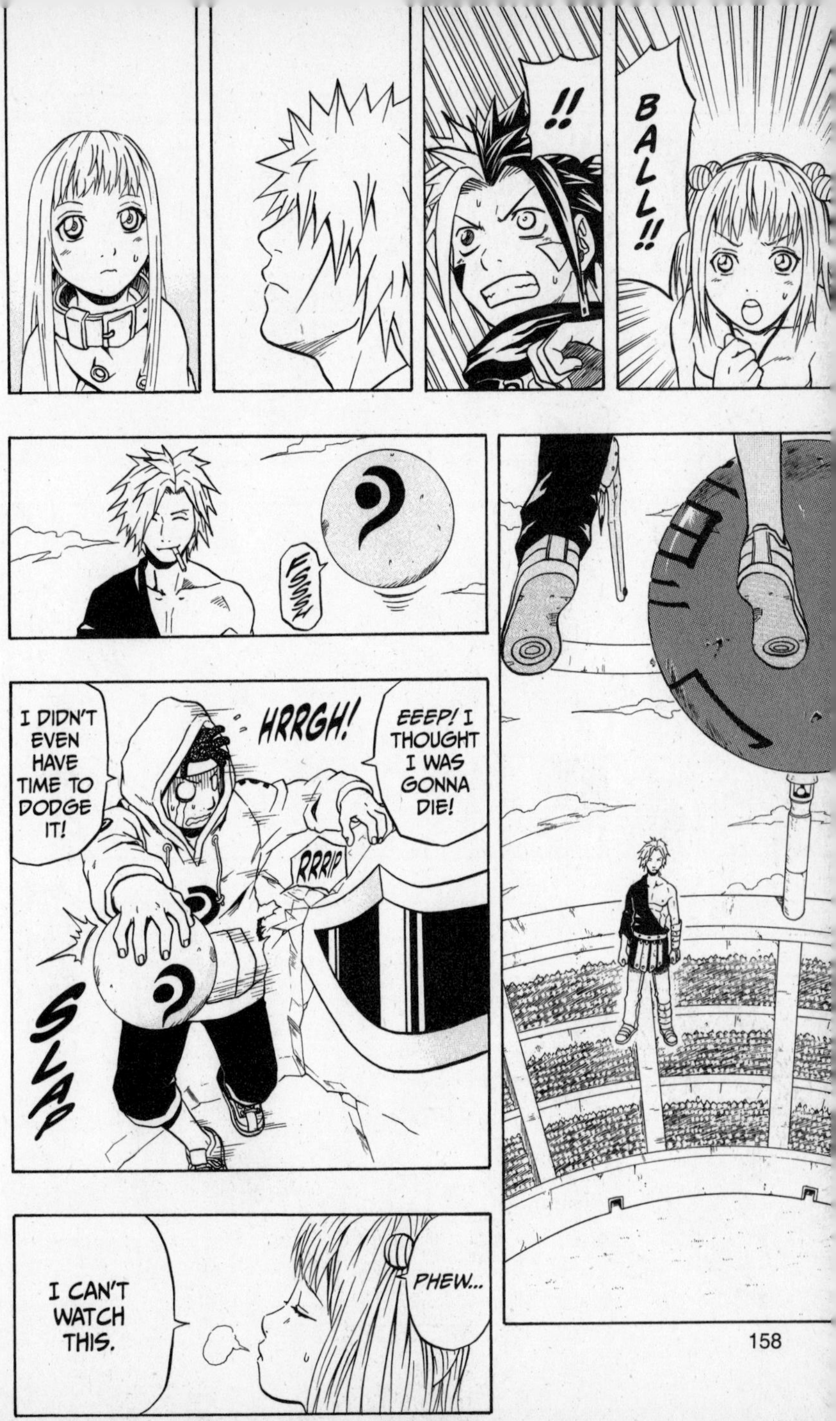
BALL!!
!!
EEEP! I THOUGHT I WAS GONNA DIE!
HRRGH!
I DIDN'T EVEN HAVE TIME TO DODGE IT!
RRRIP
SLAP
PHEW...
I CAN'T WATCH THIS.

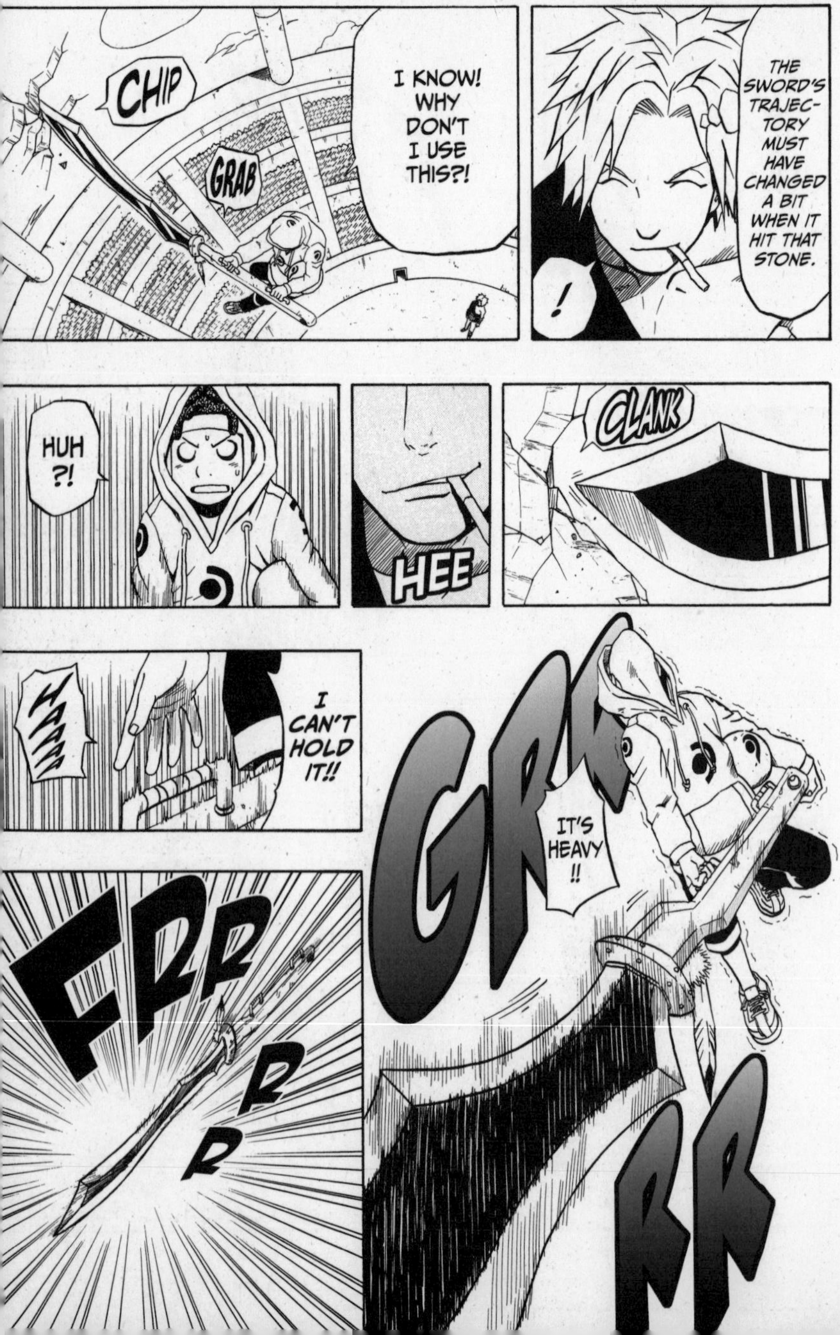
THE SWORD'S TRAJECTORY MUST HAVE CHANGED A BIT WHEN IT HIT THAT STONE.
!
I KNOW! WHY DON'T I USE THIS?!
CHIP
GRAB
CLANK
HEE
HUH ?!
GRRRR
IT'S HEAVY !!
I CAN'T HOLD IT!!
FRRRR

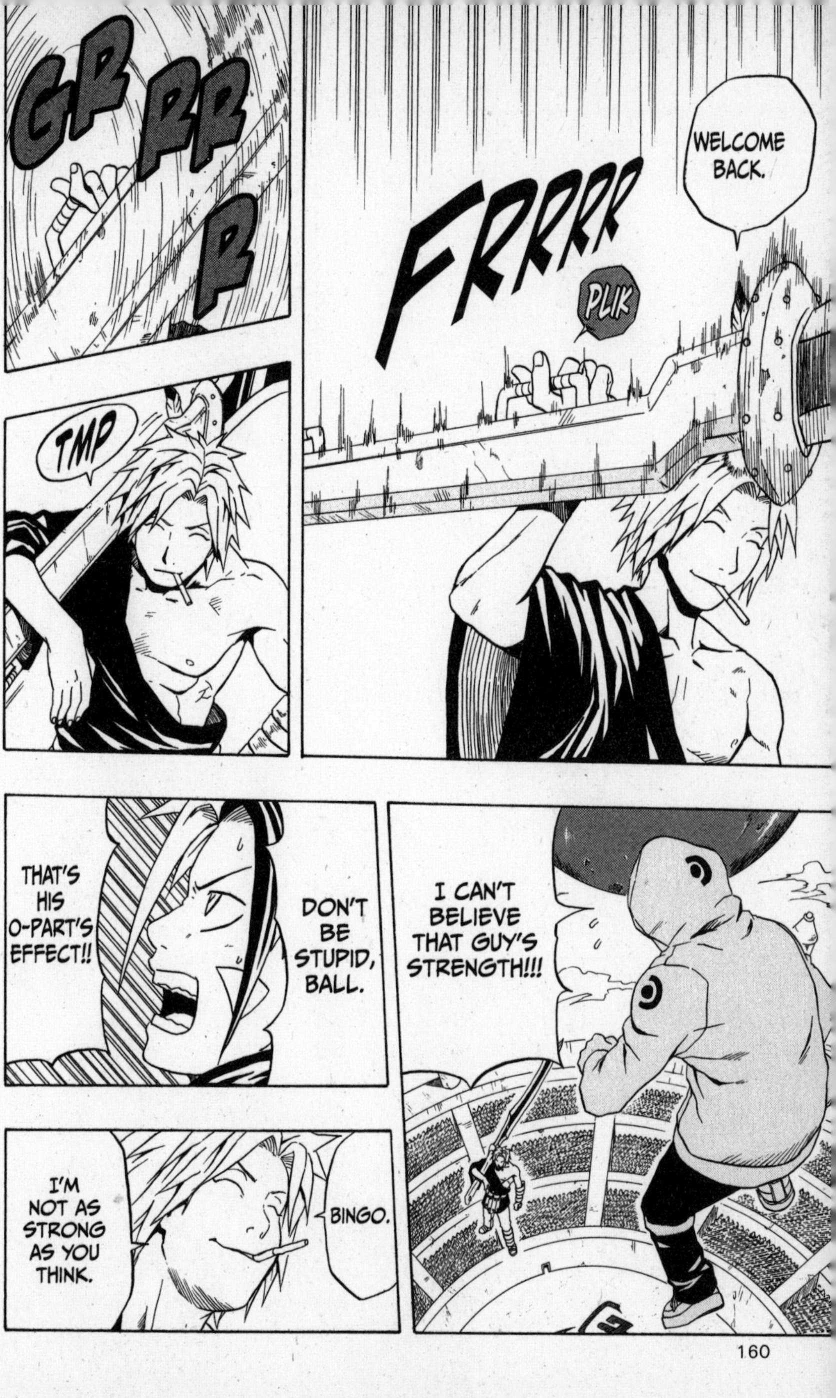
WELCOME BACK.
FRRRRR
PLIK
GRRRR
TMP
I CAN'T BELIEVE THAT GUY'S STRENGTH!!!
DON'T BE STUPID, BALL.
THAT'S HIS O-PART'S EFFECT!!
BINGO.
I'M NOT AS STRONG AS YOU THINK.

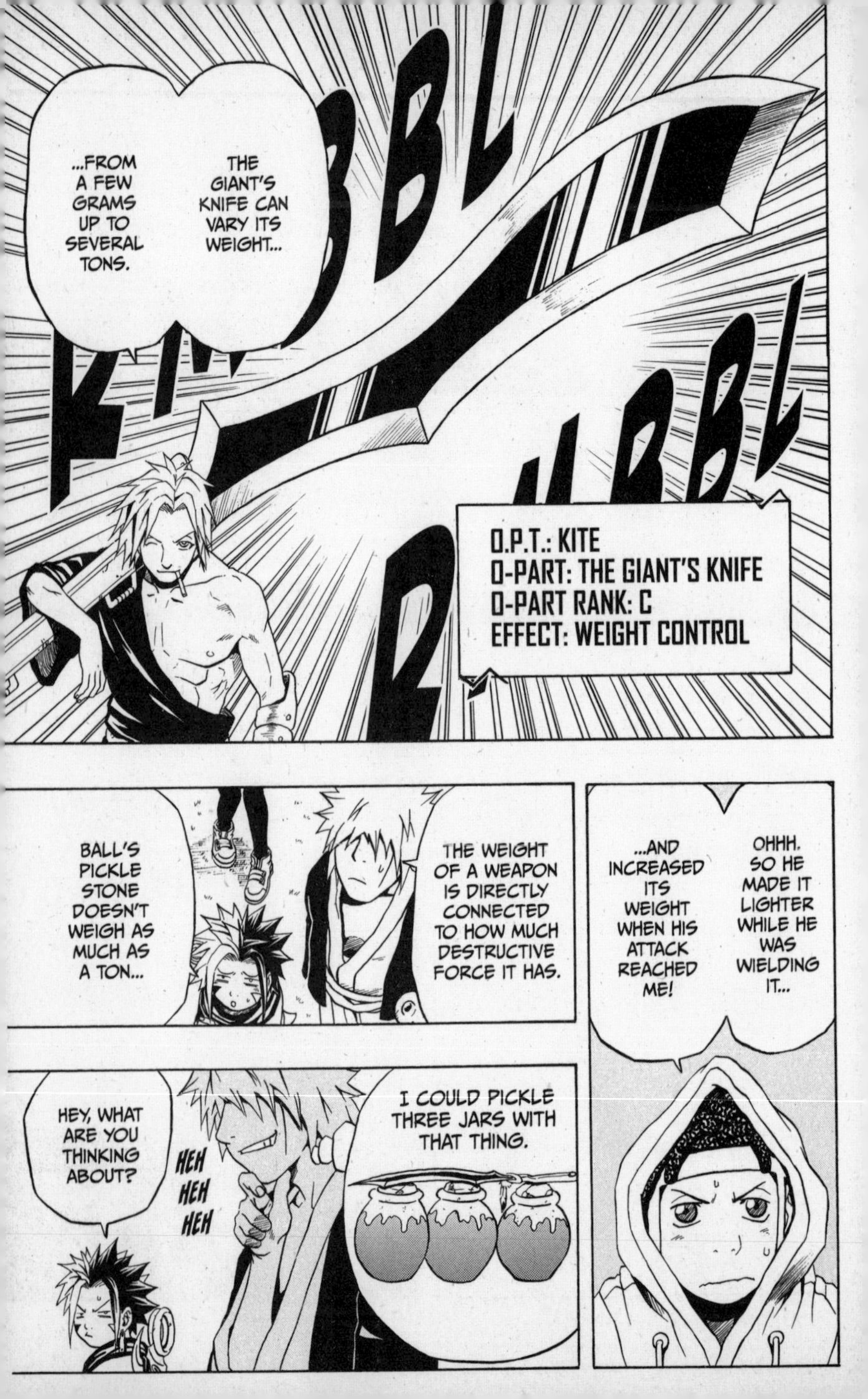
THE GIANT'S KNIFE CAN VARY ITS WEIGHT...
...FROM A FEW GRAMS UP TO SEVERAL TONS.
O.P.T.: KITE
O-PART: THE GIANT'S KNIFE
O-PART RANK: C
EFFECT: WEIGHT CONTROL
OHHH. SO HE MADE IT LIGHTER WHILE HE WAS WIELDING IT...
...AND INCREASED ITS WEIGHT WHEN HIS ATTACK REACHED ME!
THE WEIGHT OF A WEAPON IS DIRECTLY CONNECTED TO HOW MUCH DESTRUCTIVE FORCE IT HAS.
BALL'S PICKLE STONE DOESN'T WEIGH AS MUCH AS A TON...
I COULD PICKLE THREE JARS WITH THAT THING.
HEH HEH HEH
HEY, WHAT ARE YOU THINKING ABOUT?

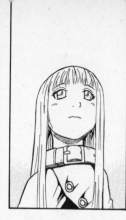

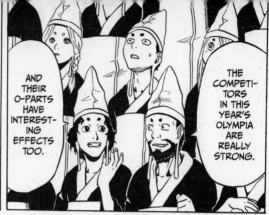

AND THEIR O-PARTS HAVE INTERESTING EFFECTS TOO.

THE COMPETITORS IN THIS YEAR'S OLYMPIA ARE REALLY STRONG.

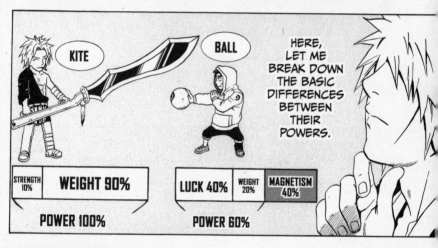

KITE

BALL

HERE, LET ME BREAK DOWN THE BASIC DIFFERENCES BETWEEN THEIR POWERS.

STRENGTH 10%	WEIGHT 90%

POWER 100%

LUCK 40%	WEIGHT 20%	MAGNETISM 40%

POWER 60%

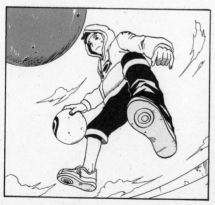

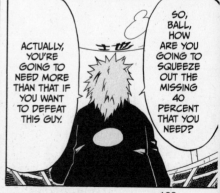

ACTUALLY, YOU'RE GOING TO NEED MORE THAN THAT IF YOU WANT TO DEFEAT THIS GUY.

SO, BALL, HOW ARE YOU GOING TO SQUEEZE OUT THE MISSING 40 PERCENT THAT YOU NEED?

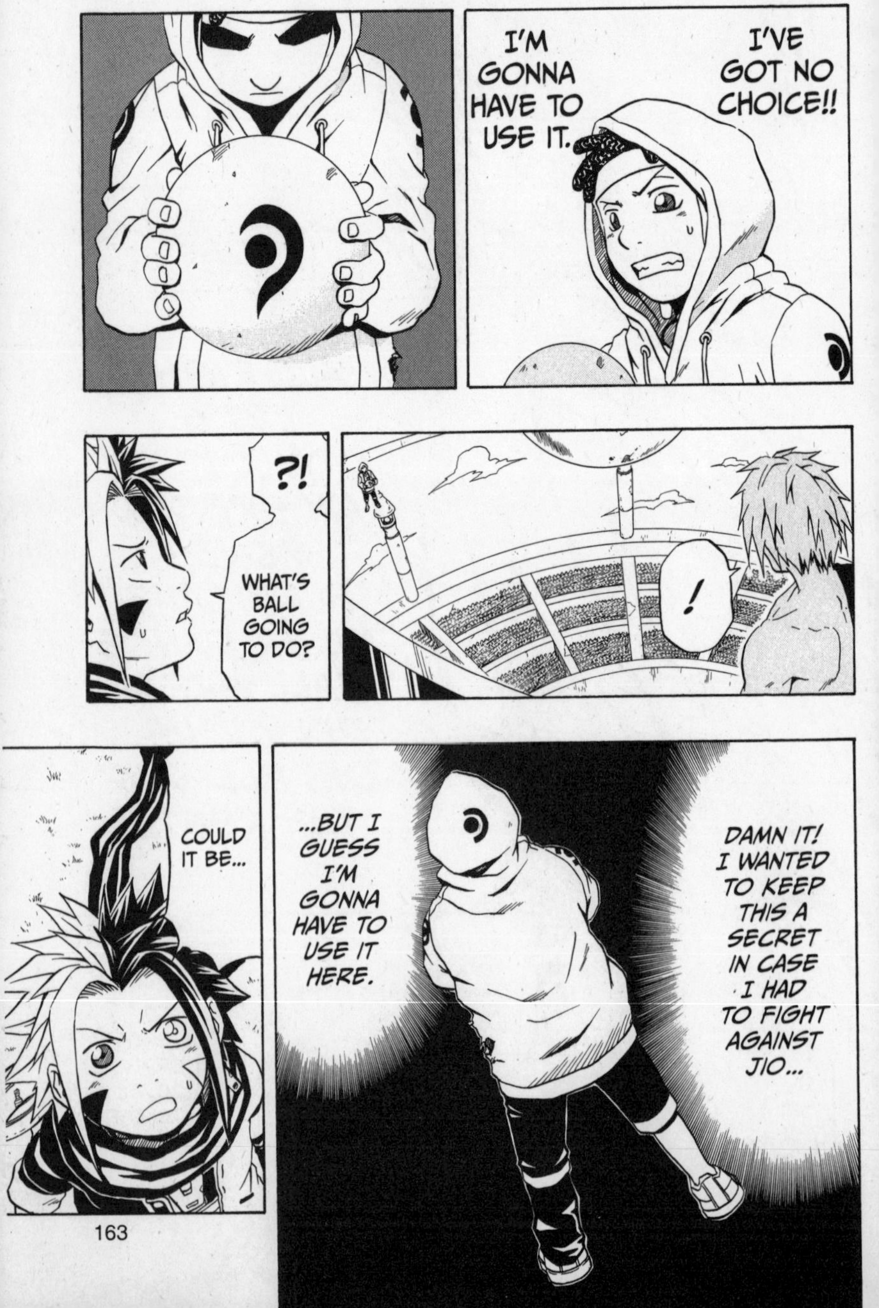
I'VE GOT NO CHOICE!!
I'M GONNA HAVE TO USE IT.
!
?!
WHAT'S BALL GOING TO DO?
DAMN IT! I WANTED TO KEEP THIS A SECRET IN CASE I HAD TO FIGHT AGAINST JIO...
...BUT I GUESS I'M GONNA HAVE TO USE IT HERE.
COULD IT BE...

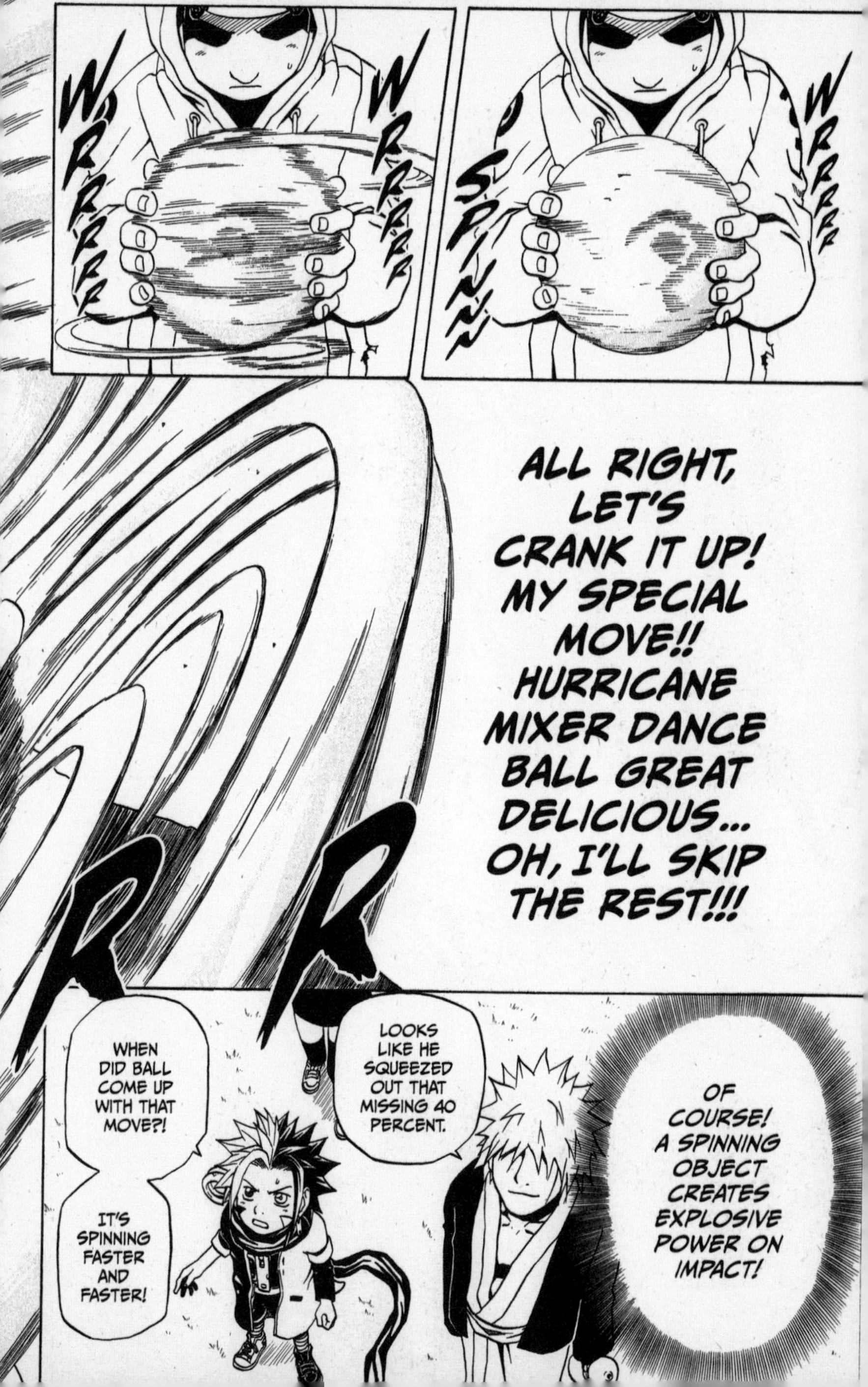
WRRRRR
SPINNN
WRRRRRR
WRRRRRR
ALL RIGHT, LET'S CRANK IT UP! MY SPECIAL MOVE!! HURRICANE MIXER DANCE BALL GREAT DELICIOUS... OH, I'LL SKIP THE REST!!!
RR
OF COURSE! A SPINNING OBJECT CREATES EXPLOSIVE POWER ON IMPACT!
LOOKS LIKE HE SQUEEZED OUT THAT MISSING 40 PERCENT.
WHEN DID BALL COME UP WITH THAT MOVE?!
IT'S SPINNING FASTER AND FASTER!

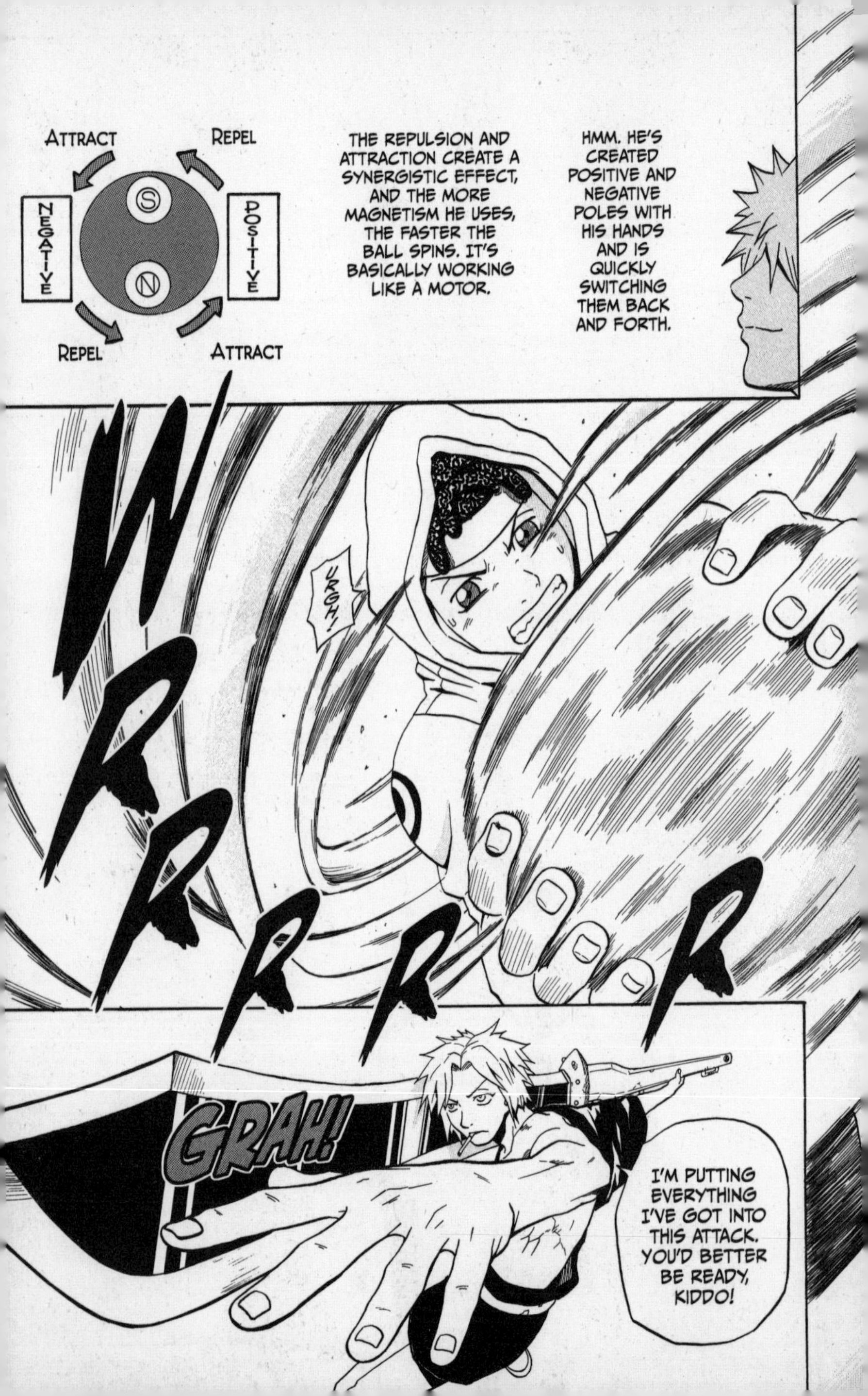
HMM. HE'S CREATED POSITIVE AND NEGATIVE POLES WITH HIS HANDS AND IS QUICKLY SWITCHING THEM BACK AND FORTH.
THE REPULSION AND ATTRACTION CREATE A SYNERGISTIC EFFECT, AND THE MORE MAGNETISM HE USES, THE FASTER THE BALL SPINS. IT'S BASICALLY WORKING LIKE A MOTOR.
REPEL
ATTRACT
POSITIVE
NEGATIVE
S
N
ATTRACT
REPEL
URGH!
WRRRRRR
GRAH!
I'M PUTTING EVERYTHING I'VE GOT INTO THIS ATTACK. YOU'D BETTER BE READY, KIDDO!

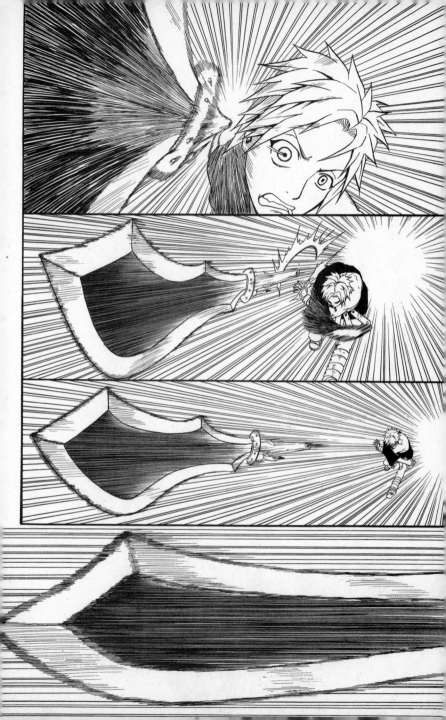

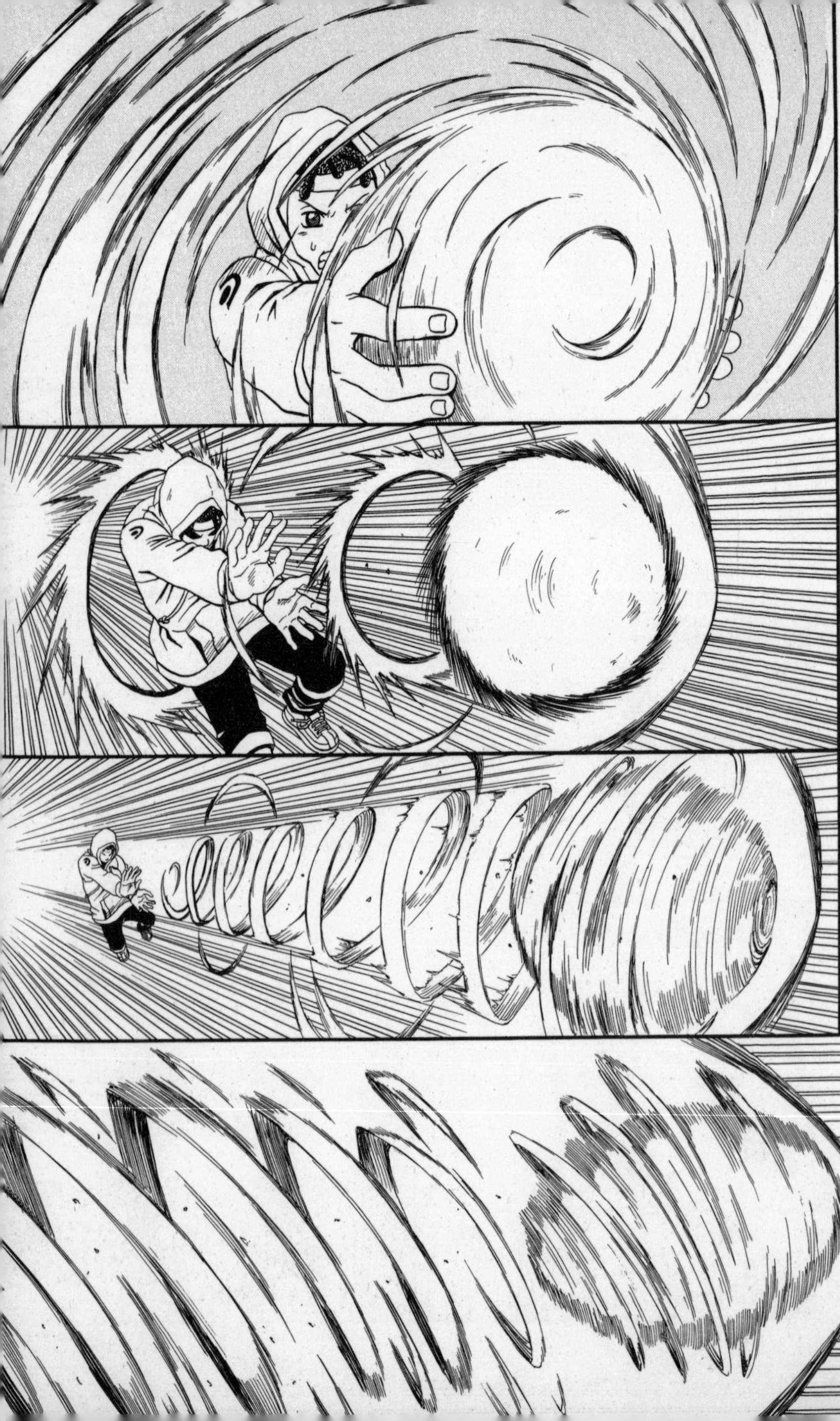

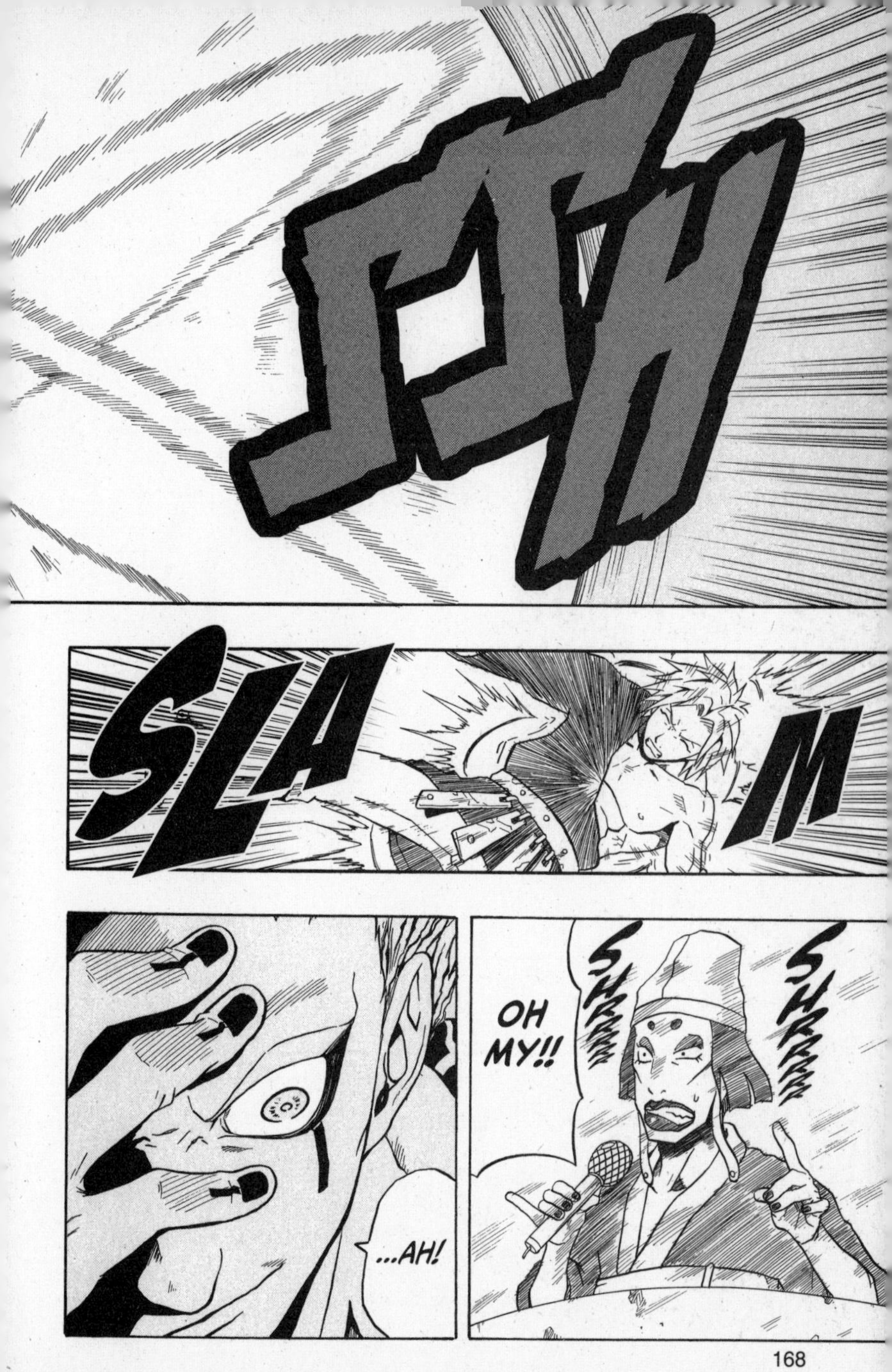
SLAM
OH MY!!
...AH!

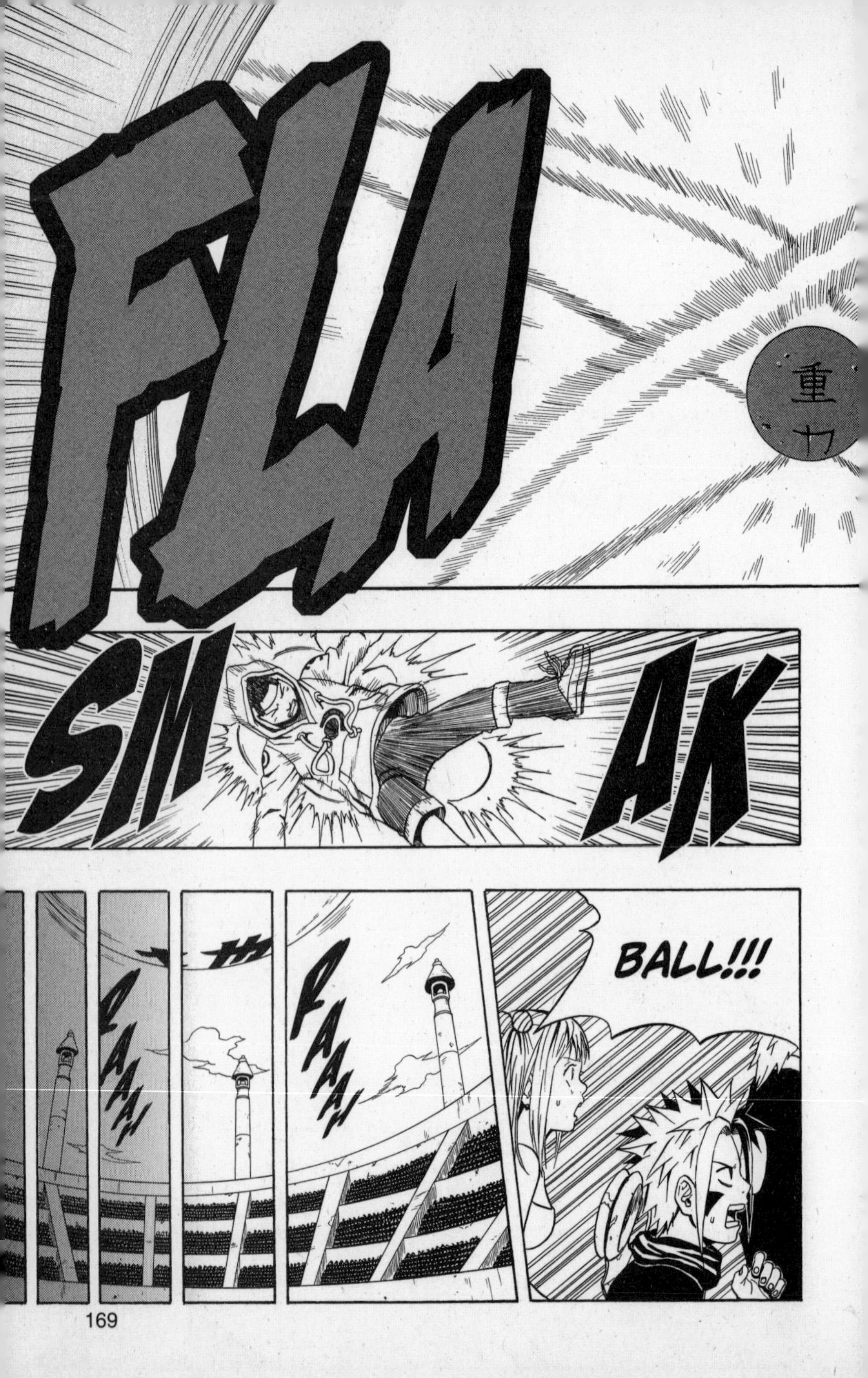
FLA
重力
SM AK
BALL!!!

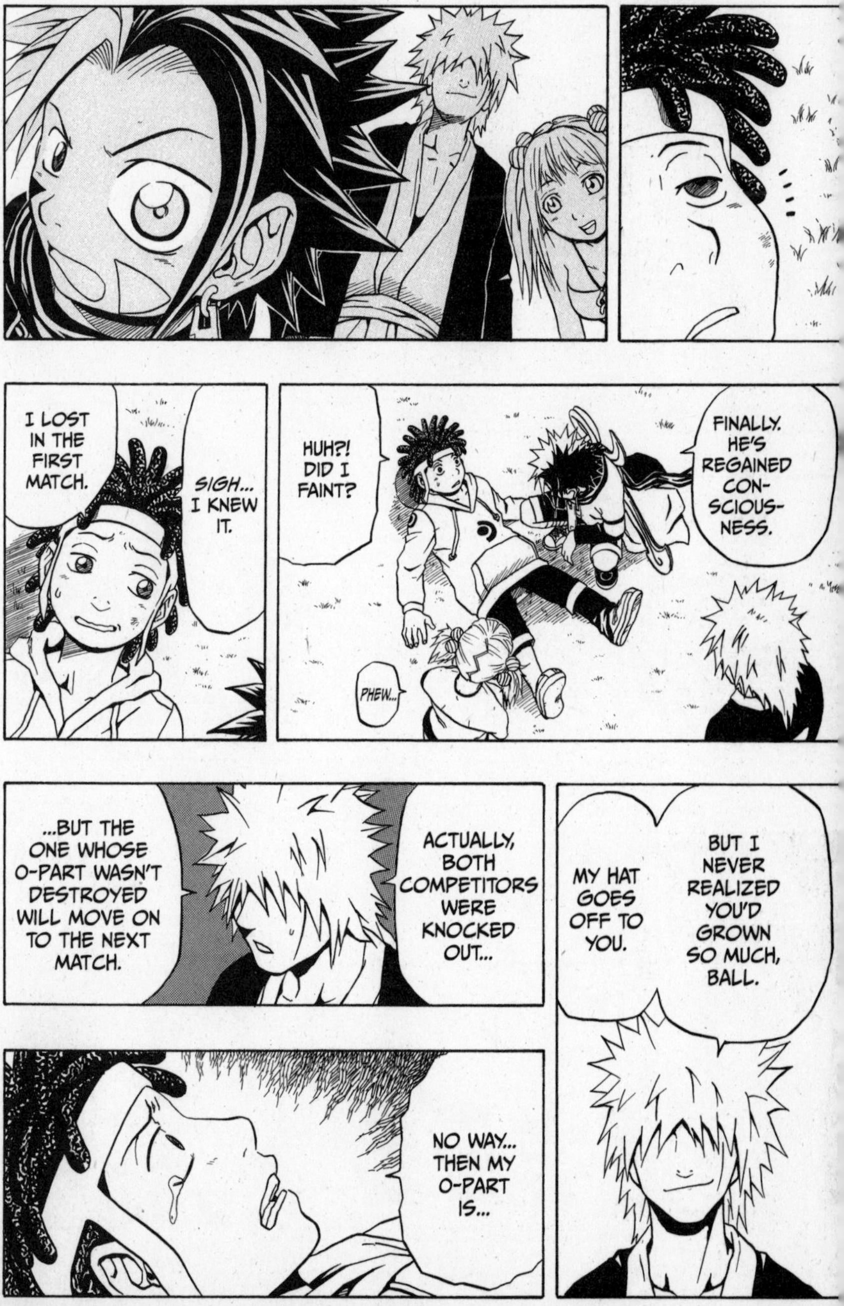
FINALLY. HE'S REGAINED CON-SCIOUS-NESS.
HUH?! DID I FAINT?
PHEW...
SIGH... I KNEW IT.
I LOST IN THE FIRST MATCH.
BUT I NEVER REALIZED YOU'D GROWN SO MUCH, BALL.
MY HAT GOES OFF TO YOU.
ACTUALLY, BOTH COMPETITORS WERE KNOCKED OUT...
...BUT THE ONE WHOSE O-PART WASN'T DESTROYED WILL MOVE ON TO THE NEXT MATCH.
NO WAY... THEN MY O-PART IS...

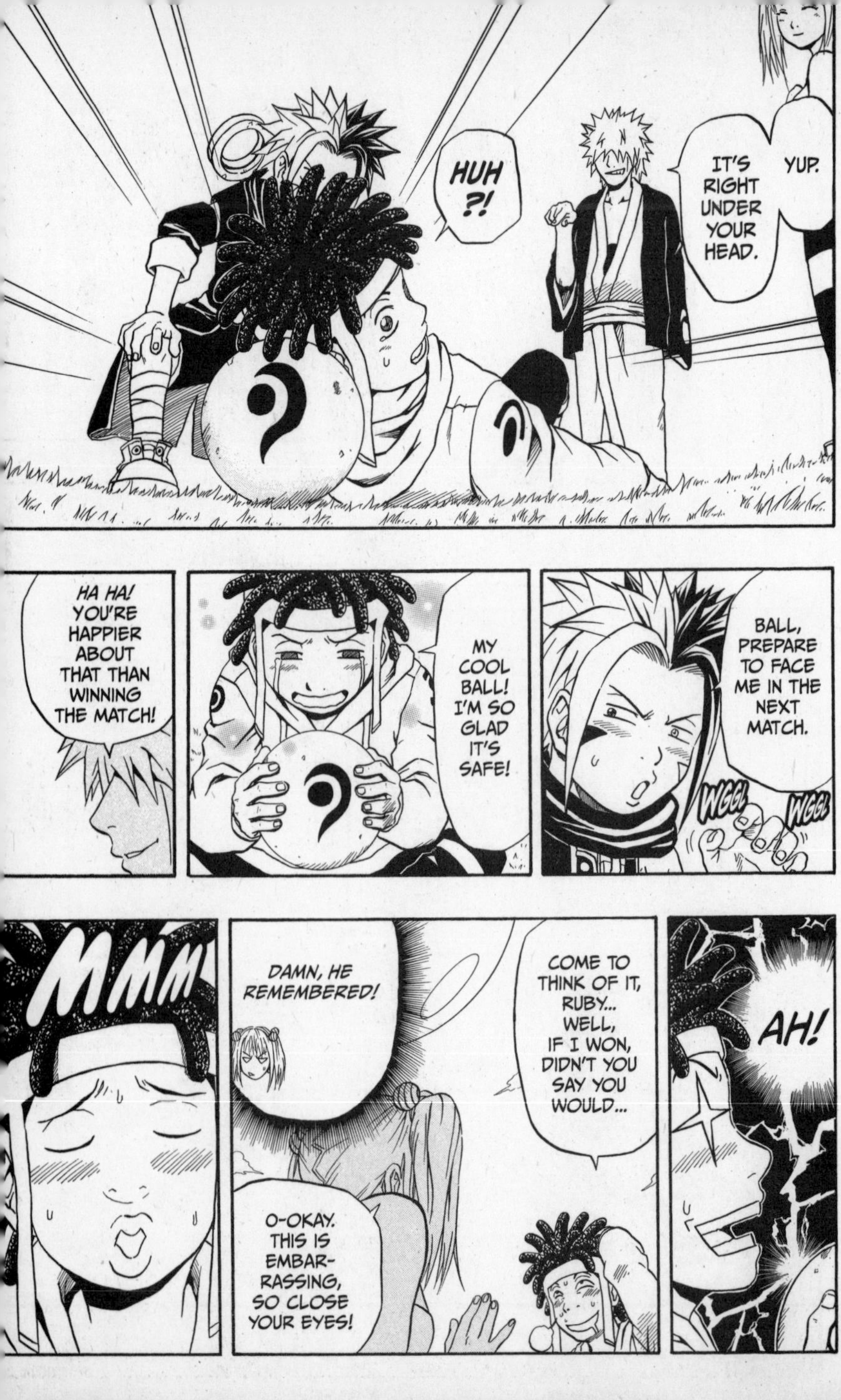
YUP.
IT'S RIGHT UNDER YOUR HEAD.
HUH ?!
BALL, PREPARE TO FACE ME IN THE NEXT MATCH.
WGGL
WGGL
MY COOL BALL! I'M SO GLAD IT'S SAFE!
HA HA! YOU'RE HAPPIER ABOUT THAT THAN WINNING THE MATCH!
AH!
COME TO THINK OF IT, RUBY... WELL, IF I WON, DIDN'T YOU SAY YOU WOULD...
DAMN, HE REMEMBERED!
O-OKAY. THIS IS EMBARRASSING, SO CLOSE YOUR EYES!
MMM

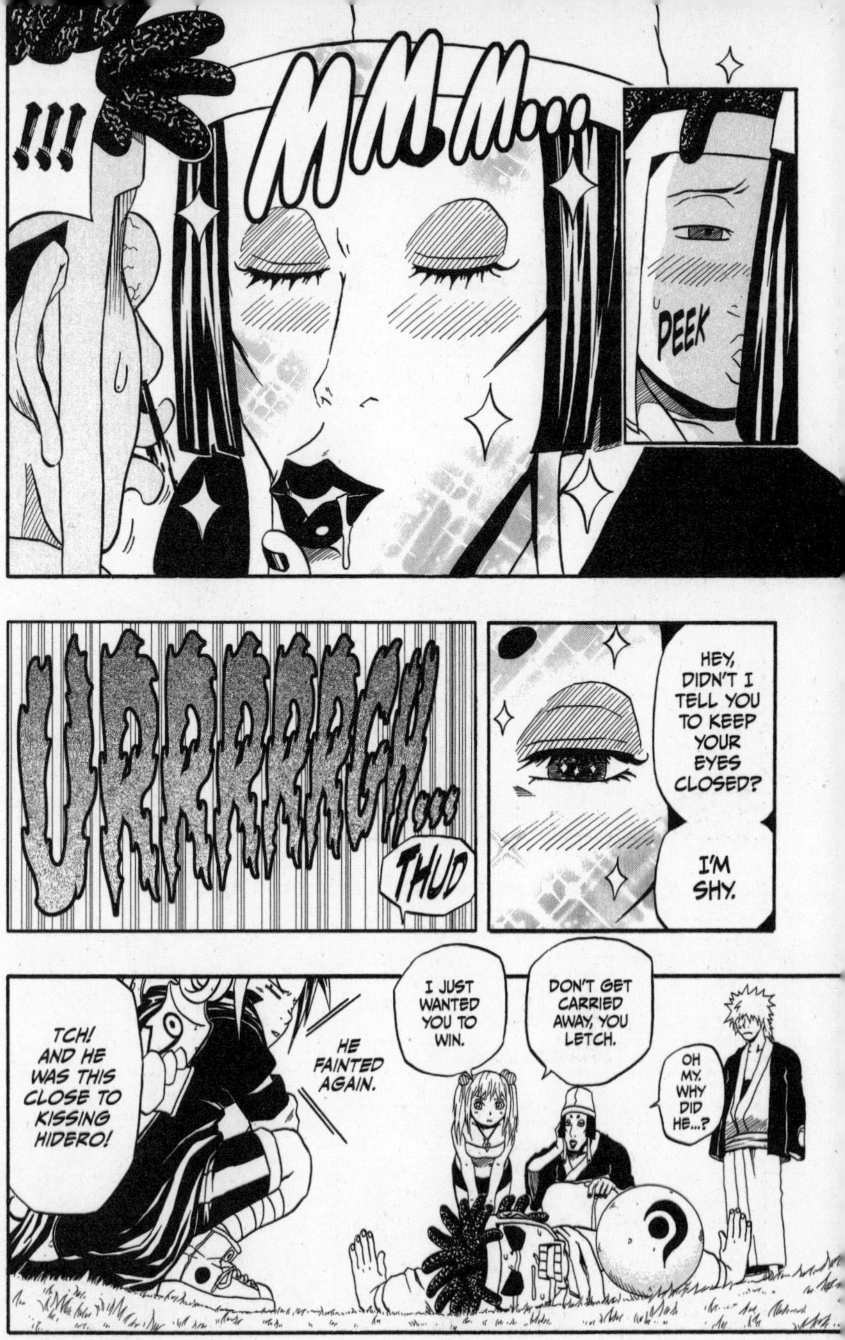
PEEK
MMM...
!!!
HEY, DIDN'T I TELL YOU TO KEEP YOUR EYES CLOSED?
I'M SHY.
URRRRRCH...
THUD
OH MY. WHY DID HE...?
DON'T GET CARRIED AWAY, YOU LETCH.
I JUST WANTED YOU TO WIN.
HE FAINTED AGAIN.
TCH! AND HE WAS THIS CLOSE TO KISSING HIDERO!

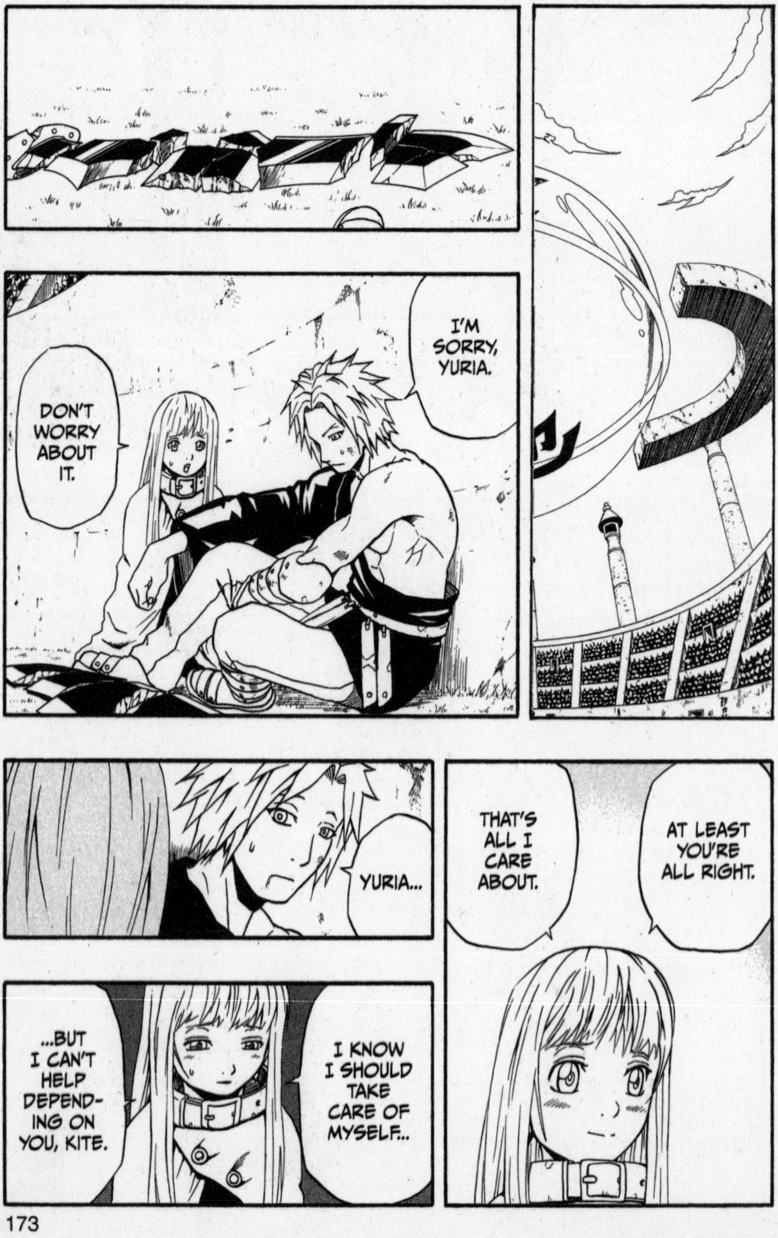
I'M SORRY, YURIA.
DON'T WORRY ABOUT IT.
AT LEAST YOU'RE ALL RIGHT.
THAT'S ALL I CARE ABOUT.
YURIA...
I KNOW I SHOULD TAKE CARE OF MYSELF...
...BUT I CAN'T HELP DEPENDING ON YOU, KITE.

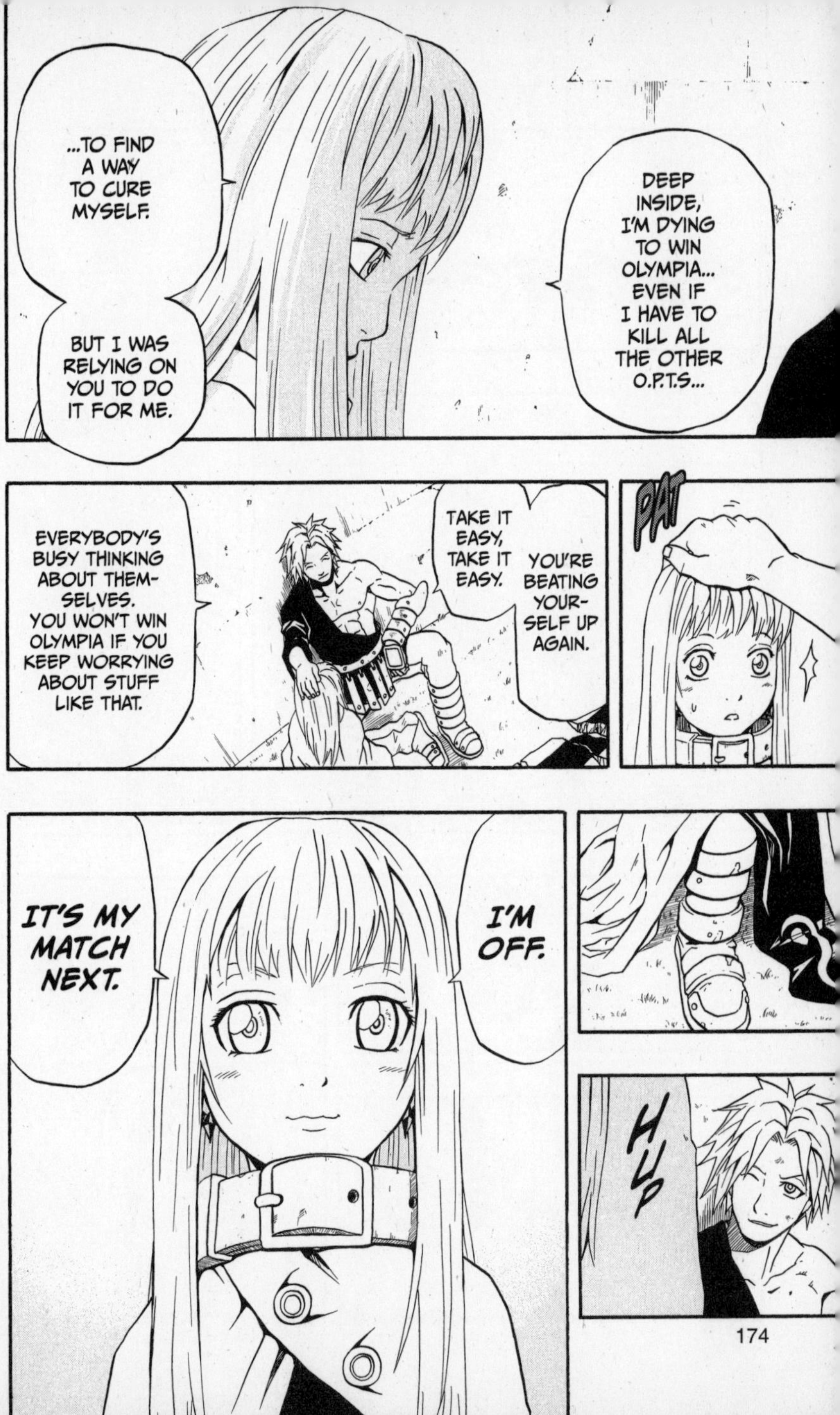
DEEP INSIDE, I'M DYING TO WIN OLYMPIA... EVEN IF I HAVE TO KILL ALL THE OTHER O.P.T.S...
...TO FIND A WAY TO CURE MYSELF.
BUT I WAS RELYING ON YOU TO DO IT FOR ME.
PIAT
TAKE IT EASY, TAKE IT EASY.
YOU'RE BEATING YOURSELF UP AGAIN.
EVERYBODY'S BUSY THINKING ABOUT THEMSELVES. YOU WON'T WIN OLYMPIA IF YOU KEEP WORRYING ABOUT STUFF LIKE THAT.
HUP
I'M OFF.
IT'S MY MATCH NEXT.

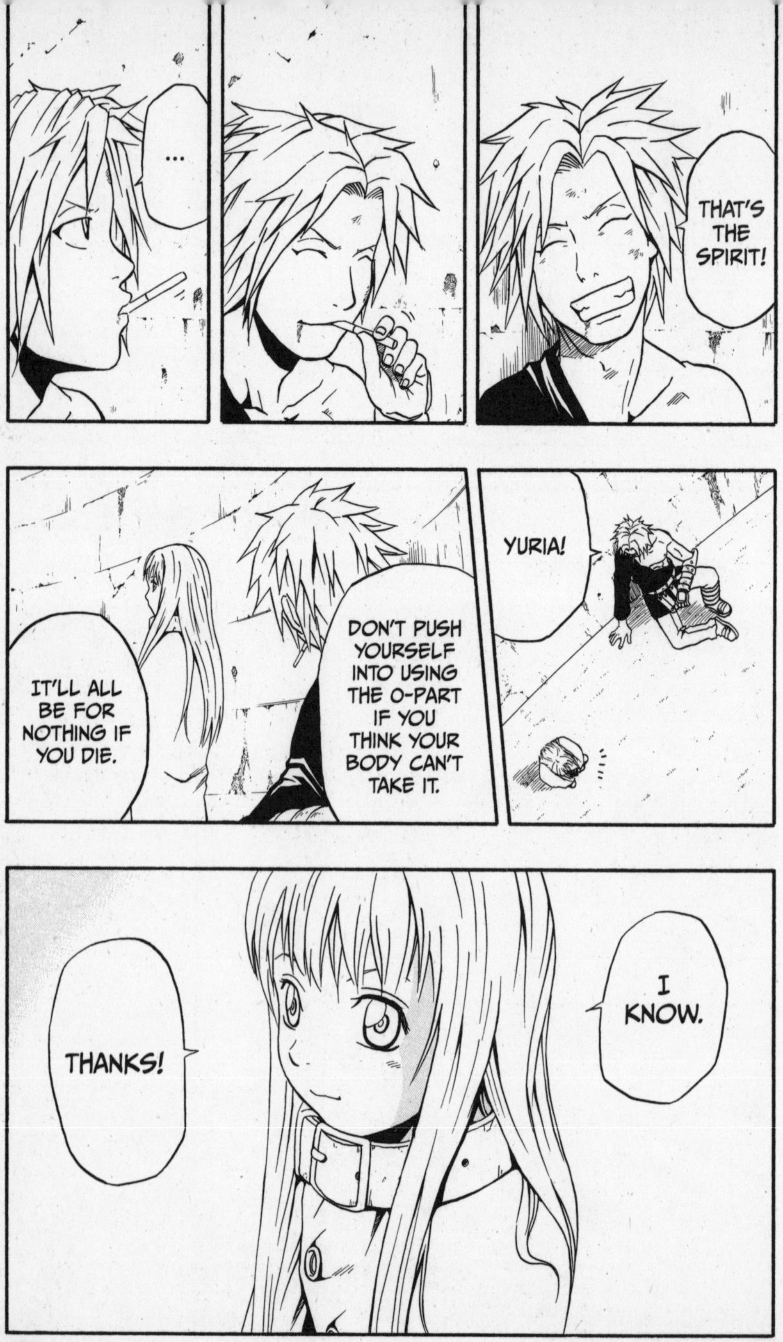
THAT'S THE SPIRIT!
...
YURIA!
DON'T PUSH YOURSELF INTO USING THE O-PART IF YOU THINK YOUR BODY CAN'T TAKE IT.
IT'LL ALL BE FOR NOTHING IF YOU DIE.
I KNOW.
THANKS!

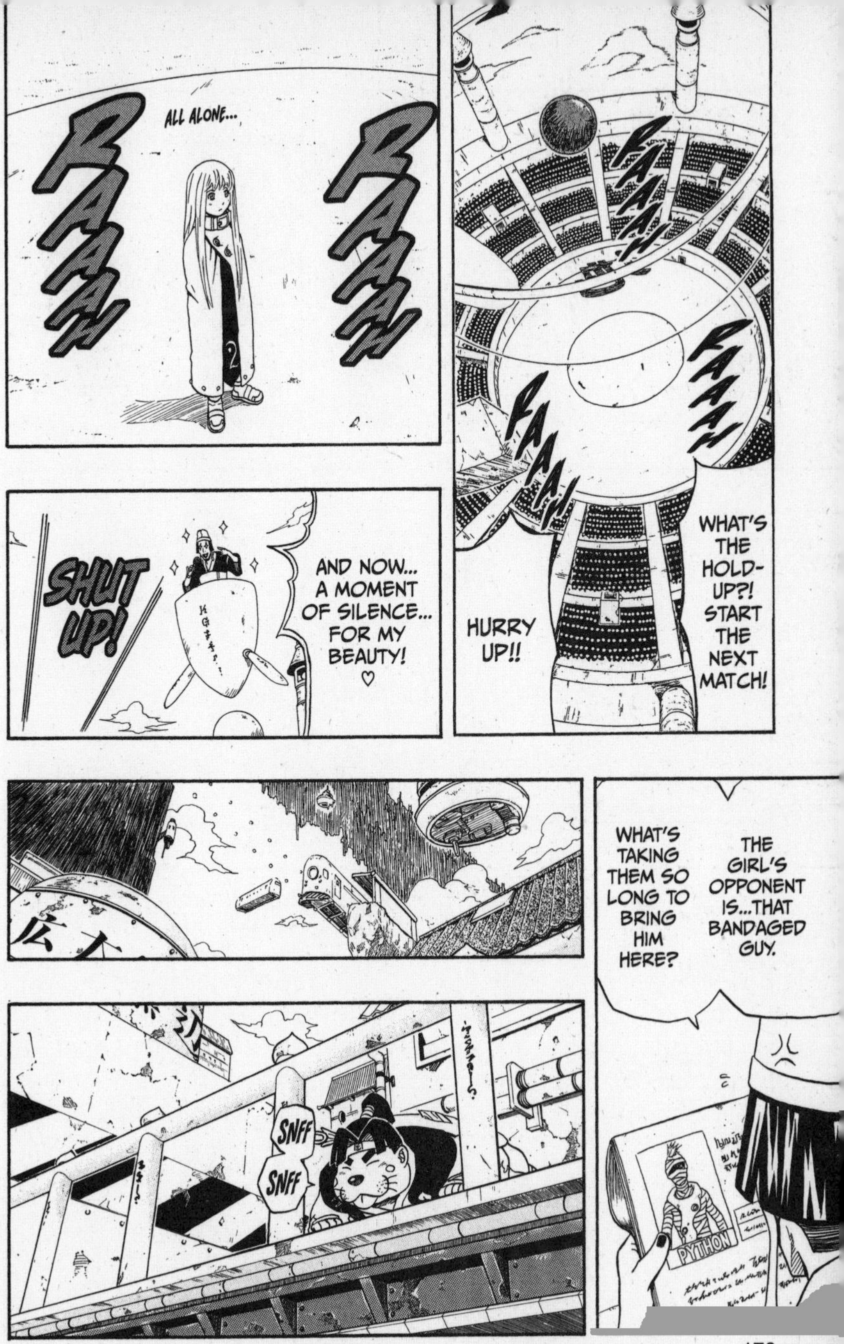
RAAAAH
RAAAAH
RAAAAH
WHAT'S THE HOLD-UP?! START THE NEXT MATCH!
HURRY UP!!
ALL ALONE...
RAAAAH
RAAAAH
AND NOW... A MOMENT OF SILENCE... FOR MY BEAUTY! ♡
SHUT UP!
THE GIRL'S OPPONENT IS...THAT BANDAGED GUY.
WHAT'S TAKING THEM SO LONG TO BRING HIM HERE?
PYTHON
SNFF
SNFF

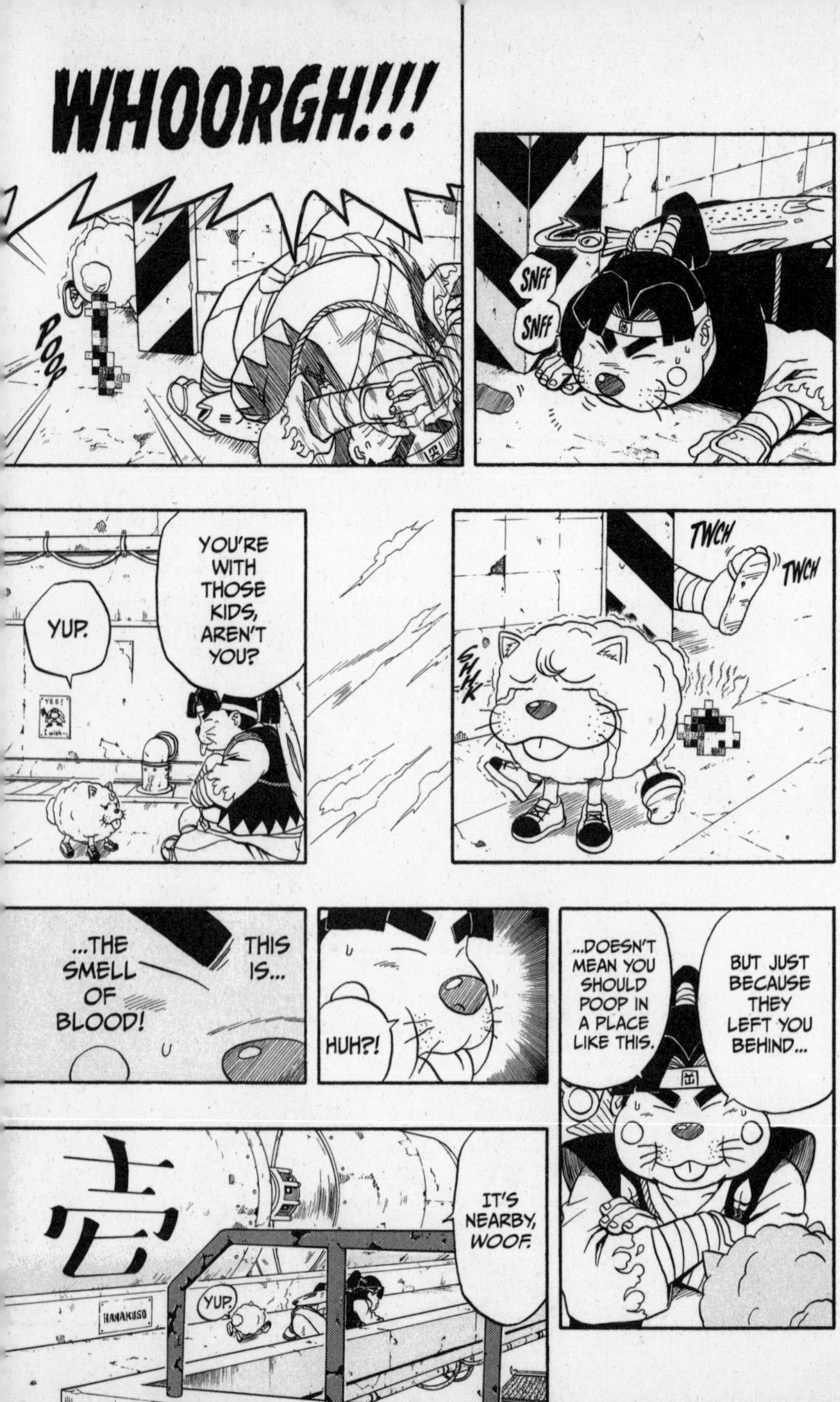
SNFF
SNFF
WHOORGH!!!
POOP
TWCH
TWCH
SHHK
YOU'RE WITH THOSE KIDS, AREN'T YOU?
YUP.
BUT JUST BECAUSE THEY LEFT YOU BEHIND...
...DOESN'T MEAN YOU SHOULD POOP IN A PLACE LIKE THIS.
HUH?!
THIS IS...
...THE SMELL OF BLOOD!
IT'S NEARBY, WOOF.
YUP.
HANAKUSO

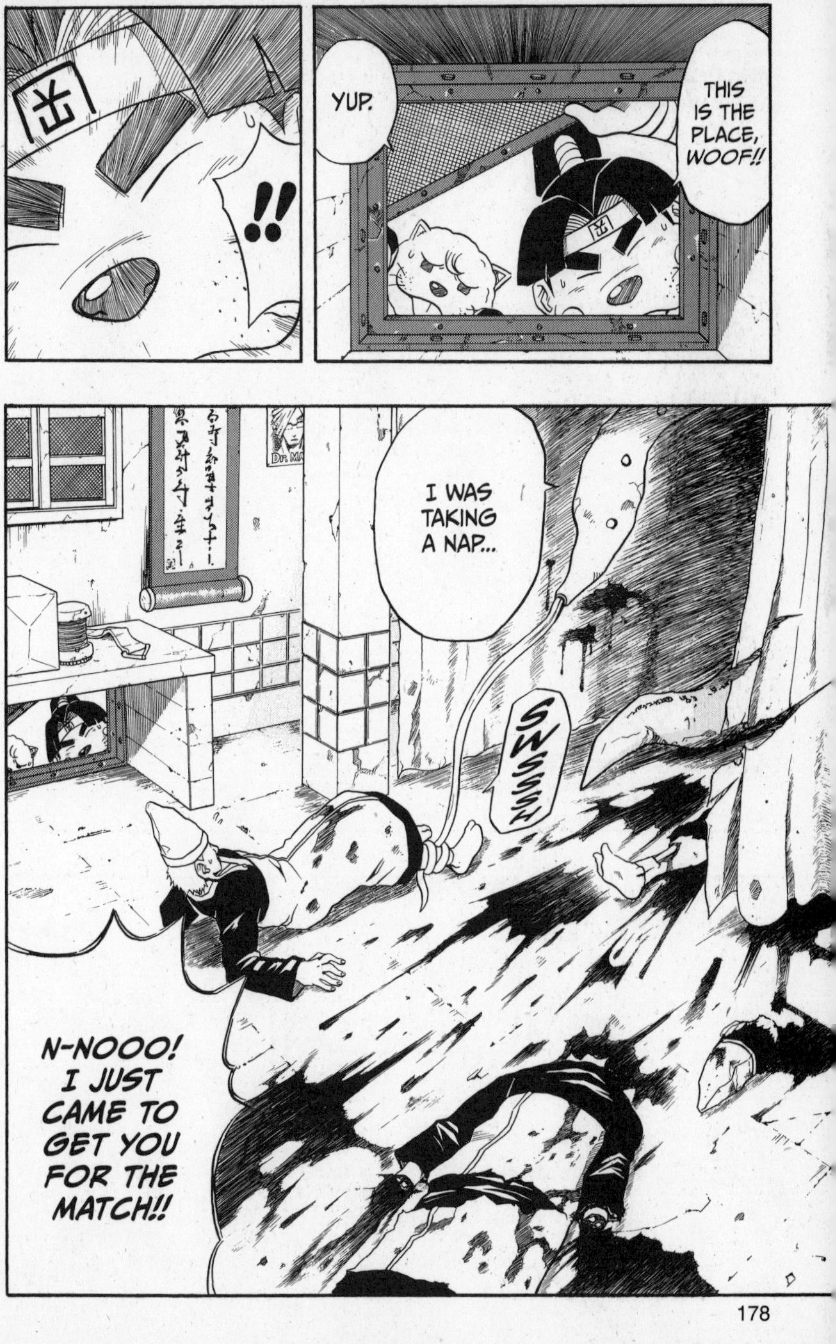
THIS IS THE PLACE, WOOF!!
YUP.
!!
I WAS TAKING A NAP...
SWSSSH
N-NOOO! I JUST CAME TO GET YOU FOR THE MATCH!!

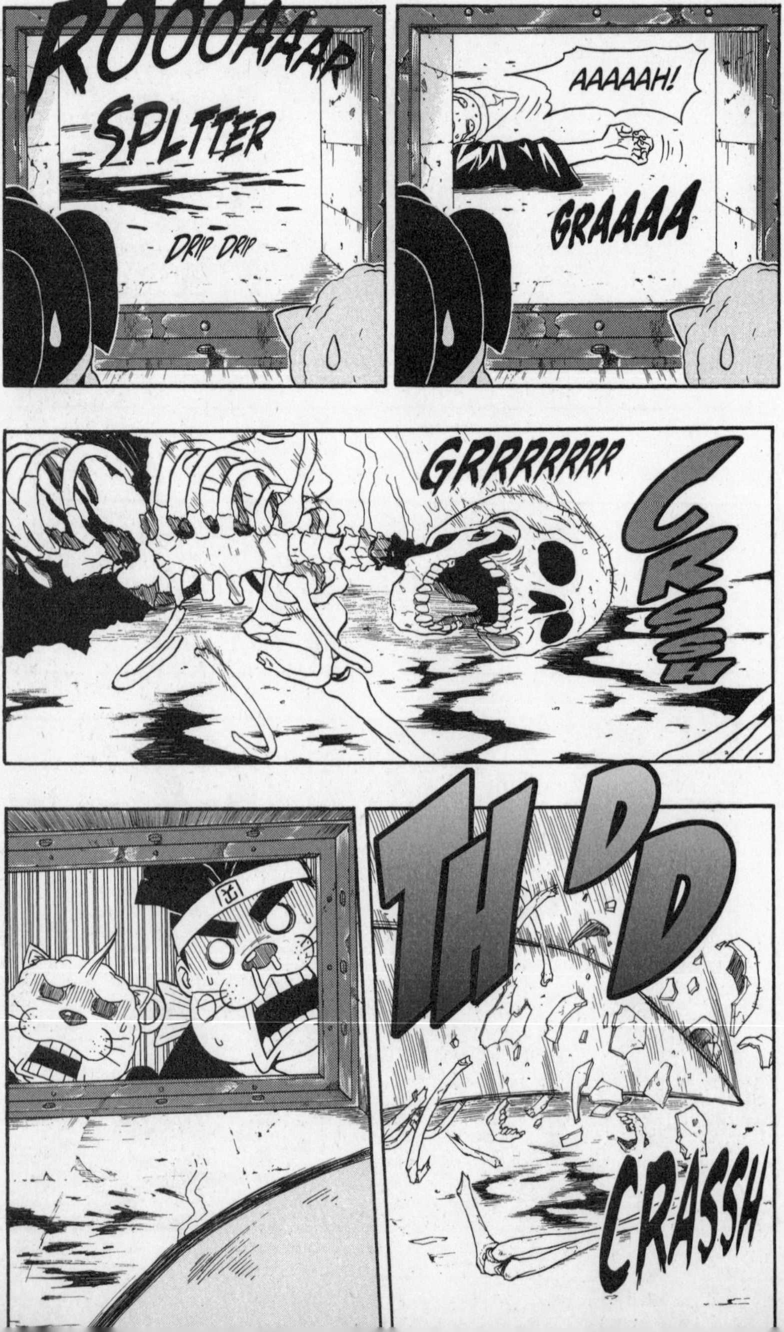
AAAAAH!
GRAAAA
ROOOAAAR
SPLTTER
DRIP DRIP
GRRRRRRR
THDD
CRASSH

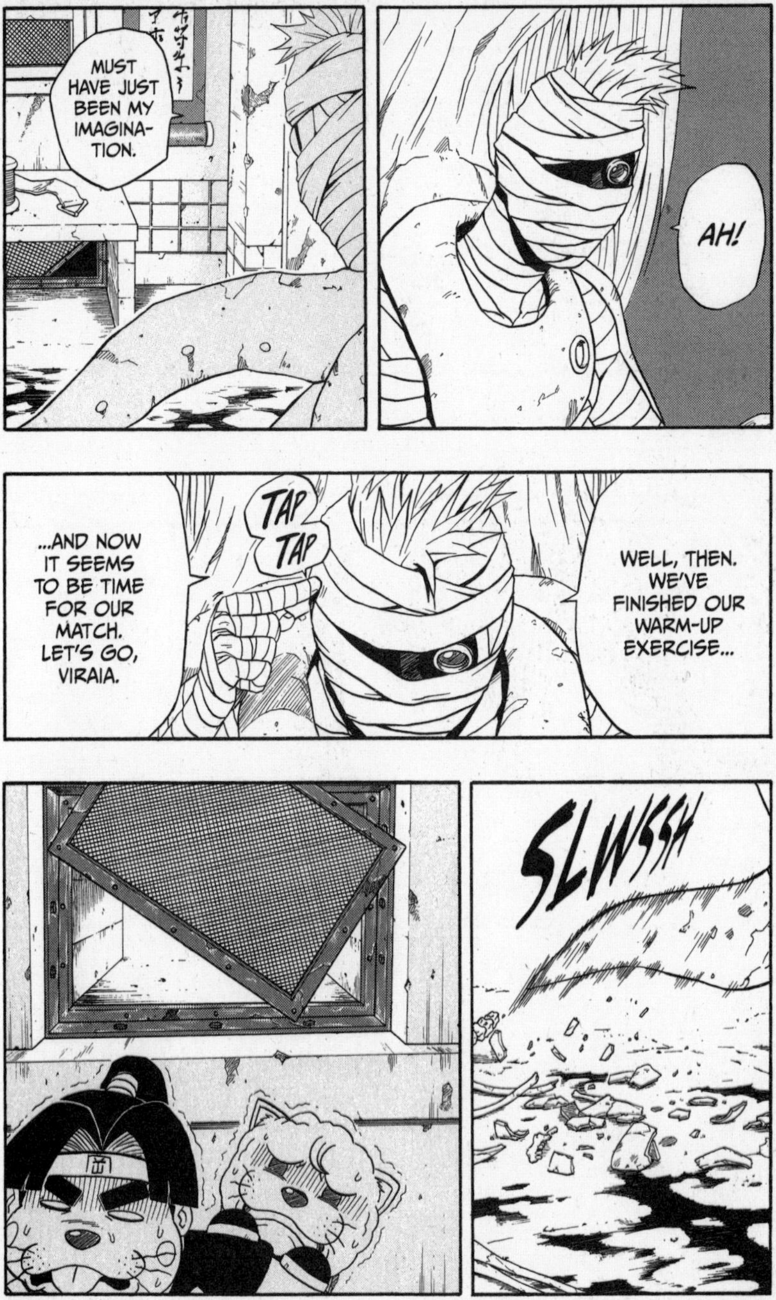
AH!
MUST HAVE JUST BEEN MY IMAGINATION.
WELL, THEN. WE'VE FINISHED OUR WARM-UP EXERCISE...
TAP TAP
...AND NOW IT SEEMS TO BE TIME FOR OUR MATCH. LET'S GO, VIRAIA.
SLWSSH

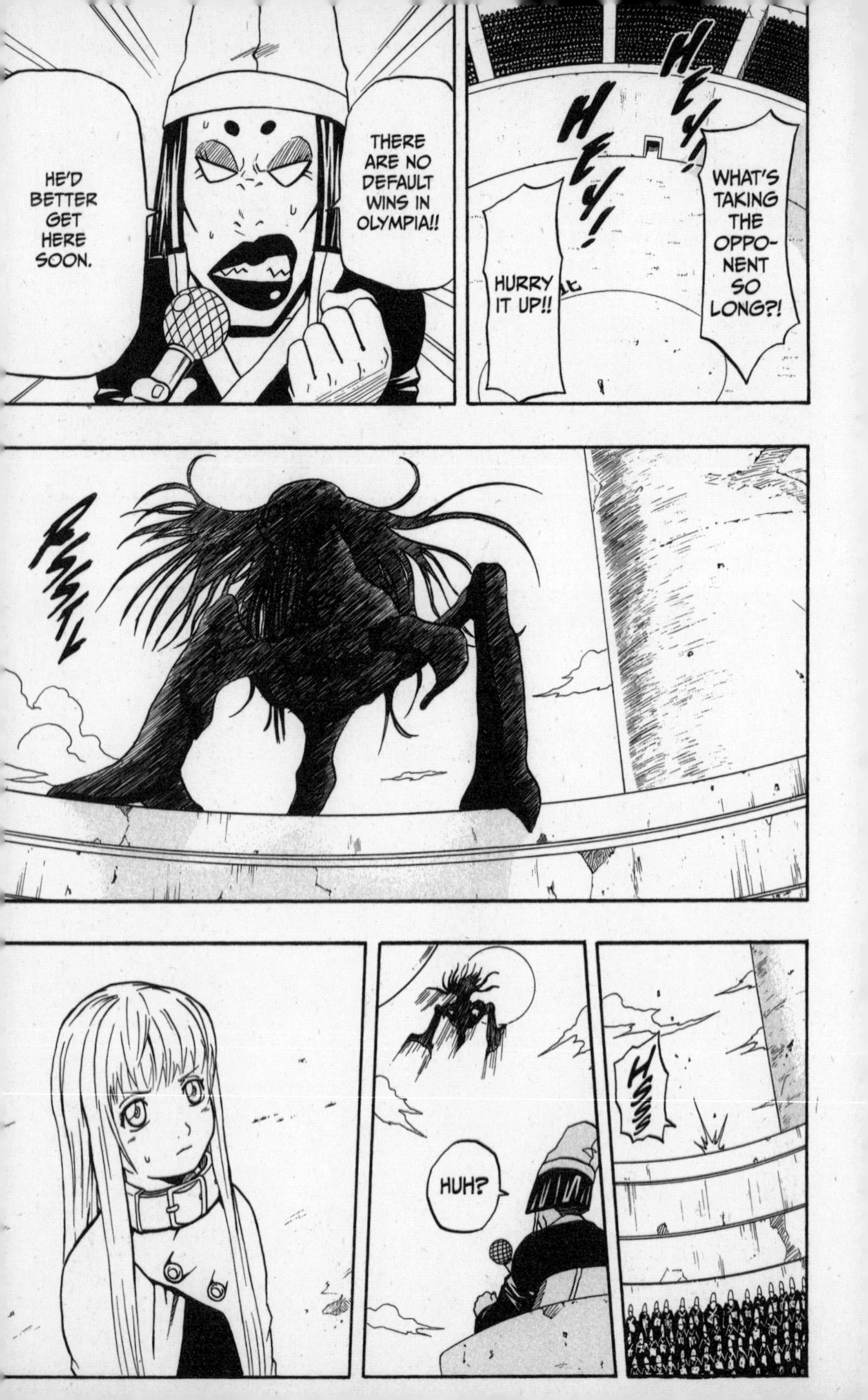
HEY! HEY!
WHAT'S TAKING THE OPPONENT SO LONG?!
HURRY IT UP!!
THERE ARE NO DEFAULT WINS IN OLYMPIA!!
HE'D BETTER GET HERE SOON.
HSSSS
HUH?

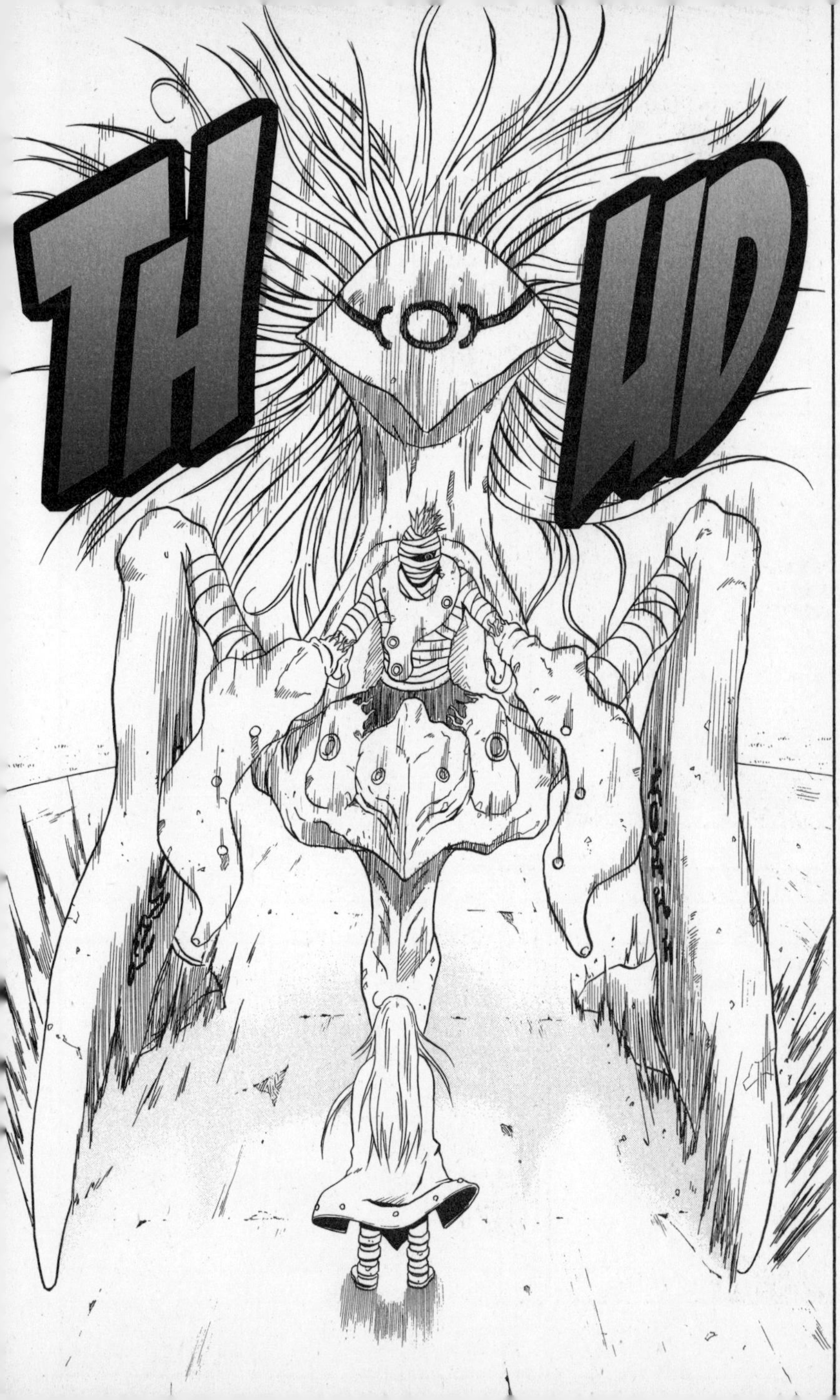
THUD

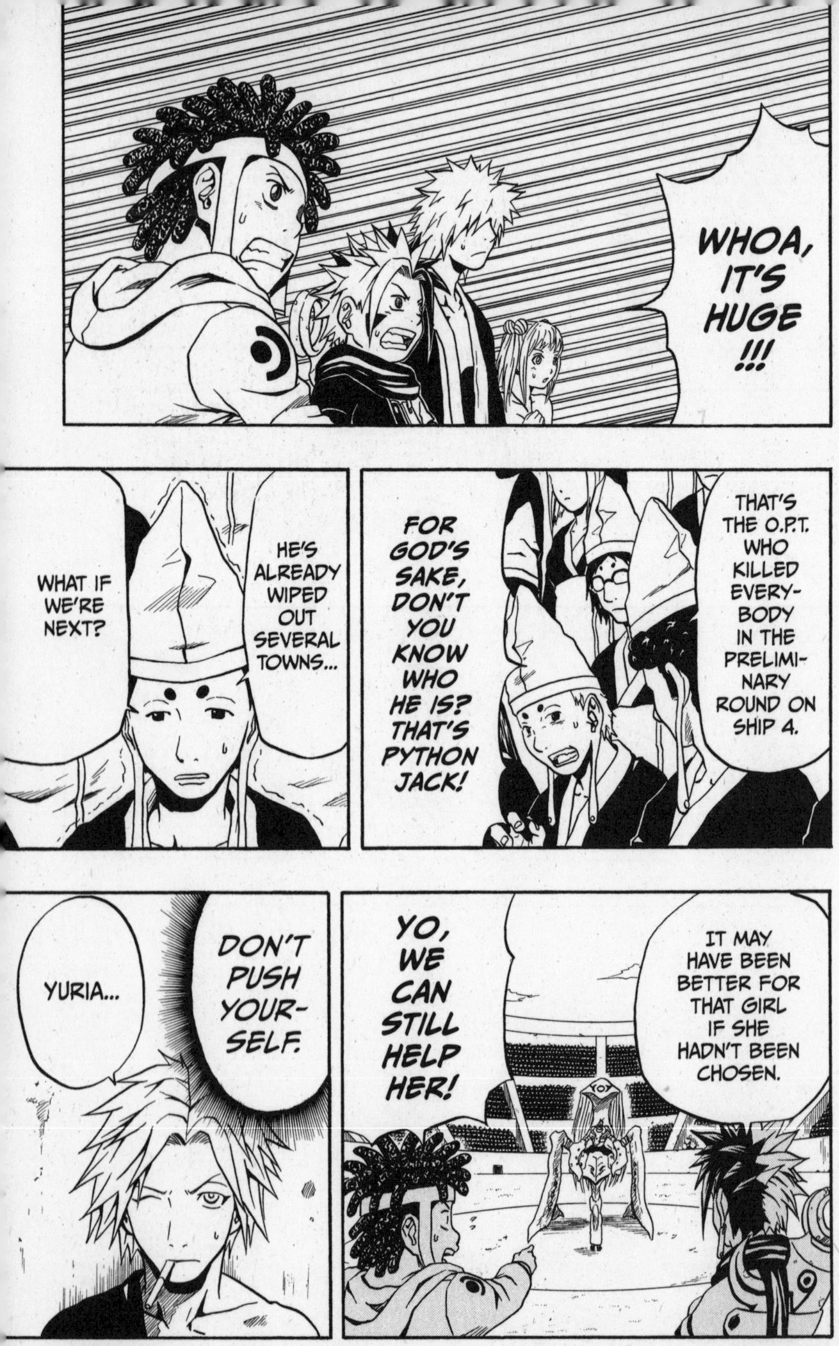
WHOA, IT'S HUGE!!!
THAT'S THE O.P.T. WHO KILLED EVERY-BODY IN THE PRELIMI-NARY ROUND ON SHIP 4.
FOR GOD'S SAKE, DON'T YOU KNOW WHO HE IS? THAT'S PYTHON JACK!
HE'S ALREADY WIPED OUT SEVERAL TOWNS...
WHAT IF WE'RE NEXT?
IT MAY HAVE BEEN BETTER FOR THAT GIRL IF SHE HADN'T BEEN CHOSEN.
YO, WE CAN STILL HELP HER!
DON'T PUSH YOUR-SELF.
YURIA...

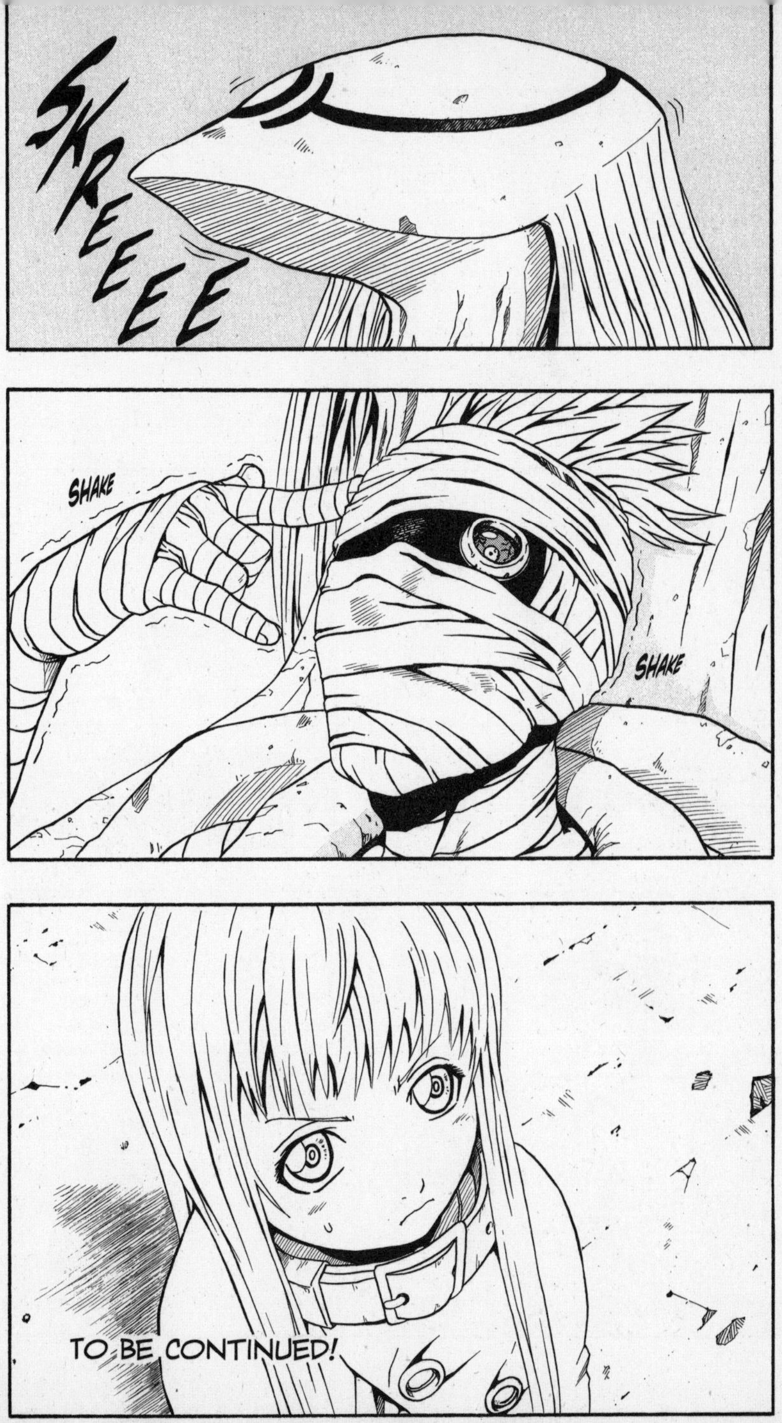
SKREEEE
SHAKE
SHAKE
TO BE CONTINUED!

SEISHI & THE CHICKEN & EGG BOWL

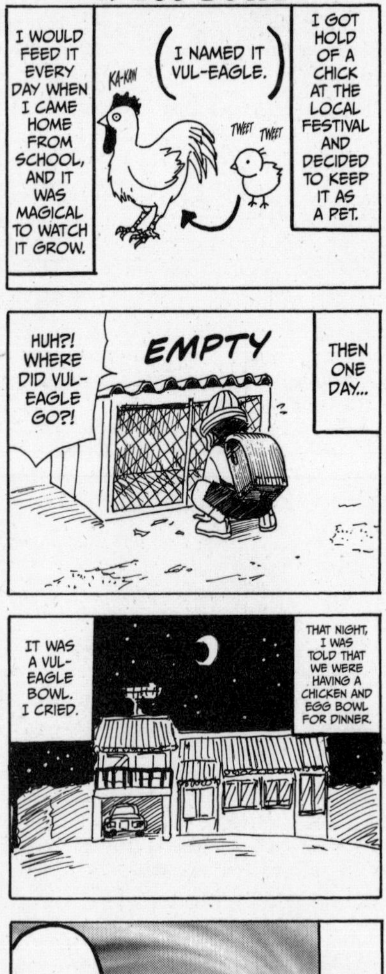

I GOT HOLD OF A CHICK AT THE LOCAL FESTIVAL AND DECIDED TO KEEP IT AS A PET.
I NAMED IT VUL-EAGLE.
TWEET TWEET
KA-KAW
I WOULD FEED IT EVERY DAY WHEN I CAME HOME FROM SCHOOL, AND IT WAS MAGICAL TO WATCH IT GROW.
THEN ONE DAY...
EMPTY
HUH?! WHERE DID VUL-EAGLE GO?!
THAT NIGHT, I WAS TOLD THAT WE WERE HAVING A CHICKEN AND EGG BOWL FOR DINNER.
IT WAS A VUL-EAGLE BOWL. I CRIED.
AND I CRIED... AND THEN I SAID...
MORE, PLEASE.

SEISHI & THE PHONE

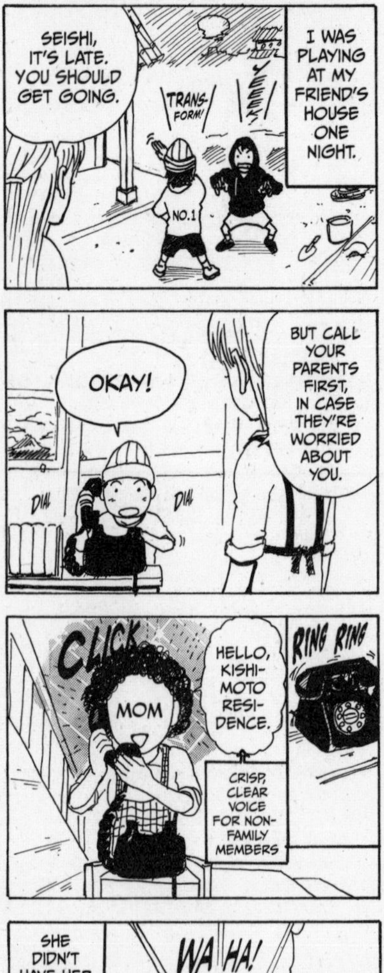

I WAS PLAYING AT MY FRIEND'S HOUSE ONE NIGHT.
TRANS-FORM!
NO.1
SEISHI, IT'S LATE. YOU SHOULD GET GOING.
BUT CALL YOUR PARENTS FIRST, IN CASE THEY'RE WORRIED ABOUT YOU.
OKAY!
DIAL
DIAL
RING RING
HELLO, KISHIMOTO RESIDENCE.
CRISP, CLEAR VOICE FOR NON-FAMILY MEMBERS
CLICK
MOM
S-SORRY! WRONG NUMBER!!
WA HA!
SHE DIDN'T HAVE HER USUAL GROWL, SO LITTLE KISHIMOTO ASSUMED HE HAD THE WRONG NUMBER.
CLICK
THUNK

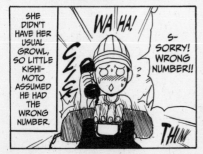

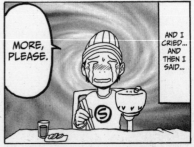

O—Parts CATALOGUE⑨

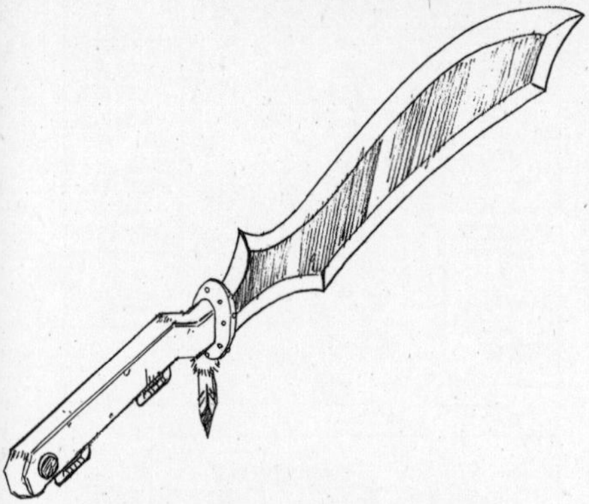

O-PART: THE GIANT'S KNIFE
O-PART RANK: C
EFFECT: WEIGHT CONTROL
PURPOSELY MADE TO LOOK HEAVY AND SLOW.

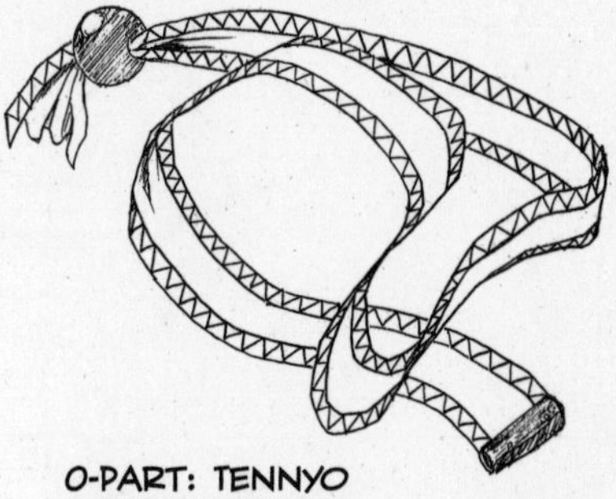

O-PART: TENNYO
O-PART RANK: C
EFFECT: HANDLING + HARDNESS TRANSFORMATION
MORE THAN JUST A C-RANKED O-PART WHEN ANNA USES IT. IT CAN CHANGE INTO VARIOUS THINGS SUCH AS A SWORD, A SPEAR, A SHIELD, A WHIP, AND SO ON.

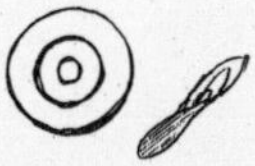

O-PART: LEVITATION STICKER
O-PART RANK: E
EFFECT: LEVITATION
THE LEVITATION STICKER CANNOT BE USED ON ITS OWN.
IT ONLY WORKS WHEN USED WITH THE GRAVITY BALL.

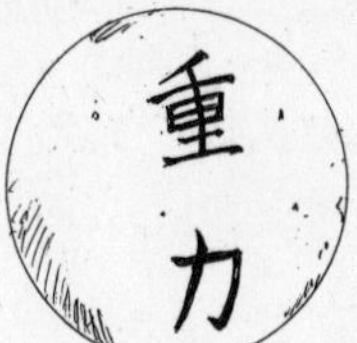
重
力

O-PART: GRAVITY BALL
O-PART RANK: C
EFFECT: GRAVITY CONTROL
IT CAN ONLY CONTROL THE GRAVITY WITHIN A LIMITED AREA.
THIS BALL CAN ALSO BE USED TO CREATE A GRAVITATIONAL PULL.

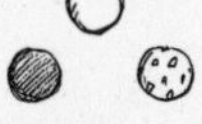

O-PART: DOG, MONKEY, PHEASANT MILLET DUMPLINGS
O-PART RANK: E
EFFECT: TRANSFORMATION
THESE TASTE DISGUSTING, SO FUTOMOMO-TARO IS THE ONLY PERSON CAPABLE OF EATING THEM.
FUTOMOMO-TARO HIMSELF THINKS THEY ARE QUITE GOOD.

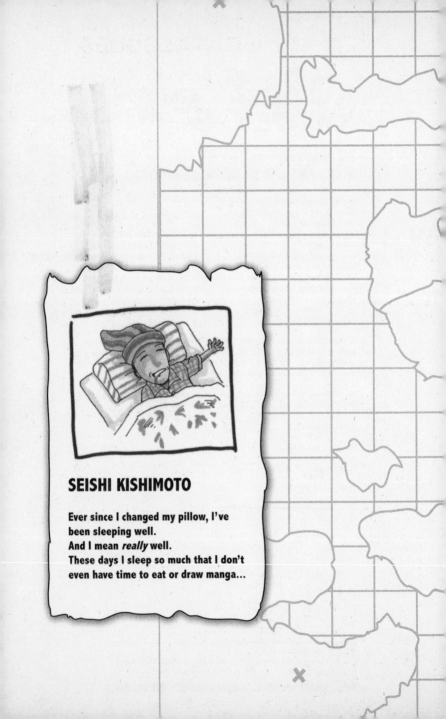

SEISHI KISHIMOTO

Ever since I changed my pillow, I've
been sleeping well.
And I mean *really* well.
These days I sleep so much that I don't
even have time to eat or draw manga...

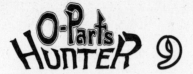

O-Parts HUNTER 9

VIZ Media Edition
STORY AND ART BY SEISHI KISHIMOTO

English Adaptation/Tetsuichiro Miyaki
Touch-up Art & Lettering/Gia Cam Luc
Cover Design/Amy Martin
Interior Design/Andrea Rice
Editor/Carol Fox

Editor in Chief, Books/Alvin Lu
Editor in Chief, Magazines/Marc Weidenbaum
VP of Publishing Licensing/Rika Inouye
VP of Sales/Gonzalo Ferreyra
Sr. VP of Marketing/Liza Coppola
Publisher/Hyoe Narita

Printed in the U.S.A.

Published by VIZ Media, LLC
P.O. Box 77010
San Francisco, CA 94107

10 9 8 7 6 5 4 3 2 1
First printing, April 2008

viz media
www.viz.com
store.viz.com

PARENTAL ADVISORY
RATED T+ FOR OLDER TEEN
O-PARTS HUNTER is rated T+ for Older Teen and is recommended for ages 16 and up. This volume contains realistic and fantasy violence and adult situations.
ratings.viz.com

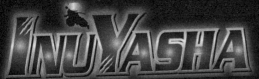
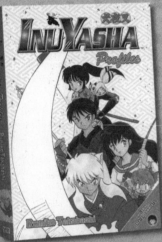
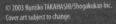

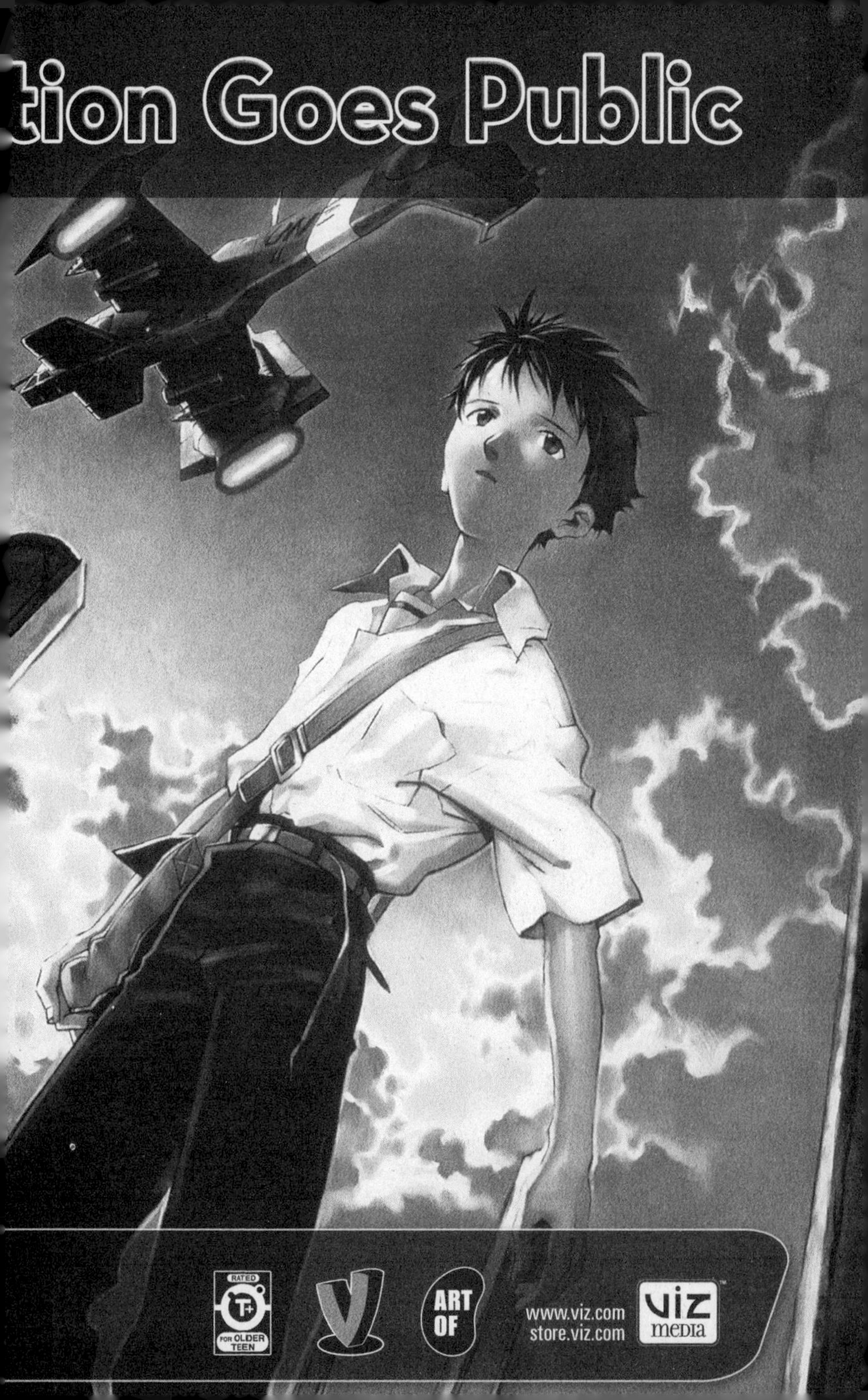
tion Goes Public
RATED T+ FOR OLDER TEEN
ART OF
www.viz.com
store.viz.com
viz media

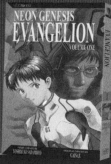
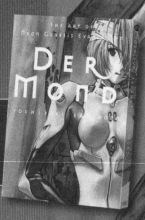

LOVE MANGA?
LET US KNOW WHAT YOU THINK!

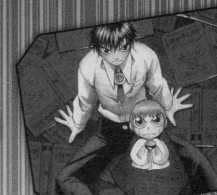

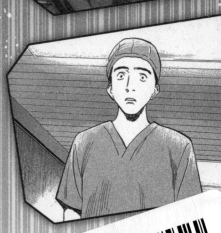

HELP US MAKE THE MAN[...]
YOU LOVE BETTER!